SOUP

*The Ultimate Book
of Soups and Stews*

13-Digit ISBN: 978-1-60433-809-6
10-Digit ISBN: 1-60433-809-1

This book may be ordered by mail from the publisher. Please include $5.99 for postage and handling.
Please support your local bookseller first!

Books published by Cider Mill Press Book Publishers are available at special discounts for bulk purchases in the United States by corporations, institutions, and other organizations. For more information, please contact the publisher.

Cider Mill Press Book Publishers
"Where Good Books Are Ready for Press"
PO Box 454
12 Spring Street
Kennebunkport, Maine 04046
Visit us online! www.cidermillpress.com

Typography: Adobe Garamond, Brandon Grotesque, Lastra, Sackers English Script
Image Credits: Photos by Derek Bissonnette, with the exception of the images
on pages 107 and 396-397, which are used under official license from Shutterstock.com.
Front cover image © StockFood / Eisling Studio-Food Photo & Video

Printed in China
4 5 6 7 8 9 0

SOUP

The Ultimate Book of Soups and Stews

DEREK BISSONNETTE

CIDER MILL PRESS

BOOK
PUBLISHERS
KENNEBUNKPORT, MAINE

"With Chef Derek Bissonnette in your kitchen, you have casual, approachable and electric cooking. This book on soups will bring pure joy, warmth and flavor to the table and the beautiful photography will transport you to a dream workplace."

Daniel Boulud
Chef/Owner of The Dinex Group

"The world does not have enough good books on the art of soup making. Leave it to Derek Bissonnette, a multi-talented New England chef, to provide us with a wonderful collection of soups for all seasons and all tastes. Gloriously photographed by the chef/author, the book sizzles with inspirational ideas from cuisines around the world. *Soup* is an irresistible gift for home cooks as well as professional chefs."

Patrick O'Connell
Chef/Proprietor The Inn at Little Washington

"A mentor once told me, 'You can always tell the level of training and talent in a chef by the quality of his or her soups.' Simple or exotic, soup is one of my favorite things to cook! Follow along with Derek Bissonnette as he guides you through the delicious layers of flavors, textures, and creativity while developing these beautiful, seasonal soups."

Jason Bangerter
Executive Chef, Langdon Hall Country House Hotel and Spa

"For nearly twenty years, Derek has exemplified the spirit of the Grand Chefs of Relais & Chateaux with a career spanning some of our most prestigious properties from the Inn at Little Washington to the White Barn Inn. It is said that the mark of a great chef is in his soups and sauces, for in their simplicity the chef must be perfect in his/her execution. In this book Derek illustrates that ideal from beginning to end, with a variety of techniques, ingredients, and tools and enough recipes to keep you happily exploring the topic for a very long time."

Daniel A. Hostettler
President, North American Delegation, Relais & Chateaux

"A collection of amazing soups from Chef Derek Bissonnette. Tried and tested recipes from Derek's wealth of experience in luxury Relais & Chateaux properties both in the U.S. and in Europe. Be inspired by these recipes and creative photography and immerse yourself in these soups for every occasion."

Steven Titman
Executive Chef, Summer Lodge Country House Hotel

"Since I have known Derek I have witnessed the evolution of a chef. His style in the kitchen is sophisticated, confident, and driven by passion. In this book, you'll find all of that passion and knowledge balanced with the heart and soul of a true hospitality professional. His love and appreciation of soup, and food that warms the soul, shines through the pages and will help you share your own love of warmth and hospitality with your friends and family."

Warren Barr
Executive Chef, The Pointe Restaurant at the Wickaninnish Inn

CONTENTS

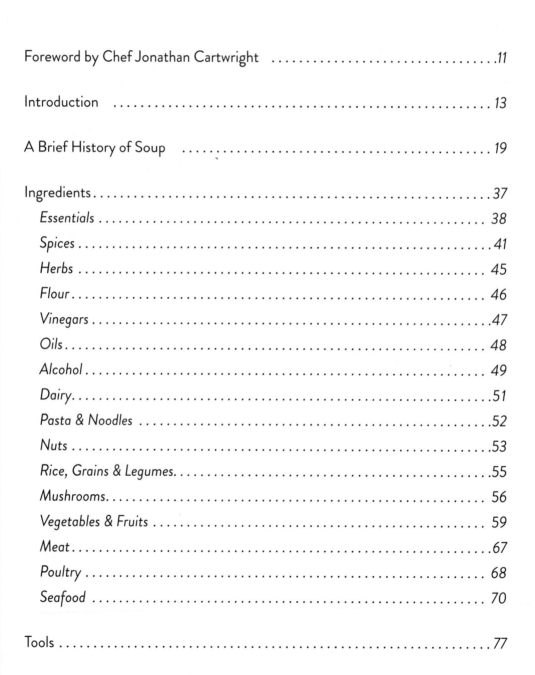

FOREWORD

*S*oup! A forgotten art, until now!

I have a good friend who always says no one makes good soups anymore. Steven, my friend, I am sure that if you follow Derek's recipes here your faith will be restored.

I remember first meeting Derek in the kitchen of The White Barn Inn in Kennebunk, Maine. He was there to try out for the position of Pastry Chef. Eagerly, Derek scurried around helping in pastry and preparing his sample dessert. He didn't fall short that day and has continued to grow as a chef every day since.

As a young pastry chef filled with desire and drive, Derek mastered the role despite all of the curveballs hospitality throws at you. Always working diligently within the team, he would scale all obstacles that came his way, producing breathtaking pastries and baked goods for our discerning guests. During Derek's first tour of duty at The Barn, he was fortunate to cross paths with our friend and mentor, the late Laurie Bongiorno, who owned the restaurant. As I'm sure Derek would agree, Laurie's never-say-die attitude rubbed off on both of us.

During his second stint at The White Barn Inn, Derek took over as Chef De Cuisine. He excelled at this position as well, showing a rare ability to teach and motivate young team members. His team-oriented leadership during this period earned The Barn more accolades and happier guests than ever before.

Together, we've opened new restaurants and cooked for many events, both at The Barn and off-property. Whether it be cooking at the James Beard House or preparing the dinner for Barbara Bush's 90th Birthday, Derek has proven himself to be a true, loyal lieutenant every time.

Over the decades of knowing Derek, I have watched him develop, and have grown to appreciate his attention to detail, which is ever-present in these recipes and photographs. Now, he has taken his two talents and produced a work of art, providing insight into his whimsical culinary mind, and working tirelessly to put his own spin on these recipes. As I'm sure you'll find, his efforts will benefit anyone who follows them.

Bon Appétit

Jonathan Cartwright

INTRODUCTION

*D*r. Seuss' *Green Eggs and Ham*, where Sam-I-am's persistence pays off for his very stubborn, very vocal counterpart, taught me a valuable lesson at an early age: never be afraid to try something new. If you're willing to treat every day as a learning opportunity, and continue to challenge your taste buds, there's no limit to your culinary abilities.

The danger in insisting that "You know what you like, and what you don't," is that I've often found that it was not a particular ingredient I didn't like, but a particular preparation of it. If you can keep this in mind, and remain open in spite of previous lackluster experiences, you'll eventually have that moment we all search for—having your expectations of unpleasantness transformed into joy, thanks to a perfect mixture of seasoning, acidity, texture, and execution.

I grew up in a household where food was seen as secondary—eating dinner together as a family was far more important than whatever was put in front of us. Because of this, I grew up on food so simple that it wasn't until I went to culinary school that I was introduced to salt! My mother avoided it due to a hereditary cholesterol problem in our family, but once I got to school I finally saw what I'd been missing—salt is not there to provide flavor, but to provide a balance that enhances the other flavors in a dish.

If I had remained stuck in my ways, and toed the familial line on salt, it's safe to say I wouldn't have had the career I've had. Not just because salt is so important to cooking, but also because it provided a philosophy to guide me—by vowing to remain open, I figured my experiences would always lead me somewhere interesting.

Because, Lord knows, I needed *something* to guide me. When I graduated culinary school, my response to the oft-asked questions about career goals was that I only wanted "to have no goals." This was often greeted with a frown, but what those people took to be a lack of drive was actually me not wanting to miss out on an opportunity simply because I was blindly chasing some *goal*. Back then, I didn't know anywhere near enough to do that.

And I can say that with confidence, because if I knew what I wanted back then, I wouldn't be here, working on this book right now. I started off as a baker in Searsport, Maine, at the age of 16. Looking back, I am appalled by the employee I was. But I was very fortunate to be in the presence of someone highly skilled, who had the uncanny ability to look through all the warning signs and see potential in me. That individual was Sean Hogan, who taught me that consistency, speed, and constant refinement of your craft are essential to a career in the culinary arts. I didn't grasp the value of these lessons until much later, but I'm forever grateful that a man as talented as Sean took the time to teach them to a knucklehead like me.

From there, I went to the Culinary Institute of America and received an associate's degree in baking and pastry. My time at the school was valuable, but even still, I was a million miles away from thinking I'd be an executive chef someday. A cookbook like this existed only in my dreams.

After school, I returned to my parents' house so I could save a little money before making my way in the world. That summer, I was lucky enough to land a job at the Youngtown Inn in Lincolnville, Maine, taking care of desserts and cold appetizers. While there, I got the first hint of my future forays into both pastry and savory, and I also got my first big break. At the end of the summer, the head chef Manuel Mercier recommended that I apply at The White Barn Inn in Kennebunk, Maine—the best restaurant north of New York City (not that I'm biased).

I was offered a position as a pastry cook, and—even at that humble station—I was in way over my head. Each day was filled with tasks I'd never done, things I never even considered being part of working in a kitchen. I was not only learning technique—I was learning how to become organized, efficient, fast, and consistent, those qualities that truly separate a great chef from a good one.

I learned fast enough to hold on to the gig, and then steadily climbed the ranks until I was promoted to pastry chef. I thought this was the greatest gift I had ever been given, but then Grand Chef Jonathan Cartwright gave me an even greater one: he let me know that this position, which I believed to be at the pinnacle of my profession, was nowhere near my ceiling as a chef. Jonathan suggested that I leave the cozy confines of The White Barn Inn. Sure, I could stay and soak up some of the glory that the place received during that time. But to do that would not be in my best interest, it would be in someone else's. So Chef Cartwright and I looked around and decided that the Inn at Little Washington in Washington, Virginia, was the best place for me, allowing me to work with the "Pope of American Cuisine," Patrick O'Connell.

So I packed my little hatchback, hit the road, and walked onto the frontlines of American cuisine. The kitchen at the Little Washington literally ran 24 hours a day, 365 days a year. We had an overnight baking team, an AM crew, a butcher, and a passel of chefs that worked throughout the night. And all those bodies were necessary—the place's reputation meant that even a slow day there would have been a killer at The White Barn.

This kind of traffic not only meant that the kitchen staff had to be considerable; it also required all those bodies to work in perfect harmony. My co-workers and I got to where we were by becoming parts of the same well-oiled machine, all synced up, helping the Little Washington achieve the almost-impossible task of maintaining its flawless reputation.

Not to say it always went according to plan. There are too many variables at play in a restaurant for that to happen, even in the best of places. What great restaurants do is keep those flaws out of the customers' sight—they learn how to disguise, how to *appear* perfect. If this sounds a bit miraculous, it's supposed to: I've spent long enough in the service industry to know that the staffs at certain restaurants are the world's true miracle workers.

After nearly two years at the Little Washington, I received a call from Steven Titman, who I had known during my time at The Barn. Steven was back in Great Britain, and wanted me to come over and help him out. I wasn't quite ready to leave Virginia, but I had a feeling that the opportunity awaiting overseas was too good to pass up. So I packed a suitcase and crossed the pond.

Europe was a huge adjustment. Over there, lunch is an important meal, and it's not uncommon for people to sit through a four-course lunch or afternoon tea. This makes balancing your breakfast, lunch, and dinner menus a huge challenge. Luckily, Steven, who had been trained by Chef Cartwright, ran his kitchen the same way as The White Barn did. So there was a little bit of familiarity to help me get on my feet. And that little bit was all I needed. Chef Titman allowed us to create dishes and involve ourselves anywhere we could be helpful.

This freedom was what I'd been craving. My original visa was for two years, but I was growing so much as a chef that I stayed an additional three.

Eventually, it was time to head home. Steven was doing a guest chef visit at The White Barn Inn when I was planning to return, so I offered to help. One thing led to another, and while working next to Chef Cartwright we

talked about the possibility of me returning. A week later I was putting on my whites and heading back to work at The Barn. Shortly after, the sous chef decided to leave, and I was offered his position.

I worked side-by-side with Chef Cartwright for several years, and when he decided to move on to his next challenge, I was offered his position. For the first time in my life, I was ultimately responsible for the success or failure of a restaurant. Not only that, I had massive shoes to fill, since Chef Cartwright had built The White Barn into one of the nation's best restaurants. I knew I would make mistakes, but I vowed to learn from them, and refused to fail.

I decided to document this experience, and purchased a camera. I knew little about photography, but from cooking I knew that whatever knowledge is out there is accessible if you embrace the fact that there is always something new to learn.

Over time, I grew to love taking photos as much as I loved cooking. And now, still pushing into new territory, I've decided to combine those two loves. My hope is that this book, by getting you to try a few new things, sets you on a path similar to mine.

A BRIEF HISTORY
of SOUP

THE ONLY UNIVERSAL DISH

The world contains countless cuisines, techniques, and ingredients. These differences might be due to availability, religious beliefs, etc., but there's no debate that food varies drastically from culture to culture.

But there is one thing that bonds them all—every single culture has some form of soup.

However, what each culture thinks of soup also varies. They can be thick or thin, can feature seafood, meat, or vegetables, and can even be clarified with gastronomic ingredients, as consommé is.

Whatever they contain, soups have been around for some time. Broths show up in the historical record around the year 1000 CE, and in the 15th century, soup dishes known as potages became a staple in the lives of peasants around the world. In fact, soups are such a vital part of what we eat that the word stems from the same Latin word that supper does: *suppare*.

EARLY CLASSIFICATIONS

At first, soups were classified based on their viscosity, whether they were thick or thin. Then the *Larousse Gastronimique*, an encyclopedia of cuisine, subdivided thin soups into broth, bouillon, consommé, those served with or without garnish, and soups that were served hot or cold. Thick soups were categorized as cream, puree, and veloute. Later on, to deal with the popularity of bouillabaisse—the famous Provencal soup created by fisherman in Marseille—Larousse added a separate category for soups featuring fish.

UTENSILS AND GROWTH

It is commonly held that cooking food was an accident, stumbled upon sometime after our ancient ancestors discovered fire 1.8 million years ago. This happy accident launched a revolution that is still underway.

The best way to cook, and the most efficient use of fire's precious heat, is boiling. Boiling kills any potential parasites in the flesh, preserves nutrients, increases the amount of antioxidants, and makes things easier to chew. Most important, the cooking liquid retains the meat's tasty juices, which would be lost if cooked over an open flame.

But finding containers that could support a boiling meal was a challenge early on. Prehistoric cooks utilized a technique called pitcooking: digging a hole in the ground, building a fire within, and covering the hole so that it functioned as a rudimentary oven. This made it possible to steam the evening meal, but boiling remained evasive. Eventually, hollowed-out rocks, turtle shells, or large pieces of bark were used for boiling. And, on occasion, the animal itself was used as a pot, with water and heated rocks inserted into the carcass so that the animal cooked itself.

Eventually, humans discovered how to fire clay, and vessels that could hold liquid as it cooked became commonplace. At first, these pots were cooked directly in the fire, but over time handles were added, allowing the cook to control the temperature by altering the pot's distance from the heat source.

Clay pots were a big step, but the true revolution came once humans learned to work with metal. This was such a giant leap forward that we utilize metal pots and pans to this day.

Different metals offer different advantages and hindrances. Copper provides the highest thermal conductivity of metals and has an unparalleled heat distribution. Cast iron is slow to heat, but once it is at temperature it provides even heating. Cast iron can also withstand very high temperatures, making it ideal for searing. But since iron is highly reactive, it can have adverse responses to high-acid foods such as wine or tomatoes. Stainless steel is resistant to corrosion, scratching, and denting, making it a dependable workhorse. But it is a relatively poor conductor of heat and doesn't adequately spread that heat over the cooking surface.

THE SPOON

There are over 50 types of spoons used in the preparation and consumption of foods. That variety is born out of the utensil's prolonged use in cultures across the world—even the pharaohs of Egypt utilized them. In Ancient Greece and Rome, bronze and silver spoons were seen as symbols of great wealth. In the Middle Ages, commoners gained access to this versatile tool, but it always remained a special oject for the upper classes—every king of England was presented a special spoon at their coronation. In the modern age, they have come to be standardized, the exact measurements provided by the tablespoon and the teaspoon making them invaluable tools for cooks all across the world.

THE FORK

The creation of the fork was huge for soup, as the fork's ability to hold a piece of meat in place while cutting it made it possible to separate solid foods from the potages they had been served in. This made multi-course meals possible, and they became increasingly popular in the 1700s, with the easy-to-digest soup serving as the first course—a position that it holds in fine restaurants to this day.

THE TABLE KNIFE

Designed to cut prepared foods, knives are typically made from stainless or carbon steel. Fun fact: knives with rounded edges were created to prevent dinner guests from indulging their questionable habit of picking their teeth with the knife's point.

EARLY MANUSCRIPTS

History documents that peasants ate the same potage for every meal, using ingredients that were easily accessible. The wealthy, however, always had a vast number of dishes at their disposal. *De re coquinaria* (On the subject of cooking), a collection of Roman recipes gathered from the 1st century to the 5th, shows that they enjoyed a large variety of "soups" featuring a number of exotic ingredients.

The first-known English cookbook is the *Forme of Cury*, which was written by the master cooks of King Richard II in the late 1300s. This text contains a number of "soup-like" recipes, and a number of dishes referred to as broths. It also features the preparation for decadent items such as whale, crane, seal, and porpoise.

The earliest German cooking manuscript is *Ein Buch con gutter spise*, which was composed in the mid-1300s. Included in the text is a recipe for *Ein spise von bonen* (a food of beans), which features a "broth" consisting of beer, vinegar, caraway seeds, and ground saffron. The recipe follows in German:

Siude grüene bonen. biz daz sie weich werden. so nim denne schoen brot. und ein wenic pfeffers. dristunt als vil kümels mit ezzige und mit biere. mal daz zu sammene. und tu dar zu saffran. und seige abe daz sode. und giuz dar uf daz gemalne. und saltz ez zu mazzen. und laz ez erwallen in dem condiment. und gibz hin.

(Translation: Boil green beans until they become soft. So take then fine bread and a little pepper. Three times as much caraway with vinegar and beer. Grind that together and add saffron thereto. And strain the broth and pour color thereon and salt it to mass and let boil in the condiment and give it out.)

As you can see, food was always something people were interested in. But it wasn't until the 17th century that the culinary arts really developed. This development was due to increased knowledge of vegetables and grains, wider access to a larger variety of ingredients, and an explosion in the publication of cookbooks.

SOUP IN CULTURE

Soups came to be known as something that promotes healing—so much so that they essentially were the health care system until the advent of modern medicine. Medical textbooks of the time read more like diet books. In China, snakes were used to make soups that were believed to help with joint pain. The meat of a strong animal was thought to strengthen a weak man. And special, protein-rich soups featuring pigs' feet were prepared for mothers following a successful childbirth, the idea being that the added protein would bolster milk production.

Of course, there is the age-old belief in chicken soup's healing capabilities. This stems from the Ancient Greeks, who recommended the meat of hens and roosters, and broth made from their bones, for many treatments. As it turns out, scientists have confirmed that this was not just an ancient superstition. Chicken actually contains a compound called carnosine that slows or blocks the migration of white blood cells, which reduces the amount of inflammation in the respiratory tract that results from the common cold. Researchers have also found that chicken soup may improve one's ability to deflect a virus and weaken it upon entry into the body. On top of all this, it also allows mucus to escape the body more freely, which keeps airways clear and eases the effects of congestion. So, with chicken soup, as with most things, it turns out that the Ancient Greeks, and your mother, have it right.

SOUP KITCHENS

In the late 1700s, flour was in short supply and expensive due to a stretch of poor wheat harvests. This development dramatically affected the poor, as bread was a staple in their households. The English government responded to the situation by opening soup kitchens in London. The measure was so successful that by the beginning of the 1800s, 55,000 individuals a week were being fed in these establishments, all for relatively little cost.

By the late 19th century, they could be found in many American and European cities. During The Great Depression, they became even more prominent in America, so much so that mobsters such as Al Capone used them to curry favor with the locals (and recruit soldiers for criminal enterprises, some would claim). Soup kitchens waned in the boom following World War II, but they are on the rise again, both in America and abroad, due to a 2006 increase in global food prices.

PRISON FOOD

At a cost of less than a penny per serving, soup also became very popular in prisons during the 19th century. Utilizing affordable ingredients such as barley, peas, and leeks, and upping the nutritional value with marrow bones, minced herring, and grated cheese, soup was seen as an easy way to keep the imprisoned nourished. It became such a staple in prisons that inmates in England in the 1830s were issued a spoon and a bowl upon incarceration.

COMFORT

Even in in the hardest of times, soup has always been a source of comfort—during the horror that was 9/11, warm cups of soup were being offered to survivors and rescue workers.

In times of emotional stress, soup can evoke feelings of warmth, happiness, satisfaction, and human connection.

This is true in any culture. Here are a few examples of popular comfort soups in countries around the globe:

Australia and New Zealand:	Chicken Soup, Lamb and Vegetable Soup, Irish Stew, Pea and Ham Soup, Pumpkin Soup
Great Britain:	Beef Stew with Dumplings, Brown Windsor Soup, Irish Stew, Potato, Leek, and Stilton Soup
Canada:	Pea Soup, Seafood Chowder, Chicken Soup with Matzo, Tomato Soup (with Grilled Cheese)
France:	Consommé, Bouillabaisse, Bisque, French Onion Soup
Hungary:	Clear Broth with Noodles and Vegetables, Stuffed Cabbage Soup, Goulash
Japan:	Ramen, Udon, Miso Soup
Philippines:	Coconut Dessert Soup, Beef Bone and Marrow Soup, Pork Offal Soup
Poland:	Clear Beetroot Soup with Pierogis, Hunter's Stew, Goulash
Russia:	Borscht, Cold Vegetable Soup, Pickled Soup
United States of America:	Tomato Soup (with Grilled Cheese), Corn Chowder, Seafood Chowder, Chicken Soup

PORTABLE SOUP

The next big movement in soup was making it portable, so that it could be enjoyed on the battlefield, and nourish weary travelers. A large share of the provisions packed on the Lewis and Clark Expedition was soup that had been boiled into a gelatin and then dried. Reports state that it was hardly a favorite among those on the journey, but it saved a lot of men from starvation.

Dried soups are advantageous for military rations, in that they only require a mug and some hot water. Mix these with tablets made from peas and rye, and, suddenly, you have a filling and nutritious meal.

Then, in 1942, dehydrated soups that tasted like they were homemade arrived on the scene. The event was momentous enough that

The New York Times detailed the development in an article. There were three types available: French Onion, Vegetable, and Green Pepper and Cornmeal. Mixed with four cups of water and cooked for 25 minutes, a delicious meal with minimal effort was available, a must in an increasingly busy world.

CANNED SOUPS

A can of soup is such a staple of mainstream culture that the pop artist Andy Warhol chose it as the subject of one of his most famous paintings. A fundamental part of the American home, it actually started out as a solution for the army, as modern military forces grew too large to live off the land, as they had historically. Once this issue had been resolved, marketers turned their attention to the home, and an icon was born.

EATING OFF THE LAND: SOUP AROUND THE WORLD

To nail down where a soup originated is very challenging. When people migrate to a new area, they add their own ingredients and techniques to what they find, transforming them quickly, and often for the better. Soups evolve quickly, making it tough to figure out the original form, and which culture was responsible for it.

However, sometimes it is obvious. Cabbage is a large crop in Germany, and is an essential ingredient in a number of German soups. Beets are grown in the Slavic countries, and Borscht—a chilled soup made from beets—is popular in the Ukraine, Poland, and Russia.

MIDDLE EAST

The Middle East's impact on European cuisine is strong, particularly in soups. Across the Middle East, the emphasis on spice and citrus lightened up a number of soups and unlocked a plethora of variations. The popular Greek

soup Avgolemono, with its lemon-flavored broth and emulsified eggs, is a perfect example of this influence.

AFRICA

Europe's colonization of African countries also added a good deal of variety to African soups, which were transformed by ingredients that were not native to the continent. Proof of this can be found in the presence of peanuts in many African soups, despite them being native to Central and South America. However, a few soups did retain their roots, such

as Ogbono, a soup made of wild mango, and Mbanga, a soup made from the ground seeds of a watermelon.

ASIA

In Asia, soup is such a staple that it is almost unthinkable to have a meal that does not incorporate either a soup or a broth. Just consider miso soup—fermented soy beans in a broth made from seaweed and bonito—is the traditional breakfast in Japan, and various potages are popular breakfasts all across the continent.

ANTARCTICA

As there are originally no native people on the frozen continent, it seems like there would be no cuisine. But soup is powerful enough to overcome even this. Those who have braved this frozen land have created a soup called Hoosh—a thick stew made from whatever's available: dried meat, powdered milk, seal blubber, biscuits, dried fruit, alcohol, and, occasionally, even pieces of sled dog.

AUSTRALIA

The use of indigenous ingredients in Australia fell out of favor almost immediately following the mass migration to the country in the 16th century, so much so that it seemed they would be lost to history. But since the 1990s there have been multiple culinary movements that emphasize these local delicacies. The latest to do so has been led by Chef Rene Redzepi, founder of the world-famous Noma restaurant in Copenhagen, Denmark. He recently opened a pop-up restaurant in Sydney that utilized local ingredients and techniques, and if his track record is any indication, it means big things in the world of Australian cooking.

CANADA

Early in the 17th century, the explorations of French explorer Samuel Champlain were powered by hearty ingredients such as salt fish, cured meats, and dried beans and peas. As luck would have it, these ingredients inspired the recipe for pea soup, a tradition which has been handed down through Canadian families for well over 400 years.

COLD SOUPS

When you think of soup, you no doubt picture a steaming bowl, ready to provide comfort on a cold day. But cold soups have their place in the world as well and are versatile enough to serve as an appetizer, a main course, or even a dessert.

Skeptical? Well, if you think about it, the contemporary smoothie is technically a soup—a liquid concoction of fruits and vegetables.

And there are a few cold soups that are as classic as any of their warmer counterparts. For instance, Vichyssoise, is a classic summer soup that was created in the early 1900s by Louis Diat, a French expatriate who was then chef at the Ritz-Carlton in New York City.

A thick soup made of boiled and puréed leeks, onions, potatoes, cream, and chicken stock, it is traditionally served cold, but is also lovely hot. Vichyssoise is a perfect start to a great meal, as it is tasty and easy on the stomach.

Another classic cold soup is Gazpacho, which has spread far from its country of origin—Spain—to provide refreshment all over the world on hot summer days. Originally just bread, garlic, oil, and vinegar ground into a paste with a mortar and pestle, gazpacho is a great example of how quickly and drastically soups can evolve.

And as we mentioned earlier, Borscht is an extremely popular soup throughout Eastern Europe. A well-made Borscht provides a wonderful sour taste that distracts you from how nourishing it is.

SOUP IN THE MODERN KITCHEN

Soups are not just placeholders on a menu. They are often the key to running a successful restaurant: one that provides the customer with a memorable experience, and does so without waste.

This is because soups are a great way to use trimmings and unused parts. In my kitchen, whether I'm at work or at home, I keep a vegetable scrap bucket. It's a way to cut costs, sure. But it's also a way to honor the efforts of those who have been a part of a particular vegetable's journey. More than 100 people could have been involved in its trip to the kitchen, and not taking them for granted means you won't take your customers for granted either. When you're running a kitchen, you have a responsibility to make sure that absolutely nothing edible goes to waste. If it does, you'll not only lose money, you'll lose a chance to experiment with a particular dish and add a bit more complexity.

From the bucket of vegetable trimmings, I'll make a beautiful, rich vegetable stock that becomes the foundation for a number of soups. In fact, the resulting stock is so lovely that, so long as time isn't a factor, I'd encourage you to ignore the Vegetable Stock recipe on page 115 and make yours with the trimmings and peels that you've saved.

And don't think those trimmings are only for vegetable stock. They're also great for adding flavor to chicken, beef, and fish stock.

The same goes for the leftover bits of a chicken: it doesn't look like much, but you can make a stock from the carcass and the legs, braise the thighs to use in a chicken noodle soup, and even make a pate from the innards. Do this, and you've managed to save yourself a bundle, all while making your future meals far more enjoyable. Trust me, this is an invaluable habit to get into—both for your wallet and for your creativity in the kitchen.

Soups also make for a great amuse-bouche or intermezzo (palate cleanser) at a restaurant, allowing the chef to keep the customer happy and entertained while they work through a five-course, prix fixe menu.

It's enjoyable for the customer, but it's a life-saver for the kitchen. With that many courses, there's bound to be a mistake or two once the pace picks up. By having a lovely, inventive soup on hand, chefs can buy themselves time by sending out a little something—and the good-will this extra, special taste engenders doesn't hurt either.

This is one of those ways great restaurants are able to appear flawless, and the only way they can afford that appearance. Without that soup, chances are the customer would be unhappy, and some tasty morsels would have gone to waste.

Not to say that soup can't be more than just a distraction. To me, it's the perfect lunch. On

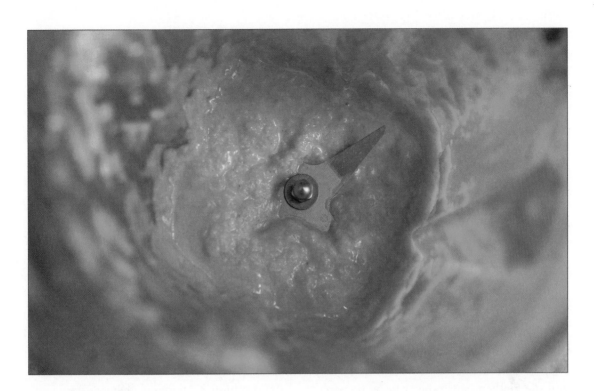

a cold, crisp fall day, I can't think of anything I want more than to warm my body, soul, and mind with a bowl of soup and a roll. As long as the soup's good, that's heaven.

Soup is also a good way to celebrate the season, and enjoy ingredients when they are fresh. In spring, it's time to pile the fiddleheads, peas, broccoli, and fava beans into a pot and get to work. In the summer, it's time to highlight corn, spinach, and bell peppers. And during the fall and winter, we move on to the heartier vegetables such as sweet potatoes, pumpkin, and squash.

THE MOTHER SOUPS

Auguste Escoffier was a French chef, restaurateur, and culinary writer. He modernized French cuisine, refined the concepts of the kitchens by simplifying, organizing, and turning them into the assembly lines that still function in most restaurants around the globe, regardless of caliber. His influence is so great that it is not too much to think of him as the Henry Ford of the culinary world. In his legendary *Le Guide Culinaire*, he defined the five mother sauces of French cuisine, those that would birth every sauce to come: Béchamel, Veloute, Espagnole, Tomato, and Hollandaise.

As a nod to Escoffier, I'd like to offer what I believe to be the six mother soups.

BROTHS
Made from meat, poultry, fish, or vegetables, a broth is a clear soup that can be consumed "as is" or used as the base in stews, soups, sauces, and braised dishes. The aroma of the broth is intended to stimulate one's appetite. They should be translucent to golden brown, with a rich, well-balanced flavor.

CONSOMMÉS
The key to a great consommé is a perfectly balanced and flavorful stock that has been clarified with a raft (made from lean meats, egg whites, tomatoes, and aromatics). When making consommé, remember this: The raft is there to

develop flavor, not provide it. It cannot compensate for a weak stock. A well-made consommé will be rich in flavor, translucent, and completely free of fat.

VEGETABLE SOUPS

The key to these soups is cooking the vegetables so that the flavor of the vegetables penetrates the base. This preparation will make the soup slightly cloudy and incredibly flavorful. Think of French Onion Soup as a perfect example of this group.

CREAM SOUPS AND VELOUTES

Traditionally, a cream soup is thickened with both cream and a *roux* (a combination of butter and flour). A veloute is a stock that has been thickened with a *roux*, cream, and eggs. Cream soups are luxurious both for the customer and the kitchen, since they can be prepared in advance and reheated to serve. Not so for veloutes, which need to be finished with the egg and served right away.

When making these soups, make sure to add the cream at the last possible moment, so that it does not curdle. Though tradition demands it, I try to avoid using a roux in these soups whenever possible, preferring to cook them low and slow in order to thicken them.

PUREED SOUPS

Pureed soups are similar to the cream soups, but more appropriate to dried beans, lentils, and starchy vegetables such as squash, potatoes, and carrots. These soups should not be strained and should have a slightly coarse texture. You'll know you've done well with one of these when the flavor is robust and the soup is not too watery and not too thick.

BISQUES

A combination of both pureed and cream soups, a bisque is traditionally made with crustaceans, which are used both in the cooking process and in garnishing the dish. A bisque is typically thickened with rice.

STORING AND REHEATING

One of the best things about soups is that not only are they OK to reheat, they are often even better the second and third time around. So make a double batch and enjoy some for lunch the following day, or use what remains to surprise your friends and neighbors with a little treat.

Please know that every single soup in this book was tested in my home kitchen. As a chef, I had several friends generously offer me use of their kitchens when they heard about my latest escapade. But I knew that those of you at home wouldn't have access to the kind of equipment, storage space, and power that a professional kitchen provides, so I wanted to make sure each of these recipes would translate to the typical home kitchen.

And yes, I have a typical home kitchen: 4-burner gas range, an oven, dishwasher, refrigerator-freezer combo, a 6-foot island

for prep, and a chest freezer in my garage—nothing crazy or extravagant. If you don't have a chest freezer, I highly recommend picking one up, since it will allow you to prepare a number of items in advance. If you're worried about the cost, keep an eye on Craigslist, where they pop up for free on occasion, so long as you're willing to handle transportation.

STOCKS

Flavorful stocks are a crucial piece to preparing these soups, so you're going to want to make a big batch every time. If you do this, and freeze whatever you don't use immediately, you'll never be stuck with grocery store stock again—meaning your soups will never lack flavor, body, or character.

Stocks freeze very well, and if you can vacuum seal the bags you store them in, much the

better. If you don't have this option, make sure to leave a little space in your container before placing it in the freezer, because the water in the stock will expand as it freezes. You can also use an ice cube tray to store your stocks, a method that comes in handy if you just want to use a little bit in a pan sauce.

Here's how you do it: When you're cooking a protein, you start it in a sauté pan and then finish it in the oven. Hang onto the juices the protein leaves behind, deglaze it with whatever wine you've chosen to enjoy with your meal, and then add a couple stock cubes and some aromatics—voila! You've got a delicious sauce to top your protein with.

Your freezer will also come in handy for storing the components you use to make the stocks. After roasting a chicken for dinner, you probably won't have the time or the energy to toss that carcass into a pot and whip up a stock.

No problem! Just wrap up the carcass and toss it into the freezer until you have some time. Do the same with your vegetable trimmings and you'll always be well on the way toward a delicious soup.

STORING SOUP

When storing a soup, be sure not to place them in the refrigerator while they are still hot. Let them cool to room temperature to avoid the development of any bacteria and prevent the temperature inside your refrigerator from rising to unsafe levels.

Not only that, depending on the size of your leftover soup, you can create an "igloo" effect, where the outsides will cool first and insulate the interior, slowing its ability to cool.

And if you are preparing a soup ahead of time and planning to reheat it for dinner the next day, make sure you leave out any fragile ingredients—such as finishing herbs—before storing in the fridge. Instead, you'll want to add these when you reheat the soup.

REHEATING

I don't often recommend using a microwave, but soup is the exception. Not to finish the soup, but using it to raise the temperature and adjust the viscosity before heating.

Once it's on the stovetop, you want to go slowly. Since soups will often coagulate when chilled due to the gelatin in the stock, you want it to thin out gradually and evenly—otherwise, you risk burning ingredients in the soup or curdling the cream.

PREPARING THE DAY BEFORE

Letting a pot of soup sit overnight allows the harsh flavors to soften, the ingredients to take on the flavors of the broth, and everything to harmonize.

Because of this, preparing them ahead of time is a great idea—except for those that are thickened with eggs, those colored by their ingredients (specifically gentle herb and spinach soups), and those containing fragile seafood.

But even these exceptions can be worked around. For soups that are thickened with eggs or feature delicate seafood, leave these ingredients out until you reheat it the next day. Soups that soak up the color of their ingredients should be frozen if not enjoyed in 24 hours, so that the chlorophyll can stabilize and the color will last.

WARMING BOWLS

When appropriate, it is very important to serve your soups in prewarmed bowls. If you shadowed me at work you would often here me repeat "Hot food, hot plates." Most china or pottery will hold a significant temperature for an extended period of time. After investing the effort to prepare a beautiful soup, it's best to extend its life by presenting and enjoying it in a warm serving dish. This will retain the soup's appropriate temperature.

INGREDIENTS

Great food begins with great ingredients. Recipes, techniques, and skills are all second to quality ingredients. I would often tell my young cooks that we are "magicians," that it is impossible to create a great recipe with a poor foundation.

In this chapter, I have outlined most of the ingredients in this book.

ESSENTIALS

Apple cider: The unfiltered and unsweetened juice of an apple. For the purposes of this book, we'll be using the nonalcoholic version.

Baking powder: A mixture of acid, carbonate, and bicarbonate that is used as a leavening agent.

Baking soda: A salt composed of sodium and bicarbonate, it is a leavening agent that responds to the acidic components in a recipe.

Brown sugar: Sucrose with molasses added to it, providing color and rich taste.

Caper: The pickled bud of the caper bush, which is also referred to as Flinders rose. It is most at home in Mediterranean cuisine, where it is used as a seasoning or garnish.

Coconut milk: The liquid that results from the grated meat of a coconut. It is used in Asian, Caribbean, and South American cuisines.

Cornmeal: The result of ground corn, it can be used in batter or as a breading.

Cornstarch: A carbohydrate extracted from the endosperm of the corn kernel, it is used to thicken sauces and soups.

Dijon mustard: This mixture of brown mustard seeds, white wine, vinegar, and salt has a sharp flavor that adds complexity wherever it appears.

Duck or Chicken fat: Natural poultry fat that has been rendered down.

Fish sauce: A regular seasoning in Asian cuisine, it is the product of fermented fish that is coated in salt and aged for up to two years. It has an extremely pungent smell and intense flavor.

Gelatin: A flavorless material that is made from the collagen in bones, and used to hold food together. You can get it as a powder or in sheets, with one sheet equaling one teaspoon of powder.

Jaggery: An unrefined sugar that typically comes from the sap of palm trees. It is used in both Middle Eastern and Asian cuisines.

Kalamata olives: A large black or brown olive that can only be grown in the Greek Peloponnese. They are usually preserved in wine vinegar or olive oil.

Kombu: An edible dried kelp that acquires a bitterness when boiled. It is used to make Dashi Broth.

Maple syrup: Forty-three gallons of sap from a maple tree are required to make one gallon of this sweet, delicious nectar.

Matzo meal: The result of finely ground matzo, the famous unleavened flatbread of Jewish cuisine.

Miso: Fermented soybeans that are used as a seasoning in a number of traditional Japanese dishes.

Panko: Bread crumbs made from bread without a crust. The result is a lighter bread crumb that absorbs less oil when fried and remains crunchy.

Sauerkraut: This fermented cabbage product is valued for its distinctive sour flavor and digestive benefits.

Semolina: This golden, aromatic flour is made from durum wheat, and most often appears in Italian dishes.

Sesame seed: These small seeds may not look like much, but they're rich in vitamins like copper, magnesium, and calcium.

Shredded coconut: The dried and grated meat of the coconut. It is available sweetened or unsweetened, and in fine or coarse textures. For the recipes in this book, I recommend using fine, unsweetened coconut.

Sliced bamboo shoots: A frequent ingredient in Asian dishes, fresh shoots can be difficult to find. For this book, the canned variety will work just fine.

Soy sauce: A dark, salty liquid made from fermented soybeans. With close ties to Asian cuisines, its earthy flavor makes it an extremely versatile seasoning.

Tabasco™: A classic hot sauce made from nothing more than tabasco peppers, vinegar, and salt.

Tapioca pearls: The result of pressing moist tapioca starch through a sieve, they are used to thicken and add texture to dishes.

Tapioca starch: Made from the cassava root, which thrives in poor soil and tropical climates. This native of Brazil can be used in place of cornstarch.

Tofu: Coagulated soy milk that is high in protein and often used as a meat substitute. As it has a neutral flavor, it takes on the taste of whatever it is cooked in.

V8™: A juice consisting of beets, celery, carrots, lettuce, parsley, watercress, spinach, and tomato. It is somewhat similar to an instant *mirepoix*, the slow-cooked vegetable mélange frequently used as a base for stews, soups, and stocks.

Wakame: A dried, edible kelp with a sweet flavor. It typically appears in soups and salads.

Whole grain mustard: Mustard featuring whole and bruised seeds.

Worcestershire sauce: The formula for this fermented sauce remains a secret, but everyone acknowledges that its flavor and aroma are one-of-a-kind.

SPICES

Allspice: This is the dried, unripe fruit of the Peimenta dioica, a tree native to Mexico and Central America. It has the flavor of cinnamon, nutmeg, and cloves.

Bay leaf: An aromatic with a bitter taste, it is more valuable for the fragrance it lends to foods.

Caraway seed: Its anise-like flavor makes it a useful addition to traditionally bland foods like bread or cabbage.

Cardamom: This floral, aromatic spice may be expensive, but it is worth every penny. Toss a little bit in your rice the next time you make it, and you'll see why.

Cayenne pepper: This chili packs a serious amount of heat but don't be afraid to use it—the spice it provides can take a dish to the next level.

Chili flakes: Also known as crushed red pepper, the spice these flakes provide is as potent as what you get from the cayenne. Commonly used in Italian cooking.

Chili powder: A combination of paprika, garlic powder, cayenne, onion powder, dried oregano, and cumin.

Cinnamon: Functional in both sweet and savory preparations, a recipe gets a bit cozier when this ingredient is added.

Clove: A very aromatic spice that is primarily used in Asian, African, and Middle Eastern cuisine.

Coriander: When ground, the floral qualities of the cilantro give way to nuttiness.

Cumin: Popular in Mexican and Indian cuisines, this spice is earthy and has a pungent aroma.

Curry powder: Traditionally, a blend of coriander, turmeric, cumin, fenugreek, and chili peppers. Sometimes spices such as ginger, garlic, fennel seed, cinnamon, caraway, cardamom, nutmeg, and black pepper are added.

Fennel pollen: Dried, small flowers from wild fennel, they have notes of anise, citrus, and vanilla, and carry a very hefty price tag.

Fennel seed: An extremely aromatic, anise-flavored spice that instills warmth into any dish it is utilized in.

Five-spice: Most commonly used in Asian and Arabic cuisine, this combination of star anise, cloves, cinnamon, Sichuan peppercorns, and fennel seeds provides each of the five basic flavors: sour, bitter, sweet, salty, and umami.

Mustard seed: Often used in pickling, and a prominent spice in Indian cuisine, its tanginess is too much for most of us to resist.

Nutmeg: A sweet spice often used in desserts. However, it is able to stand on its own, and pairs wonderfully with vegetables and gamey meats.

Old Bay: A North American seasoning mixture made from celery salt, black pepper, and crushed red pepper flakes, it is most at home in seafood dishes.

Paprika: A ground spice commonly made from red bell peppers, the smoked version adds depth to any soup or sauce it touches.

Pepper: Usually referring to ground black peppercorns; however, white peppercorns are often used in fine dining establishments so that the prepared food doesn't look "dirty."

Poppy seeds: Nutty and sometimes fruity, these seeds are most often used in pastries and breads.

Saffron: The world's most expensive spice, which is due in part to it being hand-picked. Its spicy, pungent, bitter flavor features in a number of classic dishes, from bouillabaisse to paella.

Salt: There is much debate about which version of this staple is best for cooking. In this book, and in the kitchens I have worked in, I recommend using kosher salt, which has a larger grain and does not contain iodine—which I believe lends salt a slight bitterness.

Sichuan (Szechuan) peppercorn: Its name makes it seem as though it would be spicy, but

it's actually not. Instead, it has slightly citrusy notes, allowing other spices to come to the fore.

Star anise: The product of an evergreen shrub native to Southwest China, this spice is noted for both its flavor and health benefits.

Turmeric: A popular spice in Indian cuisine, it brings warmth to whatever dish it is added to, and its golden color is a treat for the eyes.

Vanilla bean: This one's an old standby when something sweet is being prepared. Keep in mind that both the seeds and the pod are aromatic, meaning you'll want to scrape out the seeds before using both to infuse.

HERBS

Basil: Initially peppery, basil rapidly escalates into a sweet, aromatic flavor. When using in cooking, make sure to add during the final stages, since heat removes the flavor.

Chives: A delicate onion flavor makes them a wonderful garnish.

Cilantro: Also known as coriander, this herb is a true divider. Those who like it can't get enough of its citrusy taste, while those who don't like it bemoan its soapy flavor.

Dill: The extremely aromatic leaves of this herb make it perfect for those dishes with a strong taste, such as smoked salmon or Borscht.

Marjoram: It has the pine and citrus flavors of oregano, but is sweeter and more delicate.

Mint: The leaves of this aromatic can be used in both savory and sweet preparations, and its cool aftertaste ensures that your mouth is always ready for the next bite.

Oregano: An intense, slightly bitter herb that spices up any dish.

Parsley: A slightly bitter herb that provides balance when added to savory dishes. There are two popular varieties, flat leaf and curly, with the former being more flavorful.

Rosemary: This hardy herb has been known to flower in early December, and its fragrant nettles are famous for the wonders they work with poultry.

Sage: Used more often in Europe than it is in the U.S., this herb has an astringent but warm flavor.

Tarragon: One of the *fines herbes* of traditional French cuisine, it is best known for its role in béarnaise sauce.

Thyme: The slightly minty flavor of this herb makes it a natural for both poultry and soups. If you just want to use the leaves in a dish, use the back of a knife to remove them easily from the stem.

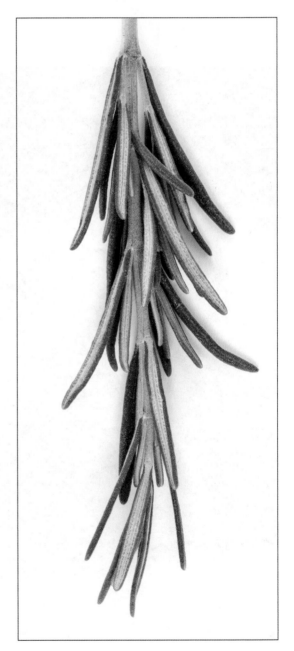

FLOUR

All-purpose: A wheat flour that is ideal for everyday baking due to its moderate levels of gluten protein.

Bread: A wheat flour that is high in gluten protein, which results in a stronger rise and a chewier crumb.

Graham: A sweet, whole wheat flour that contains all three parts of the wheat berry: the germ, endosperm, and bran.

VINEGARS

Apple cider: Made from fermented apple cider. For cooking, make sure you're purchasing an unfiltered version.

Balsamic: This black, intensely flavored vinegar is made from grape must, and is traditionally aged in a series of wooden barrels.

Champagne: Produced with the same grapes used to make the famous bubbly beverage, this is lighter than white wine vinegar.

Red wine: Red wine that is fermented until it turns sour, the flavor of this vinegar becomes muted as it ages.

Rice wine: Produced by fermenting the sugars in rice, this is less acidic than most vinegars and carries a mild, sweet flavor.

Sherry: Don't hesitate to be seduced by the handsome, dark mahogany color of this vinegar—at around $10 a bottle, it is typically a better bet than similarly priced balsamic vinegars.

White distilled : The vinegar itself is not distilled, but produced by the fermentation of distilled alcohol. Its lower acidity makes it ideal for cooking.

White wine: Its flavor is not as potent as its brethren, but this makes it more versatile—it adds a clean fruitiness to any dish.

OILS

Extra virgin olive oil: Mostly used in salad dressings. When using it to cook, be aware of the oil's temperature—the taste will deteriorate once it exceeds 210°F.

Peanut oil: Often used in American and Asian cuisines, this oil has a high smoke point, making it ideal for use in frying.

Sesame oil: A very flavorful, aromatic oil with a high smoke point. Often used in Indian, African, and Asian cuisines.

Truffle oil: Infused with the famous mushroom, it is used to finish dishes rather than cook them. Beware, there are many artificial impostors out there.

Vegetable oil: For the purpose of this book, it refers to canola oil. Canola is low in saturated fat, is high in Omega-6 fatty acids, and has a high smoke point, making it perfect for normal cooking procedures and frying.

ALCOHOL

Brandy: A spirit that results from distilled wine. In cooking, it is typically used to intensify the flavor of a soup or sauce.

Calvados: A dry, apple-flavored brandy produced in the Normandy region in France. In the kitchen, it can find its way into pan sauces, soups, and pastry.

Kirsch: A clear, fermented cherry-flavored brandy that is often used in pastry.

Kvass: A low-alcohol, fermented beverage that is made from rye bread. It is used in Borscht.

Madeira: A sweet, fortified wine produced in Portugal's Madeira Islands.

Myers's Rum: A dark Jamaican rum that appears in both savory and sweet preparations.

Mirin: A low-alcohol rice wine that is similar in flavor to sake. In Japanese cuisine, it is used as a condiment.

Pernod: A green, anise-flavored liquor from France.

Port wine: Both Madeira and White port are utilized in this book.

Red wine: For the purposes of this book, I used Cabernet Sauvignon in my preparations. Don't go overboard and use an expensive bottle of it—in my kitchens, we often use open bottles that are no longer good enough to sell.

Riesling: A sweet wine with a strong, flowery aroma.

Sambuca: An anise-flavored liqueur from Italy.

Sherry: Fortified wine made from white grapes. It comes in a number of varieties, and is probably used in cooking as much as it is imbibed.

White wine: For the recipes in this book, I used Chardonnay, preferring its fruitiness. Again, make sure you don't break the bank when you're using it for cooking.

DAIRY

Butter: Typically up to 80% butterfat, it has a melting temperature of 90 to 95°F. For the purpose of this book, all the butter is unsalted, since this will ensure that it is fresh.

Buttermilk: The liquid remaining after the butter is churned has a slightly sour taste and is mostly used for baking pastry or making drinks.

Crème fraiche: A thick cream that is slightly sour and has the consistency of sour cream. It is traditionally made by leaving unpasteurized cream at room temperature. There are pasteurized versions available at the grocery store, which typically have buttermilk added in order to provide flavor and thickness.

Cashel blue cheese: A semi-soft pasteurized cheese that is made in Ireland from cow's milk, its flavor is round and full.

Feta cheese: Made from sheep's or goat's milk, it is rich and salty. Most of the feta that is made in North America and Greece has been pasteurized.

Fontina: A nutty, delicate semi-soft cheese from Italy. Made from cow's milk, it features a dark brown rind and is typically unpasteurized.

Greek yogurt: Yogurt is the result of milk that yogurt cultures have been added to, heated, and then cooled before fermenting for several hours. Greek yogurt is the result of yogurt that has been strained to remove the whey. It has a slightly sour, zesty taste.

Gruyere: An unpasteurized, semi-soft cheese from Switzerland that is famous for its sweet, slightly salty flavor.

Halloumi: This is an unripe, brined, semi-hard cheese made from goat's or sheep's milk. Because of its high melting point, it is great for grilling and frying.

Heavy cream: Milk with a fat content of 36 to 40%. Also referred to as whipping cream, it is used frequently as an ingredient in this book.

Kefalotiri: A hard cheese made from goat's or sheep's milk. It has a sharp flavor and a dry texture.

Mascarpone: An Italian cream cheese thickened by the addition of citric acid. It is known for its milky flavor.

Monterey Jack: One of the few American cheeses, it is produced on the central California coast from pasteurized cow's milk.

Parmesan: Properly known as Parmigiano-Reggiano, this unpasteurized cheese is known for its bold aroma.

Queso fresco: A Mexican cheese that is made from cow's milk or a combination of goat's and cow's milk. It resembles feta, but lacks feta's saltiness.

Sharp cheddar: Made from cow's milk, this is originally from Somerset, a village in England. It is typically pasteurized and aged 3 to 24 months.

Sour cream: Made by adding lactic acid, this has a similar texture to yogurt, but lacks yogurt's zest.

Stilton: A semi-soft, crumbly pasteurized blue cheese from England that is notorious for its strong flavor.

PASTA & NOODLES

Egg noodles: Made from unleavened dough, these are a staple in many Asian countries.

Elbow macaroni: A curved pasta often made with durum wheat.

Farfalle: Also known as bow-tie pasta, its name is derived from the Italian word for butterfly.

Israeli couscous: A pearl-shaped pasta with a very nutty flavor.

Orzo: Pasta that is shaped like a grain of rice, it is versatile and cooks up relatively quickly, making it a good option for a busy individual to keep around.

Rice noodles: Traditionally made from rice flour and water, this staple of Asian cuisine occasionally has cornstarch or tapioca added to make the noodles chewier.

NUTS

Almond: Bursting with healthy fats, fiber, and protein, in its various forms—slivered, blanched, roasted—this native of North Africa is able to dress up a number of dishes.

Cashew: This tasty nut can be enjoyed on its own, utilized in sweet and savory dishes, and even turned into milk.

Chestnut: Native to the temperate regions of the Northern Hemisphere, these are typically roasted, just as the famous Christmas song suggests. Before roasting, you'll want to score the shell and let them dry out for a few days to get that sweet, delicate flavor they are known for.

Pine nut: Also called the pignoli, pine nuts are best known as a component in traditional pesto recipes.

Walnut: This nutrient-dense nut is often included in baked goods, as its relatively bitter taste balances the sugars.

RICE, GRAINS & LEGUMES

Arborio rice: A short-grain, high-starch rice that provides the foundation of the classic dish risotto.

Barley: This hearty grain was one of the first cultivated by man.

Black beans: A staple of Latin American cuisine, its dense, meaty texture makes it a natural in vegetable-rich dishes.

Black-eyed peas: Also known as cow peas, these are loaded with fiber, potassium, and phosphorus.

Chickpeas: Also known as garbanzo beans, this staple of Middle Eastern cuisine is best known as the basis of hummus.

Split pea: This flavorful legume is often used in Greek cuisine, and comes in yellow and green varieties.

Kidney beans: Named for their resemblance to the organ, they are popular in Southwestern and Caribbean cooking. Famously red, there is also a white variety known as cannellini beans.

Lentils: Loaded with nutrition, and available in a number of varieties. Le Puy lentils are often a solid default choice, as they hold their shape and flavor well during cooking.

Long-grain rice: Similar in taste to short-grain rice, but it does not stick together when cooked, as short-grain rice tends to do.

Peanut: This legume is best known for its butter, and its ability to effectively convey just about any seasoning it is paired with.

MUSHROOMS

Baby brown pearl: One of the most commonly used varieties of oyster mushrooms, they are at their best when baked, steamed, or sautéed.

Beech: Also known as brown clamshells, this is among the gourmet varieties of oyster mushrooms.

Button/Cremini/Portobello: Also called the common, or commercial, mushroom. True button mushrooms are picked very young, when the mushroom cap is still closed. Cremini mushrooms are the adolescent version of the button mushroom, and Portobello the adult. Each version has a different look and flavor.

Enoki: Very popular in Asian cuisine, this interesting looking and delicately flavored mushroom is at its best raw or lightly cooked.

Shiitake: Believed to have medicinal properties, they are prominent in Asian cuisines.

Truffle: Highly prized for their pungent aroma, these mushrooms can carry astronomical price tags. The most prized varieties are Alba, Perigord, and Burgundy, which are often sliced thin and used as a garnish. Although I prefer a fresh truffle, I used truffle paste and truffle oils in this book in the interest of keeping costs down. But if you feel like spoiling yourself, don't hesitate to use fresh truffles in your preparations.

VEGETABLES & FRUITS

Acorn squash: Indigenous to North and Central America, this is great baked, sautéed, steamed, or in soups.

Asparagus: A part of the onion and garlic family, it is native to Europe, Northern Africa, and Western Asia. It has many uses, but its heartiness makes it perfect for soups. Keep an eye out for the white varietal, which is prized in Europe.

Avocado: Its subtle flavor and smooth texture allow this fruit to be used in both savory and sweet preparations. The key to the avocado is choosing a ripe one. Look for those that yield slightly to gentle, even pressure—you don't want anything that's mushy or firm.

Beets: Known for their vibrant color and earthy flavor, beets seem to rise in popularity each year. They are also key to one of the world's classic soups, Borscht.

Bell pepper: A sweet pepper that comes in a variety of colors. The colors are indicative of different stages of ripeness.

Blueberry: Blueberries have been growing in Maine for over 10,000 years, way before the state had its name. This versatile, sweet, and healthy berry is almost as synonymous with my home state as lobster.

Broccoli: A member of the cabbage family, broccoli's crispness and mild nutty undertone make it a natural for soup. The deep green color it adds is also a welcome addition to any stockpot.

Burdock root: Burdock is used as a food on occasion but is best known for its ability to provide pollen and nectar for honeybees. Its root provides a sweet, earthy flavor to whatever it is added to.

Butternut squash: Technically a fruit, the flavor of its orange pulp is sweet and robust enough that it can function as a soup all by itself.

Cabbage: In this book we use the green, red, and savoy varieties of cabbage, but there are over 400 different kinds in the world. A true workhorse, its mild, earthy flavor fits in a surprising number of places.

Cantaloupe: A round melon with creamy orange flesh, it is known for its subtle, fresh flavor.

Carrot: High in vitamins, and naturally sweet, the carrot is a key to developing flavor in soups.

Cauliflower: Looking like a crown of broccoli that the color has been removed from, cauliflower is incredibly versatile, able to provide either texture or flavor, whichever is needed.

Celeriac: Valued for its tenderness and flavor, this can be roasted, stewed, or pureed.

Celery: The mild, fresh flavor of this vegetable has garnered it a lot of attention in a number of classical preparations.

Cherry: This stone fruit is mainly featured in desserts, but it pairs nicely with gamey food and rich sauces.

Chipotle pepper: Smoked and dried jalapeños, they will add wonderful heat and smokiness to any dish they are included in.

Collard greens: This bold, bitter green is a member of the cabbage family. Extremely popular in the American South, collard greens are hearty enough to turn a soup into a meal.

Corn: A staple in many parts of the world, corn's sweetness and versatility allow it to take on a number of guises.

Cucumber: There are many varieties of cucumber, but the three main ones are slicing, pickling, and seedless. Valued for their fresh, clean flavor, they are commonly used raw in salad or as a garnish.

Eggplant: This meaty vegetable can be pureed, grilled, sautéed, or used in soups. Most commonly used in Mediterranean and Middle Eastern cuisine, the Thai variety mentioned in this book is often used in Southeast Asia.

Fennel: Featuring a strong anise flavor, this member of the parsley family adds complexity to any soup or salad.

Fennel fronds: These are slightly sweet, and can work well as a garnish with the right dish.

Fiddleheads: This fern that is popular in the Northern United States is a great source of Omega-3s. Only available for a short period of time, fiddleheads are great sautéed or in soup.

Figs: The Black Mission Fig is the one used in this book. But it's only one of 600 varieties in the world. Its ruby interior provides a honey-like sweetness and berry notes.

Galangal root: A close relative to ginger that is famed for its healing properties, it is used primarily in Asian cuisines.

Garlic: Native to Central Asia, it has by now taken root in almost every cuisine. It's strong, spicy aroma marks the start of countless dishes.

Ginger: This root is known for its fragrant spiciness and ability to promote healing. One of the first spices imported into Europe, it is widely used around the world.

Globe artichoke: Only the heart of these are worth your time, and you'll have to work through a flower of tough leaves to get there. However, the heart oxidizes quickly, so it's important to submerge in water with citrus juice added while preparing it. The labor is worth it though, as the artichoke's mild, nutty flavor has been beloved since ancient Romans pickled the hearts in honey and vinegar.

Grape: This sweet fruit features in a number of delicious products, most famously wine and jelly.

Hearts of palm: Harvested from palm trees, these are difficult to find fresh in a lot of places. They are available canned in most grocery stores, and feature a delicate, artichoke-like flavor.

Hominy: A kernel of corn that has had the hull and germ removed. Ground hominy is the basis for grits, the classic Southern dish.

Honeydew melon: The green, glowing flesh of this gourd often finds its way into a dessert, but as you'll see, it can also work in soup.

Horseradish: A very spicy, pungent root vegetable that can be used when you're looking to provide a serious kick.

Jalapeño pepper: A hot pepper that is typically picked while unripe.

Kale: This leafy, beefy green has soared in popularity over the past few years. Rich in vitamins, minerals, calcium, and potassium, its sturdiness makes it perfect for soup.

Leek: The bottom part is the edible part of this cousin of the onion, garlic, shallot, chive, and scallion. In this book I refer to using the white part of the leek, but it is truly the white and slightly green part of the stem. The leaves can also be cooked.

Lemongrass: Indigenous to Asia, Africa, and Australia, and utilized for medicinal purposes as much as it is for culinary ones, lemongrass has a distinct lemon scent and flavor.

Lime: This sour green citrus fruit is wonderful at accentuating other flavors, whether it be in a beverage or a dish.

Lime leaves: From the Kaffir Lime tree, they are used in a number of Asian cuisines and also work well in seafood dishes.

Mango: A delicious, vitamin-packed fruit native to South Asia, the key to enjoying the mango is finding a ripe one. Look for those mangoes that are soft with very little green on the peel. If none of these are available, try wrapping it in newspaper and leaving it on the counter overnight.

Okra: A fan of warmer climates, okra has come to prominence due to its starring role in most gumbos.

Onion: Another member of the amaryllis family that is charged with laying the groundwork for a countless number of flavorful dishes, and a large component of a majority of the soups in this book.

Papaya: Sweet with just a little bit of peppery musk, this tropical fruit is the perfect ingredient to spice up your standard fruit salad.

Parsnip: Don't be fooled by the pale flesh of this member of the parsley family—its spicy flavor adds color to any dish, soup, or stew.

Pasilla pepper: This chili has a dark, wrinkled skin and features mild to medium heat.

Pea: Sweet and bursting with freshness, the quickness with which they can be prepared should help make peas a staple in your kitchen.

Pea tendrils: The shoots and young leafs of the snow pea plant, their taste is somewhere between spinach and peas.

Potato: This starchy vegetable is the world's fourth-most popular vegetable, and when you consider the amount of dishes it can participate in, it seems like it should be the most popular.

Pumpkin: The lighter the flesh, the sweeter the pumpkin. Useful roasted, pureed, and in desserts, the seeds of a pumpkin can be removed, dried, and toasted to make a wonderful snack or garnish.

Radish: After originating in Europe, these crunchy, peppery vegetables have taken root all across the globe. Use them to dress up salads, or a crudité.

Rhubarb: The leaves are poisonous, but the stalk is edible and offers a similar flavor to sour green apples.

Rutabaga: A cross between a turnip and a cabbage, this vegetable features a mild bitterness that works wonderfully in salads and soups.

Scallion: Also known as a green onion, these have a milder flavor than most onions. Generally, the white bulb is used in cooking, and the green stem as a garnish.

Shallot: Think of this as a sweeter, milder onion. They also contain a hint of garlic.

Spinach: The neutral flavor and bright green color of this vegetable make it a worthy addition to any soup that needs just a bit more flash.

Sunchoke: Also known as the Jerusalem artichoke, this native of North America has a slightly sweet flavor.

Sweet potato: There are a number of varieties of the sweet potato, each one offering slightly different characteristics. The lovely thing about all of them is how well they can play off both salty and sweet flavors.

Swiss chard: Less vegetal tasting than kale but just as nutritious, this green leafy vegetable is frequently used in Mediterranean cooking.

Tamarind: Sweet and tart, with incredibly complex flavor, tamarind tendsto be the star of any dish that includes it. Because it can be difficult to find fresh in the United States, for the purposes of this book tamarind paste is used.

Thai chili pepper: Also known as the bird's eye chili, this small, tapered pepper is far spicier than the jalapeño, but falls short of habanero's extreme heat.

Tomatillo: When removed from its husk, this tart treat looks like a tomato that was picked too soon. A staple of Mexican cuisine, it plays nicely off of spice.

Tomato: An iconic vegetable that works as well cooked as it does fresh. Chances are, its sweet, fresh flavor is a major part of your favorite dishes.

Watercress: A semi-aquatic, rapidly growing plant that has a slight peppery flavor. This appears most often in salads, or as a garnish.

Watermelon: The flesh of this sweet, refreshing fruit is often enjoyed raw and mysteriously improves as the temperature rises.

Zucchini: The light, delicate flavor provided by this member of the squash family really shines in ratatouille, the famous French dish.

MEAT

Andouille sausage: This famous component of Creole cuisine is double-smoked, meaning the meat is smoked before and after being put into a casing.

Beef shank: The upper part of a steer's leg, it is a tough, lean, dry cut of meat that should be cooked low and slow.

Brisket : A cut from the chest of beef or veal. Keep the fat cap on when cooking to prevent the meat from drying out.

Corned beef: Its name is the result of the beef being cured with "corns" of salt. Nitrates are often added to reduce the risk of botulism developing during curing.

Ham hocks: A joint connecting the ankle to the ham in a pig's leg. Its meat is tough, and is cooked on the bone in order to impart more flavor.

Lamb leg: Meat from the hind leg of a baby sheep, it is typically braised to counter its natural toughness. It is often cooked on the bone, but for the purposes of this book, you'll want to purchase it with the bone removed.

Lamb loin: A cut from the lamb's back, between the ribs and hip, it is lean and tender. It should be cooked at high heat.

Lamb shank: Meat from the portion of the leg below the knee, it is often braised for optimal flavor.

Lamb shoulder: Versatile and flavorful, it can be cubed for stews and soups, or braised on the bone and enjoyed on its own.

Marrow bones: The leg bones of a steer contain a soft, fatty tissue that is a delicacy in many European countries. In this book, they are used to make a delicious stock.

Oxtail: The tail of any cattle, this gelatin-rich meat is usually braised or used as the base of a stock.

Pork butt: Also referred to as pork shoulder, this flavorful cut requires slow cooking to make the most of it. It is the most common cut used in pulled pork.

Pork tenderloin: A lean, tender cut of meat from a muscle that sits along the pig's spine, it demands cooking at high heat.

Round roast: Refers to three different cuts of meat: eye of the round, bottom round, and top round. The eye of the round is a very lean, circular muscle from the bottom round. The bottom round, also referred to as a rump roast, is a cut from the outside of the hind leg. The top round is from the inside of the hind leg. These are all budget cuts of meat; for this book I used bottom round.

Salt pork: Cured fat from the belly or back of a pig. Think of it as bacon that has not yet been smoked.

Sirloin: A cut from the rear portion of an animal that is divided into three cuts: the prized top sirloin, bottom, and tip roast.

Smoked ham: A cut from the leg of a pig that is cured with salt and spices before being slowly smoked.

Spanish Chorizo: A cured, fermented, and smoked sausage that traditionally can be eaten without cooking. Its famous smokiness and deep red color is a result of dried, smoked red peppers.

Stewing steak: Meat typically from the chuck or the round that has been cut into small, bite-sized pieces. This meat is very flavorful and tender when cooked slowly.

POULTRY

Chicken: Chickens are common the world over and are bred mainly as a source of food, whether raised to be butchered or to lay eggs. Because it is such a common fowl, I think the most important piece of advice I can impart about chicken is to buy it from a local producer. Most of the meat and eggs found in supermarkets are mass produced on factory farms. I wont touch on the ethical issues, as this is a sensitive debate, but I will say that the difference in the quality and flavor of sustainably and responsibly raised meat and eggs is undebatable. So, head down to your local farm or farmers market and you will not be disappointed. Practice your butchery techniques and save the bones for stock.

Duck: Ducks are a species of waterfowl that can be found in both fresh and sea water. One of my favorite ducks to cook with is a hybrid raised in New York State, which is a blend of the heritage Mallard and the Pekin; I order mine from D'Artagnan Gourmet Foods. It is not the tenderest of birds but packs a lot of flavor. It has a nice even fat cap, perfect for roasting, searing, grilling, or confiting. Don't throw away your duck fat either, render it down and use it in recipes as the stuffed matzo balls.

Goose: A favored holiday tradition in Europe, goose is often compared to duck; it's all dark meat and has a rich, lean, and robust flavor. The fat is known as "liquid gold" and is perfect for rendering down and using to replace any recipe that calls for duck fat.

Guinea Hen: A personal favorite fowl, guinea hens look like a partridge but taste like a cross between a chicken and a pheasant. Native to Africa, the dark and lean meat of the guinea hen is incredibly delicious. Because they are so lean, it is best to cook guinea hen with bacon or duck fat.

Quail: Quail is a great introduction to game birds. Like chicken, its meat is white and very mild in flavor. Quail is cooked quickly and best enjoyed medium rare. Separating the breasts and thighs can make for a great appetizer, or try roasting the bird whole as a main course.

Pheasant: Often considered the world's favorite game bird, pheasants feature lean, pinkish white meat and are low in fat and cholesterol. Often the breast is removed and pan seared, and the legs are braised or confited. When sourcing your birds I highly recommend ones that are free range, or even better free flight. Netted free-flight fields allow the animal to be contained yet engage in natural behaviors such as flight.

Squab : Squab is a young domesticated pigeon, typically under the age of four weeks and harvested when it is adult sized, prior to flying. It tastes like dark chicken meat, very tender and moist, and is considered a delicacy. Squab meat has a fatty skin, like duck, and the meat is rich in proteins and vitamins. The practice of domesticating pigeons is said to have originated in the Middle East.

Turkey: Native to the Americas, turkey is a large bird in the genus Meleagris. Called a snood, the males have a fleshy protuberance that hangs from the top of the beak and are larger and more colorful than the females. Prized for their meat and feathers, domesticated turkeys, selectively bred to grow larger in size compared to wild turkeys, are a staple of American holidays, especially Thanksgiving. Most of the turkey recipes in this book are focused on holiday party leftovers. Keep the bones to create a nice stock and the cooked meat for finishing off your soups.

SEAFOOD

Anchovy: An oily fish consisting of more than 140 species. For this book, I use a wild-caught white anchovy.

Bonito: Similar to the mackerel, this predatory fish is very oily, but great fried. Bonito flakes are a major component of Dashi Broth, which is famously used in miso soup.

Caviar: The salt-cured roe of those fish comprising the sturgeon species. Available fresh or pasteurized.

Clam: This lovely shellfish works fried, baked, and, of course, in chowder. In this book, we use two of over 30,000 species: little neck and steamer.

Cod: The mild flavor and dense, flaky flesh make this fish perfect for frying, the results of which can be found in the extremely popular fish-and-chips.

Haddock: Related to the cod, but the mildly sweet taste of its flesh means that it stands on its own better than its cousin. When purchasing haddock, look for fillets that are firm and translucent.

Halibut: Overfishing has this fish headed toward the endangered list, which is unfortunate because its extremely clean taste and firm texture make for a memorable dining experience.

Lobster: Once known as the cockroach of the sea, contemporary culinary tastes have elevated the lobster to delicacy status. It is known for its sweet, tender meat, but the carcass has some value, too—in this book, we show you how to use it to make an exquisite lobster bisque.

Monkfish: This fish has a mildly sweet taste that draws favorable comparisons to scallops. When purchasing, steer clear of fillets that have a strong odor and/or discolored edges.

Mussel: Occurring in both fresh and salt water, the flesh of the mussel is both larger and softer than that of the clam.

Oyster: Hold out for those that are harvested during cooler months—the cooler water makes it less likely that the oyster will have pathogens.

Peekytoe crab: An Atlantic rock crab that can be found as far south as the Carolinas and as far north as Iceland, this was considered a nuisance until recently, when its sweet, delicate flesh came to be seen as a delicacy.

Salmon: An oily fish that is high in protein and Omega-3 fatty acids. It is also extremely versatile, and is delicious even when consumed raw.

Salmon roe: These salt-cured eggs of the salmon are popular in Korean cuisine.

Scallops: Sweet and delicious, these bivalves are prized by great chefs because of their interesting texture. When purchasing, always make sure they are labeled as "dry packed," which means they are free of additives.

Shrimp: Its clean flavor and firm flesh make it the ideal canvas upon which to paint a masterful meal.

Shrimp paste: A condiment in Asian cuisine that is made from fermented shrimp.

Sole: Found in both salt and fresh water, sole is mild and sweet, with a firm, flaky flesh.

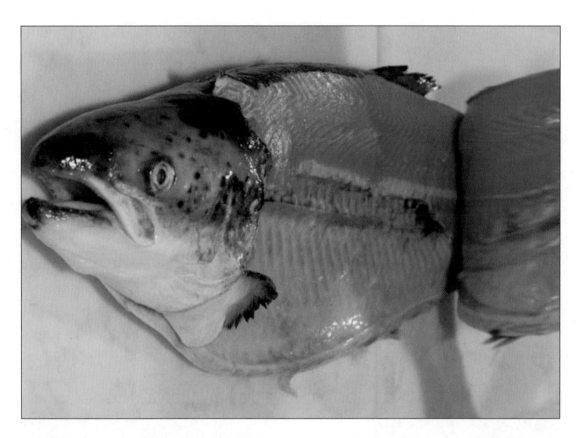

Squid: If you can get past their odd looks, you're in for a treat—they infuse whatever they touch with the sought-after umami flavor. In this book we also utilize dried squid.

Swordfish: This highly desired trophy fish also makes for good eating—its relatively high fat content makes it perfect for the grill.

Tuna: The only species that can maintain a body temperature that is higher than that of the water they exist in, tuna are both the stars and workhorses of seafood—good enough to be served raw in the world's best sushi restaurants, and versatile enough to be packed in a lunchbox.

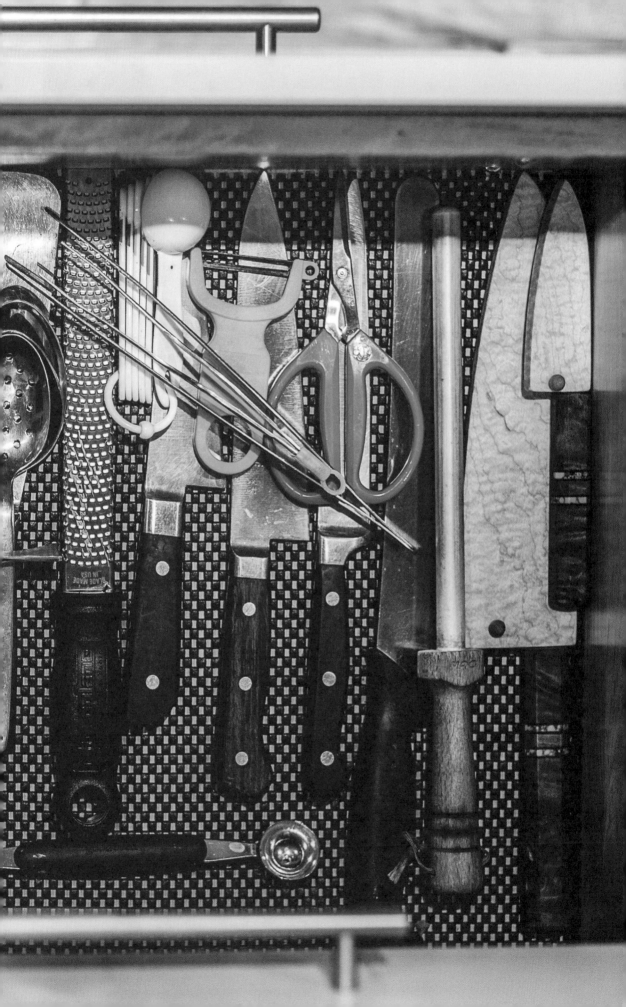

TOOLS

Most of the tools needed for this cookbook are likely already in your cupboards. There are a couple specialty tools, but I specifically chose recipes that could work around them. I have also highlighted some techniques with visual illustrations to give you extra assistance with your preparations.

MANDOLIN:
In a professional kitchen there are typically three types of mandolins. One is a Japanese mandolin, which is typically plastic with a very sharp blade and a few attachments that allow for different-sized julienne cuts. A French mandolin is metal and has fixed attachments that allow it to make julienne cuts with the addition of ruffles, which enhance the aesthetics of a dish significantly. The third is known as a truffle slicer, which is typically wood or metal, and looks much more elegant than its brethren. It is often used to shave truffles tableside.

These tools are very helpful in a professional kitchen, since they make preparation much quicker, more efficient, and consistent. However, the mandolin should only be used once you are confident and comfortable using a knife. Knife skills are essential to this book, and all cooking—to take the easy way out and use a mandolin exclusively is to shortchange your dishes.

KITCHEN SCISSORS:
This utensil should be used only for the sake of kitchen preparations that involve a sanitary purpose. The scissors will go beyond just food preparations, i.e. cutting parchment paper and twine, but you don't want to use the ones you also employ for household chores.

The scissors I prefer are made by Joyce Chen, which I like because their shape provides tremendous leverage, and their strong, thin blade promotes precision.

BONING KNIFE:
There are two standard boning knifes, one from the West—which features a heavier, bulkier blade that is beveled on both sides—and one from the East—which is more triangular and features a single bevel.

PARING KNIFE:
Primarily used to peel and chop vegetables, a great paring knife is an essential piece of equipment. Some are thick and some are thin, while some have a serrated blade and others a straight blade. I have both straight and serrated, and both come in handy. But if I had to choose one, I would invest my money in a nice, large serrated knife.

CHEF'S KNIFE:
The small chef's knife (6–10 inches) is your go-to knife for most jobs. While there are a lot of knives for specific jobs, this is a great all-around knife that can

handle almost anything. Once you find one you like, it will become an extension of your arm. There are Eastern and Western styles, and I prefer Eastern for its sharpness and lighter weight; however, there is no definitive answer with the chef's knife—all that matters is that you find one that feels right in your hand. A large chef's knife (10 to 16 inches) is a great secondary knife that just might become your go-to. I mainly use the heel of the blade with my larger knife.

SERRATED KNIFE:

A serrated knife has teeth that run along the edge of the blade. It is best for items that have a hard exterior and a softer interior, such as a loaf of bread. When using a serrated blade, mimic the movements you would employ while using a saw.

HONING STEEL:

There are three types of honing steel: steel, diamond-coated, and ceramic. Each is designed for a typical kind of knife. The steel blade has ridges and the diamond-coated are smooth with diamond particles embedded. The ceramic, which I use, is designed for Eastern knives that are thinner and made with softer metals. Using the other two with Eastern knives would greatly depreciate the blade's quality. Save them for Western knives. And remember that honing is not the same as sharpening—honing is used for light maintenance and keeping the blade precise.

GRATER:

The most common form is the box grater, which features different-sized holes on all four sides. They are most frequently used for grating cheeses and vegetables. You may also want to invest in a microplane, which is handy when

you have to zest a citrus, grate nutmeg, or perform some other fine task.

WHISK:

Used to blend ingredients to a smooth consistency, or add air to egg whites and heavy cream, I recommend having at least one small whisk and one large one in order to handle tasks of different sizes.

TONGS AND TWEEZERS:

Tongs allow you to handle food with the dexterity of your hand, without any risk of burning yourself. Helpful when turning meat or removing items from a soup, they are an essential part of any kitchen. Kitchen tweezers are also helpful. They are smaller than tongs, but offer much more finesse, and are a wonderful aid when garnishing a dish.

BUTCHER'S TWINE:

Also known as kitchen twine, this is a thick cotton string used to truss or tie animal proteins in a manner that ensures even, consistent cooking. When using butcher's twine, I recommend using a knot with two loops, which will allow for its removal without scissors.

OYSTER KNIFE:

Used to open oysters and other shellfish.

SMALL SPATULA:

Often found on a chef's person. Typically used for dessert, this tool is also very helpful when garnishing dishes.

FISH SPATULA:

A short-handled, metal spatula that is often slotted. I would recommend getting one without slots, as I find they often destroy the skin of the fish.

CAKE TESTER:

An aluminum rod used to test whether cakes are done. I often use mine to check the internal temperature of a protein, as it can be inserted without releasing the natural juices. To do this, insert the cake tester, remove it, and quickly touch it to your bottom lip, which is extremely sensitive to heat.

PIPING TIPS:

For more than garnishing cakes and cookies. They are also great for taking the presentation of your mashed potatoes and butter up a notch.

KUNZ SPOON:

Designed by a chef, for a chef. They come in various sizes, and can be slotted or without slots. I love the slotted spoons, which are perfect for removing a poached egg from its cooking water.

LADLE:

Since you'll be making plenty of soups and stocks, you'll want a variety of differently sized ladles.

FINE SIEVE:

Having sieves of different sizes and thickness is important, so that you can get the desired consistency for a particular ingredient. Having a few different sieves is also handy when you're bouncing back and forth between wet and dry ingredients—there's nothing worse than needing to sieve dry ingredients right after you just sieved your soup.

GARLIC PRESS:

Handy when you have a lot of garlic to mince, since it cuts down on the prep time considerably.

MEASURING SPOONS AND CUPS:

A crucial part of the recipes in this book. A lot of savory chefs brag about their ability to cook without measuring. But if you want consistent results, and help from others, use those teaspoons, tablespoons, and measuring cups.

MORTAR AND PESTLE:

Used to grind ingredients into a powder, it is great when working with quantities too small for a food processor. For instance, if you have whole cloves in your cupboard, but the recipe requests ground, don't run out to the store—just get to work with that mortar and pestle.

RING CUTTER:

These are great for cutting pastries, scones, and pasta, but also a tremendous help when trying to shape something on a plate. Use them to layer your garnishes and slide them onto the plate. They are typically made from aluminum, but these rust very quickly. If it's in your budget, I recommend purchasing stainless steel or plastic. If you are using aluminum, clean and dry directly after use.

SCALE:

The most valuable tool in the kitchen. All the recipes in this book have been changed to cups and tablespoons, but were all originally created using metric weight. Doing it by weight makes it much easier to cook larger batches and still get consistent results. For instance, if a recipe calls for three egg yolks, the size of the yolks will affect how the recipe turns out.

MELON BALLER:

Not a necessity, but it is nice to have when you're looking to make your mark with the presentation of a particular dish.

HAND BLENDER:

An awesome tool for soups, as just a quick blitz with it will make the soup, particularly cream soups, nice, light, and airy. It is also handy when pureeing small amounts of ingredients.

SMOKING GUN:

This is a toy, but it's an extremely cool one. You place your wood chips in the little compartment, light it with a stick lighter, and turn it on. At the restaurant we would place a cloche over a plate, fill it with smoke and then carry it to the table. When the cloche was removed it would release the smoke in front of the guest, making for a memorable, magical dining experience. These guns are also great for cold smoking indoors.

BAKING TRAY (BAKING SHEET):

These come in various shapes and sizes, but if you are stuck having to choose just one, I recommend a 13" x 18" tray made from aluminum. This will be perfect for a number of tasks, whether it be roasting proteins or stock bones, or baking a delicate pastry.

BAKING MAT:

Add these to your wish list. Made from silicone, they are reusable, dishwasher-safe, and non-stick. Never again will you be frustrated by the oven's fan blowing the parchment paper around. These mats are also perfect for dealing with gooey ingredients.

PARCHMENT PAPER:

This thin paper has many uses, whether it be lining a baking tray or rolling into a cornet to pipe your garnishes onto a plate.

CERAMIC BAKING PAN (WITH LID):

The baking pan I used for this book was 10" x 10", which is the smallest I would recommend. These are great for finishing soups in the oven. If you don't already have a set, I recommend taking a look at your local Goodwill.

PASTA STRAINER:
A bowl-shaped colander that is typically made from metal or plastic. It is perforated to allow liquid to pass through while retaining the solids.

ISI WHIPPING GUN:
This uses pressure and gas to create foams and whip cream. Can also be used to make sparkling beverages.

MIXING BOWLS:
I would recommend having a few differently sized mixing bowls on hand. I prefer either metal or plastic.

NESPRESSO™ MILK FROTHER:
I wouldn't suggest going out to buy this for food preparations, but if you have one, use it. You can achieve almost the same result with a stick blender, but this supplies heat as well. I used this for the Five-Spice Dusted Mussel Cappuccino recipe (see page 537) in this book.

VITA PREP:
This is the food processor used in most professional kitchens. It is great for pureeing soups, making smoothies, and a number of other preparations. It has a waterproof container with an attachment fixed to the base, so it cannot leak. It also has a plunger that keeps the contents moving.

ROBOT COUPE:
Another great food processor, it is better for pureeing or grinding thicker ingredients than the Vita prep. It has a removable base and blade, which has its benefits, but not the best machine to use for soups.

FRYING THERMOMETER:
A thermometer rated for temperatures up to 500° F. There are manual and digital versions available. To get a proper reading, the thermometer should be halfway into the oil. You don't want it too close to the bottom or the top, as this will provide an inaccurate reading.

STOCKPOT:
A wide, tall pot that is typically 16 quarts or larger. Used primarily for stocks, it can also be used for other large-batch preparations.

HEAVY-BOTTOM SAUCEPAN:
A pan with a thicker base, typically made out of stainless steel or cast iron. They absorb and distribute heat more evenly than a thin pot. For the purpose of this book, when I refer to a large pan, I am using an eight-quart heavy-bottom pan; a medium pan is 3½ quarts; and a small pan is 2½ quarts.

HEAVY-BOTTOM SAUTÉ PAN:
This uses the same principle as the saucepan, in that it will distribute heat evenly. Used to pan-fry foods in a shallow layer of fat over high heat. When I refer to a medium sauté pan in this book, I am referring to a 10-inch; when I say small, I am talking about the 8-inch pan.

LARGE CARVING KNIFE:

The long blade is perfect for slicing large pieces of meat. If I am filleting a large fish such as salmon, this is my knife of choice.

CARVING FORK:

Used in conjunction with the carving knife. You use it to hold the meat in place as you slice it.

KITCHENAID™ MIXER:

An invaluable tool when working with large batches. However, for a majority of the recipes in this book, I recommend doing the mixing by hand, as the quantities are small enough that a powerful machine may ruin them. These mixers are very sturdy—I've had mine for almost two decades—and come with a number of useful attachments.

FISH FILLET KNIFE:

The blade is typically 6" to 11" long and it allows you to move easily along the backbone and under the skin of a fish.

FISH PIN BONER:

A food-safe pair of pliers used to remove the very thin pin bones in a fish.

CAN OPENER:

Used to open tins, there are several different sizes available.

PEELER:

Used to remove the skin from vegetables and fruits, these come in two main varieties: A Y peeler (aka a Speed peeler), and a straight peeler. I prefer the former, as it feels much more efficient.

FISH SCALER:

Used to remove the inedible scales of a fish. For best results, move the scaler from the tail to the head, going against the grain.

BENCH SCRAPER:

A rectangular tool that is used to scrape work surfaces or cut dough. I like to cut dough with it, as its blunt edge won't destroy the work surface.

SQUEEZE BOTTLES:

They provide excellent control of your liquid components and are wonderful for refined plating.

EYE DROPPER:

A great way to control the amount of liquid being distributed into a dish, or for a very refined plating.

WOODEN SPOON:

You'll want to have a variety of these, as they are very sturdy and don't scratch the surfaces of nonstick pans.

TEMPERATURE-RESISTANT RUBBER SPATULA:

These can withstand temperatures up to 600° F, and are great for getting into the tight corners of a pot and gently folding ingredients together.

KNIFE SHARPENING:

The first thing you need to know is your knife, and what angle you want to sharpen it at. Eastern knives should be beveled at a 30° angle (15° on each side). If you have a Western knife it should be beveled at a 40° angle (20° on each side).

The smaller the bevel, the sharper the knife. But the downside of knives with small bevels is that the blade doesn't stay sharp for long.

There are several tools to help you sharpen you knife. You can use an electronic machine, a whetstone, a diamond stone, or my favorite: a Spyderco sharpening system. Before we discuss the differences, it's very important that you know what you're doing if you go with a diamond or whetstone. If you do it wrong, you will do more harm than good.

A whetstone is a natural or artificial stone that is offered in several grains, fine to coarse. Which one you choose depends on the knife, and the state of it.

A diamond stone has small diamonds embedded into it that sharpen the blade through friction. If you're using one of these, know that oil is typically added as a lubricant.

I have never actually used a sharpening machine, but I've researched them while considering a purchase. There are a number of systems available, and if the reviews are to be believed, you get what you pay for.

For a beginner, I highly recommend the Spyderco sharpening system. It is very simple, and the angles are preset for you.

Most important, do not sharpen your knife if you do not feel comfortable. Not only could you damage your knife, it can also be dangerous.

TECHNIQUES

*T*he following techniques are used in multiple recipes; for specific techniques only used in a single recipe the instructions are found with the respective recipes.

REMOVING THE OUTER LEAVES AND EXPOSING THE MEAT OF AN ARTICHOKE

The tough leaves of the artichoke protect its edible heart. It looks like a lot of work to remove them, but with this method it's not so bad. First, cut the stem and pull off the outer leaves. When you get to the tender yellow leaves, grab the top of the leaves in the center and pull them off, revealing the heart. Dig out the heart with a spoon, and use a small paring knife to remove the bottom leaves and anything clinging to the stem.

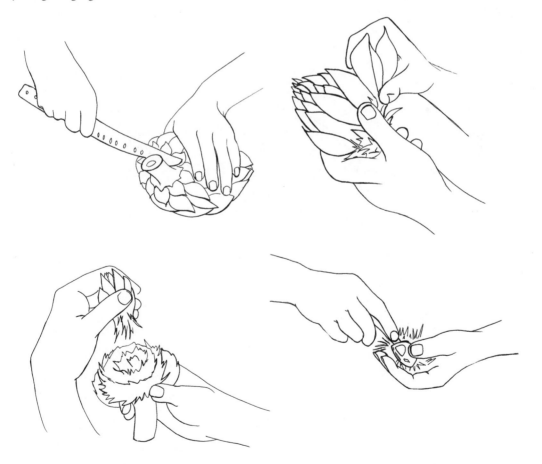

BOUQUET GARNI

Cut a 2' section of butcher twine. Tie one side of the rope around the herbs and tightly knot it. Attach the other end of the twine to the pot. For the purpose of this book we will use the traditional preparation of bay leaf and fresh sprigs of thyme and parsley.

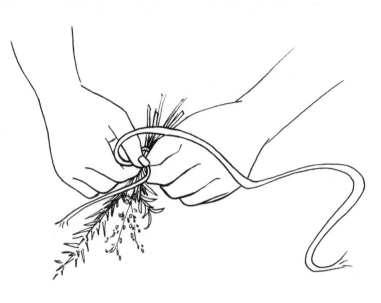

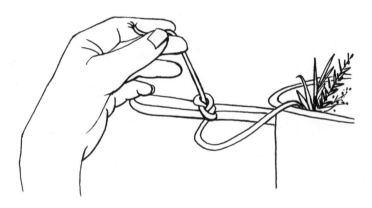

TOMATO CONCASSE

Boil enough water for a tomato to be submerged and add a pinch of salt. While it is heating, prepare an ice bath and score the top of the tomato with a paring knife, taking care not to cut into the meat of the tomato. Place the tomato in the boiling water for 30 seconds, or until the skin begins to blister. Carefully remove it from the boiling water and place it in the ice bath. Once the tomato is cool, remove it from the ice bath and use a paring knife to peel the skin off, starting at the scored top. Cut the tomato into quarters, remove the seeds, and cut according to instructions.

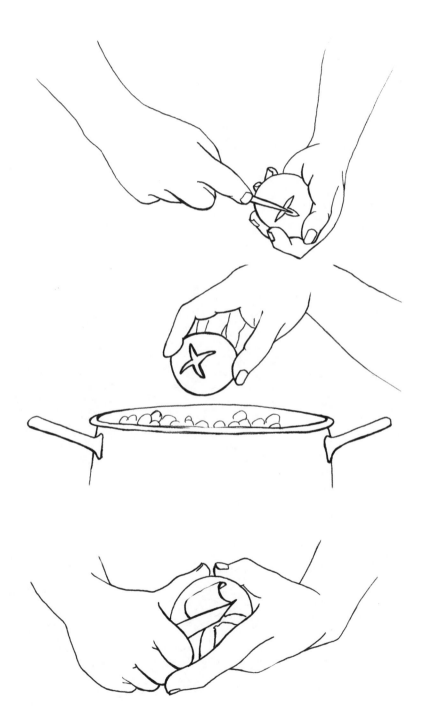

SACHET D'EPICES

Cut a 4" square of cheesecloth and a 12" piece of butcher twine. Place 3 parsley stems, ¼ tsp. thyme leaves, ½ bay leaf, ¼ tsp. cracked peppercorns, and ½ garlic clove, minced, in the middle of the cheesecloth and lift each corner to create a purse. Tie one side of the twine around the corners and make a knot. Tie the other side of the twine to the handle of your pot and then toss the sachet d'epice in.

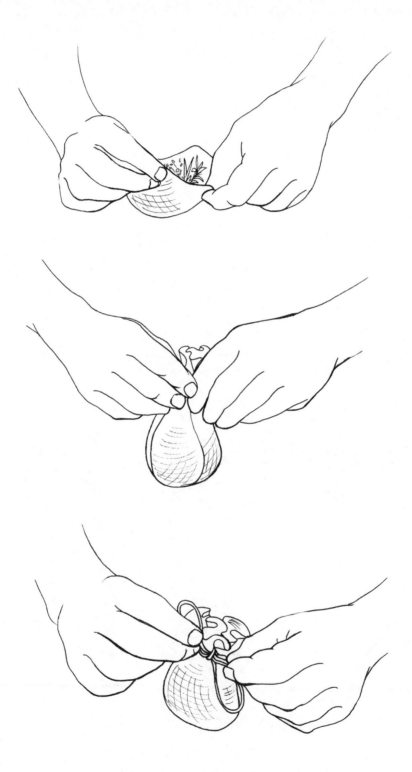

PREPARING A VANILLA BEAN, CUTTING IT IN HALF, AND SCRAPING SEEDS

Lay the vanilla bean down on a cutting board and run your finger over it from end to end, pressing down gently, several times. This will make it easier to cut. Use the tip of a sharp paring knife to slice the vanilla bean in half. Separate the two halves and flip them up, so that the cut side is facing up. Use the tip of the knife to scrape out the seeds, going over each half a few times to make sure you get all the seeds. Don't forget to save the bean pod so that you can use it to infuse your liquid. If using the seeds for a non-liquid recipe, store with some granulated sugar. This will make some beautiful-infused vanilla sugar for another recipe.

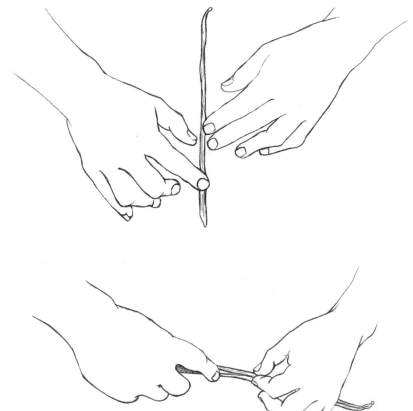

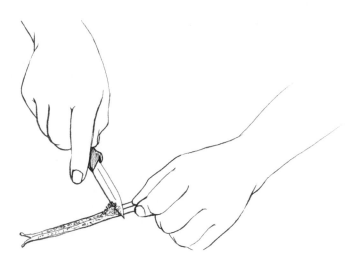

CLEANING COOKED STEAMER CLAMS

Open the cooked clams with your hands and remove the mussel and the belly. Place the belly in a container of cold water to clean and remove the outer skin from the mussel (this looks like a sock on an elephant's trunk). Place the cleaned mussel in another container of cold water and then follow the instructions for the remainder of the preparation.

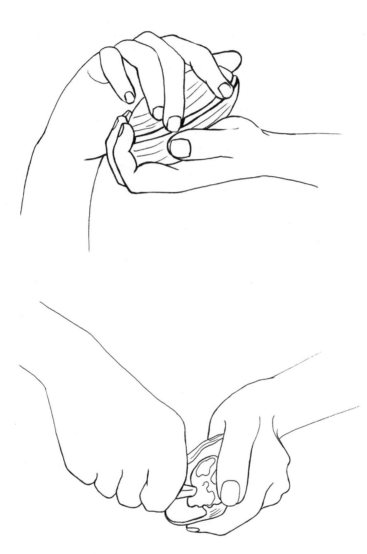

SHUCKING AN OYSTER

Fold a kitchen towel into a rectangle, and then fold it in half. Place the oyster in the center with the hinge facing toward you. Fold the towel over the oyster, place the oyster knife in the hinge, and gently twist it to loosen. Don't jam the oyster knife directly in, or you risk cutting into the meat. Turn the knife so it is perpendicular to the oyster and pry it open. Discard the top shell and carefully run the knife under the meat to release the oyster from the shell.

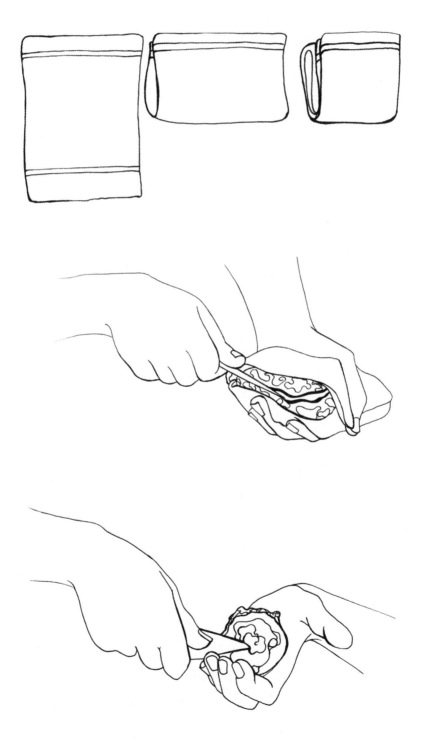

FILLING AND SHAPING WONTONS

When working with wonton dough, you want to leave it covered until you're going to use them. When you are ready, lay a few wrappers out on your work surface and place your filling in the center. Dip your finger into some water and wet the edge of the wonton wrapper. Not too much water, or the dough will become sticky and unworkable. Take two opposite corners and lift until they meet. Secure with a little pinch, and then lift the two remaining corners, one at a time.

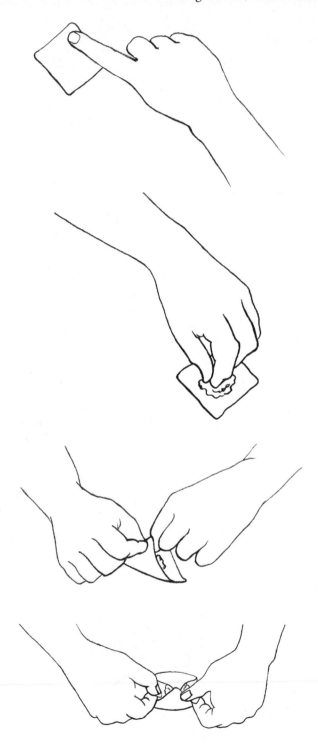

KNEADING BREAD

Place your dough on a floured work surface. Using your dominant hand, press down with your palm and gently push the dough away from you while holding onto it with your other hand. Repeat, while spinning the dough, being careful not to tear. Continue until the dough starts to resemble a firm, smooth ball.

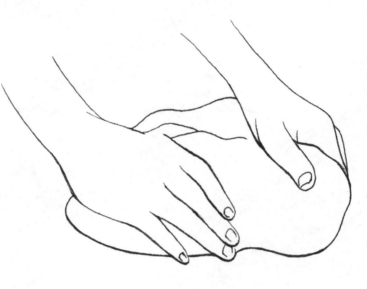

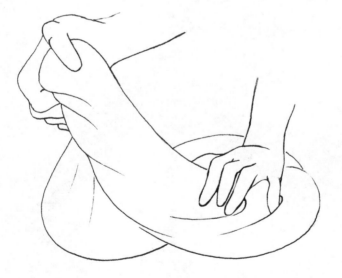

BROTHS & STOCKS

*I*n French cuisine, a basic stock is referred to as a *fonds*, which translates to "foundation." Some soups require the solid foundation a stock can provide, while others need nothing more than the proper combination of ingredients, time, and patience.

When you're preparing a stock, soup, or stew, resist the temptation to tinker and leave your seasoning until the end. Since there are a lot of salts and minerals naturally occurring in your ingredients, these will enter the soup as it cooks. Think of time and heat as doing the seasoning for you, as the flavor of almost every soup is indicative of the time invested.

A stock is traditionally a base for broths and consommés made from the bones and carcasses of a protein (vegetable stock is an obvious exception), and often features vegetables and aromatics. It is important that the bones are cooked for hours so that every last bit of flavor makes its way into the stock.

There are white stocks, and brown stocks. The former is made from the bones of white proteins, such as chicken, and lighter colored vegetables. Brown stocks are made from the bones of darker meats, such as beef.

I cannot emphasize this enough: try and save the bones from what you cook at home to use in your stocks. You can buy bones from a butcher or a fish monger, but you're paying money to haul away their garbage. If you happen to be on good terms with your butcher or fish monger and can get the bones for free, go right ahead. (There is one good thing about buying your bones from the butcher: you can have them cut there, which will maximize the amount of gelatin and flavor that can be extracted.)

If you have time—and to be a master of soup, you'd better—then you can get more flavor and more stock out of the same group of bones. Here's how: when your first stock is finished, strain it, set the bones, vegetables, and aromatics aside, and place everything in the refrigerator overnight. The next day, reuse the bones, vegetables, and aromatics, and make a second stock.

When the second stock is done, strain it and chill. Naturally, this second stock won't contain as much flavor or gelatin as the first, which is why, on the third day, you're going to combine them. You'll want to reduce this combo stock nice and slowly, making sure to skim as much fat and as many impurities out as you can. No matter what, you won't be able to get them all, which is why it's important to refrigerate your stock prior to using or freezing. When the stock is cold, the fat and the remaining impurities will settle on top, making it easy to remove.

If the fat is from chicken or duck meat, feel free to save/freeze it. This is not the traditional way of rendering these fats, but it yields the same results.

While making your own stock is essential to making great soup, stocks are available at your local grocery store. And some of them are actually decent. But nothing store bought will replicate the stock you will produce at home—so save the packaged stuff for absolute emergencies.

To keep those emergencies from occurring, you'll want to purchase a large stockpot. But don't go too large—for a home range, I recommend no larger than a 16-quart stockpot, since a majority of stoves won't burn hot enough to handle a stock larger than this.

Broths are often used to describe stocks; even among chefs the terms are often interchangeable. But they are technically different: broths are stocks that have been enhanced with

whole pieces of meat, vegetables, and, often, the addition of carbohydrates such as potatoes, pasta, or beans. Think of a broth as a finalized product, rather than a concentrate to be dressed up.

Consommé, when made properly, is a crystal clear, rich soup that is free of impurities and fat. A consommé starts with a cold stock. Egg whites, tomatoes, lean meats, and aromatics are then added, and the pot is placed over a very low flame.

As the stock heats up, the egg whites and lean meat will coagulate and rise to the top of the soup: this is known as a raft. As the stock simmers, the impurities will be filtered out and the soup's overall flavor fortified. Consommé only needs to simmer for approximately 30 minutes before being left to settle and strained through cheese cloth.

Consommé gets a bad rap, and is often criticized for being weak. But this is inevitably due to a weak stock. There is no secret to making great consommé—it's as wonderful as your starting stock. It sounds intimidating, but it's that simple. So get to work—trust me, there's not many things more pleasing than getting the taste just right and then seeing the liquid pass clear through the cheesecloth.

VEAL, BEEF, *or* LAMB STOCK

YIELD: 6 QUARTS / **ACTIVE TIME:** 30 MINUTES / **TOTAL TIME:** 5 HOURS AND 20 MINUTES

When I am making a dish that utilizes a brown stock, I try to use veal bones. Veal are cows aged from six months to a year, and it has a smoother taste than beef. It's also more tender, lighter, and finer in texture. This superiority extends to the bones as well—to me, the gelatin in stock made with veal bones has a better sheen.

That said, beef bones are much cheaper and more accessible than veal bones, so these will often be what you're working with. When using lamb bones in a brown stock, my recommendation is to use half lamb and half veal or beef bones. The lamb bones have a particularly strong flavor, which can overwhelm a soup if you are not careful.

1. Preheat oven to 350°F.

2. Lay the bones on a flat baking tray, place in oven, and cook for 30 to 45 minutes, until they are golden brown. Remove and set aside.

3. Meanwhile, in a large stockpot, add the vegetable oil and warm over low heat. Add the vegetables and cook until any additional moisture has evaporated. This allows the flavor of the vegetables to become concentrated.

4. Add the water to the stockpot. Add the bones, aromatics, and tomato paste to the stockpot, raise heat to high, and bring to a boil.

5. Reduce heat so that the stock simmers and cook for a minimum of 2 hours. Skim fat and impurities from the top as the stock cooks. As for when to stop cooking the stock, let the flavor be the judge. I typically like to cook for 4 to 5 hours total.

6. When the stock is finished cooking, strain through a fine strainer or cheesecloth. Place stock in refrigerator to chill.

7. Once cool, skim the fat layer from the top and discard. Use immediately, refrigerate, or freeze.

TIPS:

1. Stocks can stay in a freezer for up to six months.

2. This is a large recipe, which can easily be reduced to half or one-quarter the amount. However, as the same amount of time is required, I always recommend making a larger quantity and saving some for the future.

INGREDIENTS:

10	POUNDS VEAL, BEEF, OR LAMB BONES
½	CUP VEGETABLE OIL
1	LEEK, TRIMMED, AND CAREFULLY WASHED, CUT INTO 1-INCH PIECES
1	LARGE YELLOW ONION, UNPEELED, CLEANED ROOT, CUT INTO 1-INCH PIECES
2	LARGE CARROTS, PEELED AND CUT INTO 1-INCH PIECES
1	CELERY STALK WITH LEAVES, CUT INTO 1-INCH PIECES
8	OZ. TOMATO PASTE
8	PARSLEY SPRIGS
5	THYME SPRIGS
2	BAY LEAVES
10	QUARTS WATER
1	TEASPOON PEPPERCORNS
1	TEASPOON SALT

CHICKEN STOCK

YIELD: 6 QUARTS / **ACTIVE TIME:** 20 MINUTES / **TOTAL TIME:** 5 HOURS AND 20 MINUTES

Chicken stock falls under the category of a white stock. If a "true" white stock is called for, they are telling you not to cook the bones. However, I do not see any benefit in this. The color will be improved, but, unfortunately, the flavor will suffer. And while it is true that we eat with our eyes, flavor always needs to be the top priority.

As with most of these stocks, the more time, the merrier. I don't want to set a standard time, since there are too many variables. Instead, use your palate to judge what the stock needs. If you're unsure whether it's ready, it's probably not. Cook until you would consider eating it on its own. This recipe will also work with duck and rabbit as the protein.

1. Preheat oven to 350°F.

2. Lay the bones on a flat baking tray, place in oven, and cook for 30 to 45 minutes until they are golden brown. Remove and set aside.

3. Meanwhile, in a large stockpot, add the vegetable oil and warm over low heat. Add the vegetables and cook until any additional moisture has evaporated. This allows the flavor of the vegetables to become concentrated.

4. Add the water and the salt to the stockpot. Add the chicken carcasses and/or stewing pieces and the aromatics to the stockpot, raise heat to high, and bring to a boil.

5. Reduce heat so that the stock simmers and cook for a minimum of 2 hours. Skim fat and impurities from the top as the stock cooks. As for when to stop cooking the stock, let the flavor be the judge. I typically like to cook for 4 to 5 hours total.

6. When the stock is finished cooking, strain through a fine strainer or cheesecloth. Place stock in refrigerator to chill.

7. Once cool, skim the fat layer from the top and discard. Use immediately, refrigerate, or freeze.

INGREDIENTS:

10 POUNDS CHICKEN CARCASSES AND/OR STEWING CHICKEN PIECES

½ CUP VEGETABLE OIL

1 LEEK, TRIMMED AND CAREFULLY WASHED, CUT INTO 1-INCH PIECES

1 LARGE YELLOW ONION, UNPEELED, CLEANED ROOT, CUT INTO 1-INCH PIECES

2 LARGE CARROTS, CUT INTO 1-INCH PIECES

1 CELERY STALK WITH LEAVES, CUT INTO 1-INCH PIECES

10 QUARTS WATER

8 PARSLEY SPRIGS

5 THYME SPRIGS

2 BAY LEAVES

1 TEASPOON PEPPERCORNS

1 TEASPOON SALT

CRAB STOCK

YIELD: 4 QUARTS / ACTIVE TIME: 30 MINUTES / TOTAL TIME: 2 TO 4 HOURS

This stock is made with cooked crab. If using raw crab, combine all the ingredients except for the crab in the stockpot and bring to a boil. Add the crab legs and cook for 8 minutes, remove, and submerge in ice water. Reduce the heat so that the stock simmers, remove the crab meat from the shells and return the shells to the stock.

1. In a large stockpot, add the vegetable oil and warm over low heat. Add the vegetables and cook until any additional moisture has evaporated. This will allow the flavor of the vegetables to become concentrated.

2. Add the crab shells, the remaining ingredients, and enough water to cover the shells by 1-inch.

3. Raise heat to high and bring to a boil. Reduce heat so that the stock simmers and cook for a minimum of 2 hours. Skim fat and impurities from the top as the stock cooks. As for when to stop cooking the stock, let the flavor be the judge. I typically like to cook for 4 hours total.

4. When the stock is finished cooking, strain through a fine strainer or cheesecloth. Place stock in refrigerator to chill.

5. Once cool, skim the fat layer from the top and discard. Use immediately, refrigerate, or freeze.

INGREDIENTS:

- 2 TABLESPOONS VEGETABLE OIL
- 1 ONION, CHOPPED
- 1 CARROT, PEELED, ROUGHLY CHOPPED
- 1 CELERY STALK, ROUGHLY CHOPPED
- 3 POUNDS CRAB LEGS, COOKED IN THE SHELL, MEAT REMOVED AND RESERVED, SHELLS USED IN STOCK
- ½ CUP WHITE WINE
- 4 TABLESPOONS TOMATO PASTE
- 2 THYME SPRIGS
- 2 PARSLEY SPRIGS
- 3 SPRIGS TARRAGON
- 1 BAY LEAF
- ½ TEASPOON BLACK PEPPERCORNS
- 1 TEASPOON SALT
- 8 CARDAMOM PODS

DASHI STOCK

YIELD: 6 CUPS / ACTIVE TIME: 10 MINUTES / TOTAL TIME: 40 MINUTES

Dashi stock has only two very flavorful ingredients, one of which goes bitter if cooked at too high a temperature. Because of this, it's a quick and easy stock to make. You certainly can freeze any excess, but I recommend making this closer to the preparation of the soup. Kombu is edible dried kelp and bonito is a fish that is dried and fermented.

1. In a medium saucepan, add the water and the kombu. Soak for 20 minutes, remove the kombu, and score gently with a knife.

2. Return the kombu to the saucepan and bring to a boil.

3. Remove the kombu as soon as the water boils, so that the stock doesn't become bitter.

4. Add the bonito flakes and return to a boil. Turn off heat and let stand.

5. Strain through a fine sieve and chill in refrigerator.

INGREDIENTS:

8   CUPS COLD WATER

2   OZ. KOMBU

1   CUP BONITO FLAKES

HAM STOCK

YIELD: 4 CUPS / ACTIVE TIME: 15 MINUTES / TOTAL TIME: 1 HOUR AND 15 MINUTES

This stock finds itself in this book just a few times, so I have provided a quick recipe. The standard pork stock uses bones, and if you wish to go that route, you can substitute pork bones and use the veal/beef stock recipe.

1. Combine all ingredients in a stockpot and bring to a boil.

2. Reduce heat so that the stock simmers and cook for 1 hour. Strain stock through a fine sieve and chill in refrigerator.

INGREDIENTS:

12   OZ. HAM

6   CUPS WATER

2   GARLIC CLOVES, MINCED

1   ONION, CHOPPED

1   BAY LEAF

1   THYME SPRIG

FISH STOCK

YIELD: 6 QUARTS / ACTIVE TIME: 20 MINUTES / TOTAL TIME: 3 HOURS AND 20 MINUTES

This stock is a quick and simple preparation, with the aromatics helping to round out the great flavor. I often like to add star anise and citrus, depending on the recipe that I am using it for. For this book, these flavors are best left out, but great to consider for other recipes. Traditionally only white fish should be used; the reasons for this are twofold: it is a good way to avoid incorporating extra oil into the stock, and fish like tuna and salmon add an overpowering flavor to stock. That said, if using this stock for a creamed or thickened soup, I wouldn't hesitate to use a salmon carcass if you have one on hand. Fish mongers always have extra bones that they are happy to sell, or they might be game to just give them to you, one of many reasons to be friendly with the people from whom you buy ingredients.

1. In a large stockpot, add the vegetable oil and warm over low heat. Add the vegetables and cook until any additional moisture has evaporated. This will allow the flavor of the vegetables to become concentrated.

2. Add the whitefish bodies, the aromatics, the peppercorns, the salt, and the water to the pot.

3. Raise heat to high and bring to a boil. Reduce heat so that the stock simmers and cook for a minimum of 2 hours. Skim fat and impurities from the top as the stock cooks. As for when to stop cooking the stock, let the flavor be the judge. I typically like to cook for 2 to 3 hours total.

4. When the stock is finished cooking, strain through a fine strainer or cheesecloth. Place stock in refrigerator to chill.

5. Once cool, skim the fat layer from the top and discard. Use immediately, refrigerate, or freeze.

INGREDIENTS:

½ CUP VEGETABLE OIL

1 LEEK, TRIMMED AND CAREFULLY WASHED, CUT INTO 1-INCH PIECES

1 LARGE YELLOW ONION, UNPEELED, CLEANED ROOT, CUT INTO 1-INCH PIECES

2 LARGE CARROTS, CUT INTO 1-INCH PIECES

1 CELERY STALK WITH LEAVES, CUT INTO 1-INCH PIECES

10 POUNDS WHITEFISH BODIES

8 PARSLEY SPRIGS

5 THYME SPRIGS

2 BAY LEAVES

1 TEASPOON PEPPERCORNS

1 TEASPOON SALT

10 QUARTS WATER

LOBSTER STOCK

YIELD: 8 CUPS / ACTIVE TIME: 20 MINUTES / TOTAL TIME: 4 HOURS AND 20 MINUTES

If you are a lover of lobsters, you will appreciate having this stock readily available. It's great in pasta dishes, sauces, and many other recipes. This is made with the cooked bodies and shells of the lobster, which are very flavorful when roasted. The V8™ helps add a nice touch of red and even more flavor. When straining this stock, be sure to press on the lobster bodies with a ladle for every last bit of flavor.

1. Preheat oven to 350°F.

2. Lay the lobster bodies on a baking tray, place in oven, and cook for 30 to 45 minutes. Remove and set aside.

3. Meanwhile, in a large stockpot, add the vegetable oil and warm over low heat. Add the root vegetables and cook until any additional moisture has evaporated. This allows the flavor of the vegetables to become concentrated.

4. Add the lobster bodies, tomatoes, V8™, herbs, garlic, and white wine to the stockpot. Add enough water to cover the shells, raise heat to high, and bring to a boil. Reduce heat so that the stock simmers and cook for a minimum of 2 hours. Skim fat and impurities from the top as the stock cooks. As for when to stop cooking the stock, let the flavor be the judge. I typically like to cook for 3 to 4 hours total.

5. When the stock is finished cooking, strain through a fine strainer or cheesecloth. Place stock in refrigerator to chill.

6. Once cool, skim the fat layer from the top and discard. Use immediately, refrigerate, or freeze.

INGREDIENTS:

- 5 **POUNDS LOBSTER SHELLS AND BODIES**
- 2 **TABLESPOONS VEGETABLE OIL**
- 1 **POUND MIXED ROOT VEGETABLES (CARROT, LEEK, ONION, CELERY), CHOPPED**
- 10 **TOMATOES, CHOPPED**
- 1 **CUP V8™**
- 1 **BUNCH THYME**
- 1 **BUNCH PARSLEY**
- 1 **BUNCH TARRAGON**
- 1 **BUNCH DILL**
- 1 **GARLIC CLOVE**
- 2 **CUPS WHITE WINE**

MUSHROOM STOCK

YIELD: 6 CUPS / ACTIVE TIME: 20 MINUTES / TOTAL TIME: 3 HOURS AND 20 MINUTES

Making a nice mushroom risotto? Replace the chicken stock with mushroom stock to enhance the dish's flavor. Any mushroom is perfect for this stock, so try to find the most affordable option. The trick to a great mushroom stock is cooking out as much of the mushroom's natural liquid prior to adding the water. This will speed up the cooking time and make for a more concentrated, flavorful stock.

1. In a large stockpot, add the oil and mushrooms and cook over low heat for 30 to 40 minutes. The longer you cook the mushrooms, the better.

2. Add onion, garlic, bay leaves, peppercorns, and thyme and cook for 5 minutes.

3. Add the white wine, cook 5 minutes, and then add the water.

4. Bring to a boil, reduce heat so that stock simmers, and cook for 2 to 3 hours, until you are pleased with the taste.

INGREDIENTS:

2	TABLESPOONS VEGETABLE OIL
3	POUNDS MUSHROOMS
1	ONION, CHOPPED
1	GARLIC, MINCED
2	BAY LEAVES
1	TABLESPOON BLACK PEPPERCORNS
2	THYME SPRIGS
1	CUP WHITE WINE
8	CUPS WATER

VEGETABLE STOCK

YIELD: 6 CUPS / **ACTIVE TIME:** 20 MINUTES / **TOTAL TIME:** 2 HOURS AND 20 MINUTES

A vegetable stock is very important to have on hand in a professional kitchen in order to accommodate dietary preferences. This recipe is a classical version, but there is no reason not to keep your vegetable trimmings and use them for a stock. I recommend avoiding starchy vegetables, such as potatoes, as they will make the stock cloudy. Also try to avoid very colorful vegetables, such as beets, as their color will leech into the stock. This stock can be used to replace the meat stock in a majority of the recipes in this book.

1. In a large stockpot, add the vegetable oil and the vegetables and cook over low heat until any additional moisture has evaporated. This will allow the flavor of the vegetables to become concentrated.

2. Add parsley, thyme, bay leaf, water, peppercorns, and salt. Raise heat to high and bring to a boil. Reduce heat so that the soup simmers and cook for 2 hours. Skim fat and impurities from the top as the stock cooks.

3. When the stock is finished cooking, strain through a fine strainer or cheesecloth. Place stock in refrigerator to chill.

4. Once cool, skim the fat layer from the top and discard. Use immediately, refrigerate, or freeze.

INGREDIENTS:

2   TABLESPOONS VEGETABLE OIL

2   LARGE LEEKS, TRIMMED AND CAREFULLY WASHED

2   LARGE CARROTS, PEELED AND SLICED

2   CELERY STALKS, SLICED

2   LARGE ONIONS, SLICED

3   GARLIC CLOVES, UNPEELED BUT SMASHED

2   PARSLEY SPRIGS

2   THYME SPRIGS

1   BAY LEAF

8   CUPS WATER

½   TEASPOON BLACK PEPPERCORNS

     SALT, TO TASTE

PASTA
& NOODLES

The recipes in this chapter focus on everyone's favorite: pasta and noodles. For the sake of this book, we elected to use dried pasta and noodles in most of these soups. Fresh pasta and noodles are fine, but to be perfectly honest, dried will give these soups a better mouthfeel.

You can make your own pasta and dry it, of course. If you're interested, check out another book Cider Mill Press put out in this series, which focuses on pasta. We highly recommended you add it to your collection.

One thing: you're going to see a lot of Ramen noodles pop up in this chapter. You probably associate them with being too broke and too young to care about what you ate, but they are actually perfect for the bases and stocks in this book.

BROKEN PASTA SOUP

YIELD: 4 SERVINGS / ACTIVE TIME: 20 MINUTES / TOTAL TIME: 45 MINUTES

This is a great healthy soup, which becomes much easier to eat with the broken pasta.

1. In a medium saucepan, add the oil and cook over medium heat until warm. Add the onion and cook for 5 minutes, or until soft. Add the garlic, carrots, zucchini, and celery, and cook for 5 minutes. Add the tomatoes and stock, and bring to a boil.

2. Reduce heat so that the soup simmers and cook for 15 minutes.

3. Add the spaghetti and cook for 8 to 10 minutes, or until the pasta is tender.

4. Stir in the parsley, season with salt and pepper, and serve in warm bowls with the pesto.

INGREDIENTS:

2 TEASPOONS EXTRA VIRGIN OLIVE OIL

1 ONION, CHOPPED

2 GARLIC CLOVES, MINCED

2 CARROTS, PEELED AND CHOPPED

1 ZUCCHINI, SEEDS REMOVED AND CHOPPED

4 CELERY STALKS, CHOPPED

2 14 OZ. CANS STEWED TOMATOES

4 CUPS VEGETABLE STOCK

2 OZ. SPAGHETTI, BROKEN INTO 2-INCH PIECES

2 TABLESPOONS PARSLEY, LEAVES REMOVED AND CHOPPED

SALT AND PEPPER, TO TASTE

TO SERVE:

PESTO (SEE RECIPE ON PAGE 597)

VIETNAMESE PHO

YIELD: 4 SERVINGS / ACTIVE TIME: 30 MINUTES / TOTAL TIME: 3 HOURS AND 50 MINUTES

Pho, is a soup consisting of broth, rice noodles, spices, and either beef or chicken, and is a popular street food in Vietnam that has slowly spread to the rest of the world.

1. Preheat oven to 350°F.

2. Place the bones in the oven and roast for 20 minutes, or until golden brown.

3. Meanwhile, over an open flame, char your onion and ginger.

4. Place all of the spices in a nonstick pan and cook over medium heat for 2 to 3 minutes, until they become nice and fragrant.

5. Add the bones, the charred onion and ginger, spices, cilantro and the water in a large saucepan and bring to a boil.

6. Reduce heat so that the soup simmers and cook for 3 hours.

7. Strain the soup into a fresh clean pot. Season with fish sauce, hoisin, black pepper, and Sriracha. Return to a simmer.

8. Place the rice noodles into a bowl and cover with boiling water. Let soak for 4 minutes, or according to manufacturer's instructions.

9. Place the rice noodles into warm bowls. Ladle the soup over the noodles and garnish with sliced jalapeño, bean sprouts, lime wedges, and Thai basil.

INGREDIENTS:

- 2 POUNDS BEEF OR CHICKEN BONES
- 1 SMALL YELLOW ONION, HALVED
- 1-INCH PIECE OF GINGER, UNPEELED
- 2 CINNAMON STICKS
- 3 STAR ANISE
- 2 CARDAMOM PODS, SEEDS REMOVED AND CHOPPED
- 1 TABLESPOON BLACK PEPPERCORNS
- 5 CLOVES
- 1 TABLESPOON CORIANDER SEED
- 1 TABLESPOON FENNEL SEED
- 1 CUP CILANTRO, LEAVES AND STEMS
- 8 CUPS WATER
- 1 TABLESPOON FISH SAUCE
- 1 TABLESPOON HOISIN
- BLACK PEPPER, TO TASTE
- 1 TEASPOON SRIRACHA
- 3 OZ. RICE NOODLES
- JALAPEÑO, SLICED, FOR GARNISH
- BEAN SPROUTS, FOR GARNISH
- LIME WEDGES, FOR GARNISH
- THAI BASIL, FOR GARNISH

CHICKEN LIVER *and* PASTA
with BAKED HERB BAGUETTE SLICES

YIELD: 4 SERVINGS / ACTIVE TIME: 25 MINUTES / TOTAL TIME: 55 MINUTES

Although chicken livers can be purchased separately, I save and freeze my livers whenever I butcher chickens.

1. Add the oil and butter to a medium saucepan and cook over medium-high heat until warm. Add the chicken livers and garlic and sauté for 3 minutes, or until the chicken livers are golden brown.

2. Add the wine and cook until it evaporates. Stir in the herbs and cook for 2 minutes. Remove pan from heat and set aside.

3. In a large saucepan, add the chicken stock and bring to a boil.

4. Reduce heat so that the stock simmers, add the peas, and cook for 5 minutes.

5. Return to a boil and add the farfalle. Reduce the heat so that the stock simmers and cook for 10 minutes, until the pasta is *al dente*.

6. Add the chicken livers and scallions and simmer for 3 minutes. Season with salt and pepper, ladle into warm bowls, and serve with Baked Herbed Baguette Slices.

BAKED HERBED BAGUETTE SLICES

1. Preheat oven to 350°F.

2. Place the herbs and olive oil in a bowl and mix until combined.

3. Place the slices of baguette on a baking tray.

4. Drizzle the oil over the slices, season with salt and pepper, place in oven, and bake for 10 minutes, or until golden brown. Remove and serve.

INGREDIENTS:

1	TABLESPOON EXTRA VIRGIN OLIVE OIL
1	TABLESPOON BUTTER
½	CUP CHICKEN LIVERS, CUT INTO ¼-INCH PIECES.
4	GARLIC CLOVES, MINCED
3	PARSLEY SPRIGS, LEAVES REMOVED AND CHOPPED
3	MARJORAM SPRIGS, LEAVES REMOVED AND CHOPPED
3	SAGE SPRIGS, LEAVES REMOVED AND CHOPPED
1	THYME SPRIG, LEAVES REMOVED AND CHOPPED
6	BASIL LEAVES, CHOPPED
6	CUPS CHICKEN STOCK
2	TABLESPOONS WHITE WINE
2	CUPS PEAS
1	CUP FARFALLE PASTA
3	SCALLIONS, WHITE PART ONLY, SLICED
	SALT AND PEPPER, TO TASTE

TO SERVE:
BAKED HERBED BAGUETTE SLICES

BAKED HERBED BAGUETTE SLICES

1	TEASPOON PARSLEY, CHOPPED
1	TEASPOON MARJORAM, CHOPPED
1	TEASPOON SAGE, CHOPPED
1	TEASPOON THYME, CHOPPED
1	TEASPOON BASIL, CHOPPED
1	CUP EXTRA VIRGIN OLIVE OIL
	BAGUETTE, SLICED INTO 8 PIECES, ¼-INCH THICK
	SALT AND PEPPER, TO TASTE

HOMEMADE MEATBALLS
and CONCHIGLIE PASTA SOUP

YIELD: 4 SERVINGS / ACTIVE TIME: 45 MINUTES / TOTAL TIME: 1 HOUR AND 15 MINUTES

With orange-scented meatballs and a hearty sauce thickened by cannellini beans, this is a surefire Italian classic.

MEATBALLS

1. Place the bread and milk in a bowl and let stand for 10 minutes.

2. Add the veal, onion, parsley, orange zest, garlic, and egg. Mix with your hands until well-combined.

3. Season with salt and pepper and roll the mixture into balls that are about the size of a grape.

4. In a large sauté pan, add the oil and cook over medium heat until warm. Add the meatballs and cook for 5 minutes, or until browned all over.

5. Remove from pan with a slotted spoon and set on paper towels to drain.

SOUP

1. Place the cannellini beans and 1 cup of the stock in a food processor, puree until smooth, and set aside.

2. In a medium saucepan, add the olive oil, onion, garlic, Thai chili, celery, and carrot and cook for 5 minutes, or until the vegetables are soft.

3. Add the tomato paste, the cannellini puree, and the remaining stock, and bring to a boil.

4. Reduce heat so that the soup simmers and cook for 10 minutes.

5. Add the pasta and cook for 8 minutes, until tender. Add the meatballs, cook for 5 minutes until heated through, and then season with salt and pepper.

6. Serve in warm bowls and garnish with pecorino and basil.

INGREDIENTS:

MEATBALLS

2   SLICES OF WHITE BREAD, CRUST REMOVED AND TORN INTO SMALL PIECES

6   TABLESPOONS MILK

12   OZ. GROUND VEAL

½   ONION, CHOPPED

3   TABLESPOONS PARSLEY, LEAVES REMOVED AND CHOPPED

1   TABLESPOON ORANGE ZEST

2   GARLIC CLOVES, MINCED

1   EGG, BEATEN

  SALT AND PEPPER, TO TASTE

2   TABLESPOONS EXTRA VIRGIN OLIVE OIL

SOUP

1   14 OZ. CAN CANNELLINI BEANS, RINSED AND DRAINED

4   CUPS VEAL STOCK

2   TABLESPOONS EXTRA VIRGIN OLIVE OIL

1   ONION, CHOPPED

1   GARLIC CLOVE, MINCED

1   THAI CHILI, SEEDS REMOVED AND CHOPPED

1   CELERY STALK, CHOPPED

1   CARROT, PEELED AND CHOPPED

1   TABLESPOON TOMATO PASTE

8   OZ. CONCHIGLIE PASTA

  SALT AND PEPPER, TO TASTE

  PECORINO CHEESE, FOR GARNISH

  BASIL, FINELY CHOPPED, FOR GARNISH

FIVE-SPICE *and* CHICKEN RAMEN

YIELD: 4 SERVINGS / ACTIVE TIME: 15 MINUTES / TOTAL TIME: 45 MINUTES

Here is a very quick, simple ramen that is perfect for a cold day.

1. In a medium saucepan, add the chicken stock, garlic, ginger, soy sauce, Worcestershire sauce, five-spice powder, and chili powder, and bring to a boil.

2. Reduce heat so that the soup simmers and cook for 5 minutes. Turn off the heat and let stand.

3. Season with sugar, salt, and pepper.

4. Add the sesame oil to a medium sauté pan and cook over medium heat.

5. Bring 4 cups of water to boil in a medium saucepan. Add udon noodles and cook according to manufacturer's instructions.

6. Add the chicken to the sauté pan and cook for 8 minutes, or until browned on all sides.

7. Add the corn kernels to the chicken and cook for 2 minutes. Add the cooked udon noodles and spinach and cook for 1 minute.

8. Strain the broth through a fine sieve, and discard the solids. Place the broth in a clean pan and bring to a boil.

9. Place the udon noodles in warm bowls. Pour the broth over the top and garnish with the hardboiled eggs, scallions, and nori.

INGREDIENTS:

- 6 CUPS CHICKEN STOCK
- 4 GARLIC CLOVES, MINCED
- 2-INCH PIECE OF GINGER, MINCED
- ½ CUP SOY SAUCE
- 2 TEASPOONS WORCESTERSHIRE SAUCE
- 1 TEASPOON FIVE-SPICE POWDER
- ⅛ TEASPOON CHILI POWDER
- 1 TABLESPOON SUGAR, OPTIONAL
-   SALT AND PEPPER, TO TASTE
- 2 TABLESPOONS SESAME OIL
- 8 OZ. UDON NOODLES
- 2 CHICKEN BREASTS, CUT INTO 1-INCH CUBES
- 1 CUP CORN KERNELS
- 1 CUP SPINACH
- 4 HARDBOILED EGGS, HALVED, FOR GARNISH
- 8 SCALLION GREENS, FOR GARNISH
- 1 SHEET NORI, SHREDDED, FOR GARNISH

HARDBOILED EGGS

1. Bring enough water to a boil in medium saucepan so that it will cover eggs by at least 1 inch.

2. Once boiling, reduce to a simmer, add the eggs, and cook for 10 minutes.

3. Remove and refresh in iced water and leave for 10 minutes.

4. Once cooled down, peel and use.

ITALIAN WEDDING SOUP

YIELD: 4 SERVINGS / ACTIVE TIME: 30 MINUTES / TOTAL TIME: 1 HOUR AND 15 MINUTES

The term wedding soup comes from the phrase *minestra maritata*, which means "married soup," a reference to the combination of leafy greens and meat.

MEATBALLS

1. Preheat oven to 350°F.

2. In a bowl, add all the ingredients and mix with a fork until well-combined.

3. Divide the mixture into 16 balls, roll with your hands until nice and round, and then place on a baking tray.

4. Place tray in oven and bake for 20 to 25 minutes, until nicely browned and cooked through. Remove from oven and set aside.

SOUP

1. In a medium saucepan, add the olive oil and cook over medium heat until warm. Add the onion, carrots, and celery and cook for 5 minutes, or until soft.

2. Add the stock and the wine, and bring to a boil.

3. Reduce heat so that the soup simmers, add the pasta, and cook for 8 minutes.

4. Add the cooked meatballs and simmer for 5 minutes. Add the dill and the spinach and cook for 2 minutes, or until the spinach has wilted.

5. Ladle into warm bowls and garnish with parmesan.

INGREDIENTS:

MEATBALLS

12	OZ. GROUND CHICKEN
⅓	CUP PANKO BREAD CRUMBS
1	GARLIC CLOVE, MINCED
2	TABLESPOONS PARSLEY, LEAVES REMOVED AND CHOPPED
¼	CUP PARMESAN CHEESE, GRATED
1	TABLESPOON MILK
1	EGG, BEATEN
⅛	TEASPOON FENNEL SEEDS
⅛	TEASPOON RED PEPPER FLAKES
½	TEASPOON PAPRIKA
	SALT AND PEPPER, TO TASTE

SOUP

2	TABLESPOONS EXTRA VIRGIN OLIVE OIL
1	ONION, CHOPPED
2	CARROTS, FINELY CHOPPED
1	CELERY STALK, FINELY CHOPPED
6	CUPS CHICKEN STOCK
¼	CUP WHITE WINE
½	CUP TUBETINI PASTA
2	TABLESPOONS DILL, CHOPPED
6	OZ. BABY SPINACH
	SALT AND PEPPER, TO TASTE
	PARMESAN CHEESE, GRATED, FOR GARNISH

TOMATO SOUP
with CHEDDAR CHEESE DUMPLINGS

YIELD: 4 SERVINGS / ACTIVE TIME: 30 MINUTES / TOTAL TIME: 1 HOUR

Do you like tomato soup and grilled cheese? Then you are certain to love this soup that puts a slightly different twist on this classic.

1. Place the butter in a large saucepan and cook over medium heat until melted.

2. Add the onion and cook for 5 minutes, or until soft.

3. Stir in the tomatoes, carrots, chicken stock, parsley, and thyme, reduce to low and simmer for 20 minutes, or until the vegetables are tender.

4. Transfer the soup to a food processor, puree, and then pass through a fine sieve.

5. Return the soup to the pan and add the cream. Reheat gently, season with salt and pepper, and let simmer while you prepare the Cheddar Cheese Dumplings.

CHEDDAR CHEESE DUMPLINGS

1. Combine the flour, baking powder, and salt in a mixing bowl. Add the cheddar cheese, buttermilk, and parsley, and mix with a fork until a dough forms.

2. When the dough becomes thick, use your hands and knead it until it is nice and smooth. Add water or flour, as necessary.

3. Drop tablespoon-sized dumplings into the simmering tomato soup.

4. Once all the dough has been incorporated, simmer for 10 minutes. Turn off heat and let stand for a few minutes. Ladle into warm bowls, and garnish with parmesan, a splash of heavy cream, and parsley.

INGREDIENTS:

2	TABLESPOONS BUTTER
1	ONION, CHOPPED
2	POUNDS TOMATOES, CHOPPED
5	CUPS CHICKEN STOCK
2	CARROTS, PEELED AND CHOPPED
2	TABLESPOONS PARSLEY LEAVES, CHOPPED, PLUS MORE FOR GARNISH
½	TEASPOON THYME LEAVES, CHOPPED
6	TABLESPOONS HEAVY CREAM, PLUS MORE FOR GARNISH
	SALT AND PEPPER, TO TASTE
	PARMESAN CHEESE, SHAVED, FOR GARNISH

CHEDDAR CHEESE DUMPLINGS

¾	CUP ALL-PURPOSE FLOUR
1	TEASPOON BAKING POWDER
¼	TEASPOON SALT
⅓	CUP SHARP CHEDDAR CHEESE, GRATED
½	CUP BUTTERMILK
3	TABLESPOONS PARSLEY, LEAVES REMOVED AND CHOPPED

CHICKEN PARM SOUP

YIELD: 4 SERVINGS / ACTIVE TIME: 20 MINUTES / TOTAL TIME: 1 HOUR

By turning this famous Italian-American dish into a soup, your work in the kitchen is certain to garner a few devotees.

1. In a medium saucepan, add the oil and warm over medium-high heat. Add the chicken and cook for 5 minutes, while turning, until golden brown.

2. Add the onion and garlic and cook for 5 minutes, or until the onion is soft.

3. Add the red pepper flakes, tomato paste, tomatoes, and stock, and bring to a boil.

4. Reduce heat so that the soup simmers and cook for 10 minutes.

5. Add the penne and cook for 12 minutes. Add the mozzarella and parmesan and stir until they melt. Season with salt and pepper, ladle into bowls, and garnish with basil and parmesan.

INGREDIENTS:

- 2 TABLESPOONS EXTRA VIRGIN OLIVE OIL
- 2 CHICKEN BREASTS, CUT INTO ½-INCH PIECES
- 1 ONION, CHOPPED
- 2 GARLIC CLOVES, MINCED
- 1 TEASPOON CRUSHED RED PEPPER FLAKES
- ¼ CUP TOMATO PASTE
- 1 14 OZ. CAN DICED STEWED TOMATOES
- 6 CUPS CHICKEN STOCK
- 2 CUPS PENNE
- 2 CUPS MOZZARELLA, SHREDDED
- 1 CUP PARMESAN CHEESE, GRATED, PLUS MORE FOR GARNISH

  SALT AND PEPPER, TO TASTE

  BASIL, CHOPPED, FOR GARNISH

CHICKPEA *and* PASTA SOUP

YIELD: 4 SERVINGS / ACTIVE TIME: 15 MINUTES / TOTAL TIME: 14 HOURS AND 30 MINUTES

This simple Italian soup is perfect for your vegan friends or family members. Ditalini is a small, tube-shaped pasta.

1. Rinse the chickpeas and then place in a medium saucepan. Cover with 6 cups of water, add the seaweed and the cloves of garlic, and bring to a simmer. Cook for 2 hours, or until the chickpeas are nice and tender.

2. Reserve ¼ of the cooked chickpeas. Transfer the remaining contents of the saucepan to a food processor and puree.

3. In a medium heavy-bottom pan, add the olive oil and warm over medium-high heat.

4. Gently place the whole rosemary sprig into the pan and cook for a few minutes, until it is soft and fragrant. Remove the rosemary sprig and discard. Add the chickpea puree and reserved chickpeas. Add the pasta and cook for 10 minutes. If the soup becomes too thick, add more water.

5. Add the chopped rosemary, season with salt and pepper , and ladle into warm bowls. Garnish with a splash of olive oil and black pepper, and serve with crusty bread.

INGREDIENTS:

1¼ CUP DRIED CHICKPEAS, SOAKED OVERNIGHT

1 TABLESPOON DRIED KOMBU SEAWEED

3 GARLIC CLOVES

2 TABLESPOONS EXTRA VIRGIN OLIVE OIL, PLUS MORE FOR GARNISH

2 ROSEMARY SPRIGS, 1 LEFT WHOLE, LEAVES REMOVED AND CHOPPED FROM THE OTHER

1 CUP DITALINI PASTA

SALT AND PEPPER, TO TASTE, PLUS MORE PEPPER FOR GARNISH

CREAM OF MUSHROOM
with FUSILLI PASTA

YIELD: 4 SERVINGS / ACTIVE TIME: 20 MINUTES / TOTAL TIME: 45 MINUTES

This soup is quick, but rich. I prefer the texture of fusilli for this preparation, but feel free to use your favorite, or whatever's in the cupboard.

1. In a medium saucepan, add the butter and cook over medium heat until melted. Add the onions and garlic and cook for 5 minutes, or until soft.

2. Add the Madeira and cook until it evaporates.

3. Add the mushrooms and cook until all of their moisture has been released.

4. Add the mushroom stock and bring to a boil. Reduce heat so that the soup simmers and cook for 10 minutes.

5. Transfer the soup to a food processor, puree until creamy, and then strain through a fine sieve.

6. Return the soup to a clean pan and bring to a simmer. Add the pasta and cook for 8 to 10 minutes, or until pasta is tender.

7. Add the heavy cream and simmer for 2 minutes. Season with salt and pepper and serve in warm bowls garnished with the parsley.

INGREDIENTS:

- 4 TABLESPOONS BUTTER
- 1 ONION, CHOPPED
- 2 GARLIC CLOVES, CHOPPED
- ⅓ CUP MADEIRA
- 12 OZ. WILD MUSHROOMS
- 4 CUPS MUSHROOM STOCK
- 1½ CUP FUSILLI PASTA
- 1 CUP HEAVY CREAM
  SALT AND PEPPER, TO TASTE
  PARSLEY, CHOPPED, FOR GARNISH

KHAO SOI GAI
with RICE NOODLES

YIELD: 4 SERVINGS / ACTIVE TIME: 30 MINUTES / TOTAL TIME: 1 HOUR

Enjoy this classic from Northern Thailand. Don't let the exotic name intimidate you: it's delicious!

1. In a nonstick sauté pan, add chili, shallots, garlic, lemongrass, lime zest, Galangal root, ginger, cilantro stalks, coriander seeds, and cardamom seeds and cook over low heat for 5 minutes, or until the mixture becomes fragrant.

2. Transfer the contents of the saucepan to a mortar and pestle. Add a pinch of salt and the shrimp paste and grind until a very fine paste is formed. Set aside.

3. Place the vegetable oil in a Dutch oven and cook over medium-high heat until it reaches 325°F.

4. Place 1 oz. of rice noodles into the oil and cook until nice and crispy. Remove with a slotted spoon, set to drain on a paper towel, and season with salt. Reserve for garnish.

5. In a medium saucepan, add 1 tablespoon of the hot vegetable oil and 2 tablespoons of the creamy fat from the top of the coconut milk. Cook over high heat until the coconut fat breaks up and begins to smoke. Add the paste and cook for 45 seconds, while stirring constantly.

6. Reduce heat and whisk in the remaining coconut milk, chicken stock, and sugar.

7. Add the chicken pieces and simmer, while turning the chicken occasionally, for 30 minutes, or until the chicken is tender.

8. In the meantime, bring a pot of salted water to a boil and add the remaining rice noodles. Turn off heat, cover, and let stand for 3 minutes.

9. Place the noodles into warm bowls. Season the soup with fish sauce, salt, and pepper, and pour the soup over the noodles. Garnish with sliced shallots, lime wedges, and crispy rice noodles.

INGREDIENTS:

1	THAI CHILI, SEEDS REMOVED AND CHOPPED
2	SHALLOTS, PEELED AND CUT INTO QUARTERS, PLUS MORE FOR GARNISH
4	GARLIC CLOVES, MINCED
1	LEMONGRASS STALK, BRUISED WITH THE BACK OF A KNIFE
1	TEASPOON LIME ZEST
	1-INCH PIECE OF GALANGAL ROOT, PEELED AND FINELY CHOPPED
	1-INCH PIECE OF GINGER, PEELED AND FINELY CHOPPED
	SMALL BUNCH OF CILANTRO, LEAVES REMOVED, STEMS RESERVED
1	TEASPOON CORIANDER SEEDS
1	CARDAMOM POD, SEEDS REMOVED, SHELL DISCARDED
1½	TABLESPOONS SHRIMP PASTE
1	CUP VEGETABLE OIL
4	OZ. RICE NOODLES
2	14 OZ. CANS COCONUT MILK
1	CUP CHICKEN STOCK
2	TABLESPOONS SUGAR
4	CHICKEN LEGS, SPLIT INTO DRUMSTICKS AND THIGHS
	FISH SAUCE, TO TASTE
	SALT AND PEPPER, TO TASTE
	LIME WEDGES, FOR GARNISH

MISO RAMEN
with SPICY BEAN SPROUT SALAD

YIELD: 4 SERVINGS / ACTIVE TIME: 20 MINUTES / TOTAL TIME: 45 MINUTES

This is a great, quick miso with a bit of heat that is balanced out by the pickled ginger.

1. In a medium saucepan, warm the sesame oil over medium heat. Add the garlic, ginger, and shallots, and cook for 3 minutes, or until fragrant.

2. Increase the heat to medium-high and add the ground pork. Cook for 5 minutes, or until nicely browned. Add the chili bean paste, miso, sesame paste, sugar, sake, and chicken stock and stir to combine.

3. Bring to a boil. Reduce heat so that the soup simmers and season with salt and pepper.

4. Cook the noodles according to manufacturer's instructions.

5. Place the noodles in warm bowls. Pour the soup over the noodles and garnish with the Spicy Bean Sprout Salad, pickled red ginger, and poached eggs.

SPICY BEAN SPROUT SALAD

1. Bring a pot of water to a boil. Add the bean sprouts and cook for 2 minutes. Remove, strain through a fine sieve, and let cool.

2. Combine the remaining ingredients together in a bowl. Add the cooled bean sprouts, mix gently until combined, and serve.

POACHED EGGS

1. Crack each egg into a small, individual bowl.

2. In a medium saucepan, add 3 cups water and 2 tablespoons white vinegar and bring to a boil.

3. Reduce the heat so that the water simmers and gently add the eggs to the water one at a time.

4. Cook for 3 minutes, gently basting the eggs with the poaching water as they cook.

5. Gently remove the eggs with a slotted spoon and place on a paper towel to dry.

6. Season each egg with salt and pepper and serve immediately.

INGREDIENTS:

2	TABLESPOONS SESAME OIL
4	GARLIC CLOVES, MINCED
	2-INCH PIECE OF GINGER, PEELED AND MINCED
2	SHALLOTS, FINELY CHOPPED
8	OZ. GROUND PORK
2	TEASPOON CHILI BEAN PASTE
6	TABLESPOONS MISO
4	TABLESPOONS SESAME SEEDS, MIXTURE OF BLACK AND WHITE, TOASTED AND GROUND INTO A PASTE
2	TABLESPOONS SUGAR
2	TABLESPOONS SAKE
8	CUPS CHICKEN STOCK
	NOODLES FROM 2 PACKETS OF RAMEN
	SALT AND PEPPER, TO TASTE
	PICKLED RED GINGER, FOR GARNISH
	POACHED EGGS, FOR GARNISH

TO SERVE:
SPICY BEAN SPROUT SALAD

SPICY BEAN SPROUT SALAD

12	OZ. BEAN SPROUTS
1	TABLESPOON BLACK SESAME SEEDS
2	GREEN ONIONS, THINLY SLICED
2	TABLESPOONS SESAME OIL
2	TEASPOONS SOY SAUCE
⅛	TEASPOON RED CHILI FLAKES
	PINCH OF GROUND GINGER
	ZEST OF 1 ORANGE

LEFTOVER TURKEY PASTA SOUP

YIELD: 4 SERVINGS / ACTIVE TIME: 20 MINUTES / TOTAL TIME: 45 MINUTES

Everybody loves Thanksgiving, and I think everybody enjoys the day after even more. Make that day even better with the help of this soup.

1. In a medium saucepan, warm oil over medium heat. Add the onion, celery, and carrots and cook for 5 minutes, or until soft.

2. Add the stock, bay leaf, and rosemary and bring to a boil.

3. Reduce heat so that the soup simmers and cook for 10 minutes.

4. Add the orzo and simmer for 8 to 10 minutes, or until the pasta is tender.

5. Add the turkey meat and parsley. Season with salt and pepper, and serve in warm bowls.

INGREDIENTS:

- 1 TABLESPOON EXTRA VIRGIN OLIVE OIL
- 1 ONION, CHOPPED
- 2 CELERY STALKS, CHOPPED
- 2 CARROTS, PEELED AND CHOPPED
- 6 CUPS TURKEY STOCK
- 1 BAY LEAF
- 1 TEASPOON ROSEMARY, LEAVES REMOVED AND CHOPPED
- ½ CUP ORZO
- 2 CUPS LEFTOVER TURKEY MEAT, CHOPPED
- 1 TEASPOON PARSLEY, LEAVES REMOVED AND CHOPPED
- SALT AND PEPPER, TO TASTE

OLD FASHIONED CHICKEN BROTH
and DUMPLING SOUP

YIELD: 4 SERVINGS / ACTIVE TIME: 30 MINUTES / TOTAL TIME: 1 HOUR AND 15 MINUTES

This one may be "Old Fashioned," but for comfort food, it can't be beat.

BROTH

1. Add the oil to a medium saucepan and warm over medium heat. Add the onions and cook for 5 minutes, or until soft. Add the remaining vegetables and cook until tender.

2. Add the thyme and the chicken stock and bring to a boil. Reduce the heat so that the soup simmers and cook for 20 minutes.

3. Season with salt and pepper, ladle into bowls with the chicken dumplings, and garnish with parsley.

CHICKEN DUMPLINGS

1. Place the bread and parsley in a food processor and pulse until combined. Add the flour and the baking powder, pulse, then slowly add the milk, egg, and butter. Pulse until a smooth paste forms and transfer to a mixing bowl.

2. Fold in the chopped chicken meat and season with salt and pepper. Refrigerate for 1 hour.

3. Drop tablespoon-sized balls into the simmering broth. Cover and cook for 12 minutes.

INGREDIENTS:

BROTH

1	TABLESPOON VEGETABLE OIL
½	ONION, FINELY CHOPPED
1	CARROT, PEELED AND FINELY CHOPPED
1	CELERY STALK, FINELY CHOPPED
1	THYME SPRIG, LEAVES REMOVED AND CHOPPED
4	CUPS CHICKEN STOCK
	SALT AND PEPPER, TO TASTE
	PARSLEY, CHOPPED, FOR GARNISH

CHICKEN DUMPLINGS

4	SLICES OF BREAD, CHOPPED
½	CUP PARSLEY, LEAVES REMOVED AND CHOPPED
1¼	CUP ALL-PURPOSE FLOUR
1	TEASPOON BAKING POWDER
½	CUP MILK
1	EGG
¼	CUP BUTTER, MELTED
1	CUP COOKED CHICKEN LEG MEAT, CHOPPED
	SALT AND PEPPER, TO TASTE
4	CUPS CHICKEN STOCK

ORECCHIETTE PASTA
with BROCCOLI *and* ANCHOVY

YIELD: 4 SERVINGS / ACTIVE TIME: 20 MINUTES / TOTAL TIME: 45 MINUTES

This Southern Italian dish celebrates the wonderful combination of broccoli and anchovies, which is common in the region.

1. In a medium saucepan, add the olive oil and butter and warm over low heat. Add the onion, garlic, Thai chili, and anchovy and cook for 5 minutes, or until the onion is soft.

2. Add the tomatoes and the white wine and simmer, while stirring occasionally, for 10 minutes.

3. Add the stock, raise the heat to medium-high, and bring to a boil.

4. Reduce the heat so that the soup simmers. Add the broccoli florets and cook for 5 minutes.

5. Add the pasta and cook, while stirring occasionally, for 8 minutes, or until *al dente*.

6. Season with salt and pepper, ladle into bowls, and garnish with parmesan cheese.

INGREDIENTS:

- 1 TABLESPOON EXTRA VIRGIN OLIVE OIL
- 1 TABLESPOON BUTTER
- 1 ONION, CHOPPED
- 1 GARLIC CLOVE, MINCED
- 1 THAI CHILI, SEEDS REMOVED AND CHOPPED
- 2 WHITE ANCHOVY FILLETS, FINELY CHOPPED
- 1 CUP TOMATO, CONCASSE AND CHOPPED (SEE PAGE 89)
- ¼ CUP WHITE WINE
- 4 CUPS VEGETABLE STOCK
- 2 CUPS BROCCOLI FLORETS
- 1½ CUPS ORECCHIETTE PASTA
- SALT AND PEPPER, TO TASTE
- PARMESAN CHEESE, GRATED, FOR GARNISH

PORK *and* CRAB WONTON SOUP

YIELD: 4 SERVINGS / ACTIVE TIME: 40 MINUTES / TOTAL TIME: 1 HOUR

This quick and refreshing soup can work as an appetizer or a main course. The sweetness in this dish is balanced by the spiciness of the radish.

1. In a medium saucepan, add the sesame oil and cook over medium heat until warm. Add the onion and carrots and cook for 5 minutes, or until soft.

2. Add the garlic and cook for 2 minutes. Add mirin, crab stock, lemongrass, soy sauce, and fish sauce. Simmer for 10 minutes, and then remove the lemongrass.

3. Bring the soup to a boil and add the wontons. Reduce heat so that the soup simmers and cook for 5 minutes, or until the wontons float to the top.

4. Place 3 wontons in each bowl, pour the soup over the wantons, and garnish with toasted sesame seeds, cilantro, sesame oil, and the broken nori.

PORK AND CRAB WONTONS

1. Combine all ingredients in a bowl, save the wonton wrappers, and mix until well-combined.

2. Place 2 teaspoons of the mixture in the center of a wonton wrapper.

3. Dip a finger into cold water and rub it around the entire edge of the wonton. Bring each corner of the wrapper together and seal together. Repeat with remaining wonton wrappers and refrigerate until ready to use. (See instructions on page 94)

INGREDIENTS:

1	TABLESPOON SESAME OIL
1	ONION, FINELY CHOPPED
2	CARROTS, FINELY CHOPPED
2	GARLIC CLOVES, FINELY CHOPPED
1	CUP MIRIN
4	CUPS CRAB STOCK
1	LEMONGRASS STALK, BRUISED WITH THE BACK OF A KNIFE
1	TABLESPOON SOY SAUCE
1	TABLESPOON FISH SAUCE
12	WONTONS
	SALT AND PEPPER, TO TASTE
	SESAME SEEDS, TOASTED, FOR GARNISH
	CILANTRO, CHOPPED, FOR GARNISH
	SESAME OIL, FOR GARNISH
1	SHEET OF NORI, BROKEN, FOR GARNISH

PORK AND CRAB WONTONS

4	OZ. CRAB MEAT, CLEANED, COOKED, FINELY CHOPPED
4	OZ. GROUND PORK
1	TABLESPOON SHALLOTS, MINCED
1	TABLESPOON CHIVES, CHOPPED
1	TABLESPOON FISH SAUCE
2	TABLESPOONS MISO
2	TABLESPOONS RADISH, CHOPPED
1	TABLESPOON SESAME SEEDS, TOASTED
1	TEASPOON SESAME OIL
1	TEASPOON SHERRY
12	WONTON WRAPPERS

PORK *and* SHRIMP WONTON SOUP

YIELD: 4 SERVINGS / ACTIVE TIME: 40 MINUTES / TOTAL TIME: 1 HOUR

This is an instant classic—seafood and pork in an aromatic broth. How can you go wrong?

1. In a medium saucepan, add the sesame oil and cook over medium heat until warm. Add the onion and carrots and cook for 5 minutes, or until soft.

2. Add the garlic and cook for 2 minutes. Add the sake, chicken stock, lemongrass, soy sauce, and fish sauce, simmer for 10 minutes, and then remove the lemongrass.

3. Bring the soup to a boil and add the wontons. Reduce the heat so that the soup simmers and cook for 5 minutes, or until the wontons float to the top. Season with salt and pepper.

4. Place 3 wontons in each bowl, pour the soup over the top of the wontons, and garnish with the shallots, bean sprouts, and cilantro.

PORK AND SHRIMP WONTONS

1. Combine all ingredients in a bowl, save the wonton wrappers, and mix until well-combined.

2. Place 2 teaspoons of the mixture in the center of a wonton wrapper.

3. Dip your finger into cold water and rub it around the entire edge of the wonton. Bring each corner of the wrapper together and seal together. Repeat with remaining wonton wrappers and refrigerate until ready to use. (See instructions on page 94)

INGREDIENTS:

1	TABLESPOON SESAME OIL
1	ONION, FINELY CHOPPED
2	CARROTS, FINELY CHOPPED
2	GARLIC CLOVES, FINELY CHOPPED
1	CUP SAKE
4	CUPS CHICKEN STOCK
1	LEMONGRASS STALK, BRUISED WITH THE BACK OF A KNIFE
1	TABLESPOON SOY SAUCE
1	TABLESPOON FISH SAUCE
12	WONTONS
	SALT AND PEPPER, TO TASTE
	SHALLOTS, SLICED, FOR GARNISH
	BEAN SPROUTS, FOR GARNISH
	CILANTRO, CHOPPED, FOR GARNISH

PORK AND SHRIMP WONTONS

4	OZ. SHRIMP, PEELED AND DEVEINED, FINELY CHOPPED
8	OZ. GROUND PORK
1	TABLESPOON SHALLOTS, MINCED
1	TABLESPOON CHIVES, CHOPPED
1	TABLESPOON FISH SAUCE
2	TABLESPOONS MISO
1	TABLESPOON SHRIMP PASTE
2	TABLESPOONS RADISH, CHOPPED
1	TABLESPOON SESAME SEEDS, TOASTED
1	TEASPOON SESAME OIL
1	TEASPOON SHERRY
12	WONTON WRAPPERS

PORK TERIYAKI *and* RED MISO RAMEN

YIELD: 6 SERVINGS / **ACTIVE TIME:** 30 MINUTES / **TOTAL TIME:** 2 HOURS AND 30 MINUTES

This recipe is a version of a Sapporo-style Ramen. Typically served with pork belly, I adjusted and went with the Pork Teriyaki. Since it does take some time to make, you can prepare the stock, hardboiled eggs, and chili-garlic oil the night before.

1. In a stockpot, bring 8 cups of water to boil. Add the pork bones and boil for 5 minutes.

2. Remove the bones, discard the water, and clean the pot.

3. Bring 12 cups of water to boil and add the pork bones, onion, and ginger. Reduce heat so that the water simmers and cook for 1 hour and 30 minutes.

4. In a mixing bowl, add the soy sauce, mirin, brown sugar, and water. Stir until combined and then set aside.

5. In a large sauté pan, add 2 tablespoons of the oil and warm over medium-high heat.

6. Add the pork tenderloin and cook for 5 minutes, or until browned on all sides.

7. Pour the contents of the mixing bowl into the pan, reduce heat to low, and cook for 25 minutes, stirring halfway through.

8. Remove pan from heat and let cool.

9. While waiting for stock to finish cooking, prepare the Chili-Garlic Oil, Buttered Corn Kernels, and Cooked Bean Sprouts and Noodles (see next page).

10. When the stock is done cooking, strain through a fine sieve. Add 1 cup of the stock to a clean pan and bring to a boil. Remove the pan from heat and add the red miso.

11. In a medium saucepan, add the remaining vegetable oil and warm over medium-high heat.

12. Add the scallions and sauté for 1 minute. Add the remaining stock and bring to a boil.

13. Reduce heat to low and add the miso. Mix until combined and then shut off the heat. Season with salt and pepper.

14. Place the pork, hardboiled eggs, Buttered Corn Kernels, and Cooked Bean Sprouts and Noodles into warm bowls. Pour the broth on top and then garnish with bamboo shoots, nori, and Chili-Garlic Oil.

INGREDIENTS:

1½	POUNDS PORK BONES
1	ONION, CHOPPED
	2-INCH PIECE OF GINGER, PEELED AND MINCED
¼	CUP SOY SAUCE
1	CUP MIRIN
1	TABLESPOON BROWN SUGAR
1	CUP WATER
3	TABLESPOONS VEGETABLE OIL
1¼	POUNDS PORK TENDERLOIN, CHOPPED INTO 1-INCH PIECES
⅔	CUP RED MISO
4	SCALLIONS, SLICED
	SALT AND PEPPER, TO TASTE
	BAMBOO SHOOTS, FOR GARNISH
6	HARDBOILED EGGS, HALVED, FOR GARNISH
	NORI, FOR GARNISH

TO SERVE:

BUTTERED CORN KERNELS

COOKED BEAN SPROUTS AND NOODLES

CHILI-GARLIC OIL

BUTTERED CORN KERNELS

In a small saucepan, add the butter and cook over medium heat until warm. Add the corn, cook for 3 minutes, and season with salt and pepper. Set aside until ready to serve.

COOKED BEAN SPROUTS AND NOODLES

1. Bring 8 cups of water to a boil in a large saucepan. Add the sprouts, boil for 1 minute, remove, and set aside.

2. Add the noodles and cook according to manufacturer's instructions. Remove noodles from the pan and place in a mixing bowl. Add the bean sprouts and the sesame oil, stir until combined, and set aside.

CHILI-GARLIC OIL

1. In a small saucepan, add the oil and warm over low heat.

2. After 2 minutes, add the garlic and red pepper flakes and cook for an additional 2 minutes.

3. Remove from heat, let cool, and season with soy sauce.

4. Stir to combine and reserve until ready to use.

HARDBOILED EGGS

1. Bring enough water to a boil in medium saucepan so that it will cover eggs by at least 1 inch.

2. Once boiling, reduce to a simmer, add the eggs, and cook for 10 minutes.

3. Remove and refresh in iced water and leave for 10 minutes.

4. Once cooled down, peel and use.

INGREDIENTS (CONTINUED):

BUTTERED CORN KERNELS

2   TABLESPOONS BUTTER

1   CUP CORN KERNELS, COOKED

     SALT AND PEPPER, TO TASTE

COOKED BEAN SPROUTS AND NOODLES

8   OZ. BEAN SPROUTS

12   OZ. RAMEN NOODLES

1   TABLESPOON SESAME OIL

CHILI-GARLIC OIL

¼   CUP VEGETABLE OIL

3   GARLIC CLOVES, MINCED

1   TEASPOON RED PEPPER FLAKES

     SOY SAUCE, TO TASTE

PORK WONTON BROTH

YIELD: 4-6 SERVINGS / ACTIVE TIME: 30 MINUTES / TOTAL TIME: 1 HOUR

This beautiful, nourishing, and satisfying soup features vegetables a[...] perfect balm after a hard day.

1. In a mixing bowl, add the cornstarch and mirin. Stir until combined.

2. Add the pork, scallions, sesame seeds, soy sauce, ginger, sesame oil, and sugar and stir to combine. Season with salt and pepper, and refrigerate for 30 minutes.

3. Place 1 tablespoon of the pork filling in the center of a wonton wrapper. Dip a finger into the beaten egg and rub it around the edge of the wonton wrapper. Bring each corner of the wonton wrapper together and seal it shut. (See instructions on page 94)

4. Repeat Step 3 with remaining wonton wrappers. Refrigerate until ready to use.

5. In a medium saucepan, add the chicken stock and bring to a boil.

6. Reduce heat so that the stock simmers, season with salt and pepper, and add the carrot and bok choy. Cook for 3 minutes.

7. Add the sugar snap peas and cook for an additional 3 minutes, or until all the vegetables are tender.

8. Use a slotted spoon to remove the vegetables. Place into warm bowls.

9. Return the stock to a simmer and add the wontons in two batches. Cook each batch for 8 minutes, remove, and place into the bowls containing the cooked vegetables.

10. Once all the wontons have been cooked, ladle 1 cup of broth into each bowl and garnish with scallion greens and edible flowers.

INGREDIENTS:

1 TEASPOON CORNSTARCH

2 TABLESPOONS MIRIN

12 OZ. GROUND PORK

4 SCALLIONS, WHITES CHOPPED, GREENS RESERVED FOR GARNISH

1 TABLESPOON SESAME SEEDS, TOASTED

1½ TABLESPOONS SOY SAUCE

1 TEASPOON GINGER, MINCED

2 TEASPOONS SESAME OIL

½ TEASPOON SUGAR

SALT AND PEPPER, TO TASTE

24 WONTON WRAPPERS

1 EGG, BEATEN

6 CUPS CHICKEN STOCK

1 CARROT, THINLY SLICED

4 BOK CHOY, SEPARATED INTO INDIVIDUAL LEAVES

24 SUGAR SNAP PEAS

EDIBLE FLOWERS, FOR GARNISH

PORTOBELLO MUSHROOM RAVIOLI
in BEET SOUP

YIELD: 4 SERVINGS / ACTIVE TIME: 1 HOUR / TOTAL TIME: 1 HOUR AND 45 MINUTES

A beautifully light and elegant meal to serve your guests. Once you get some practice with making ravioli, try making some into heart shapes to serve your love on Valentine's Day—they'll look great in the beet soup.

PASTA DOUGH

1. Place the flour and salt on a clean work surface and make a well in the center of it.

2. Place the egg yolks and the olive oil in the middle of the well and use a fork to beat the yolks, while drawing in the flour to make a paste.

3. Once the mixture becomes too hard to mix with a fork, use your hands to knead the dough.

4. Knead for 5 minutes, or until smooth. Wrap the dough in plastic wrap to keep it from drying out and let stand at room temperature for 30 minutes.

PORTOBELLO MUSHROOM FILLING

1. In a medium saucepan, add the butter and cook over medium heat until melted. Add the mushrooms and cook for 5 minutes. Add the shallot, garlic, and thyme and cook for 5 minutes.

2. Remove the pan from the stove and strain to remove any excess liquid. Let cool.

3. Once cool, place in a small bowl and add the mascarpone. Stir to combine, season with salt and pepper, and reserve until ready to use.

INGREDIENTS:

PASTA DOUGH

1   CUP "00" PASTA FLOUR

⅛   TEASPOON SALT

1   CUP EGG YOLKS

1   TEASPOON EXTRA VIRGIN OLIVE OIL

PORTOBELLO MUSHROOM FILLING

1   TABLESPOON BUTTER

2   CUPS PORTOBELLO MUSHROOMS, CHOPPED

1   SHALLOT, FINELY CHOPPED

1   GARLIC CLOVE, MINCED

1   THYME SPRIG, LEAVES REMOVED AND CHOPPED

2   TABLESPOONS MASCARPONE CHEESE

SALT AND PEPPER, TO TASTE

RAVIOLI

1. Cut the pasta dough into 2 pieces.

2. Using a pasta maker, roll each piece into long, thin rectangles. Place one of the rectangles over a floured ravioli tray and place a teaspoon of the filling into the depressions.

3. Combine the beaten egg and water in a small bowl. Dip a pastry brush or a finger into it and run lightly over the edge of each ravioli.

4. Gently lay the remaining rectangle of pasta on top of the other piece. Use the included rolling pin to gently cut out the ravioli.

5. Remove ravioli and place on a floured baking tray.

BEET SOUP

1. In a large saucepan, add the oil and cook over medium heat.

2. Add the onion, garlic, and fennel seeds and cook for 5 minutes, or until the onion is soft.

3. Add the beet and cook for 5 minutes.

4. Add the stock and orange juice, and bring to a boil.

5. Reduce heat so that the soup simmers and cook for 15 minutes, or until the beet is tender.

6. Season with salt and pepper and return to a boil. Once boiling, drop the ravioli into the pan and cook for 3 minutes.

7. Ladle the soup into shallow bowls and garnish with fennel fronds.

INGREDIENTS (CONTINUED):

RAVIOLI

1   BATCH OF PASTA DOUGH

1   BATCH PORTOBELLO MUSHROOM FILLING

1   EGG, BEATEN WITH A FORK

1   TABLESPOON WATER

BEET SOUP

1   TABLESPOON EXTRA VIRGIN OLIVE OIL

1   ONION, PEELED AND CHOPPED

2   GARLIC CLOVES, MINCED

1   TEASPOON FENNEL SEEDS

1   LARGE BEET, PEELED AND FINELY CHOPPED

6   CUPS CHICKEN STOCK

¼   CUP ORANGE JUICE

   SALT AND PEPPER, TO TASTE

   FENNEL FRONDS, FOR GARNISH

POT STICKER BROTH

YIELD: 4 SERVINGS / **ACTIVE TIME:** 30 MINUTES / **TOTAL TIME:** 1 HOUR

This very simple and flavorful broth will work well with either pork or shrimp pot stickers, whatever your preference.

POT STICKERS

1. In a bowl, add the pork or shrimp. Add the cabbage, ginger, scallion whites, soy sauce, and 2 tablespoons of the water and stir until combined.

2. Lay 6 wrappers on a clean, dry work surface. Dip a finger into the egg and rub it over the edge of each wonton wrapper.

3. Place a teaspoon of the filling in the middle of each wrapper. Fold over wrapper and seal by pinching the edges together. (See page 94)

4. Repeat with the remaining wrappers.

5. Once complete, warm a large sauté pan over medium-high heat.

6. Add the oil and warm for 1 minute. Add the pot stickers and cook for 2 minutes, or until nicely browned.

7. Add the remaining water to the pan, cover, and cook for 3 minutes. Remove and place in serving bowls or refrigerate if using later.

SOUP

1. In a medium saucepan, add the chicken stock and bring to a boil. Add the cabbage, mushrooms, and carrot, and cook for 3 minutes.

2. Add the peas and cook for 2 minutes. Add the soy sauce, and then season with salt and pepper.

3. Ladle over pot stickers and garnish with scallion greens and sesame oil.

INGREDIENTS:

POT STICKERS

6	OZ. GROUND PORK OR SHRIMP
½	CUP CABBAGE, FINELY CHOPPED
1	TABLESPOON GINGER, MINCED
4	SCALLIONS, SLICED, WHITES AND GREENS SEPARATED
1	TABLESPOON SOY SAUCE
4	TABLESPOONS WATER
24	WONTON WRAPPERS
1	EGG, BEATEN
2	TABLESPOONS OIL

SOUP

6	CUPS CHICKEN STOCK
3	CUPS SAVOY CABBAGE, THINLY SLICED
2	CUPS SHIITAKE MUSHROOM CAPS, SLICED
1	CARROT, PEELED AND CUT INTO MATCHSTICKS
½	CUP PEAS
2	TABLESPOONS SOY SAUCE
	SALT AND PEPPER, TO TASTE
	SCALLION GREENS, FOR GARNISH
	SESAME OIL, FOR GARNISH

SIMPLE DUMPLING SOUP

YIELD: 4 SERVINGS / ACTIVE TIME: 30 MINUTES / TOTAL TIME: 1 HOUR

This is a very simple, yet satisfying soup. Feel free to add additional vegetables and/or beans if you want to make it heartier.

DUMPLINGS

1. Add the flour, baking powder, and salt to a mixing bowl and stir until combined.

2. Add the oil, egg, water, and chives and stir with a fork until a loose dough forms. Cover dough and set aside.

SOUP

1. In a medium saucepan, add the butter and cook over medium heat until warm.

2. Add the bacon and onion and cook for 5 minutes, or until the bacon is crispy and the onion is soft.

3. Add the potato and cook for 3 minutes. Add the stock and bring to a boil.

4. Reduce heat so that the soup simmers and cook for 10 minutes, or until the potatoes are tender.

5. Season with salt and pepper. Drop tablespoon-sized dumplings into the broth.

6. Once all of the dumplings have been incorporated, simmer for 3 minutes then turn off the heat.

7. Let stand a few minutes, then ladle into warmed bowls and serve.

INGREDIENTS:

DUMPLINGS

1	CUP ALL-PURPOSE FLOUR
½	TEASPOON BAKING POWDER
½	TEASPOON SALT
½	TABLESPOON EXTRA VIRGIN OLIVE OIL
1	EGG
6	TABLESPOONS WATER
1	TABLESPOON CHIVES, CHOPPED

SOUP

2	TABLESPOONS BUTTER
4	SLICES THICK-CUT BACON, CHOPPED
1	ONION, CHOPPED
4	CUPS POTATO, PEELED AND CHOPPED
6	CUPS CHICKEN STOCK
	SALT AND PEPPER, TO TASTE

SHRIMP *and* PORK WONTON BROTH

YIELD: 4 SERVINGS / ACTIVE TIME: 40 MINUTES / TOTAL TIME: 1 HOUR AND 30 MINUTES

A lovely Asian-inspired sausage and wonton soup. It reheats very well, so make sure to make enough for lunch tomorrow.

1. Add the ham stock, onion, garlic, cinnamon stick, star anise, cloves, and Thai chili to a medium saucepan. Bring to a boil, reduce heat so that the soup simmers and cook for 10 minutes. Remove from heat and let stand for 30 minutes.

2. Strain through a fine sieve. Return the broth to a clean pan and bring to a simmer. Add the scallion whites, fish sauce, and soy sauce. Add the wontons and cook for 5 minutes, or until they float to the top. Season with salt and pepper, ladle into bowls, and garnish with scallion greens.

INGREDIENTS:

6   CUPS HAM STOCK

1   ONION, CHOPPED

1   GARLIC CLOVE, MINCED

1   CINNAMON STICK

2   STAR ANISE

2   CLOVES

1   RED THAI CHILI

2   SCALLIONS, SLICED, WHITES AND GREENS SEPARATED

1   TABLESPOON FISH SAUCE

1   TABLESPOON SOY SAUCE

PORK AND SHRIMP WONTONS (SEE PAGE 150)

SALT AND PEPPER, TO TASTE

SCALLION GREENS, FOR GARNISH

SZECHUAN SPICED SHOYU RAMEN

YIELD: 4 SERVINGS / ACTIVE TIME: 30 MINUTES / TOTAL TIME: 1 HOUR AND 15 MINUTES

This dish has a great aroma and spiciness. Tip: The Ramen noodles cook very quickly, so make sure to have them ready by the time you prepare the poached eggs.

1. In a medium saucepan, add the sesame oil and warm over medium heat. Add the garlic and ginger and cook for 3 minutes, or until fragrant. Add the chili bean sauce and cook for 1 minute.

2. Add the chicken stock, dashi stock, soy sauce, and sake. Bring to a boil and then reduce heat so that the soup simmers. Cook for 5 minutes, adjust the seasoning with sugar, salt, and pepper and turn off the heat.

3. Meanwhile, cook the Ramen noodles to the manufacturer's instructions. When cooked, place in warm bowls.

4. Bring the broth to a boil and then pour over the Ramen noodles. Garnish with Poached Eggs, Szechuan Peppercorn and Chili Oil, Crispy Scallions, and scallion greens.

SZECHUAN PEPPERCORN AND CHILI OIL

1. In a small saucepan, add the vegetable oil, star anise, cinnamon stick, bay leaves, and Szechuan peppercorns. Cook over the lowest-possible heat for 20 minutes, being careful not to burn.

2. Place the red pepper flakes in a small bowl. Strain the warm oil over the flakes. Let cool, season with salt, and reserve until ready to use.

CRISPY SCALLIONS

1. Place the oil in a Dutch oven and cook over medium-high heat until it reaches 350°F.

2. Bring a pot of water to boil. Add the scallion whites and cook for 2 minutes. Remove, submerge in ice water, and then dry thoroughly.

3. Place the scallion whites into the oil. Stir constantly and fry until golden brown.

4. Remove with a slotted spoon or large tweezers. Set on paper towels to drain, season with salt and pepper, and serve.

INGREDIENTS:

2	TABLESPOONS SESAME OIL
4	GARLIC CLOVES, MINCED
	3-INCH PIECE OF GINGER, MINCED
2	TABLESPOONS CHILI BEAN SAUCE
3	CUPS CHICKEN STOCK
3	CUPS DASHI STOCK
¼	CUP SOY SAUCE
1	TABLESPOON SAKE
2	TEASPOONS SUGAR
	SALT AND PEPPER, TO TASTE
	NOODLES FROM 2 PACKETS OF RAMEN
	SCALLION GREENS, FOR GARNISH

TO SERVE:
SZECHUAN PEPPERCORN AND CHILI OIL

CRISPY SCALLIONS

POACHED EGGS

SZECHUAN PEPPERCORN AND CHILI OIL

1½	CUPS VEGETABLE OIL
5	STAR ANISE
1	CINNAMON STICK
2	BAY LEAVES
3	TABLESPOONS SZECHUAN PEPPERCORNS
⅓	CUP RED PEPPER FLAKES
1	TEASPOON SALT

CRISPY SCALLIONS

4	SCALLIONS, WHITE PART CUT INTO THICK MATCHSTICKS, GREENS RESERVED FOR GARNISH
1	CUP OIL
	SALT AND PEPPER, TO TASTE

POACHED EGGS

1. Crack each egg into a small, individual bowl.

2. In a medium saucepan, add 3 cups water and 2 tablespoons white vinegar and bring to a boil.

3. Reduce the heat so that the water simmers and gently add the eggs to the water one at a time.

4. Cook for 3 minutes, gently basting the eggs with the poaching water as they cook.

5. Gently remove the eggs with a slotted spoon and place on a paper towel to dry.

6. Season each egg with salt and pepper and serve immediately.

VEGETARIAN RAMEN

YIELD: 4 SERVINGS / ACTIVE TIME: 15 MINUTES / TOTAL TIME: 45 MINUTES

This is a great vegetarian Ramen, which gets its spice from the Chili Bean Sauce. If you want to make this a bit heartier, add a hardboiled or poached egg.

VEGETARIAN DASHI STOCK

1. In a heavy saucepan, add the water and the kombu. Soak for 20 minutes.

2. Remove the kombu and score the surface gently with a knife.

3. Return the kombu to the water and bring to a boil. Remove the kombu immediately, so that the broth doesn't become bitter.

4. Add the dried shiitakes and return to a boil. Turn off heat and let stand until cool.

5. Pass the stock through a fine sieve and refrigerate until ready to use.

RAMEN

1. In a medium saucepan, add the sesame oil and cook over medium heat until warm.

2. Add the garlic and ginger, and cook for 3 minutes, or until fragrant.

3. Add the scallions, chili bean paste, and miso, and cook for 1 minute. Add the sake and cook until half of it has evaporated.

4. Add the sesame seed paste, stock, and soy milk, and bring to a boil.

5. Season with salt and pepper, and remove pan from heat.

6. Cook the noodles per manufacturer's instructions. Place the noodles into warm bowls and pour the broth over them. Garnish with scallion greens, toasted sesame seeds, and bean sprouts.

INGREDIENTS:

VEGETARIAN DASHI STOCK

3 CUPS WATER

1 OZ. KOMBU

4 DRIED SHIITAKE MUSHROOMS

RAMEN

2 TABLESPOONS SESAME OIL

4 GARLIC CLOVES, MINCED

2-INCH PIECE OF GINGER, MINCED

4 SCALLIONS, SLICED, GREENS RESERVED FOR GARNISH

2 TABLESPOONS CHILI BEAN PASTE

2 TABLESPOONS MISO

¼ CUP SAKE

4 TABLESPOONS BLACK-AND-WHITE SESAME SEEDS, TOASTED AND GROUND INTO A PASTE, PLUS MORE FOR GARNISH

2 CUPS VEGETARIAN DASHI STOCK

3 CUPS UNSWEETENED SOY MILK

NOODLES FROM 2 PACKAGES OF RAMEN

SALT AND PEPPER, TO TASTE

BEAN SPROUTS, FOR GARNISH

POACHED EGGS

1. Crack each egg into a small, individual bowl.

2. In a medium saucepan, add 3 cups water and 2 tablespoons white vinegar and bring to a boil.

3. Reduce the heat so that the water simmers and gently add the eggs to the water one at a time.

4. Cook for 3 minutes, gently basting the eggs with the poaching water as they cook.

5. Gently remove the eggs with a slotted spoon and place on a paper towel to dry.

6. Season each egg with salt and pepper and serve immediately.

THAI COCONUT BROTH
with LOBSTER WONTONS

YIELD: 4 SERVINGS / ACTIVE TIME: 30 MINUTES / TOTAL TIME: 1 HOUR

A wonderful fusion of Thailand and the great state of Maine!

THAI CURRY PASTE

Place all ingredients in a food processor and puree until smooth. Refrigerate until ready to use.

LOBSTER WONTONS

1. Place the lobster meat, scallion, salt, and pepper in a mixing bowl, and stir to combine.

2. Place 1 tablespoon of lobster filling in the center of a wonton wrapper. Dip a finger into the egg and then rub it around the edge of the wrapper. Bring each corner of the wrapper together, and seal. (See page 94)

3. Repeat Step 2 with remaining wonton wrappers. When all of the wontons have been made, refrigerate until ready to use.

SOUP

1. In a medium saucepan, add the sesame oil and warm over low heat. Add the red Thai curry paste and cook, while stirring constantly, for 5 minutes.

2. Meanwhile, bring 8 cups of water to boil in a large saucepan. Add the wontons and cook for 3 minutes.

3. Remove the wontons from the water with a slotted spoon and place in warm bowls.

4. Add the sugar, fish sauce, and coconut milk to the medium saucepan. Cook on low heat for 4 minutes, while stirring constantly. Season with the lime juice, salt, and pepper, while taking care not to bring to a boil.

5. Pour the soup over the wontons. Garnish with the cilantro and Thai chilies, and serve.

INGREDIENTS:

THAI CURRY PASTE

2   SHALLOTS, FINELY CHOPPED

     2-INCH PIECE OF LEMONGRASS, FINELY CHOPPED

     1-INCH GALANGAL ROOT, GRATED

3   GARLIC CLOVES, MINCED

LOBSTER WONTONS

1½   CUPS LOBSTER MEAT, COOKED, FINELY CHOPPED

1   SCALLION, FINELY SLICED

     SALT AND PEPPER, TO TASTE

1   EGG, BEATEN

24   WONTON WRAPPERS

SOUP

1   TABLESPOON SESAME OIL

1   TABLESPOON RED THAI CURRY PASTE

2   TEASPOONS SUGAR

3   TABLESPOONS FISH SAUCE

1   14 OZ. CAN OF COCONUT MILK

     JUICE OF 1 LIME

     SALT AND PEPPER, TO TASTE

     THAI CHILIES, SLICED, FOR GARNISH

     CILANTRO, CHOPPED, FOR GARNISH

TOMATO SOUP
with CHICKPEAS *and* PASTA

YIELD: 4 SERVINGS / ACTIVE TIME: 20 MINUTES / TOTAL TIME: 45 MINUTES

The canned tomatoes help provide consistent flavor year-round in this hearty, healthy soup.

1. In a large saucepan, add the oil and cook over medium heat until warm.

2. Add the onion and cook for 5 minutes, or until soft. Add the garlic and cook for 2 minutes.

3. Add the pureed tomatoes, thyme, and stock and bring to a boil.

4. Reduce heat so that the soup simmers. Add the pasta and cook for 8 to 10 minutes, or until the pasta is tender.

5. Add the chickpeas, parsley, and parmesan and cook for 3 minutes.

6. Season with salt and pepper and serve in warm bowls garnished with parmesan and basil.

INGREDIENTS:

2   TABLESPOONS EXTRA VIRGIN OLIVE OIL

1   ONION, CHOPPED

2   GARLIC CLOVES, MINCED

4   14 OZ. CANS OF STEWED TOMATOES, PUREED

2   THYME SPRIGS, LEAVES REMOVED AND CHOPPED

4   CUPS CHICKEN STOCK

½   CUP DITALINI PASTA

1   14 OZ. CAN OF CHICKPEAS, RINSED AND DRAINED

¼   CUP PARSLEY, LEAVES REMOVED AND CHOPPED

¼   CUP PARMESAN CHEESE, GRATED, PLUS MORE FOR GARNISH

    SALT AND PEPPER, TO TASTE

    BASIL, CHOPPED, FOR GARNISH

AVGOLEMONO
with ORZO SALAD

YIELD: 4 SERVINGS / ACTIVE TIME: 45 MINUTES / TOTAL TIME: 1 HOUR AND 15 MINUTES

One of the most popular soups in Greek cuisine. Avgolemono means egg and lemon, and these two ingredients combine to produce a nourishing soup that is still nice and light.

1. Pour the stock into a large saucepan and bring to a boil.

2. Reduce the heat so that the broth simmers. Add the chicken thighs and cook for 20 minutes.

3. Remove the chicken thighs and set aside. Add the orzo and cook for 5 minutes.

4. Meanwhile, remove the meat from the chicken thighs, discard the skin and bones and chop the meat into bite-sized pieces.

5. Strain the orzo from the broth and set aside. Return the broth to the pan and bring to a simmer.

6. In a mixing bowl, add the eggs and beat until frothy. Add the lemon juice and cold water and whisk. Add approximately ½ cup of the stock to bowl and stir constantly.

7. Add another cup of hot stock to the egg mixture and then add the contents of the bowl to the saucepan. Be careful not to let the stock boil once you add the egg mixture, otherwise it will curdle.

8. Add half of the cooked orzo and the chicken to the saucepan. Season with salt and pepper and ladle into warmed bowls. Garnish with parsley and lemon slices and serve with Orzo Salad.

ORZO SALAD

1. In a medium-sized mixing bowl, add the orzo, feta cheese, bell pepper, Kalamata olives, scallions, capers, garlic, parsley, and pine nuts and stir until combined.

2. In a small bowl, add the lemon juice, vinegar, mustard, and cumin and stir until combined. Gradually whisk in the olive oil and then add the dressing to the orzo mixture. Toss to blend, season with salt and pepper, cover, and refrigerate until ready to serve.

INGREDIENTS:

6	CUPS CHICKEN STOCK
2	CHICKEN THIGHS
1	CUP ORZO PASTA
3	EGGS
1	TABLESPOON LEMON JUICE
1	TABLESPOON COLD WATER
	SALT AND PEPPER, TO TASTE
	LEMON SLICES, FOR GARNISH
	PARSLEY, CHOPPED, FOR GARNISH

TO SERVE:
ORZO SALAD

ORZO SALAD

½	CUP OF ORZO, COOKED
¼	CUP CRUMBLED FETA CHEESE
¼	CUP RED BELL PEPPER, CHOPPED
3	TABLESPOONS YELLOW BELL PEPPER, CHOPPED
3	TABLESPOONS KALAMATA OLIVES, CHOPPED
1	SCALLION, SLICED
1	TEASPOON CAPERS, DRAINED AND CHOPPED
1	TEASPOON GARLIC, MINCED
1	TEASPOON PARSLEY, LEAVES REMOVED AND CHOPPED
1	TABLESPOON PINE NUTS, TOASTED AND CHOPPED
2	TEASPOONS LEMON JUICE
1	TEASPOON WHITE WINE VINEGAR
1	TEASPOON DIJON MUSTARD
½	TEASPOON CUMIN
3	TABLESPOONS EXTRA VIRGIN OLIVE OIL
	SALT AND PEPPER, TO TASTE

VEGETABLES

*S*ome of my favorite soups are vegetable-based, as you will see from the large amount of recipes in this chapter. Vegetables allow me to experience one of my favorite things about soup: how easily it can follow the changing seasons, allowing you to optimize what is currently available. Vegetable soups are also a great way to showcase a vegetable that is no longer at its prettiest, as this extra bit of ripening converts the carbohydrates to natural sugars and gives the soup even more flavor.

Unlike many meat-centric soups, vegetable soups do not typically need a lot of time to develop their flavors—they have them naturally. While this chapter features vegetable soups, the recipes are not all vegetarian. Because of this, feel free to pair them with seafood, as they are a perfect complement to the fresh, clean flavor that comes from the sea.

CORN *and* PLANTAIN SOUP

YIELD: 4 SERVINGS / ACTIVE TIME: 15 MINUTES / TOTAL TIME: 40 MINUTES

A traditional African soup that is both sweet and spicy.

1. In a medium saucepan, add the butter and cook over medium heat until melted. Add the onion and garlic, and cook for 5 minutes, or until soft.

2. Add the plantains, tomatoes, corn kernels, and tarragon. Cook for 5 minutes.

3. Add the stock, jalapeño, and nutmeg, and bring to a boil.

4. Reduce to a simmer and cook for 10 minutes, or until the plantains are tender.

5. Season with salt and pepper and serve in warm bowls.

INGREDIENTS:

¼ CUP BUTTER

1 ONION, CHOPPED

2 GARLIC CLOVES, MINCED

2 RIPE YELLOW PLANTAINS, PEELED AND SLICED

2 PLUM TOMATOES, CONCASSE AND CHOPPED (SEE PAGE 89)

4 EARS OF CORN, KERNELS REMOVED

1 TARRAGON SPRIG, LEAVES REMOVED AND CHOPPED

4 CUPS CHICKEN STOCK

1 TABLESPOON JALAPEÑO, FINELY CHOPPED

⅛ TEASPOON NUTMEG

SALT AND PEPPER, TO TASTE

CHILI TORTILLA SOUP

YIELD: 4 SERVINGS / ACTIVE TIME: 25 MINUTES / TOTAL TIME: 1 HOUR AND 15 MINUTES

Tortilla soup is one of Mexico's best-known soups, and with all the options available, it's easy to see why.

1. Preheat oven to 350°F.

2. Place the garlic in an ungreased, nonstick pan. Cook over medium heat for 15 minutes, or until blackened, turning occasionally. Remove the garlic from the pan and allow to cool. When cool, peel and mince.

3. Place the tomato on a baking tray. Place the tray in the oven and cook for 10 minutes. Remove and set aside, making sure to save any juices.

4. In a medium saucepan, add 1 tablespoon of vegetable oil and warm over low heat. Add the onion and cook for 10 minutes, or until golden brown.

5. Place the rehydrated chilies in a food processor with the roasted garlic, tomato, the tomato's juices, and 1 cup of the stock. Puree until smooth, strain though a fine sieve, and add to the cooked onions.

6. Add the remaining stock and simmer for 30 minutes.

7. Meanwhile, place the remaining 2 cups of oil in a Dutch oven and warm to 350°F. Place the tortilla strips into the oil and fry, turning frequently until crisp. Remove with a slotted spoon and set on paper towels to drain.

8. After 30 minutes, add the red Swiss chard to the soup and cook for 5 minutes.

9. Ladle into bowls and serve with the tortilla strips, Monterey Jack cheese, and limes.

INGREDIENTS:

2 GARLIC CLOVES, UNPEELED

1 TOMATO

2 CUPS VEGETABLE OIL, PLUS 1 TABLESPOON

1 ONION, SLICED

1½ OZ. DRIED PASILLA CHILIES, STEMMED AND SEEDED, SOAKED IN HOT WATER FOR 20 MINUTES AND THEN DRAINED

6 CUPS CHICKEN STOCK

½ TEASPOON SALT

8 CORN TORTILLAS, CUT INTO ¼-INCH STRIPS

4 CUPS RED SWISS CHARD, THINLY SLICED

2 CUPS MONTEREY JACK CHEESE, SHREDDED, FOR GARNISH

1 SMALL LIME, CUT INTO QUARTERS, FOR GARNISH

APPLE RUTABAGA SOUP
and PORK BELLY

YIELD: 6 SERVINGS / **ACTIVE TIME:** 25 MINUTES / **TOTAL TIME:** 26 HOURS

This is a great soup for the fall, where acidity and lightness balance out the richness of the pork belly.

1. In a large saucepan, add the butter and cook over medium heat until melted. Add the onion, apple, rutabaga, butternut squash, carrots, and sweet potato and cook for 10 minutes, or until vegetables are soft.

2. Add vegetable stock and bring to a boil. Reduce heat so that the soup simmers and cook for 20 minutes, or until vegetables are cooked through.

3. Transfer the soup to a food processor, puree until smooth, and strain through a fine sieve.

4. Return soup to pan and bring to a simmer. Add heavy cream and season with salt and cayenne pepper.

5. Ladle into bowls, serve with Roasted Pork Belly, and garnish with rosemary and blanched rutabaga.

INGREDIENTS:

¼ CUP BUTTER

1 CUP ONION, CHOPPED

1 CUP TART APPLE, PEELED, CORED, AND CHOPPED

1 CUP RUTABAGA, PEELED AND CHOPPED

1 CUP BUTTERNUT SQUASH, PEELED AND CHOPPED

1 CUP CARROTS, PEELED AND CHOPPED

1 CUP SWEET POTATO, PEELED AND CHOPPED

4 CUPS VEGETABLE STOCK

3 CUPS HEAVY CREAM

SALT AND CAYENNE PEPPER, TO TASTE

ROSEMARY, FOR GARNISH

BLANCHED RUTABAGA, FOR GARNISH, OPTIONAL

TO SERVE:
ROASTED PORK BELLY

Continued . . .

ROASTED PORK BELLY

1. With fat side up, score a crisscross pattern across the pork belly with a sharp knife. The cut should be approximately ¼-inch deep (see diagram below).

2. In a medium saucepan, add the water, fennel seeds, star anise, cinnamon stick, peppercorns, cloves, bay leaf, and salt. Bring to a boil, remove from heat, and let cool.

3. When cool, place the pork belly and the contents of the saucepan in a roasting pan. Place in refrigerator and marinate for 24 hours.

4. Preheat oven to 450°F.

5. Rinse the marinated pork belly and set on a rack in a baking tray, fat side up.

6. Place tray in oven and cook for 30 minutes. Lower temperature to 275°F and cook for 1 hour, until it is tender, but not mushy.

7. Remove tray from the oven, cut the pork belly into 6 pieces, and serve.

INGREDIENTS (CONTINUED):

ROASTED PORK BELLY

1½	POUNDS PORK BELLY
6	CUPS WATER
1	TEASPOON FENNEL SEEDS
2	STAR ANISE
1	CINNAMON STICK
1	TEASPOON BLACK PEPPERCORNS
6	CLOVES
1	BAY LEAF
¼	CUP SALT

SCORING CROSS-PATTERNS IN PORK BELLY

Scoring pork belly prior to cooking allows the fat to seep into the meat and keep it moist. It also allows the fat to crisp up, since it is not just bathing in itself. To score the top, use a sharp knife and make quick, gentle slices across the top in a crisscross pattern.

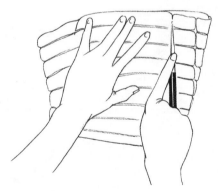

ARTICHOKE SOUP
with FENNEL SEED YOGURT

YIELD: 4 SERVINGS / ACTIVE TIME: 20 MINUTES / TOTAL TIME: 45 MINUTES

Artichokes are a vegetable that people often shy away from. So why not try them in a soup? After peeling and cleaning the artichokes, place them in lemon water to prevent oxidation.

1. Peel the artichokes and slice the hearts thin.

2. Place the oil and butter in a medium saucepan. Add the artichokes, garlic, and onion and cook over medium heat for 10 minutes.

3. Add the Riesling and thyme and cook until the wine has been reduced by half.

4. Add the heavy cream and the vegetable stock and simmer for 10 minutes.

5. Transfer the soup to a food processor, puree until smooth, and strain through a fine sieve. Season to taste with salt and pepper, ladle into warm bowls, serve with the Fennel Seed Yogurt, and garnish with dill.

INGREDIENTS:

6   ARTICHOKES

1   TABLESPOON VEGETABLE OIL

1   TABLESPOON BUTTER

1   GARLIC CLOVE, MINCED

1   ONION, DICED

1   CUP RIESLING

1   THYME SPRIG, LEAVES REMOVED AND CHOPPED

4   CUPS HEAVY CREAM

1   CUP VEGETABLE STOCK

    SALT AND PEPPER, TO TASTE

    DILL, CHOPPED, FOR GARNISH

TO SERVE:
FENNEL SEED YOGURT

Continued . . .

FENNEL SEED YOGURT

For a stronger flavor, roast and cool the fennel seeds before grinding them.

Combine all ingredients in a bowl. Place in refrigerator and chill until ready to use.

INGREDIENTS (CONTINUED):

FENNEL SEED YOGURT

1   CUP GREEK YOGURT

2   TABLESPOONS PERNOD

1   TEASPOON GROUND
    FENNEL SEED

REMOVING THE OUTER LEAVES AND EXPOSING THE MEAT OF AN ARTICHOKE

The tough leaves of the artichoke protect its edible heart. It looks like a lot of work to remove them, but with this method it's not so bad. First, cut the stem and pull off the outer leaves. When you get to the tender yellow leaves, grab the top of the leaves in the center and pull them off, revealing the heart. Dig out the heart with a spoon, and use a small paring knife to remove the bottom leaves and anything clinging to the stem.

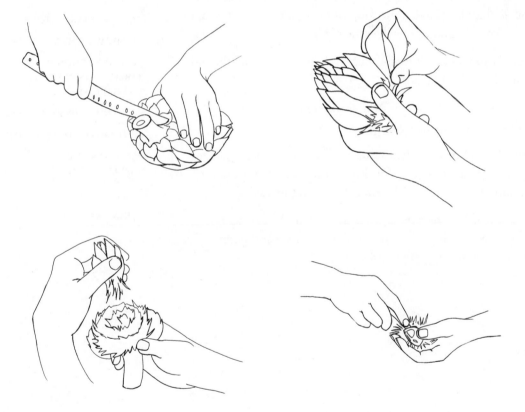

ASPARAGUS *and* PEA SOUP

YIELD: 6 SERVINGS / ACTIVE TIME: 25 MINUTES / TOTAL TIME: 1 HOUR AND 20 MINUTES

Asparagus is sold year-round. However, there is nothing better than buying it from your local farm stand when it's in season. The lemon zest is key here, as it lightens the whole soup.

1. Remove the base of the asparagus and discard. Separate the spears, remove the tips and reserve for garnish, and chop up the remaining pieces.

2. In a medium saucepan, add the butter and cook over medium heat until melted. Add the leeks and cook for 5 minutes, or until they have softened.

3. Add the chopped asparagus, 1 cup of the peas, and the parsley. Cook for 3 minutes, add the vegetable stock, and bring to a boil. Reduce heat so that the soup simmers and cook for 6 to 8 minutes, or until the vegetables are tender.

4. Transfer the soup to a food processor, puree until smooth, and strain through a fine sieve.

5. Place soup in a clean pan. Add cream and lemon zest, season with salt and pepper, and bring to a simmer.

6. Bring a small pan of salted water to a boil. Place the asparagus tips in the pan and cook for 3 to 4 minutes, or until tender. Remove tips, submerge in ice water, dry, and set aside.

7. Ladle the soup into warm bowls, garnish with the asparagus tips, reserved peas, mint leaves, reserved lemon zest, and parmesan, and serve with Parmesan Crackers.

INGREDIENTS:

- 12 OZ. GREEN ASPARAGUS
- 2 TABLESPOONS BUTTER
- 1 LEEK, CHOPPED
- 1¼ CUPS FRESH OR FROZEN PEAS, ¼ CUP RESERVED FOR GARNISH
- 1 TABLESPOON PARSLEY, CHOPPED
- 5 CUPS VEGETABLE STOCK
- ½ CUP HEAVY CREAM
- ZEST OF 1 LEMON, 1 TABLESPOON RESERVED FOR GARNISH
- SALT AND PEPPER, TO TASTE
- MINT LEAVES, FOR GARNISH
- PARMESAN CHEESE, SHAVED, FOR GARNISH

TO SERVE:
PARMESAN CRACKERS

PARMESAN CRACKERS

These are good on their own, and great with a pre-dinner drink.

1. Place the butter and sugar in a bowl and whisk until creamy. Beat one of the eggs and slowly add it to the bowl, whisking until combined.

2. Fold in the flour and then add the parmesan cheese. Stir until a dough forms, place in refrigerator, and chill for 30 minutes. Meanwhile, preheat oven to 375°F.

3. Remove dough from refrigerator and place on a lightly floured surface. Roll until ⅛ inch thick.

4. Cut with ring cutter or knife. Place crackers on a lined baking tray.

5. Combine the remaining egg and the water in a bowl. Brush the egg wash on each of the crackers, sprinkle with sea salt, cayenne pepper, and parmesan.

6. Place in oven and bake for 8 minutes, or until golden brown. Remove from oven and let cool on a wire rack.

INGREDIENTS (CONTINUED):

PARMESAN CRACKERS

- 4 TABLESPOONS BUTTER, PLUS 1 TEASPOON, SOFTENED
- 2 TABLESPOONS POWDERED SUGAR
- 2 EGGS
- 1½ CUPS ALL-PURPOSE FLOUR
- 2 CUPS PARMESAN CHEESE, GRATED, PLUS MORE FOR TOPPING
- 1 TABLESPOON WATER
  SEA SALT, TO TASTE
  CAYENNE PEPPER, TO TASTE

BASIL VICHYSSOISE *and* FLAN

YIELD: 4 SERVINGS / ACTIVE TIME: 45 MINUTES / TOTAL TIME: 1 HOUR AND 30 MINUTES

This recipe is based on the classic, but the lemon juice gives it a fresh taste that is made for summer.

1. In a medium saucepan, add the butter and cook over medium heat until melted. Add the onion and leeks and cook for 5 minutes, or until soft.

2. Add the potato and bay leaf, and cook for 5 minutes.

3. Add the stock and cook for 15 minutes, or until the potato is soft.

4. Add the lemon juice and red wine vinegar.

5. Transfer the soup to a food processor, puree until smooth, and pass through a fine sieve.

6. Place in the refrigerator until chilled.

7. Add the basil and puree again in a food processor.

8. Transfer to a bowl and gently whisk in the heavy cream.

9. Season with salt and pepper and chill in refrigerator, until ready to serve.

10. Pour the soup into chilled bowls. Serve with the Basil Flan and garnish with basil.

BASIL FLAN

Flan is a savory dish that uses eggs to bind a custard.

1. Preheat oven to 270°F.

2. In a medium saucepan add the oil and warm over medium heat.

3. Add the shallot and cook for 3 minutes, or until soft.

4. Add the basil and spinach leaves and cook for another 5 minutes, or until they are wilted.

5. Add the eggs. Transfer the mixture to a food processor, puree until creamy, and strain through a fine sieve.

6. Season with salt and pepper, pour into Pyrex bowls, and place in a deep baking tray.

7. Fill the baking tray with hot water, so that the water goes halfway up the flan.

8. Place in the oven and bake for 20 to 25 minutes, until a toothpick entered into the center comes out clean.

9. Place in refrigerator until ready to serve.

INGREDIENTS:

¼ CUP BUTTER

1 ONION, CHOPPED

2 LEEKS, CHOPPED

1 POTATO, PEELED AND CHOPPED

1 BAY LEAF

4 CUPS CHICKEN STOCK

1½ TEASPOONS LEMON JUICE

2 TABLESPOONS RED WINE VINEGAR

1 CUP BASIL LEAVES, CHOPPED, PLUS MORE FOR GARNISH

1 CUP HEAVY CREAM

SALT AND PEPPER, TO TASTE

TO SERVE:

BASIL FLAN

BASIL FLAN

1 TABLESPOON EXTRA VIRGIN OLIVE OIL

1 SHALLOT, FINELY CHOPPED

2 CUPS BASIL

2 CUPS SPINACH

3 EGGS

SALT AND PEPPER, TO TASTE

BROCCOLI *and* CHEDDAR SOU[P]
with PARMESAN CRISPS

YIELD: 4 SERVINGS / **ACTIVE TIME:** 15 MINUTES / **TOTAL TIME:** 30

This very simple and quick soup is sure to become a family favorite. Caulifl[ower] as a variation.

1. In a medium saucepan, add the oil and warm over medium heat.

2. Add the onion and cook for 5 minutes, or until soft.

3. Add the butter. When the butter is melted, slowly add the flour, while stirring constantly. Cook for 3 minutes, and then add the milk and chicken stock.

4. Bring to a boil, reduce heat so that the soup simmers, and add the broccoli florets, carrots, and celery. Cook for 8 minutes, or until vegetables are cooked through.

5. Add cheddar cheese and mix until combined.

6. Season with salt and pepper, and serve with Parmesan Crisps.

PARMESAN CRISPS

1. Preheat oven to 400°F.

2. In a mixing bowl, add the cheeses and mix until combined.

3. Sprinkle the cheese on a lined baking tray. Make 8 circles, using a ring cutter to help keep then round.

4. Place a pinch of cayenne on each crisp. Place the tray in the oven and cook for 7 minutes, or until melted.

INGREDIENTS:

2	TABLESPOONS EXTRA VIRGIN OLIVE OIL
1	ONION, CHOPPED
¼	CUP BUTTER
¼	CUP FLOUR
2	CUPS MILK
2	CUPS CHICKEN STOCK
1½	CUPS BROCCOLI FLORETS
1	CUP CARROTS, CUT INTO MATCHSTICKS
2	CELERY STALKS, SLICED
2	CUPS SHARP CHEDDAR CHEESE, GRATED
	SALT AND PEPPER, TO TASTE

TO SERVE:
PARMESAN CRISPS

PARMESAN CRISPS

1	CUP PARMESAN CHEESE, GRATED
1	CUP SHARP CHEDDAR CHEESE, GRATED
	CAYENNE PEPPER, TO TASTE

BROCCOLI *and* STILTON SOUP

YIELD: 4 SERVINGS / ACTIVE TIME: 30 MINUTES / TOTAL TIME: 45 MINUTES

A twist on the traditional broccoli and cheddar soup, with Stilton's unique flavor completely changing the dynamic.

1. In a large saucepan, add the butter and cook over medium heat until melted. Add the onion and leek and cook for 5 minutes, or until soft.

2. Add the broccoli, potato, and stock. Bring to a boil, reduce heat so that the soup simmers, and cook for 5 to10 minutes, or until the vegetables are tender.

3. Transfer the soup to a food processor, add the spinach, and puree until smooth. Pass through a fine sieve, return to a clean pan, and add milk and cream. Reheat gently and add cheese, stirring until it melts. Do not let the soup come to a boil.

4. Season with salt and pepper, ladle into warm bowls, garnish with the peanuts, and serve with Tempura Broccoli.

TEMPURA BROCCOLI

1. Place the oil in a Dutch oven and heat to 350°F.

2. Place the water and salt in a medium saucepan and bring to a boil. Add the broccoli, cook for 3 minutes, and then submerge in ice water. Remove and set on a paper towel to dry.

3. Combine ½ cup of the flour, cornstarch, and baking powder in a bowl. Pass through a sieve.

4. Add your soda water and whisk until smooth. This is the tempura mix.

5. In a small bowl, add the remaining flour and the broccoli. Mix gently until the broccoli is coated.

6. Dip the pieces of broccoli into the tempura mix. Drop in oil and fry until golden brown.

7. Use a slotted spoon to remove from the oil and set on a paper towel to drain. Season with salt and pepper, and serve immediately.

INGREDIENTS:

- 2 TABLESPOONS BUTTER
- 1 ONION, CHOPPED
- 1 LEEK, WHITE PART ONLY, CHOPPED
- 8 CUPS BROCCOLI, STEMS REMOVED
- 1 SMALL POTATO, PEELED AND ROUGHLY CHOPPED
- 3 CUPS CHICKEN STOCK
- 1 CUP SPINACH
- 1 CUP MILK
- 4 TABLESPOONS HEAVY CREAM
- 6 OZ. STILTON, RIND REMOVED

  SALT AND PEPPER, TO TASTE

  PEANUTS, CRUSHED AND TOASTED, FOR GARNISH

TO SERVE:
TEMPURA BROCCOLI

TEMPURA BROCCOLI
- 1 CUP OF OIL
- 4 CUPS WATER
- 1 TEASPOON SALT
- 12 SMALL BROCCOLI FLORETS
- ¾ CUP ALL-PURPOSE FLOUR
- ¼ CUP CORNSTARCH
- ½ TEASPOON BAKING POWDER
- 1 CUP SODA WATER

  SALT AND PEPPER, TO TASTE

MAINE FIDDLEHEAD FERN SOUP
with CARAMELIZED ONION CRÈME FRAICHE

YIELD: 4 SERVINGS / ACTIVE TIME: 30 MINUTES / TOTAL TIME: 1 HOUR

Fiddleheads or fiddlehead greens are the curled fronds of a young fern. Fiddleheads have a very small growing window in Maine but are a celebrated local vegetable nonetheless.

1. In a medium saucepan, add the butter and cook over medium heat until melted. Add the onion, garlic, and fiddlehead ferns, and cook for 5 minutes, or until soft.

2. Add the vegetable stock and bring to a boil.

3. Transfer the soup to a food processor, puree until smooth, and strain through a fine sieve.

4. Return soup to a clean pan, add cream, and bring to a simmer. Season with salt and pepper, ladle into warm bowls, garnish with chives, and serve with Caramelized Onion Crème Fraiche.

CARAMELIZED ONION CRÈME FRAICHE

1. In a medium sauté pan, add the oil and warm over low heat.

2. Add the onions and cook slowly, adding a splash of water once they start to dry. Cook until onions are caramelized.

3. Season with salt and pepper, remove from heat, and let cool.

4. Once cool, fold into the crème fraiche, and refrigerate until ready to serve.

INGREDIENTS:

3	TABLESPOONS BUTTER
1	ONION, CHOPPED
1	GARLIC CLOVE, MINCED
1	POUND FIDDLEHEAD FERNS
4	CUPS VEGETABLE STOCK
1	CUP HEAVY CREAM
	SALT AND PEPPER, TO TASTE
	CHIVES, CHOPPED, FOR GARNISH

TO SERVE:

CARAMELIZED ONION CRÈME FRAICHE

CARAMELIZED ONION CRÈME FRAICHE

1	TABLESPOON VEGETABLE OIL
1	ONION, CHOPPED
	SALT AND PEPPER, TO TASTE
	CRÈME FRAICHE

CALDO VERDE SOUP
with PAPRIKA OIL

YIELD: 4 SERVINGS / ACTIVE TIME: 25 MINUTES / TOTAL TIME: 1 HOUR

This soup is popular in Portugal, where it is typically consumed during celebrations.

1. Heat the olive oil in a large saucepan over medium heat. Add the chorizo and cook for 5 minutes, or until it releases its red oil and begins to brown. Remove chorizo from the pan and set aside. Reserve 1 tablespoon of the oil for the Paprika Oil.

2. Add the onions to the pan and cook for 5 minutes, or until they are soft. Add the garlic and cook for 2 minutes. Add the potatoes, bay leaf, and stock and bring to a boil.

3. Reduce the heat so that the soup simmers and cook for 20 minutes, or until the potatoes can be crushed with a fork.

4. In the meantime, separate the leaves of the cabbage and rinse. Remove any particularly thick ribs. Roll up each leaf as tightly as you can and then slice into thin strips.

5. When the potatoes are cooked, remove pan from heat and remove the bay leaf. Transfer the soup to a food processor and puree until smooth.

6. Return the soup to the pan, add the chorizo and the cabbage, and bring to a boil. Reduce heat so that the soup simmers and cook for 5 minutes.

7. Season with salt and pepper, ladle into bowls, and garnish with the Paprika Oil and dill.

PAPRIKA OIL

Place the ingredients in a blender and mix until combined. Strain through a fine sieve and reserve until ready to use.

INGREDIENTS:

1	TABLESPOON EXTRA VIRGIN OLIVE OIL
4	OZ. CHORIZO, CUT INTO ¼-INCH PIECES
½	LARGE ONION, DICED
4	GARLIC CLOVES, MINCED
3	MEDIUM POTATOES, PEELED AND DICED
1	BAY LEAF
6	CUPS VEGETABLE STOCK
1	POUND SAVOY CABBAGE
	DILL, CHOPPED, FOR GARNISH

TO SERVE:
PAPRIKA OIL

PAPRIKA OIL

½	CUP VEGETABLE OIL
1	TABLESPOON SMOKED PAPRIKA
1	TABLESPOON CHORIZO OIL (RESERVED FROM CALDO VERDE RECIPE)

CANH BAP CAI CUON

YIELD: 4 SERVINGS / ACTIVE TIME: 40 MINUTES / TOTAL TIME: 1 HOUR AND 40 MINUTES

This dish's name translates to stuffed cabbage soup. Variations include meats such as pork belly and other mushrooms.

1. In a large stockpot, add all the ingredients for the infused stock and bring to a boil. Turn off heat and allow to infuse for 1 hour. Strain through a fine sieve and reserve the stock, which can be prepared the night before.

2. In a large saucepan, bring water to a boil, add the cabbage leaves, and cook for 2 minutes. Remove and submerge in ice water. Add the scallion greens to the boiling water and cook for 1 minute. Remove and submerge in ice water. Place cabbage and scallion greens on paper towel to dry.

3. In a mixing bowl, combine the wood ear mushrooms, pork, shrimp, scallion whites, Thai chili, fish sauce, and soy sauce.

4. Place a tablespoon of the mixture at the bottom of each of the cabbage leaves. Roll mixture to the top of the leaves.

5. Cut the scallion greens in half lengthwise and use them to tie a cabbage leaf closed. Repeat with the remaining leaves.

6. Place the infused stock in a large saucepan and bring to a boil. Reduce the heat so that the soup simmers.

7. Gently place the cabbage leaves into the soup and simmer for 20 minutes.

8. Place 2 cabbage leaves in a warm bowl. Ladle the hot broth over the top, garnish with watercress and jalapeño, and serve.

INGREDIENTS:

INFUSED STOCK

6	CUPS CHICKEN STOCK
	1½-INCH PIECE OF GINGER, PEELED AND CHOPPED
2	TABLESPOONS FISH SAUCE
2	TABLESPOONS SOY SAUCE
2	THYME SPRIGS, LEAVES REMOVED AND CHOPPED
¼	TEASPOON SALT

SOUP

8	SAVOY CABBAGE LEAVES
4	SCALLIONS, GREEN TOPS LEFT WHOLE, WHITE PART CHOPPED
¼	CUP DRIED WOOD EAR MUSHROOMS, SOAKED IN HOT WATER FOR 10 MINUTES, SQUEEZED DRY, AND FINELY CHOPPED
4	OZ. GROUND PORK
4	OZ. SHRIMP, SHELLED, DEVEINED, AND CHOPPED
1	THAI CHILI, FINELY CHOPPED
2	TABLESPOONS FISH SAUCE
1	TABLESPOON SOY SAUCE
	WATERCRESS, FOR GARNISH
	JALAPEÑO, FINELY SLICED, FOR GARNISH

CARAMELIZED ONION SOUP
with BAKED HERBED CROUTON

YIELD: 4 SERVINGS / ACTIVE TIME: 30 MINUTES / TOTAL TIME: 1

Caramelizing the onions allows for the natural sugars to concentrate and make t.. nice and sweet. Combining them with the Madeira is sure to make everyone happy.

1. In a medium saucepan, add the butter and cook over low heat until melted. Add the onions and cook over the lowest possible heat for 30 minutes, or until golden brown. Stir the onions every few minutes and add small amounts of water when they begin to stick to the pan.

2. Add the garlic, thyme, Riesling, and Madeira and cook until the liquid has been reduced by half.

3. Add the cream and simmer for 10 minutes.

4. Transfer the soup to a food processor and blend until smooth.

5. Season to taste with salt and pepper and serve with Baked Herbed Croutons.

BAKED HERB CROUTONS

1. Preheat oven to 350°F.

2. Combine the herbs and olive oil in a small bowl. Place slices of baguette on a baking tray and drizzle with the herbed olive oil.

3. Season with salt and pepper, place in the oven, and bake for 10 minutes, or until golden brown.

INGREDIENTS:

¼ CUP BUTTER

6 SPANISH ONIONS, CHOPPED

2 GARLIC CLOVES, MINCED

1 THYME SPRIG, LEAVES REMOVED AND CHOPPED

½ CUP RIESLING

½ CUP MADEIRA

4 CUPS HEAVY CREAM

SALT AND PEPPER, TO TASTE

TO SERVE:
BAKED HERB CROUTONS

BAKED HERB CROUTONS

1 TABLESPOON PARSLEY, CHOPPED

1 TABLESPOON TARRAGON, CHOPPED

1 TABLESPOON CHIVES, CHOPPED

¼ CUP EXTRA VIRGIN OLIVE OIL

8 SLICES OF FRENCH BREAD

SALT AND PEPPER, TO TASTE

CARROT *and* GINGER SOUP
with TURMERIC CREAM

YIELD: 4 TO 6 SERVINGS / ACTIVE TIME: 25 MINUTES / TOTAL TIME: 1 HOUR

This soup is for the true ginger lover, or for when you feel a cold coming on.

1. In a medium saucepan, add the butter and cook over medium heat until melted. Add the onions and cook for 5 minutes, while stirring often, or until it is soft.

2. Add the carrots, ginger, and orange zest. Cook for 5 minutes, or until the carrot starts to break down.

3. Add the orange juice and white wine and cook until evaporated. Add the chicken stock, bring to a boil, and season with salt and pepper. Reduce heat so that the soup simmers and cook for 10 to 15 minutes, until the vegetables are tender.

4. Transfer the soup to a food processor, puree until smooth, and strain through a fine sieve.

5. Return the soup to a clean pan and adjust the seasoning. Add more stock or juice if it is too thick.

6. Ladle into warm bowls, serve with Turmeric Cream, and garnish with dill.

TURMERIC CREAM

1. Place the cream in a bowl and whip until medium peaks begin to form.

2. Add the turmeric and season with salt. Stir to combine, and refrigerate until ready to use.

INGREDIENTS:

4	TABLESPOONS BUTTER
2	ONIONS, DICED
6	CUPS CARROTS, PEELED AND CHOPPED
4	TABLESPOONS GINGER, PEELED AND MINCED
	ZEST AND JUICE OF 2 ORANGES
1	CUP WHITE WINE
8	CUPS CHICKEN STOCK OR VEGETABLE STOCK
	SALT AND PEPPER, TO TASTE
	DILL, CHOPPED, FOR GARNISH

TO SERVE:

TURMERIC CREAM

TURMERIC CREAM

½	CUP HEAVY CREAM
½	TEASPOON TURMERIC
	PINCH OF SALT

CELERIAC ROASTED GARLIC SOUP
with PICKLED TOMATOES *and* FUNNEL CAKE

YIELD: 4 SERVINGS / ACTIVE TIME: 45 MINUTES / TOTAL TIME: 13 HOURS AND 30 MINUTES

Roasting the garlic brings out an earthy, sweet, and mild flavor that is balanced by the acid from the pickled tomatoes.

1. Preheat oven to 350°F.

2. Place the whole garlic bulb on a baking tray and drizzle with the olive oil. Place in oven and bake for 30 minutes, or until it's golden brown. Remove from oven and let stand until cool. When cool, slice off top and remove individual cloves. Set aside.

3. In a medium saucepan, add the butter and cook over medium heat until melted. Add the onion and celeriac and cook for 5 minutes, or until soft.

4. Add the herbs, cover the pan with a lid, and cook for 5 minutes, while stirring often.

5. Add the wine, stock, and roasted garlic and bring to a boil.

6. Add the cream and cook for 2 minutes.

7. Reduce the heat so that the soup simmers and cook for 15 minutes, until the celeriac is tender.

8. Transfer the soup to a food processor, puree until smooth, and strain through a fine sieve.

9. Season with salt and pepper, return to a clean pan, and bring to a boil. Adjust seasoning and ladle into warm bowls. Garnish with the scallion greens and serve with the Pickled Tomatoes and the Pepper and Onion Funnel Cake.

INGREDIENTS:

1	WHOLE GARLIC BULB
1	TABLESPOON EXTRA VIRGIN OLIVE OIL
2	TABLESPOONS BUTTER
½	ONION, DICED
8	CUPS CELERIAC, DICED
1	THYME SPRIG, LEAVES CHOPPED
1	ROSEMARY SPRIG, LEAVES CHOPPED
1	CUP WHITE WINE
2	CUPS CHICKEN OR VEGETABLE STOCK
4	CUPS HEAVY CREAM
	SALT AND PEPPER, TO TASTE
	SCALLION GREENS, CHOPPED, FOR GARNISH

TO SERVE:

PICKLED TOMATOES

PEPPER AND ONION FUNNEL CAKE

PICKLED TOMATOES

1. Combine the vinegar, brown sugar, salt, garlic, mustard seeds, peppercorns, cumin, cayenne pepper, turmeric, and olive oil in a small saucepan and bring to a simmer over medium heat.

2. Remove from heat, and let cool.

3. Once cool, add chopped tomatoes, place in refrigerator, and marinate for 12 hours or overnight.

PEPPER AND ONION FUNNEL CAKE

YIELD: 4 SERVINGS

1. Place the oil in a large saucepan and heat to 375°F.

2. In a bowl, add the eggs, rice wine vinegar, Tabasco™, and Worcestershire sauce, and whisk until combined.

3. Slowly add the flour and baking powder, stirring to combine. Add the scallions, green bell pepper, and red onion, and stir until combined.

4. Drop spoonfuls of the mixture into the hot oil and fry until golden.

5. Remove with a slotted spoon, place on a paper towel to drain, and season with salt. Serve immediately.

INGREDIENTS (CONTINUED):

PICKLED TOMATOES

4   TABLESPOONS WHITE WINE VINEGAR

1½   TABLESPOONS BROWN SUGAR

2   TEASPOONS SALT

½   TEASPOON GARLIC, MINCED

2   TEASPOONS MUSTARD SEEDS

¼   TEASPOON CRACKED PEPPERCORNS

1   TEASPOON CUMIN

¼   TEASPOON CAYENNE PEPPER

¼   TEASPOON TURMERIC

1½   TABLESPOONS EXTRA VIRGIN OLIVE OIL

1   TOMATO, CONCASSE AND CHOPPED (SEE PAGE 89)

PEPPER AND ONION FUNNEL CAKE

4   CUPS VEGETABLE OIL

2   EGGS

1   TEASPOON RICE WINE VINEGAR

½   TEASPOON TABASCO™

½   TEASPOON WORCESTERSHIRE SAUCE

⅓   CUP FLOUR

¼   TEASPOON BAKING POWDER

2   SCALLIONS, WHITES CHOPPED

2   TABLESPOONS GREEN BELL PEPPER, CHOPPED

2   TABLESPOONS RED ONION, DICED

    SALT, TO TASTE

CELERIAC TRUFFLE SOUP

YIELD: 4 SERVINGS / ACTIVE TIME: 25 MINUTES / TOTAL TIME: 1 HOUR AND 15 MINUTES

This recipe was made more affordable by using truffle paste and truffle oil. In a restaurant setting we would use fresh Périgord truffles from the south of France and shave some Alba truffles over it. If you're getting fancy, this is a great intermezzo soup.

1. In a medium saucepan, add the butter and cook over medium heat until melted. Add the onion and celeriac and cook for 5 minutes, or until soft.

2. Add the herbs, cover with a lid, reduce heat, and cook for 5 minutes, stirring often.

3. Add the stock, white wine, and truffle paste, and bring to a boil. Add the cream and cook for 2 minutes. Reduce heat so that the soup simmers and cook for 15 minutes, until the celeriac is tender.

4. Transfer the soup to a food processor, puree until smooth, and strain through a fine sieve.

5. Season with salt and pepper, return to a clean pan, and bring to a boil.

6. Add the truffle oil and emulsify with a whisk for 1 minute.

7. Ladle into warm bowls, garnish with truffle paste, truffle oil, and celery leaves and serve with Truffle Croutons.

INGREDIENTS:

- 2 TABLESPOONS BUTTER
- ½ ONION, DICED
- 8 CUPS CELERIAC, DICED
- 1 THYME SPRIG, LEAVES REMOVED AND CHOPPED
- 1 ROSEMARY SPRIG, LEAVES REMOVED AND CHOPPED
- 2 CUPS CHICKEN OR VEGETABLE STOCK
- 1 CUP WHITE WINE
- 4 TABLESPOONS BLACK TRUFFLE PASTE, PLUS MORE FOR GARNISH
- 4 CUPS HEAVY CREAM
- SALT AND PEPPER, TO TASTE
- WHITE TRUFFLE OIL, FOR GARNISH
- CELERY LEAVES, FOR GARNISH

TO SERVE:
TRUFFLE CROUTONS

TRUFFLE CROUTONS

YIELD: 4 SERVINGS

1. Combine vegetable and truffle oil in a mixing bowl.

2. In a sauté pan, add oil and cook over low heat until warm. Add the bread, raise heat to medium, and cook until bread is golden brown.

3. Add truffle paste and cook for 1 minute.

4. Remove bread and set to drain on paper towels.

5. Season with salt and pepper, and serve.

TRUFFLE CROUTONS

- ¼ CUP VEGETABLE OIL
- 2 TABLESPOONS TRUFFLE OIL
- 1 CUP OF BREAD, CUT INTO ½-INCH CUBES (SOFT ENRICHED BREAD IS BEST, SOMETHING SIMILAR TO BRIOCHE)
- 1 TEASPOON TRUFFLE PASTE
- SALT AND PEPPER, TO TASTE

CELERY BISQUE
with CRISPY CELERY HEARTS

YIELD: 6 SERVINGS / ACTIVE TIME: 15 MINUTES / TOTAL TIME: 1 HOUR AND 5 MINUTES

Celeriac provides the flavor of celery and a white, creamy color. The celery heart is the center part of the celery stalk. Protected by the outer part, it is very tender and sweet.

1. In a medium saucepan, add the butter and cook over medium heat until melted. Add the onions, leek, and celery and cook for 5 minutes, or until tender.

2. Add the bay leaf, potato, and celeriac and cook for 5 minutes.

3. Add the stock and cinnamon stick and bring to a boil. Reduce heat so that the soup simmers and cook until the potatoes and celeriac are soft.

4. Remove the cinnamon stick and transfer the soup to a food processor. Puree until creamy and pass through a fine sieve.

5. Return the soup to the pan and bring to a simmer. Add the cream and nutmeg and season with salt and pepper.

6. Ladle into bowls and serve with Crispy Celery Hearts.

CRISPY CELERY HEARTS

1. Place oil in a large saucepan and heat to 350°F.

2. Combine 1 cup of the flour, cornstarch, and baking powder in a bowl. Pass through a fine sieve.

3. Add the beer and whisk until smooth. This is your tempura mix.

4. In a small bowl, add the remaining flour and celery hearts. Mix until the celery hearts are coated.

5. Dip each piece of celery heart in the tempura mix and place into the hot oil. Fry until golden brown.

6. Use a slotted spoon or tongs to remove from oil. Set to drain on a paper towel.

7. Season with salt and pepper and serve immediately.

INGREDIENTS:

- ¼ CUP BUTTER
- 1 SMALL ONION, CHOPPED
- ½ LEEK, WHITE PART ONLY, CUT INTO ¾-INCH PIECES
- 2 CELERY STALKS, CHOPPED
- 1 BAY LEAF
- 1 MEDIUM POTATO, PEELED AND CHOPPED
- 1 MEDIUM CELERIAC, PEELED AND CHOPPED
- 4 CUPS CHICKEN STOCK
- 1 CINNAMON STICK
- ½ CUP HEAVY CREAM
  FRESH GROUND NUTMEG, TO TASTE
  SALT AND PEPPER, TO TASTE

TO SERVE:
CRISPY CELERY HEARTS

CRISPY CELERY HEARTS
- 4 CUPS VEGETABLE OIL
- 1½ CUPS ALL-PURPOSE FLOUR
- ½ CUP CORNSTARCH
- 1 TEASPOON BAKING POWDER
- 1½ CUPS BEER, PREFERABLY ALE
- 18 CELERY HEARTS
  SALT AND PEPPER, TO TASTE

CHILLED SWEET *and* SOUR BEET SOUP

YIELD: 4 SERVINGS / ACTIVE TIME: 20 MINUTES / TOTAL TIME: 2 HOURS

This is a summer classic. You can even add vodka and serve it as a shooter.

1. In a large saucepan, add the butter and oil and cook over medium heat until warm.

2. Add the onion, beets, celery, red bell pepper, and apples and cook for 5 minutes, or until onion is soft.

3. Add the stock, cumin, thyme, and bay leaves and bring to a boil. Reduce heat so that the soup simmers and cook for 30 minutes, or until the vegetables are soft.

4. Transfer the soup to a food processor, puree until creamy, and strain through a fine sieve.

5. Return to a clean pan, add sour cream, heavy cream, and lemon juice and bring to a simmer. Season with salt and pepper, place in the refrigerator, and chill for 1 hour.

6. Serve in chilled bowls and garnish with sour cream and dill.

INGREDIENTS:

- 2 TABLESPOONS BUTTER
- 2 TABLESPOONS VEGETABLE OIL
- 1 RED ONION, CHOPPED
- 6 CUPS BEETS, PEELED AND CHOPPED
- 2 CELERY STALKS, CHOPPED
- 1 RED BELL PEPPER, SEEDED AND CHOPPED
- 2 SMALL APPLES, PEELED AND CHOPPED
- 6 CUPS VEGETABLE STOCK
- 1 TEASPOON CUMIN
- 1 TEASPOON THYME, LEAVES REMOVED AND CHOPPED
- 2 BAY LEAVES
- ½ CUP SOUR CREAM, PLUS MORE FOR GARNISH
- ½ CUP HEAVY CREAM
- 2 TEASPOONS LEMON JUICE
- SALT AND PEPPER, TO TASTE
- DILL, FOR GARNISH

CORN CHOWDER

YIELD: 4 TO 6 SERVINGS / **ACTIVE TIME:** 25 MINUTES / **TOTAL TIME:** 2 HOURS AND 15 MINUTES

There is nothing better than fresh corn from your local farm stand, and turning it into a soup is a great way to show off its lovely characteristics. For a more rustic version, skip the food processor.

1. In a stockpot, place the reserved cobs and cover with water. Bring to a boil, reduce heat so that the stock simmers, and cook for 1 hour. Strain the stock, measure out 4 cups, and reserve.

2. In a large saucepan, add the bacon and cook over medium heat until fat renders. Add the onion and garlic and cook for 5 minutes or until soft.

3. Add the potatoes and corn kernels and cook for another 10 minutes, while stirring occasionally.

4. Add the corn stock and cook until reduced by a third.

5. Add the cream and simmer for 30 minutes. Transfer to a food processor, puree until creamy, and strain through a fine sieve.

6. Season with salt and pepper, ladle into warm bowls, and serve with Corn Beignets.

CORN BEIGNETS

1. In a medium saucepan, add milk, salt, and butter and bring to a boil.

2. Add the flour and stir constantly until a ball of dough forms.

3. Remove the pan from heat and let the dough cool for 10 minutes.

4. Add the egg to the pan and whisk vigorously.

5. Once the egg has been combined, add the corn and cilantro and stir until combined.

6. Place the oil in a Dutch oven and heat to 350°F.

7. Spoon small amounts of the batter into the hot oil and cook until golden brown.

8. Remove with a slotted spoon and set on a paper towel to drain.

9. Serve immediately.

INGREDIENTS:

6	EARS OF CORN, KERNELS REMOVED, COBS RESERVED
4	OZ. BACON, CHOPPED
1	LARGE WHITE ONION, CHOPPED
3	GARLIC CLOVES, MINCED
2	LARGE POTATOES, PEELED AND CHOPPED
4	CUPS HEAVY CREAM
	SALT AND PEPPER, TO TASTE

TO SERVE:
CORN BEIGNETS

CORN BEIGNETS

¼	CUP MILK
⅛	TEASPOON SALT
2	TABLESPOONS BUTTER
¼	CUP FLOUR
1	EGGS
¼	CUP CORN
½	TEASPOON CILANTRO, CHOPPED
2	CUPS OIL

BUTTERNUT SQUASH *and* APPLE CIDER SOUP
with FALL SPICED CREAM

YIELD: 4 SERVINGS / ACTIVE TIME: 30 MINUTES / TOTAL TIME: 1 HOUR AND 20 MINUTES

This was always a staple at The White Barn Inn for Thanksgiving. The fall spices and apple cider complement the components of this dish, and a quenelle of cold whipped cream provides a wonderful mouthfeel.

1. In a medium saucepan, add the oil and cook over medium heat until warm. Add the onion and cook, while stirring often, for 5 minutes, or until soft.

2. Add the squash and apple. Cook, while stirring, for 5 to 10 minutes, until the squash starts to break down.

3. Add the Calvados and cook until it evaporates. Add the cider and chicken stock.

4. Bring to a boil and season with salt and pepper. Reduce heat so that the soup simmers and cook for 20 minutes, until the squash and onion are tender.

5. Transfer the soup to a food processor, puree until smooth, and strain through a fine sieve.

6. Place the soup in a clean pan and bring to a simmer. Adjust the consistency with more chicken stock if it is too thick. Adjust seasoning to taste, ladle into warm bowls, and garnish with Fall Spiced Cream, Crispy Butternut Squash Ribbons, and Toasted Pumpkin Seeds.

FALL SPICED CREAM

1. In a bowl, add cream and whisk until medium peaks start to form.

2. Add the nutmeg. Season with salt and stir to combine. Refrigerate until ready to use.

INGREDIENTS:

1	TABLESPOON VEGETABLE OIL
1	ONION, DICED
1	POUND BUTTERNUT SQUASH, PEELED AND DICED
1	APPLE, PEELED AND DICED
2	TABLESPOONS CALVADOS
½	CUP APPLE CIDER
2	CUPS CHICKEN STOCK
	SALT AND PEPPER, TO TASTE

TO SERVE:

FALL SPICED CREAM

CRISPY BUTTERNUT SQUASH RIBBONS

TOASTED PUMPKIN SEEDS

FALL SPICED CREAM

½	CUP HEAVY CREAM
½	TEASPOON NUTMEG
	PINCH OF SALT

CRISPY BUTTERNUT SQUASH RIBBONS

1. Place oil in a medium saucepan and cook over medium-high heat until 375°F.

2. After skin is removed from the butternut squash, use the peeler to make nice long ribbons.

3. In a small saucepan, bring the water to boil. Add the butternut squash ribbons, cook for 1 minute, remove with a slotted spoon, and submerge in ice water. Remove and let dry.

4. When dry, place squash ribbons in the oil and fry until golden brown. Remove, set to drain on a paper towel, and season with salt.

TOASTED PUMPKIN SEEDS

1. Preheat oven to 350°F.

2. Place the seeds on a baking tray and sprinkle with the olive oil and salt.

3. Place tray in oven and cook for 5 minutes. Remove, stir, and place back in the oven for another 5 minutes, until golden brown.

4. Remove from oven, set on paper towels to drain, and season to taste with salt.

INGR

CRIS
RIB

2

1

2

SALT, TO TASTE

TOASTED PUMPKIN SEEDS

½ CUP RAW PUMPKIN SEEDS

½ TEASPOON EXTRA VIRGIN OLIVE OIL

PINCH OF SALT

CREAM OF CAULIFLOWER SOUP
with CURRIED CAULIFLOWER FLORETS

YIELD: 4 SERVINGS / ACTIVE TIME: 15 MINUTES / TOTAL TIME: 45 MINUTES

This quick and easy soup is sure to warm you up on a cold day.

1. Remove the florets from the stem of the cauliflower. Reserve 2 large florets and then chop the remaining florets and stem.

2. In a medium saucepan, add the butter and olive oil and cook over medium heat until warm.

3. Add the onion and chopped cauliflower and cook for 5 minutes, or until soft.

4. Add the herbs and cook for 3 minutes. Add the wine and the stock, bring to a boil, reduce heat so that the soup simmers, and cook for 5 minutes.

5. Add the cream and simmer for 20 minutes, or until the cauliflower is tender.

6. Transfer the soup to a food processor, puree until creamy, and strain through a fine sieve.

7. Return to a clean pan, bring to a simmer, and season with salt and pepper.

8. Ladle into warm bowls, serve with Curried Cauliflower Florets, and garnish with toasted almonds and pea tendrils.

CURRIED CAULIFLOWER FLORETS

1. Add 1 tablespoon of the oil to a medium saucepan and warm over medium heat.

2. Add the cauliflower and cook for 2 minutes on both sides.

3. Meanwhile, place the remaining oil and the spices in a bowl. Whisk until combined.

4. Add the spiced oil to the pan and bring to a simmer.

5. Remove from heat and let cool. Season with salt and pepper, and serve.

INGREDIENTS:

- 1 HEAD OF CAULIFLOWER
- 2 TABLESPOONS BUTTER
- 1 TABLESPOON EXTRA VIRGIN OLIVE OIL
- ½ ONION, DICED
- 1 THYME SPRIG, LEAVES REMOVED AND CHOPPED
- 1 ROSEMARY SPRIG, LEAVES REMOVED AND CHOPPED
- 1 CUP CHARDONNAY
- 1 CUP CHICKEN OR VEGETABLE STOCK
- 2 CUPS HEAVY CREAM
- SALT AND PEPPER, TO TASTE
- PEA TENDRILS, FOR GARNISH
- ALMONDS, SLICED AND TOASTED, FOR GARNISH

TO SERVE:
CURRIED CAULIFLOWER FLORETS

CURRIED CAULIFLOWER FLORETS

- ½ CUP EXTRA VIRGIN OLIVE OIL
- 2 LARGE CAULIFLOWER FLORETS, SLICED INTO 8 ¼-INCH PIECES
- 1 TABLESPOON CURRY POWDER
- ⅛ TEASPOON CAYENNE PEPPER
- SALT AND PEPPER, TO TASTE

COCONUT *and* SPINACH SOUP
with TOASTED SLICED ALMONDS

YIELD: 4 SERVINGS / ACTIVE TIME: 20 MINUTES / TOTAL TIME: 45 MINUTES

While working in England, I discovered that I really liked this combination of flavors in a soup. This is not the same soup that won me over but has a similar profile.

1. Place 2 tablespoons of the butter in a medium saucepan and cook over medium heat until melted. Add the onion and cook for 5 minutes, or until soft.

2. Add the spinach, cover, and cook over low heat for 5 minutes, or until wilted.

3. Add the stock and bring to a boil.

4. Transfer the soup to a food processor, blend until creamy, and strain through a fine sieve.

5. In a clean medium saucepan, add the remaining butter and melt. Add the flour and cook for 2 minutes. Add the soup and coconut milk to the pan with the butter and flour. Cook for 5 minutes. Season with salt, pepper, and nutmeg, ladle into warm bowls, and garnish with nutmeg, chives, toasted sliced almonds, and coconut.

INGREDIENTS:

3   TABLESPOONS BUTTER

1   ONION, CHOPPED

16 CUPS SPINACH, CHOPPED

4   CUPS VEGETABLE STOCK

1   TABLESPOON ALL-PURPOSE FLOUR

2   CUPS COCONUT MILK

¼   TEASPOON NUTMEG, PLUS MORE FOR GARNISH

SALT AND PEPPER, TO TASTE

CHIVES, CHOPPED, FOR GARNISH

ALMONDS, SLICED AND TOASTED, FOR GARNISH

UNSWEETENED COCONUT, SHREDDED, FOR GARNISH

CREAM OF TOMATO
with FONTINA JALAPEÑO HUSH PUPPIES

YIELD: 4 SERVINGS / ACTIVE TIME: 30 MINUTES / TOTAL TIME: 1 HOUR AND 15 MINUTES

This revitalizing classic is a favorite with diners of all ages.

1. Place the butter in a large saucepan and cook over medium heat until melted. Add the onion and cook for 5 minutes, or until soft.

2. Add the tomatoes, chopped carrots, chicken stock, parsley, and thyme. Reduce heat to low and simmer for 20 minutes, or until the vegetables are tender.

3. Transfer the soup to a food processor, puree until smooth, and pass through a fine sieve.

4. Return the soup to the pan and add the cream. Reheat gently and season with salt and pepper. Ladle the soup into bowls and serve with Fontina Jalapeño Hush Puppies.

FONTINA JALAPEÑO HUSH PUPPIES

1. Place the oil in a Dutch oven and heat to 320°F.

2. Add the corn meal, flour, sugar, salt, baking powder, baking soda, and cayenne pepper to a small bowl and whisk until combined.

3. In a separate bowl, add the buttermilk, egg, and jalapeño. Whisk to combine.

4. Combine the buttermilk mixture and the dry mixture.

5. Add the cheese and stir until combined.

6. Drop spoonfuls of the batter into the hot oil and fry until golden brown.

7. Remove from oil with a slotted spoon and place on paper towels to drain.

INGREDIENTS:

- 2 TABLESPOONS BUTTER
- 1 ONION, CHOPPED
- 2 POUNDS TOMATOES, CHOPPED
- 2 CARROTS, PEELED AND CHOPPED
- 5 CUPS CHICKEN STOCK
- 2 TABLESPOONS PARSLEY LEAVES, CHOPPED
- ½ TEASPOON THYME LEAVES, CHOPPED
- 6 TABLESPOONS HEAVY CREAM

  SALT AND PEPPER, TO TASTE

TO SERVE:
FONTINA JALAPEÑO HUSH PUPPIES

FONTINA JALAPEÑO HUSH PUPPIES
- 2 CUPS VEGETABLE OIL
- ½ CUP CORN MEAL
- 3 TABLESPOONS ALL-PURPOSE FLOUR, PLUS 1½ TEASPOONS
- 4½ TABLESPOONS SUGAR
- ¾ TEASPOON SALT
- ¼ TEASPOON BAKING POWDER
- ⅛ TEASPOON BAKING SODA
- ⅛ TEASPOON CAYENNE PEPPER
- ¼ CUP BUTTERMILK
- 1 EGG, BEATEN
- 2 TABLESPOONS JALAPEÑO, SEEDED AND CHOPPED
- ¾ CUP FONTINA, GRATED

EGGPLANT *and* ZUCCHINI SOUP
with TZATZIKI, MINT-PICKLED CUCUMBERS, *and* PITA BREAD

YIELD: 4 SERVINGS / ACTIVE TIME: 1 HOUR / TOTAL TIME: 2 HOURS AND 30 MINUTES

This is a perfectly Greek soup, garnished with tzatziki, the country's staple condiment.

1. Preheat oven to 425°F.

2. Place the eggplant, zucchini, onion, and garlic in a roasting pan and drizzle with olive oil.

3. Place in the oven and roast for 30 minutes, stirring occasionally. Remove and let stand.

4. Place half of the vegetables in a food processor. Add the stock and blend until smooth.

5. Add the puree to a medium saucepan. Add the remaining vegetables and bring to a boil.

6. Stir in oregano and mint, and season with salt and pepper. Ladle into bowls, garnish with fresh mint sprigs, and serve with a scoop of Tzatziki, the Mint-pickled Cucumbers, and Pita Bread.

TZATZIKI

1. Place the cucumber in a bowl. Sprinkle the salt over it and let stand for 20 minutes.

2. Combine the salted cucumber with the remaining ingredients. Season to taste and place in the refrigerator until ready to use.

MINT-PICKLED CUCUMBERS

These quick pickles are a great way to add acid and texture to a dish. Marinating for only 30 minutes allows for nice acidity, while maintaining the cucumber's crunch.

1. Place all ingredients, save the cucumber, in a small saucepan and bring to a boil.

2. Turn off heat and let cool.

3. Strain through a fine sieve. Place cucumbers in the pickling liquid and marinate for 30 minutes.

INGREDIENTS:

1 LARGE EGGPLANT, PEELED AND DICED

2 LARGE ZUCCHINIS, DICED

1 ONION, DICED

3 GARLIC CLOVES, MINCED

2 TABLESPOONS EXTRA VIRGIN OLIVE OIL

3 CUPS VEGETABLE STOCK

1 TABLESPOON OREGANO, LEAVES REMOVED AND CHOPPED

1 TABLESPOON MINT, LEAVES REMOVED AND CHOPPED, PLUS MORE FOR GARNISH

SALT AND PEPPER, TO TASTE

TO SERVE:
TZATZIKI

PITA BREAD (SEE RECIPE ON PAGE 469)

MINT-PICKLED CUCUMBERS

TZATZIKI
½ CUCUMBER, PEELED, SEEDS REMOVED, DICED

½ TEASPOON SALT

1 GARLIC CLOVE, MINCED

½ CUP GREEK YOGURT

2 TABLESPOONS MINT, CHOPPED

MINT-PICKLED CUCUMBERS
⅓ CUP SUGAR

⅓ CUP WATER

⅓ CUP RICE WINE VINEGAR

1 TABLESPOON DRIED MINT

1 TEASPOON CORIANDER SEEDS

1 TEASPOON MUSTARD SEEDS

½ CUCUMBER, PEELED, SEEDED, SLICED INTO HALF-MOONS

230 | SOUP

EGGPLANT SOUP *with* SCHNITZEL, MOZZARELLA, *and* GREMOLATA

YIELD: 4 SERVINGS / ACTIVE TIME: 30 MINUTES / TOTAL TIME: 1 HOUR

Sprinkling salt over eggplant before cooking it draws out the vegetable's moisture, which can be bitter.

1. In a large saucepan, add the oil and the shallots and garlic. Cook for 5 minutes, or until soft.

2. Add the eggplant and cook for 10 minutes, while stirring occasionally.

3. Pour in the stock, bring to a simmer, and cook for 10 minutes.

4. Transfer to a food processor, puree until smooth, and strain through a fine sieve.

5. Return to a clean pan, add cream and parsley, bring to a simmer, and season with salt and pepper.

6. Ladle into warm bowls, garnish with the mozzarella pearls, and serve with the Gremolata and eggplant Schnitzel.

GREMOLATA

Combine all of the ingredients in a small bowl and set aside until ready to use.

EGGPLANT SCHNITZEL

1. Place the eggplant on a plate. Lightly salt on both sides and let stand for 30 minutes.

2. Place the flour and breadcrumbs on 2 separate plates.

3. Dip the eggplant in the flour so that both sides are coated.

4. Dip the floured eggplant into the beaten eggs until coated.

5. Gently remove the eggplant. Roll in the breadcrumbs until coated.

6. Repeat Steps 4 and 5.

7. In a large sauté pan, add the oil and cook over medium heat until warm. The oil should be ¼-inch deep, add more if necessary. Add the breaded eggplant and fry until golden brown. Remove and set to drain on paper towels.

INGREDIENTS:

1   TABLESPOON EXTRA VIRGIN OLIVE OIL

2   SHALLOTS, FINELY CHOPPED

1   GARLIC CLOVE, MINCED

1   EGGPLANT, PEELED AND ROUGHLY CHOPPED

4   CUPS CHICKEN STOCK

½   CUP HEAVY CREAM

2   TABLESPOONS PARSLEY, LEAVES REMOVED AND CHOPPED

    SALT AND PEPPER, TO TASTE

    MOZZARELLA PEARLS, FOR GARNISH

TO SERVE:
GREMOLATA

EGGPLANT SCHNITZEL

GREMOLATA

2   GARLIC CLOVES, MINCED

    ZEST OF 2 LEMONS

1   TABLESPOON PARSLEY, CHOPPED

EGGPLANT SCHNITZEL

4   SLICES OF EGGPLANT, ¼-INCH THICK

    SALT, TO TASTE

⅔   CUP BREADCRUMBS

⅓   CUP FLOUR

2   EGGS, BEATEN

¼   CUP OIL

SPICY TOMATO *and* EGG DROP SOUP *with* SZECHUAN PEPPERCORN *and* CHILI OIL

YIELD: 4 SERVINGS / ACTIVE TIME: 20 MINUTES / TOTAL TIME: 45 MINUTES

These wispy eggs in boiled chicken broth can take on many forms—I elected to go with a spicy version.

1. Place the oil in a medium saucepan and warm over medium heat. Add the shallots, garlic, and chilies and cook for 3 minutes, or until fragrant.

2. Add the tomatoes, sugar, fish sauce, and lime leaves. Pour in the stock and bring to a boil. Reduce heat so that the soup simmers and cook for 15 minutes. Season with salt and pepper.

3. Introduce a small amount of the soup to the scrambled eggs and whisk until combined. Add egg mixture to the saucepan.

4. Reduce heat to the lowest setting and stir constantly with a wooden spoon. Cook for 3 to 5 minutes until the soup starts to thicken.

5. Pour soup into warm bowls, and garnish with scallions and Szechuan Peppercorn and Chili Oil.

SZECHUAN PEPPERCORN AND CHILI OIL

1. In a small saucepan, add the vegetable oil, star anise, cinnamon stick, bay leaves, and Szechuan peppercorns. Stir to combine and cook over lowest heat setting for 20 minutes, being careful not to burn.

2. Place the red pepper flakes in a bowl and strain the oil over them. Let cool, season with salt, and reserve until ready to use.

INGREDIENTS:

2	TABLESPOONS VEGETABLE OIL
4	SHALLOTS, FINELY DICED
2	GARLIC CLOVES, MINCED
2	THAI CHILIES, SEEDED AND FINELY CHOPPED
8	LARGE RIPE TOMATOES, CONCASSE AND FINELY CHOPPED (SEE PAGE 89)
1	TABLESPOON SUGAR
6	TABLESPOONS FISH SAUCE
4	LIME LEAVES
6	CUPS CHICKEN STOCK
	SALT AND PEPPER, TO TASTE
2	EGGS, SCRAMBLED
	SCALLION GREENS, CHOPPED, FOR GARNISH

TO SERVE:

SZECHUAN PEPPERCORN AND CHILI OIL

SZECHUAN PEPPERCORN AND CHILI OIL

1½	CUPS VEGETABLE OIL
5	STAR ANISE
1	CINNAMON STICK
2	BAY LEAVES
3	TABLESPOONS SZECHUAN PEPPERCORNS
⅓	CUP RED PEPPER FLAKES
1	TEASPOON SALT

FOREST MUSHROOM SOUP
with TRUFFLED MADEIRA CREAM

YIELD: 4 SERVINGS / ACTIVE TIME: 20 MINUTES / TOTAL TIME: 1 HOUR

This is one of my all-time favorite soups. The secret is to cook as much moisture as possible out of the mushrooms, which concentrates the flavor.

1. In a medium saucepan, add the butter, onion, and garlic. Cook for 5 minutes, or until soft.

2. Add the Madeira and cook until it evaporates. Add the mushrooms and cook until all the moisture has been released.

3. Add mushroom stock and bring to a boil. Reduce heat so that the soup simmers and cook for 10 minutes.

4. Transfer the soup to a food processor, puree until creamy, and strain through a fine sieve.

5. Return soup to a clean pan, add cream and Worcestershire sauce, and season with salt and pepper. Bring to a simmer.

6. Ladle into warm bowls, garnish with sautéed mushrooms, a dollop of Truffled Madeira Cream, and parsley.

TRUFFLED MADEIRA CREAM

1. In a small saucepan, add the Madeira and simmer until it is reduced to a syrup. Remove from heat and let cool.

2. Place the cream in a bowl and whip until soft peaks begin to form.

3. Add the Madeira reduction and whip until medium peaks form.

4. Add the parsley and truffle paste and stir to combine. Season with salt and pepper and refrigerate until ready to use.

INGREDIENTS:

4	TABLESPOONS BUTTER
1	ONION, CHOPPED
2	GARLIC CLOVES, CHOPPED
⅓	CUP MADEIRA
8	OZ. WILD MUSHROOMS (WORKS WITH ALL VARIETIES)
5	OZ. PORTOBELLO MUSHROOMS
4	CUPS MUSHROOM STOCK
1	CUP HEAVY CREAM
1	TABLESPOON WORCESTERSHIRE SAUCE
	SALT AND PEPPER, TO TASTE
	SAUTÉED MUSHROOMS, FOR GARNISH
	PARSLEY, CHOPPED, FOR GARNISH

TO GARNISH:
TRUFFLED MADEIRA CREAM

TRUFFLED MADEIRA CREAM

1	CUP MADEIRA
½	CUP HEAVY CREAM
1	TEASPOON PARSLEY, CHOPPED
1	TABLESPOON TRUFFLE PASTE
	SALT AND PEPPER, TO TASTE

FRENCH ONION SOUP

YIELD: 4 SERVINGS / ACTIVE TIME: 30 MINUTES / TOTAL TIME: 1 HOUR AND 15 MINUTES

S hould you only make one recipe from this book, let it be this one. I've yet to meet someone who dislikes this soup.

1. Place the halved onion over an open flame and char. Set aside.

2. Place the oil in a medium saucepan. Add the remaining onions and cook on the lowest heat setting for 30 minutes or until golden brown. Stir the onions every few minutes and add small amounts of water when the onions begin to stick.

3. Deglaze the pan with the sherry and Worcestershire sauce. Cook until liquid has been reduced by half.

4. Add the thyme, stock, and half-charred onion and reduce by half.

5. Meanwhile, preheat your oven's broiler.

6. Remove the half-charred onion, season the soup with salt and pepper, and pour into ceramic bowls.

7. Cover with a slice of bread and the cheese, and cook on the highest shelf to melt the cheese.

INGREDIENTS:

- 5 ONIONS, 1 HALVED, THE REMAINING 4 SLICED VERY THIN
- 2 TABLESPOONS VEGETABLE OIL
- ½ CUP SHERRY
- 1 TABLESPOON WORCESTERSHIRE SAUCE
- 2 TEASPOONS THYME, CHOPPED
- 8 CUPS CHICKEN STOCK
  SALT AND PEPPER, TO TASTE
- 4 SLICES OF SOURDOUGH BREAD
- 1½ CUPS GRUYERE CHEESE, GRATED

GREEN ASPARAGUS SOUP
with CURED LEMON SLICES

YIELD: 4 SERVINGS / ACTIVE TIME: 30 MINUTES / TOTAL TIME: 1 HOUR

A delicious and simple soup prepared with one of the best ingredients Mother Nature blessed us with.

1. In a medium saucepan, add the butter and cook over medium heat until melted. Add the onion, leeks, and celery and cook for 5 minutes, or until soft.

2. Add the potato and bay leaf and cook for 5 minutes. Add the stock, bring to a boil, reduce heat so that the soup simmers, and cook for 15 minutes, or until the potatoes are soft.

3. In a large sauté pan, add the oil and warm over medium-high heat. Add the asparagus and cook for 4 minutes, until nicely green and firm. Reserve 12 of the asparagus tips for garnish.

4. Add the asparagus to the soup and simmer for 5 minutes, or until soft.

5. Transfer the soup to a food processor, puree until smooth, and pass through a fine sieve.

6. Return soup to pan, add cream, and season with salt and pepper. Ladle into warm bowls and garnish with the asparagus tips and Cured Lemon Slices.

INGREDIENTS:

- 2 TABLESPOONS BUTTER
- 1 ONION, CHOPPED
- 2 CUPS LEEKS, WHITE PART ONLY, CHOPPED
- 2 CELERY STALKS, CHOPPED
- 1 LARGE POTATO, PEELED AND CHOPPED
- 1 BAY LEAF
- 4 CUPS CHICKEN STOCK
- 2 TABLESPOONS EXTRA VIRGIN OLIVE OIL
- 3 CUPS GREEN ASPARAGUS, QUARTERED, WHITE BOTTOMS DISCARDED
- ¾ CUP CREAM
- SALT AND PEPPER, TO TASTE

TO SERVE:
CURED LEMON SLICES

CURED LEMON SLICES
- 1 LEMON, THINLY SLICED, SEEDS REMOVED
- 1 TABLESPOON SALT
- 3 TABLESPOONS SUGAR

CURED LEMON SLICES

These are also great garnishes for any fish or chicken dishes that you prepare.

1. Spread your lemon slices on a baking tray.

2. Combine the salt and sugar in a bowl. Sprinkle half on the lemon slices.

3. Let lemon stand for 15 minutes.

4. Flip the lemon slices over, sprinkle remaining mixture on them, and let stand for 15 minutes.

5. Bring a pot of water to boil. Add the lemon slices and boil for 30 seconds. Submerge in ice water, dry, and set aside until ready to serve.

HEART OF PALM SOUP
with PALM FONDANT

YIELD: 4 SERVINGS / ACTIVE TIME: 20 MINUTES / TOTAL TIME: 45 MINUTES

Heart of palm, also called palm heart, chonta, palmito, palm cabbage, swamp cabbage, or burglar's thigh, is a vegetable harvested from the inner core and growing bud of certain palm trees. It can be purchased fresh or canned. For my preparation, I used canned, since fresh was not available.

1. Place the butter and oil in a medium saucepan and cook over medium heat until warm. Add the onion and leek and cook for 5 minutes, or until soft.

2. Sprinkle the flour evenly over the vegetables and cook, while stirring, for 2 minutes.

3. Add the stock and the potatoes. Bring to a boil, lower the heat so that the soup simmers, and cook for 10 minutes. Stir in the hearts of palm and simmer for another 10 minutes.

4. Once the potatoes and hearts of palm have been cooked through, transfer soup to a food processor, puree until smooth, and strain through a fine sieve.

5. Place soup in a large saucepan. Reheat gently, add the cream, and season with salt and pepper.

6. Ladle the soup into bowls. Serve with the Hearts of Palm Fondant and garnish with chives and a sprinkle of cayenne pepper.

PALM FONDANT

1. Melt butter in a medium saucepan.

2. Add hearts of palm and cook over medium heat, while turning every few minutes, until the butter is brown and nutty and the hearts of palm are golden brown on all sides. Remove and serve immediately.

INGREDIENTS:

- 2 TABLESPOONS BUTTER
- 2 TEASPOONS EXTRA VIRGIN OLIVE OIL
- 1 ONION, FINELY CHOPPED
- 1 LARGE LEEK, CHOPPED
- 1 TABLESPOON ALL-PURPOSE FLOUR
- 6 CUPS CHICKEN STOCK
- 12 OZ. POTATOES, PEELED AND CUBED
- 2 14 OZ. CANS HEART OF PALM, DRAINED AND CHOPPED
- 1 CUP HEAVY CREAM
- SALT AND PEPPER, TO TASTE
- CHIVES, CHOPPED, FOR GARNISH
- CAYENNE PEPPER, FOR GARNISH

TO SERVE:
PALM FONDANT

PALM FONDANT
- ½ CUP BUTTER
- 4 HEARTS OF PALM, 3 INCHES LONG

IRISH LEEK *and* CASHEL BLUE CHEESE SOUP
with BLUE CHEESE FRITTERS

YIELD: 6 SERVINGS / ACTIVE TIME: 30 MINUTES / TOTAL TIME: 1 HOUR

If you like blue cheese and haven't tried Cashel blue, remedy that immediately. If you have, you know that it is perfect for this traditional Irish soup.

1. In a medium saucepan, add the butter and oil and warm over low heat. Add the leeks and gently cook for 5 minutes, or until softened.

2. Break the Cashel blue into small pieces and add to the saucepan. Cook, while stirring, until the cheese is melted.

3. Add the flour and cook for 2 minutes, while stirring constantly, then season to taste with the mustard.

4. Slowly add the stock, stirring to prevent any lumps from forming. Bring to a boil, reduce heat so that the soup simmers, and cook for 10 minutes.

5. Season with pepper and ladle into warm bowls. Garnish with chives and mustard, and serve with the Blue Cheese Fritters.

BLUE CHEESE FRITTERS

1. Place the oil in a medium saucepan and heat to 350°F.

2. Place the eggs in a bowl and beat with a fork. Place the flour and bread crumbs in separate bowls.

3. Dredge the cheese in the flour, remove, and shake to remove any excess flour. Place the floured blue cheese in the egg wash and coat evenly. Remove from egg wash, shake to remove any excess egg, and gently coat with bread crumbs.

4. Repeat with the egg wash and bread crumbs.

5. Place the cheese in the hot oil and fry until golden brown. Use a slotted spoon to remove the fritters from the oil, set on paper towels to drain, and season with salt.

INGREDIENTS:

- ¼ CUP BUTTER
- 2 TABLESPOONS VEGETABLE OIL
- 3 LARGE LEEKS, THINLY SLICED
- 8 OZ. CASHEL BLUE
- 2 TABLESPOONS ALL-PURPOSE FLOUR
- 1 TABLESPOON WHOLE GRAIN MUSTARD, PLUS MORE FOR GARNISH
- 6 CUPS CHICKEN STOCK

  BLACK PEPPER, TO TASTE

  CHIVES, CHOPPED, FOR GARNISH

TO GARNISH:
BLUE CHEESE FRITTERS

BLUE CHEESE FRITTERS
- 2 CUPS OIL
- 3 EGGS
- ¼ CUP ALL-PURPOSE FLOUR
- 1 CUP PANKO BREAD CRUMBS, REDUCED TO A FINE POWDER IN A FOOD PROCESSOR
- 6 OZ. CASHEL BLUE, ROLLED INTO 12 BALLS OR CUT INTO 12 CUBES

  SALT, TO TASTE

MEXICAN SWEET ROASTED GARLIC SOUP

YIELD: 4 SERVINGS / ACTIVE TIME: 20 MINUTES / TOTAL TIME: 1 HOUR

This soup, when poured tableside, will really blow your guests away.

1. In a medium saucepan, add the chicken stock and confit garlic and simmer for 20 minutes.

2. Transfer to a food processor, puree until smooth, and pass through a fine sieve.

3. Return to a clean pan, bring to a simmer, and season with salt and pepper.

4. Remove from heat and whisk in the eggs.

5. Garnish serving bowls with the avocado, Queso Fresco or feta, tomato, chipotles, Garlic Roasted Scallions, Garlic Croutons, and cilantro leaves. Carry the bowls into the dining room and pour the soup tableside.

CONFIT GARLIC

1. Place the olive oil in a small saucepan and warm. Reduce heat to lowest setting, add the garlic, and cook for 15 minutes, while stirring frequently, until soft and golden.

2. Strain and set garlic aside. Reserve oil.

GARLIC CROUTONS

1. In a small sauté pan, add the oil and warm over medium heat.

2. Add the bread cubes, and cook until golden brown on all sides.

3. Season with salt and pepper, and set on a paper towel to drain.

GARLIC ROASTED SCALLIONS

1. Preheat oven to 350°F.

2. Place the scallions on a baking tray, drizzle with the oil, and season with salt and pepper.

3. Place tray in oven and bake for 8 minutes, or until soft and lightly colored. Remove, let cool, and serve.

INGREDIENTS:

5	CUPS CHICKEN STOCK
1	BULB CONFIT GARLIC (SEE RECIPE)
	SALT AND PEPPER, TO TASTE
2	EGGS, LIGHTLY BEATEN
1	RIPE AVOCADO, PEELED, PITTED, AND QUARTERED, FOR GARNISH
3	OZ. QUESO FRESCO OR FETA, FOR GARNISH
1	LARGE TOMATO, CONCASSE AND CHOPPED, FOR GARNISH (SEE PAGE 89)
4	CHIPOTLES EN ADOBO, SEEDED, AND THINLY SLICED, FOR GARNISH
	CILANTRO, FOR GARNISH

TO SERVE:
GARLIC CROUTONS

GARLIC ROASTED SCALLIONS

CONFIT GARLIC

1	BULB OF GARLIC, CLOVES REMOVED, PEELED AND MINCED
½	CUP EXTRA VIRGIN OLIVE OIL

GARLIC CROUTONS

3	TABLESPOONS OIL RESERVED FROM CONFIT GARLIC
4	SLICES OF BREAD, CRUST REMOVED, CUT INTO CUBES
	SALT AND PEPPER, TO TASTE

GARLIC ROASTED SCALLIONS

4	SCALLIONS
3	TEASPOONS OIL RESERVED FROM CONFIT GARLIC
	SALT AND PEPPER, TO TASTE

MISO BROTH *with* FRIED TOFU

YIELD: 4 SERVINGS / ACTIVE TIME: 30 MINUTES / TOTAL TIME: 1 HOUR

I used Azuki Bean Miso from South River Miso, in Conway, Massachusetts for this recipe. If you have yet to try their miso, you certainly should. They are a family-run company and their products are outstanding.

1. In a stockpot, add the scallion greens, cilantro stalks, ginger, star anise, cinnamon stick, cardamom seeds, bay leaf, red pepper flakes, and dashi stock. Cook over medium heat until boiling, reduce the heat, and simmer for 10 minutes.

2. Strain the broth through a fine sieve. Return to the stockpot and bring to a simmer.

3. Add the bok choy and cook for 5 minutes. Add the scallion whites and cook for an additional 2 minutes.

4. Place the miso in a small bowl, add a bit of the hot stock, and then place in the soup.

5. Add soy sauce. Ladle into warm bowls, garnish with the cilantro and Thai chili, and serve with Fried Tofu and Crispy Wonton Skins.

FRIED TOFU

For all the people who think they don't like tofu, this recipe is a good introduction—crispy and hot.

1. Place oil in a medium saucepan and heat to 350°F.

2. Place the eggs, flour, and panko bread crumbs in 3 separate bowls.

3. Dredge the tofu in the flour, remove, and shake to remove any excess flour. Place the coated tofu in the egg wash. Remove from egg wash, shake to release any excess egg, and gently coat with bread crumbs.

4. If there is any tofu exposed, return to the egg mix and repeat with bread crumbs.

5. Once all the tofu is coated, place in oil and fry in batches until golden brown. Remove with a slotted spoon, place on a paper towel, and season with salt.

Continued . . .

INGREDIENTS:

- 4   SCALLIONS, WHITES SLICED THIN, GREENS RESERVED FOR BROTH
- 4   CILANTRO SPRIGS, LEAVES RESERVED FOR GARNISH, STALKS RESERVED FOR BROTH
-     1-INCH PIECE OF GINGER, SLICED
- 1   STAR ANISE
- 1   CINNAMON STICK
- 4   CARDAMOM PODS, SEEDS REMOVED FROM SHELL AND CRUSHED
- 1   BAY LEAF
- ½   TEASPOON RED PEPPER FLAKES
- 4   CUPS OF DASHI STOCK
- 3   BOK CHOY, CUT LENGTHWISE INTO EIGHTHS
- ¼   CUP RED MISO
- 2   TABLESPOONS SOY SAUCE
-     THAI CHILI, SEEDS REMOVED, THINLY SLICED, FOR GARNISH

TO SERVE:

FRIED TOFU

CRISPY WONTON SKINS

6. Reduce the heat of the oil to 300°F and reserve for the Crispy Wonton Skins.

CRISPY WONTON SKINS

1. Place the wonton wrappers in the reserved oil and turn frequently until they are crisp and golden brown.

2. Use a slotted spoon to remove the fried wonton wrappers from oil and set on paper towels to drain.

3. Season with salt, and serve.

INGREDIENTS (CONTINUED):

FRIED TOFU

2	CUPS VEGETABLE OIL
2	EGGS, WHISKED TOGETHER
¼	CUP FLOUR
1½	CUPS PANKO BREAD CRUMBS, GROUND TO A FINE POWDER IN FOOD PROCESSOR
5	OZ. TOFU, CUT INTO ¾-INCH CUBES, DRIED ON A PAPER TOWEL
	SALT, TO TASTE

CRISPY WONTON SKINS

4	WONTON WRAPPERS, CUT INTO TRIANGLES
	SALT, TO TASTE

PARSNIP SOUP
with BUTTERNUT SQUASH CROUTON

YIELD: 6 SERVINGS / **ACTIVE TIME:** 30 MINUTES / **TOTAL TIME:** 2 HOURS AND 20

A great combination for my favorite time of year: autumn.

1. In a large saucepan, add the butter and melt over medium heat. Add the parsnips, carrot, onion, and celery and cook for 5 minutes or until soft, while stirring often.

2. Add the stock and bay leaf, bring to a boil, reduce heat so that the soup simmers, and cook for 20 minutes, or until vegetables are tender. Remove the bay leaf.

3. Transfer the soup to a food processor, puree until smooth, and strain through a fine sieve.

4. Return soup to the pan and add the cream, salt, pepper, and nutmeg. Return to a simmer.

5. Ladle into bowls and serve with Butternut Squash Croutons

BUTTERNUT SQUASH BREAD
YIELD: 1 LOAF

The butternut squash bread makes a full loaf, which is way more than you need for the croutons. Good news—breakfast is sorted for the morning!

1. Preheat oven to 350°F.

2. In a medium bowl, add the flour, baking powder, baking soda, salt, and cinnamon and stir to combine. Set aside.

3. Place the butter in the bowl of a mixer and beat, using the paddle attachment, until creamy. Add sugar and brown sugar and mix until fluffy.

4. Add the eggs one at a time and beat until smooth.

5. Add butternut squash and mix until smooth.

6. Add the dry ingredients and slowly mix until just combined. Be careful not to overmix.

7. Pour batter into a 9" x 5" loaf pan that has been greased and lined with paper.

Continued . . .

INGREDIENTS:

2	TABLESPOONS BUTTER
6	CUPS PARSNIPS, PEELED AND CHOPPED
1	CARROT, PEELED AND CHOPPED
½	ONION, CHOPPED
1	CELERY STALK, CHOPPED
8	CUPS VEGETABLE STOCK
1	BAY LEAF
2	CUPS HEAVY CREAM
	SALT AND PEPPER, TO TASTE
	FRESHLY GROUND NUTMEG, TO TASTE

TO SERVE:
BUTTERNUT SQUASH BREAD

BREAD

1½	CUPS ALL-PURPOSE FLOUR
1	TEASPOON BAKING POWDER
¼	TEASPOON BAKING SODA
¼	TEASPOON SALT
¼	TEASPOON CINNAMON
½	CUP BUTTER, ROOM TEMPERATURE
½	CUP GRANULATED SUGAR
½	CUP LIGHT BROWN SUGAR, FIRMLY PACKED
2	LARGE EGGS
1	CUP BUTTERNUT SQUASH, COOKED, MASHED, AND COOLED

...ke for about 50 minutes, or until a toothpick inserted into bread comes out clean.

9. Remove from the oven, leave the loaf in the pan, and let cool on a wire rack.

10. Remove bread from loaf pan and continue to cool.

CROUTONS

1. Preheat oven to 350°F.

2. Place the cubes on a baking tray, sprinkle with rosemary, and drizzle with olive oil.

3. Place in oven and bake for 5 minutes. Remove, gently stir, and cook for an additional 5 minutes, or until golden brown. Remove, let cool, and serve.

INGREDIENTS (CONTINUED):

CROUTONS

1   CUP BUTTERNUT SQUASH BREAD, CUT INTO ½-INCH CUBES

1   TABLESPOON FRESH ROSEMARY, CHOPPED

1   TABLESPOON EXTRA VIRGIN OLIVE OIL

PARSNIP *and* PEAR SOUP

YIELD: 4–6 SERVINGS / ACTIVE TIME: 30 MINUTES / TOTAL TIME: 1 HOUR AND 15 MINUTES

This is a very interesting combination of sweet and savory.

1. In a medium saucepan, add the butter and cook over medium heat until melted. Add the parsnip, onion, pear, garlic, and thyme and cook for 10 minutes, or until soft, stirring often.

2. Add the white wine and cook until it has evaporated.

3. Add the chicken stock. Simmer for 30 minutes, or until the parsnip is tender.

4. Transfer the soup to a food processor, puree until smooth, and strain through a fine sieve.

5. Adjust the seasoning. Ladle into warm bowls, serve with the Poached Pears, and garnish with blue cheese.

POACHED PEARS

YIELD: 1½ CUPS

1. In a small saucepan, add the wine, sugar, lemon juice, cinnamon stick, and star anise. Bring to a boil, remove from heat, and let stand.

2. Add the chopped pear and return to a boil.

3. Remove from heat and let the pear cool in the mixture. It is best to let sit in the refrigerator overnight. Remove pear with a slotted spoon and serve.

INGREDIENTS:

2	TABLESPOONS, BUTTER
4	CUPS PARSNIP, PEELED AND DICED
1	ONION, CHOPPED
1	CUP PEAR, PEELED AND DICED
1	GARLIC CLOVE, MINCED
1	THYME SPRIG, CHOPPED
½	CUP WHITE WINE
8	CUPS CHICKEN STOCK
	BLUE CHEESE CRUMBLES, FOR GARNISH

TO SERVE:
POACHED PEARS

POACHED PEARS

1	CUP RED WINE
¼	CUP SUGAR
1	TEASPOON LEMON JUICE
1	CINNAMON STICK
1	STAR ANISE
1	PEAR, PEELED AND FINELY CHOPPED

ROASTED PUMPKIN MOLE SOUP

YIELD: 4 SERVINGS / ACTIVE TIME: 20 MINUTES / TOTAL TIME: 1 HOUR AND 30 MINUTES

Mole is a traditional Mexican sauce, with the flavor of chocolate and chili. Mole paste is a mixture of rehydrated chilies, nuts, bread, garlic, and raisins. I have opted to remove the chocolate, but if you prefer, add a small amount of dark chocolate at the very end of your preparation.

1. Preheat oven to 450°F.

2. Sprinkle 1 tablespoon of the olive oil on a baking tray. Place the two pumpkin halves on the tray, flesh side down, and bake for 30 minutes, or until the flesh is tender.

3. Remove from the oven and let stand for 30 minutes.

4. Meanwhile, reduce the oven temperature to 325°F.

5. Place the pumpkin seeds, brown sugar, cumin, salt, and remaining olive oil in a bowl. Toss until the seeds are coated, place on a baking tray, and bake for 8 minutes. Remove from oven and set aside.

6. Scoop the flesh out of the cooked pumpkin and place in a food processor with the ancho chili. Puree until smooth.

7. In a small saucepan, add the mole paste and water. Cook over low heat and whisk until it forms a thick paste. Remove from heat and set aside.

8. In a large saucepan, add the pumpkin puree, the mole sauce, and the buttermilk. Bring to a simmer, while stirring constantly. Season with salt and pepper and ladle into warm bowls. Garnish with chives, toasted pumpkin seeds, and Lime Sour Cream.

LIME SOUR CREAM

Place all of the ingredients in a bowl and stir until combined. Refrigerate until ready to use.

INGREDIENTS:

- 1½ TABLESPOONS EXTRA VIRGIN OLIVE OIL
- 1 3-POUND PUMPKIN, HALVED, SEEDS REMOVED
- ½ CUP PUMPKIN SEEDS
- 1 TEASPOON BROWN SUGAR
- ½ TEASPOON CUMIN
- ¼ TEASPOON SALT
- 1 ANCHO CHILI, SOAKED IN WARM WATER FOR 20 MINUTES, DRAINED, EXCESS WATER SQUEEZED OUT
- 1 TABLESPOON MOLE PASTE
- ¼ CUP WATER
- 2 CUPS BUTTERMILK
- SALT AND PEPPER, TO TASTE
- CHIVES, CHOPPED, FOR GARNISH

TO SERVE:
LIME SOUR CREAM

LIME SOUR CREAM
- 1 CUP SOUR CREAM
- ZEST AND JUICE OF 1 LIME
- SALT AND PEPPER, TO TASTE

ROASTED RED BELL PEPPER SOUP
with ROSEMARY CRACKERS

YIELD: 4 SERVINGS / ACTIVE TIME: 30 MINUTES / TOTAL TIME: 1 HOU

You can make a red bell pepper soup even more interesting by roasting the peppers, which concentrates the flavor.

1. Over an open flame, cook the peppers until charred on all sides.

2. Place in a bowl and cover for 10 minutes. Remove the skin, remove the seeds, chop, and set aside.

3. Melt the butter in a medium saucepan. Add the onion and rosemary and cook for 5 minutes, or until the onion is soft.

4. Add the roasted peppers, stock, tomato paste, paprika, and cayenne. Bring to a boil, reduce heat so that the soup simmers, and cook for 15 minutes.

5. Transfer the soup to a food processor, puree until creamy, and strain through a fine sieve.

6. Return to a clean pan and bring to a simmer.

7. Add the sour cream and season with salt and pepper. Ladle into warm bowls and serve with the sour cream and Rosemary Crackers.

ROSEMARY CRACKERS

1. Preheat oven to 350°F.

2. Place the yeast and the warm water in a bowl and let stand for 10 minutes.

3. Add the remaining ingredients to the bowl and knead until a smooth dough forms

4. Cover and let stand in a warm spot for 15 to 20 minutes, or until it doubles in size.

5. On a lightly floured surface, roll out the dough as thin as you can without tearing it.

6. Cut crackers to desired shape, place on a lined baking tray, and brush the crackers with a small amount of olive oil.

7. Place in oven and cook for 20 minutes, or until golden brown. Remove and let cool on a wire rack before serving.

INGREDIENTS:

4   RED BELL PEPPERS

4   TABLESPOONS BUTTER

1   ONION, CHOPPED

1   ROSEMARY SPRIG, LEAVES PICKED AND CHOPPED

5   CUPS CHICKEN STOCK

2   TABLESPOONS TOMATO PASTE

1   TEASPOON PAPRIKA

⅛   TEASPOON CAYENNE PEPPER

½   CUP SOUR CREAM, PLUS MORE FOR GARNISH

SALT AND PEPPER, TO TASTE

TO SERVE:
ROSEMARY CRACKERS

ROSEMARY CRACKERS

⅛   TEASPOON DRIED YEAST

1   TABLESPOON WARM WATER

¾   CUPS ALL-PURPOSE FLOUR

½   TEASPOON SALT

PINCH OF SUGAR

1   TABLESPOON ROSEMARY, LEAVES REMOVED AND CHOPPED

1   TABLESPOON EXTRA VIRGIN OLIVE OIL

3   TABLESPOONS COLD WATER

RUSSIAN BORSCHT *and* SOUR CREAM

YIELD: 4 TO 6 SERVINGS / ACTIVE TIME: 30 MINUTES / TOTAL TIME: 1 HOUR AND 15 MINUTES

This sour soup is popular in several Eastern European cuisines. Kvass is a fermented beverage commonly made from rye bread. If not available, I have provided a quick cheat to make it yourself.

1. In a large saucepan, add butter and melt over medium heat. Add the onion and cook for 5 minutes, or until soft.

2. Add the beets, carrot, and celery and cook for 5 minutes. Add the tomatoes and cook for an additional 2 minutes.

3. Add the sachet d'epices and stock, and bring to a boil. Reduce heat so that the soup simmers and cook for 1 hour, or until tender.

4. Stir in the kvass and season with salt and pepper. Ladle into bowls and garnish with sour cream and parsley.

SIMPLE AND QUICK KVASS

1. Combine all ingredients in a small pot and bring to a boil.

2. Cover, remove from heat, and let stand for 30 minutes.

3. Strain and reserve liquid until ready to serve.

INGREDIENTS:

- 1½ TABLESPOONS BUTTER
- 1 ONION, SLICED
- 4 CUPS BEETS, PEELED AND CHOPPED
- 1 CARROT, PEELED AND CHOPPED
- 1 CELERY STALK, CHOPPED
- 2 TOMATOES, CONCASSE AND CHOPPED (SEE PAGE 89)
- SACHET D'EPICES, WITH 2 GARLIC CLOVES ADDED (SEE PAGE 90)
- 6 CUPS BEEF OR VEAL STOCK
- ½ CUP BEET KVASS
- SALT AND PEPPER, TO TASTE
- SOUR CREAM, FOR GARNISH
- PARSLEY, FOR GARNISH

SIMPLE AND QUICK KVASS

- 1 BEET, PEELED AND CHOPPED
- ⅔ CUP BEEF OR VEAL STOCK
- 2 TEASPOON LEMON JUICE

SAFFRON *and* SUNCHOKE SOUP

YIELD: 4 SERVINGS / ACTIVE TIME: 30 MINUTES / TOTAL TIME: 1 HOUR AND 30 MINUTES

This creamy soup is balanced by a pinch of saffron and a shot of lemon, which will help brighten even the dreariest day. After preparing the sunchokes, store them in a bowl with enough water to cover and a squeeze of lemon juice.

1. In a medium saucepan, add the oil and cook over medium heat until warm. Add the onion and cook for 5 minutes, or until soft.

2. Add the garlic and sunchokes and cook for 5 minutes. Add the chicken stock and bring to a boil. Reduce heat so that the soup simmers and cook for 15 minutes.

3. Add the saffron and lemon juice. Cook for 15 minutes, or until the sunchokes are soft.

4. Transfer the soup to a food processor, puree, and then pass through a fine sieve.

5. Return the soup to the pan and bring to a simmer.

6. Serve in warm bowls sprinkled with chopped parsley, toasted whole almonds, and saffron threads and serve with Sunchoke Aioli and Crispy Skins.

SUNCHOKE AIOLI AND CRISPY SKINS

1. Preheat oven to 200°F.

2. In a small saucepan, add the sunchokes and cover with water.

3. Boil for 20 to 25 minutes, or until interior flesh is very tender.

4. Remove from boiling water and submerge in ice water. Remove, cut sunchokes in half, and remove meat with a spoon. Set aside.

5. Place the skins in the oven and cook for 20 minutes, or until crispy. Remove and let cool.

6. Meanwhile, mash the sunchoke meat with a fork. Add the egg yolks, garlic, mustard, and lemon juice, and whisk vigorously until the mixture is nice and smooth.

7. Slowly drizzle in the oil, while whisking constantly. Season with salt and pepper, and serve with Crispy Skins.

INGREDIENTS:

2	TABLESPOONS EXTRA VIRGIN OLIVE OIL
1	ONION, DICED
1	GARLIC CLOVE, MINCED
2	CUPS SUNCHOKES, PEELED AND CHOPPED
4	CUPS CHICKEN STOCK
	PINCH OF SAFFRON, PLUS MORE FOR GARNISH
	JUICE OF ½ LEMON
	PARSLEY, CHOPPED, FOR GARNISH
	TOASTED ALMONDS, FOR GARNISH

TO SERVE:
SUNCHOKE AIOLI AND CRISPY SKINS

SUNCHOKE AIOLI AND CRISPY SKINS

2	SUNCHOKES
2	EGG YOLKS
½	GARLIC CLOVE, MINCED
½	TEASPOON DIJON MUSTARD
1	TEASPOON LEMON JUICE
½	CUP EXTRA VIRGIN OLIVE OIL
	SALT AND PEPPER, TO TASTE

SHIITAKE MUSHROOM LAKSA

RVINGS / **ACTIVE TIME:** 30 MINUTES / **TOTAL TIME:** 1 HOUR AND 30 MINUTES

...soup typically features seafood, but this recipe highlights the flavor of shii-takes instead.

1. In a medium saucepan, add the vegetable stock and bring to a boil.

2. Pour the boiling stock over the dried shiitakes and let soak for 20 minutes. Strain and reserve the liquid.

3. Place the dried Pasilla peppers in a small bowl, cover with hot water, and soak for 5 minutes. Strain and reserve the liquid.

4. In a food processor, add the lemongrass, turmeric, galangal, onion, soaked Pasilla peppers, and shrimp paste. Add a bit of the Pasilla soaking water and blend to form a paste.

5. In a saucepan, add the oil and cook over low heat until warm. Add the paste and cook for 5 minutes, or until fragrant.

6. Add the tamarind paste, mushroom liquid, and jaggery. Simmer for 25 minutes.

7. Strain the soup and return the broth to a pan. Add the soaked shiitakes, return to a simmer, and season with salt and pepper.

8. Place the rice noodles into a bowl and cover with boiling water. Let soak for 4 minutes, or according to the manufacturer's instructions.

9. Place the noodles in hot bowls and ladle the soup over the top. Garnish with cucumber, mint, and Crispy Red Onion Rings.

CRISPY RED ONION RINGS

1. Place the red onion and buttermilk in a bowl and soak for 30 minutes.

2. Meanwhile, place the oil in a Dutch oven and heat to 375°F.

3. Combine the flour and cornstarch and pass through a fine sieve.

4. Dredge the marinated onions in the dry mixture until they are nicely coated.

5. Drop the onions into the hot oil one at a time and fry until golden brown.

6. Remove from oil, set to drain on a paper towel, and season with salt and pepper.

INGREDIENTS:

4	CUPS VEGETABLE STOCK
1¼	CUPS DRIED SHIITAKE MUSHROOMS
3	LARGE DRIED PASILLA PEPPERS, STEMS AND SEEDS REMOVED
1	LEMONGRASS STALK, FINELY SLICED
½	TEASPOON GROUND TURMERIC
1	TABLESPOON GALANGAL ROOT, GRATED
1	ONION, CHOPPED
½	TABLESPOON SHRIMP PASTE
1	TABLESPOON VEGETABLE OIL
1	TABLESPOON TAMARIND PASTE
1	TABLESPOON JAGGERY
	SALT AND PEPPER, TO TASTE
3	OZ. RICE NOODLES
	SMALL CUCUMBER, SEEDED, CUT INTO THIN STRIPS, FOR GARNISH
	FRESH MINT LEAVES, FOR GARNISH

TO SERVE:
CRISPY RED ONION RINGS

CRISPY RED ONION RINGS

1	SMALL RED ONION, PEELED AND FINELY SLICED INTO RINGS
1	CUP BUTTERMILK
2	CUPS VEGETABLE OIL
½	CUP FLOUR
½	CUP CORNSTARCH
	SALT AND PEPPER, TO TASTE

BABY SPINACH *and* YOGURT SOUP

YIELD: 4 SERVINGS / ACTIVE TIME: 20 MINUTES / TOTAL TIME: 1 HOUR

This very simple and quick vegetarian soup is transformed by the Turmeric Oil.

1. In a large saucepan, add the oil and cook over medium heat until warm. Add the onion and cook for 5 minutes, or until soft.

2. Add 8 cups of the spinach, cover, and cook for 5 minutes, or until all the spinach is wilted.

3. Add the scallions, rice, and vegetable stock, and simmer for 18 minutes, or until the rice is cooked.

4. Transfer the soup to a food processor, add the garlic and remaining spinach, and puree until smooth. Strain through a fine sieve, return to a clean pan, bring to a simmer, and add yogurt.

5. Season with salt and pepper, ladle into warm bowls, and serve with Shallot Wilted Spinach and Turmeric Oil.

SHALLOT WILTED SPINACH

1. In a saucepan, add the oil and warm over medium heat. Add the shallots and cook for 3 minutes, or until soft.

2. Add the spinach and cook for 5 minutes, or until wilted.

3. Season with salt and pepper and serve.

TURMERIC OIL

1. Combine the olive oil and turmeric in a bowl and whisk vigorously.

2. Season with salt and pepper, strain through a fine sieve, and reserve until ready to use.

INGREDIENTS:

- 2 TABLESPOONS VEGETABLE OIL
- 1 ONION, CHOPPED
- 12 CUPS BABY SPINACH, PACKED
- 2 SCALLIONS, CHOPPED
- 3 TABLESPOONS LONG-GRAIN RICE
- 3 CUPS VEGETABLE STOCK
- 1 GARLIC CLOVE, MINCED
- 1½ CUPS WHOLE MILK YOGURT
- SALT AND PEPPER, TO TASTE

TO SERVE:

SHALLOT WILTED SPINACH

TURMERIC OIL

SHALLOT WILTED SPINACH

- ¼ CUP EXTRA VIRGIN OLIVE OIL
- 2 SHALLOTS, MINCED
- 4 CUPS BABAY SPINACH, PACKED
- SALT AND PEPPER, TO TASTE

TURMERIC OIL

- ½ CUP EXTRA VIRGIN OLIVE OIL
- 2 TEASPOONS TURMERIC
- SALT AND PEPPER, TO TASTE

SWEET POTATO SOUP

YIELD: 4 TO 6 SERVINGS / ACTIVE TIME: 25 MINUTES / TOTAL TIME: 55 MINUTES

Do you love sweet potatoes? Then you are certain to love this soup. The curry is very subtle, but it adds a nice bit of flavor.

1. In a medium saucepan, add the butter and cook over medium heat until melted. Add the onion and cook for 5 minutes, or until soft.

2. Add the chicken stock, curry powder, sweet potato, maple syrup, thyme, and cayenne pepper. Bring to a boil, reduce heat so that the soup simmers, and cook for 25 minutes, or until the sweet potatoes are soft.

3. Remove the thyme sprigs and transfer the soup to a food processor. Puree until creamy and then pass through a fine sieve.

4. Return the soup to the pan and bring to a simmer. Add the cream, nutmeg, salt, and pepper.

5. Ladle into bowls and garnish with a dollop of Rum Cream, a sprinkle of curry powder, and cilantro.

RUM CREAM

1. In a bowl, add cream and whip until medium peaks form.

2. Add the lemon juice, lemon zest, rum, and sugar. Stir to combine and refrigerate until ready to use.

INGREDIENTS:

- 1½ TABLESPOONS BUTTER
- 1 SMALL ONION, CHOPPED
- 5 CUPS CHICKEN STOCK
- ½ TEASPOON CURRY POWDER, PLUS MORE FOR GARNISH
- 10 CUPS SWEET POTATOES, PEELED AND CHOPPED
- 2 TABLESPOONS MAPLE SYRUP
- 2 THYME SPRIGS, LEAVES REMOVED AND CHOPPED
  PINCH OF CAYENNE PEPPER
- 2 CUPS HEAVY CREAM
- 2 PINCHES OF GROUND NUTMEG
  SALT AND PEPPER, TO TASTE
  CILANTRO, FOR GARNISH

TO SERVE:
RUM CREAM

RUM CREAM
- ½ CUP HEAVY CREAM
- ¼ TEASPOON LEMON JUICE
- ⅛ TEASPOON LEMON ZEST
- 2 TABLESPOONS MYERS'S RUM
  PINCH OF SUGAR

TOMATO *and* BASIL SOUP
with GRISSINI STICKS

YIELD: 4 TO 6 SERVINGS / **ACTIVE TIME:** 45 MINUTES / **TOTAL TIME:** 1 HOUR AND 30 MINUTES

Make sure your tomatoes are nice and ripe and, preferably, from your garden.

1. In a medium saucepan, add the oil and butter and cook over medium heat until warm.

2. Add the onion and cook for 5 minutes, or until soft.

3. Stir in the tomatoes and garlic, cook for 2 minutes, and then add the stock, white wine, and tomato paste.

4. Bring to a boil, reduce to a simmer, season with salt and pepper, and cook for 20 minutes.

5. Transfer the soup to a food processor, add the basil, and puree until creamy. Strain through a fine sieve, return to a clean pan, add the heavy cream, and bring to a simmer.

6. Adjust seasoning to taste, ladle into warm bowls, garnish with a sprinkle of Romano cheese and basil, and serve with Grissini Sticks.

GRISSINI STICKS

YIELD: 24 STICKS

1. Preheat the oven to 375°F.

2. Place the bread flour, salt, yeast, and semolina flour in a bowl and mix by hand until combined. Gradually add the oil and water and mix until well combined.

3. Add the herbs and seeds and combine. Place on a floured work surface and knead for 5 minutes. Place in a bowl, cover with a moist towel, and let stand for 20 minutes.

4. Cut the dough into 4 pieces. Cut the pieces into 6 strips.

5. On a lightly floured work surface roll the strips out until they are 12 inches long. Place on a lined baking tray and let stand for 5 minutes.

6. Place in the oven and bake for 20 minutes, or until golden brown. Remove, let cool, and serve.

INGREDIENTS:

2	TABLESPOONS EXTRA VIRGIN OLIVE OIL
2	TABLESPOONS BUTTER
1	ONION, CHOPPED
2	POUNDS TOMATOES, CHOPPED
1	GARLIC CLOVE, MINCED
3	CUPS VEGETABLE STOCK
½	CUP WHITE WINE
3	TABLESPOONS TOMATO PASTE
	SALT AND PEPPER, TO TASTE
½	CUP BASIL, CHOPPED, PLUS MORE FOR GARNISH
1	CUP HEAVY CREAM
	ROMANO CHEESE, GRATED, FOR GARNISH

TO SERVE:
GRISSINI STICKS

GRISSINI STICKS

½	CUP BREAD FLOUR, PLUS 2 TABLESPOONS
1	TEASPOON SALT
1½	TEASPOONS YEAST
2½	TABLESPOONS SEMOLINA FLOUR
1½	TEASPOONS EXTRA VIRGIN OLIVE OIL
6	TABLESPOONS WARM WATER
1½	TEASPOONS POPPY SEEDS
1½	TEASPOONS DRIED PARSLEY
1½	TEASPOONS OREGANO
½	TEASPOON CARAWAY SEEDS

ROLLING GRISSINI STICKS

Place your dough on your work surface and roll it into a sphere, while gently pressing from the center out to lengthen it. Continue until it's the desired length and thickness. If it is sticking too much, add a small amount of flour to your surface. If there is not enough friction, drip a small amount of water on the work surface.

VEGETABLE SOUP
with ISRAELI COUSCOUS

YIELD: 4 TO 6 SERVINGS / ACTIVE TIME: 15 MINUTES / TOTAL TIME: 45 MINUTES

A beautiful, hearty vegan meal that will warm your heart and soul.

1. In a large saucepan, add the oil and warm over medium heat. Add the onion and carrot and cook for 5 minutes, or until softened.

2. Add the tomatoes, garlic, vegetable stock, Israeli couscous, cumin, cilantro, salt, pepper, and cayenne pepper.

3. Bring to a boil, reduce to a simmer, and cook for 8 minutes, or until the couscous is tender.

4. Ladle into warm bowls and serve.

INGREDIENTS:

2 TABLESPOONS EXTRA VIRGIN OLIVE OIL

1 ONION, CHOPPED

1 LARGE CARROT, PEELED AND DICED

1 14 OZ. CAN DICED TOMATOES

5 GARLIC CLOVES, MINCED

6 CUPS VEGETABLE STOCK

1¼ CUPS ISRAELI COUSCOUS

¼ TEASPOON CUMIN

6 CILANTRO SPRIGS, LEAVES REMOVED AND CHOPPED

SALT AND PEPPER, TO TASTE

⅛ TEASPOON CAYENNE PEPPER

TRUFFLED MUSHROOM CONSOMMÉ

YIELD: 4 SERVINGS / ACTIVE TIME: 25 MINUTES / TOTAL TIME: 1 HOUR AND 15 MINUTES

I f you would like to make this dish vegan, substitute tofu for the ground chicken meat in the consommé and olive oil for the butter in the duxelle.

1. Combine all of the ingredients in a large stockpot.

2. Slowly bring to a simmer and cook for 45 minutes, with the egg whites creating a raft which will clarify the stock.

3. Ladle the stock through cheesecloth, return to a clean pan, and bring to a boil. Season with salt and pepper, ladle into warm bowls, and garnish with parsley, truffle oil, truffle paste, and Mushroom Duxelle.

MUSHROOM DUXELLE

1. In a medium saucepan, add the butter and cook over medium heat until melted. Add the shallot and garlic and cook over medium heat for 3 minutes, or until soft.

2. Add the mushrooms and a pinch of salt, and cook for 7 minutes, until the mushrooms release their liquid.

3. Cook until all the liquid has evaporated. Season with salt and pepper, fold in chopped parsley, and serve.

INGREDIENTS:

2 CARROTS, PEELED AND CHOPPED

1 ONION, CHOPPED

2 CELERY STALKS, CHOPPED

8 OZ. GROUND CHICKEN MEAT, LEAN

6 OZ. TOMATOES, CHOPPED

6 CUPS MUSHROOM STOCK, COLD

SACHET D'EPICES, 1 CLOVE AND 1 ALLSPICE BERRY ADDED (SEE PAGE 90)

5 EGG WHITES, BEATEN

SALT AND PEPPER, TO TASTE

PARSLEY, FOR GARNISH

TRUFFLE OIL, FOR GARNISH

TRUFFLE PASTE, FOR GARNISH

TO SERVE:
MUSHROOM DUXELLE

MUSHROOM DUXELLE

1 TABLESPOON BUTTER

1 SHALLOT, FINELY CHOPPED

½ GARLIC CLOVE, MINCED

1 CUP ASSORTED MUSHROOMS, STEMS TRIMMED, FINELY CHOPPED

SALT AND PEPPER, TO TASTE

1 TEASPOON PARSLEY, CHOPPED

HEALTHY VEGETABLE MINESTRONE
with SHAVED PARMESAN

YIELD: 4 TO 6 SERVINGS / ACTIVE TIME: 45 MINUTES / TOTAL TIME: 1 HOUR AND 30 MINUTES

To keep this soup low-carb, I omitted any starch. However, pasta, beans, peas, etc. can be added at the end of preparation. I served this soup in a hollowed-out bell pepper bowl, which is a fun way to present it to your guests. This picture is particularly important to me. The big wooden spoon was part of a set that was hanging in my grandparents' kitchen. It was the only thing I wanted when they passed.

1. In a large saucepan, add the oil and warm over medium heat. Add the garlic, onions, carrot, and leek and cook for 5 minutes, or until soft.

2. Add the peppers and cook for 5 minutes. Add zucchini and cook for 3 minutes.

3. Add the tomato juice, thyme, and rosemary and bring to a boil. Reduce to a simmer and cook for 20 minutes, or until the vegetables are tender.

4. Season with salt and pepper, ladle into bowls, and garnish with Garlic Confit Vegetables and parmesan.

GARLIC CONFIT VEGETABLES

1. Place the olive oil in a small saucepan and warm.

2. Reduce heat to lowest setting, add the garlic and cook for 15 minutes, while stirring frequently, until soft and golden.

3. Strain and reserve oil.

4. Return garlic oil to a clean pan and warm.

5. Add the cherry tomatoes, zucchini, and peppers, and then remove from heat and let them cool in the oil.

6. Remove with a slotted spoon, season with salt and pepper, and serve.

INGREDIENTS:

2	TABLESPOONS EXTRA VIRGIN OLIVE OIL
1	GARLIC CLOVE, MINCED
2	ONIONS, FINELY CHOPPED
1	CARROT, PEELED AND FINELY CHOPPED
½	LEEK, WHITE PART ONLY, FINELY CHOPPED
1	YELLOW BELL PEPPER, SEEDS REMOVED AND FINELY CHOPPED
1	RED BELL PEPPER, SEEDS REMOVED AND FINELY CHOPPED
1	ZUCCHINI, SEEDS REMOVED, FINELY CHOPPED
6	CUPS TOMATO JUICE
½	TEASPOON THYME, LEAVES REMOVED AND CHOPPED
½	TEASPOON ROSEMARY, LEAVES REMOVED AND CHOPPED
	SALT AND PEPPER, TO TASTE
	PARMESAN CHEESE, SHAVED, FOR GARNISH

TO SERVE:
GARLIC CONFIT VEGETABLES

GARLIC CONFIT VEGETABLES

½	CUP EXTRA VIRGIN OLIVE OIL
1	BULB OF GARLIC, CLOVES REMOVED, PEELED, AND MINCED
8–12	CHERRY TOMATOES
8–12	ZUCCHINI, TOURNED
8–12	YELLOW BELL PEPPERS, CHOPPED
	SALT AND PEPPER, TO TASTE

WATERCRESS *and* BUTTERMILK SOUP
with POPPY SEED YOGURT

YIELD: 4 SERVINGS / ACTIVE TIME: 25 MINUTES / TOTAL TIME: 1 HOUR AND 15 MINUTES

This soup is very similar to vichyssoise. The bitterness of the watercress is balanced out by the buttermilk and the yogurt.

1. Place the oil in a medium saucepan and warm over medium heat. Add the onion and cook for 5 minutes, or until soft.

2. Add the potato and cook for 8 minutes.

3. Add the watercress stems and stock and bring to a boil. Reduce to a simmer and cook for 10 minutes, or until the potato is tender.

4. Reserve some watercress leaves for garnish, place the rest in the pan, and simmer for 2 minutes.

5. Transfer to a food processor, blend until smooth, and strain through a fine sieve.

6. Place into a clean pan and add buttermilk. Reheat gently, season with salt and pepper, ladle into warm bowls, and garnish with reserved watercress, Poppy Seed Yogurt, and Crispy Potato Strips.

INGREDIENTS:

2   TABLESPOONS VEGETABLE OIL

1   ONION, CHOPPED

1   POTATO, PEELED AND CHOPPED

5   PACKED CUPS WATERCRESS, LEAVES REMOVED, STEMS FINELY CHOPPED

2   CUPS VEGETABLE STOCK

1½   CUPS BUTTERMILK

     SALT AND PEPPER, TO TASTE

TO SERVE:
POPPY SEED YOGURT
CRISPY POTATO STRIPS

POPPY SEED YOGURT

½   CUP WHOLE MILK YOGURT

1   TABLESPOON POPPY SEEDS

     SALT AND PEPPER, TO TASTE

CRISPY POTATO STRIPS

1   YUKON GOLD POTATO, PEELED AND CUT INTO THIN STRIPS

2   CUPS VEGETABLE OIL

     SALT AND PEPPER, TO TASTE

POPPY SEED YOGURT

1. Place the yogurt and the poppy seeds in a bowl and whisk together.

2. Season with salt and pepper, and place in refrigerator until ready to use.

CRISPY POTATO STRIPS

1. In a small saucepan, add the potato and 3 cups of cold water. Cook over high heat and bring to a boil. Remove the potato strips, submerge in ice water, and set to dry on paper towels.

2. Place the oil in a Dutch oven and heat to 375°F.

3. Place the potato strips in the oil and fry until golden brown.

4. Use a slotted spoon to remove the potato strips, set on a paper towel to drain, and season with salt and pepper.

ONION *and* WHITE PORT SOUP

YIELD: 4 TO 6 SERVINGS / ACTIVE TIME: 15 MINUTES / TOTAL TIME: 45 MINUTES

A very rich and filling cream soup, with a hint of sweetness coming from the onions and white port.

1. In a medium saucepan, warm the oil over medium heat. Add the onions and cook for 5 minutes, until soft.

2. Add a pinch of salt, garlic, and thyme, reduce heat to low, and slowly cook the onions for 10 more minutes, until tender.

3. Add the white port and cook until reduced by half.

4. Add the cream and bring to a boil. Reduce to a simmer and cook for 15 minutes.

5. Transfer the soup to a food processor, puree until creamy, and strain through a fine sieve. Season with salt and pepper, and serve in warm bowls.

INGREDIENTS:

¼ CUP EXTRA VIRGIN OLIVE OIL

5 LARGE ONIONS, SLICED

1 GARLIC CLOVE, MINCED

1 THYME SPRIG, LEAVES PICKED AND CHOPPED

1 CUP WHITE PORT

4 CUPS HEAVY CREAM

SALT AND PEPPER, TO TASTE

YELLOW SPLIT PEA SOUP
with GREEK TOMATO SAUCE *and* STEWED CAPERS

YIELD: 4 SERVINGS / **ACTIVE TIME:** 30 MINUTES / **TOTAL TIME:** 1 HOUR AND 30 MINUTES

This is a delicious variation on classical Mediterranean flavors.

---

1. Place the olive oil in a large saucepan and warm over medium heat.

2. Add the onions and cook for 5 minutes, or until soft. Add the split peas and toss to coat with oil. Cook, while stirring, for 2 minutes.

3. Add 4 cups of the chicken stock, cover, and bring to a boil. Reduce to a simmer and cook for 1 hour, or until most of the chicken stock has evaporated.

4. Transfer the soup to a food processor, add the remaining chicken stock, and puree until smooth.

5. Return to the pan and bring to a simmer. Add the oregano and red wine vinegar, season with salt and pepper, and ladle into warm bowls. Garnish with oregano sprigs, Greek Tomato Sauce, and Stewed Capers.

GREEK TOMATO SAUCE

1. Place the oil in a large saucepan and warm over medium heat. Add the onion and cook for 5 minutes, or until soft.

2. Add the tomatoes, cinnamon, bay leaf, salt, and pepper. Bring to a simmer, cover, and cook, while stirring occasionally, until the sauce has thickened and the onions are tender.

STEWED CAPERS

1. Place the olive oil in a medium saucepan and warm over low heat. Add the onion and cinnamon stick and cook for 15 minutes, while stirring occasionally.

2. Add the tomato paste and stir to combine. Cook for 5 minutes, add the capers, then cook for an additional 5 minutes. Season with black pepper, remove from heat, and let cool before serving.

INGREDIENTS:

- ¼ CUP EXTRA VIRGIN OLIVE OIL
- 2 RED ONIONS, FINELY CHOPPED
- ½ CUP DRIED YELLOW SPLIT PEAS, RINSED AND DRAINED
- 6 CUPS CHICKEN STOCK
- 1 TEASPOON DRIED OREGANO
- 1 TABLESPOON RED WINE VINEGAR
- SALT AND PEPPER, TO TASTE
- OREGANO SPRIGS, FOR GARNISH

TO SERVE:
GREEK TOMATO SAUCE
STEWED CAPERS

GREEK TOMATO SAUCE

- ¼ CUP EXTRA VIRGIN OLIVE OIL
- 1 RED ONION, FINELY CHOPPED
- 2 FIRM TOMATOES, CHOPPED
- 1 CINNAMON STICK
- 1 BAY LEAF
- SALT AND PEPPER, TO TASTE

STEWED CAPERS

- ¼ CUP EXTRA VIRGIN OLIVE OIL
- 1 RED ONION, FINELY CHOPPED
- 1 CINNAMON STICK
- 1 TABLESPOON TOMATO PASTE
- ½ CUP CAPERS IN BRINE
- BLACK PEPPER, TO TASTE

WHITE TOMATO SOUP *with* BASIL OIL *and* CONFIT CHERRY TOMATOES

YIELD: 4 SERVINGS / ACTIVE TIME: 45 MINUTES / TOTAL TIME: 13 HOURS

This one tops my list of favorite soups. It does require a bit of time to get the clear tomato water. The key is letting gravity do the work—if you try to force it, it will not be clear. It is very important to choose ripe tomatoes for this dish. The riper the better. If not, this soup can be very acidic.

1. Place the tomatoes in a food processor and puree for 5 minutes.

2. Strain through cheesecloth overnight to get tomato water.

3. Place the tomato water, thyme, star anise, and rice in a medium saucepan and cook over medium heat until the liquid has been reduced by half.

4. Add the cream and cook for 30 minutes.

5. Remove the star anise, transfer the soup to a food processor, and puree until creamy. Strain through a fine sieve, return to the pan, season with salt and pepper, and bring to a simmer.

6. Ladle into bowls and serve with Basil Oil, Crispy Basil Leaves, and Confit Cherry Tomatoes.

BASIL OIL

1. In a small saucepan, bring 4 cups of water to a boil.

2. Add the basil and spinach, cook for 1 minute, remove, and submerge in ice water.

3. Squeeze out any excess water. Place the basil, spinach, and oil in a food processor and puree for 3 to 4 minutes.

4. Strain through a cheesecloth and reserve until ready to use.

CRISPY BASIL LEAVES

1. Place the oil in a Dutch oven and heat to 350°F.

2. Bring water to a boil in a small saucepan. Add the basil, cook for 1 minute, remove, and submerge in ice water.

3. Remove from water and set on paper towels to dry.

Continued . . .

INGREDIENTS:

10   LARGE RIPE TOMATOES, CHOPPED

1   THYME SPRIG, LEAVES REMOVED AND CHOPPED

1   STAR ANISE

1   TABLESPOON RICE

2   CUPS HEAVY CREAM

    SALT AND PEPPER, TO TASTE

TO SERVE:

BASIL OIL

CRISPY BASIL LEAVES

CONFIT CHERRY TOMATOES

BASIL OIL

1   CUP BASIL LEAVES

1   CUP BABY SPINACH

1   CUP VEGETABLE OIL

CRISPY BASIL LEAVES

2   CUPS VEGETABLE OIL

8   BASIL LEAVES

CONFIT CHERRY TOMATOES

12   CHERRY TOMATOES

1   GARLIC CLOVE, SLICED VERY THIN

    ZEST OF 1 LEMON

1   TABLESPOON EXTRA VIRGIN OLIVE OIL

    SALT AND PEPPER, TO TASTE

4. Place basil in hot oil and fry, while stirring constantly, until crispy.

5. Remove with a slotted spoon and set on paper towels to drain.

CONFIT CHERRY TOMATOES

1. Preheat the oven to 300°F.

2. Place the tomatoes on a baking tray and sprinkle with garlic and lemon zest.

3. Drizzle with olive oil and season with salt and pepper.

4. Place in oven and cook for 15 minutes. Remove and serve.

HAVUÇ ÇORBASI

YIELD: 6 SERVINGS / ACTIVE TIME: 20 MINUTES / TOTAL TIME: 1 HOUR

This delicious, healthy, and easy-to-make soup is finished with egg yolks, like a veloute.

1. In a medium saucepan, add the carrots and the stock and bring to a boil.

2. Add the salt, pepper, sugar, and cinnamon. Reduce to a simmer and cook for 30 minutes, or until carrots are very soft.

3. Transfer the soup to a food processor, puree until creamy, and strain through a fine sieve. Set aside.

4. Place the butter in a clean medium pan and cook over low heat until melted. Add the flour and cook for 3 minutes, while stirring.

5. Add the hot milk and cook, while stirring vigorously, until the soup thickens.

6. Add the strained soup to the pan and bring to a simmer.

7. Ladle the soup into the whisked egg yolks and whisk vigorously until combined.

8. Whisk the egg mixture into the soup and stir constantly until the soup thickens.

9. Remove from the heat, adjust seasoning, and ladle into warm bowls immediately.

10. Garnish with pistachios and serve with Crispy Carrot Ribbons.

INGREDIENTS:

5 CUPS CARROTS, PEELED AND CHOPPED

8 CUPS CHICKEN STOCK

SALT AND PEPPER, TO TASTE

2 TEASPOONS SUGAR

1 TEASPOON CINNAMON

2 TABLESPOONS BUTTER

2 TABLESPOONS FLOUR

½ CUP HOT MILK

3 EGG YOLKS, WHISKED

PISTACHIOS, TOASTED AND CHOPPED, FOR GARNISH

TO SERVE:
CRISPY CARROT RIBBONS

CRISPY CARROT RIBBONS
2 CUPS VEGETABLE OIL

2 CARROTS, PEELED

2 CUPS COLD WATER

CRISPY CARROT RIBBONS

1. Place the oil in a medium saucepan and heat to 375°F.

2. Use a peeler to cut the carrots into long ribbons.

3. In a small saucepan, add the carrots and cold water and bring to a boil over high heat.

4. Remove carrots, submerge in ice water, and place them on a paper towel to dry.

5. When dry, drop them in the hot oil and fry until crispy. Remove with a slotted spoon and set to drain on a paper towel.

6. Season with salt and pepper and serve.

INDO-CHINESE VEGETABLE
HOT *and* SOUR SOUP

YIELD: 4 SERVINGS / ACTIVE TIME: 30 MINUTES / TOTAL TIME: 45 MINUTES

The secret to this fast-cooking dish is to have all your ingredients prepped and cut in advance.

1. Place the cornstarch and the water in a bowl. Stir until cornstarch dissolves and set aside.

2. In a medium saucepan, add the oil and warm over medium heat. Add the onion, ginger, garlic, and celery and cook for 5 minutes, or until soft.

3. Add the green beans, carrot, mushrooms, cabbage, and bell pepper. Sauté for 1 minute, add the stock, and bring to a boil.

4. Reduce to a simmer and add soy sauce and vinegar.

5. Slowly add the dissolved cornstarch to the soup, whisking constantly until combined. Simmer for 5 minutes, or until thickened, stirring often.

6. Season with salt and pepper, ladle into warm bowls, and garnish with bean sprouts and scallions.

INGREDIENTS:

3	TABLESPOONS CORNSTARCH
1	CUP WATER
1	TABLESPOON SESAME OIL
½	CUP ONION, FINELY CHOPPED
2	TEASPOONS GINGER, MINCED
2	TEASPOONS GARLIC, MINCED
2	TABLESPOONS CELERY, FINELY CHOPPED
¼	CUP GREEN BEANS, FINELY SLICED
¼	CUP CARROT, PEELED AND FINELY CHOPPED
¼	CUP MUSHROOMS, FINELY CHOPPED
½	CUP GREEN CABBAGE, FINELY SLICED
¼	CUP GREEN BELL PEPPER, FINELY CHOPPED
4	CUPS VEGETABLE STOCK
3	TABLESPOONS SOY SAUCE
1	TEASPOON WHITE DISTILLED VINEGAR
	SALT AND PEPPER, TO TASTE
	BEAN SPROUTS, FOR GARNISH
2	SCALLIONS, FINELY SLICED, FOR GARNISH

RUTABAGA *and* FIG SOUP *with* HONEY-ROASTED FIGS *and* BARBEQUED CHICKPEAS

YIELD: 4 SERVINGS / ACTIVE TIME: 30 MINUTES / TOTAL TIME: 13 HOURS

This soup has a slightly sour finish, so I decided to add some honey-roasted figs to balance it out.

1. In a medium saucepan, add the oil and warm over medium heat. Add the onion and rutabaga and cook for 10 minutes, or until soft.

2. Add the honey, stock, thyme, and figs and bring to a boil.

3. Reduce to a simmer and cook for 20 minutes, or until the rutabaga is soft.

4. Transfer the soup to a food processor and puree until smooth. Return to a clean pan, add the buttermilk, and bring to a simmer.

5. Season with salt and pepper, ladle into warm bowls, and serve with Honey-Roasted Figs and Barbequed Chickpeas.

HONEY-ROASTED FIGS

1. In a medium nonstick sauté pan, add the honey and warm over medium heat.

2. Place the cut figs facedown and cook for 5 minutes, or until golden brown.

3. Sprinkle the cinnamon over the figs and gently stir to coat. Remove figs from pan and serve.

BARBEQUED CHICKPEAS

You can cheat with the chickpeas and used canned, if preferred. Make sure to make plenty of the barbeque seasoning, as it is perfect on homemade potato chips.

1. Bring 4 cups of water to a boil. Add the chickpeas, reduce to a simmer, and cook for 20 minutes, or until the chickpeas are tender. Drain the chickpeas and set on a paper towel to dry.

2. Place the oil in a Dutch oven and heat to 350°F.

3. Combine the remaining ingredients, pass through a fine sieve, and set aside. This is your barbeque seasoning.

4. Place the chickpeas in the hot oil and fry until golden brown. Remove and place into a bowl. Coat with the barbeque seasoning and serve.

INGREDIENTS:

2	TABLESPOONS VEGETABLE OIL
1	ONION, CHOPPED
4	CUPS RUTABAGA, CHOPPED
1	TABLESPOON HONEY
4	CUPS VEGETABLE STOCK
1	TEASPOON THYME, CHOPPED
16	BLACK MISSION FIGS
1	CUP BUTTERMILK
	SALT AND PEPPER, TO TASTE

TO SERVE:
HONEY-ROASTED FIGS
BARBEQUED CHICKPEAS

HONEY-ROASTED FIGS

2	TABLESPOONS HONEY
4	BLACK MISSION FIGS, HALVED
1/8	TEASPOON CINNAMON

BARBEQUED CHICKPEAS

1/4	CUP DRIED CHICKPEAS, SOAKED OVERNIGHT
2	CUPS VEGETABLE OIL
1	TEASPOON SMOKED PAPRIKA
1/2	TEASPOON ONION POWDER
1/2	TEASPOON BROWN SUGAR
1/4	TEASPOON GARLIC POWDER
1/4	TEASPOON SALT
1/8	TEASPOON CHILI POWDER

VEGAN TOM YAM GUNG
with TOFU

YIELD: 4 SERVINGS / ACTIVE TIME: 20 MINUTES / TOTAL TIME: 45 MINUTES

This hot-and-sour soup is traditionally served with shrimp. But since it's a very fragrant and healthy soup, I thought putting a vegan twist on it would be a great modification.

1. In a medium saucepan, add 2 tablespoons of the oil and cook over medium heat until warm.

2. Add the onion and garlic and cook for 5 minutes, or until soft.

3. Add the stock, lime juice, lime leaves, chilies, cilantro stalks, lemongrass, and sugar and bring to a boil.

4. Reduce the heat so that the soup simmers and cook for 20 minutes.

5. Meanwhile, in a large sauté pan, add the remaining oil and cook over medium heat until warm. Add the tofu and cook for 4 minutes, or until it is lightly browned on all sides. Remove tofu from pan and set aside.

6. Strain the broth through a fine sieve and then return to a clean pan. Add the fish sauce and shiitake mushrooms, and bring to a simmer. Add the tofu and cook for 4 additional minutes.

7. Season with salt and pepper, serve in warm bowls, and garnish with watercress, bean sprouts, and cilantro.

INGREDIENTS:

4 TABLESPOONS VEGETABLE OIL

1 ONION, FINELY CHOPPED

1 GARLIC CLOVE, MINCED

6 CUPS VEGETABLE STOCK

JUICE OF 2 LIMES

3 KAFFIR LIME LEAVES

3 THAI CHILIES, SEEDS REMOVED, SLICED

6 CILANTRO STALKS, LEAVES REMOVED, CHOPPED, AND RESERVED FOR GARNISH

1 LEMONGRASS STALK, BRUISED WITH THE BACK OF A KNIFE

1 TABLESPOON SUGAR

12 OZ. TOFU, CUT INTO ½-INCH CUBES

4 TABLESPOONS FISH SAUCE

8 SHIITAKE MUSHROOMS, SLICED

SALT AND PEPPER, TO TASTE

WATERCRESS, FOR GARNISH

BEAN SPROUTS, FOR GARNISH

VEGETARIAN GREEN GUMBO

YIELD: 4 TO 6 SERVINGS / ACTIVE TIME: 30 MINUTES / TOTAL TIME: 1 HOUR

This revitalizing and healthy gumbo will go great with a fresh baguette or toasted garlic bread.

1. In a large saucepan, add the oil and cook over medium heat until warm.

2. Add the onions, garlic, celery, and bell pepper and cook for 5 minutes, or until soft.

3. Add the cabbage, oregano, thyme, and bay leaf and cook for 5 minutes.

4. Add the stock and bring to a boil. Reduce heat so that the soup simmers and cook for 5 minutes.

5. Add the collard greens and cook for 5 minutes, then add the spinach, watercress, and tofu. Cook for 2 minutes before adding the parsley, allspice, and cayenne. Season with salt and pepper, simmer for 2 minutes, and then serve in warm bowls.

INGREDIENTS:

- 1 TABLESPOON VEGETABLE OIL
- 1 ONION, CHOPPED
- 2 GARLIC CLOVES, MINCED
- 1 CELERY STALK, FINELY CHOPPED
- 1 GREEN BELL PEPPER, CHOPPED
- ¼ GREEN CABBAGE, CORE REMOVED AND FINELY SLICED
- ½ TEASPOON OREGANO, LEAVES REMOVED AND CHOPPED
- ½ TEASPOON THYME, LEAVES REMOVED AND CHOPPED
- 1 BAY LEAF
- 6 CUPS VEGETABLE STOCK
- 2 CUPS COLLARD GREENS, FINELY SHREDDED
- 2 CUPS SPINACH, FINELY SHREDDED
- 1 BUNCH WATERCRESS
- 12 OZ. TOFU, CUT INTO ¼-INCH PIECES
- ¼ CUP PARSLEY, LEAVES REMOVED AND CHOPPED
- ½ TEASPOON ALLSPICE
- PINCH OF CAYENNE PEPPER
- SALT AND PEPPER, TO TASTE

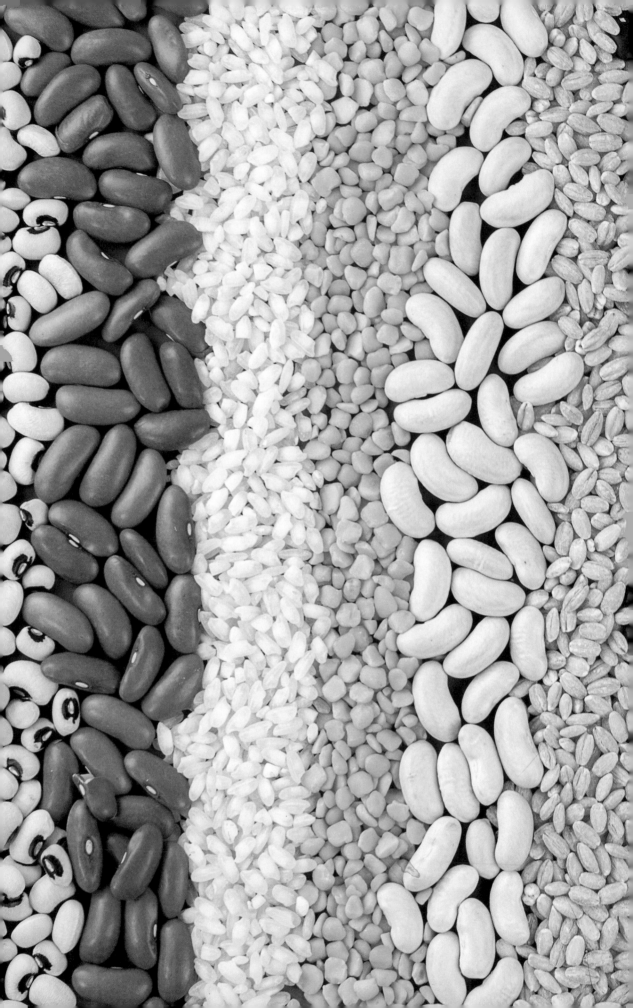

LEGUMES, NUTS
& GRAINS

*L*egumes, grains, and nuts add a great deal of nutrition, texture, and flavor to these recipes. In some of these recipes, they provide the main flavor profile, and in others they play a supporting role. This is part of the magic of these ingredients—they are versatile and capable of whatever task is assigned to them.

A note on beans: if the recipe requires dried beans, the beans need to soak overnight. Soaking the beans cleans them, removes some of their natural sugars, and softens them, which will decrease cooking time. The reduction in cooking time is the most important variable, as it will prevent you from overcooking and throwing the entire dish out of balance. So, when using dried beans, make sure you start your preparations the night before.

SAUSAGE BARLEY SOUP

YIELD: 4 SERVINGS / ACTIVE TIME: 20 MINUTES / TOTAL TIME: 1 HOUR AND 30 MINUTES

This barley soup is very hearty and flavorful. It's also a great soup for the pressure cooker.

1. In a medium saucepan, add the olive oil and cook over medium-high heat until warm.

2. Add the sausage, onion, and garlic and cook for 5 minutes, using a wooden spoon to break up the sausage as it cooks. When the sausage is nicely browned, add the herbs and stock and bring to a boil.

3. Reduce heat so that the soup simmers and add the carrot and barley.

4. Turn the heat down to its lowest setting and cover the saucepan. Cook for 1 hour, or until the barley is tender.

5. Add the spinach and cook for 5 minutes, or until wilted.

6. Season with salt and pepper and serve in warm bowls with focaccia or crusty bread.

INGREDIENTS:

- 2 TABLESPOONS EXTRA VIRGIN OLIVE OIL
- 1 POUND GROUND ITALIAN SAUSAGE
- 1 ONION, DICED
- 2 GARLIC CLOVES, MINCED
- 1 TEASPOON BASIL, LEAVES REMOVED AND CHOPPED
- 1 TEASPOON OREGANO, LEAVES REMOVED AND CHOPPED
- 1 TEASPOON THYME, LEAVES REMOVED AND CHOPPED
- 8 CUPS CHICKEN STOCK
- 1 CARROT, SLICED
- ¼ CUP PEARL BARLEY
- 10 OZ. SPINACH, CHOPPED

SALT AND PEPPER, TO TASTE

CHICKEN QUINOA SOUP

YIELD: 4 SERVINGS / **ACTIVE TIME:** 20 MINUTES / **TOTAL TIME:** 45 MINUTES

Quinoa has become very popular due to its superfood properties and nutty flavor, which make it perfect for this comforting soup.

1. In a small saucepan, bring the water to a boil. Add the quinoa, reduce heat so that the water simmers, and cover. Cook for 15 minutes, or until tender, and set aside.

2. Meanwhile, in a medium saucepan, add the oil and cook over medium heat until warm.

3. Add the chicken and cook for 5 minutes, or until evenly browned. Remove and set aside.

4. Add the onion, carrots, celery, and green pepper and cook for 5 minutes, or until soft.

5. Add the garlic and cook for another 2 minutes.

6. Add the stock and fresh herbs and bring to a boil. Reduce heat so that the soup simmers and return chicken to the pan.

7. Simmer for 10 minutes, add the quinoa and kale, and simmer for 5 more minutes.

8. Season with salt and pepper, discard the bay leaf, and serve in warm bowls.

INGREDIENTS:

- 1½ CUPS WATER
- ½ CUP QUINOA
- 1 TABLESPOON EXTRA VIRGIN OLIVE OIL
- 2 CHICKEN BREASTS, CUT INTO ½-INCH PIECES
- 1 ONION, CHOPPED
- 2 CARROTS, PEELED AND CHOPPED
- 2 CELERY STALKS, CHOPPED
- ½ CUP GREEN BELL PEPPER
- 2 GARLIC CLOVES, MINCED
- 4 CUPS CHICKEN STOCK
- 1 BAY LEAF
- 2 THYME SPRIGS, LEAVES REMOVED AND CHOPPED
- 1 OREGANO SPRIG, LEAVES REMOVED AND CHOPPED
- 1 CUP KALE, THINLY SLICED
- SALT AND PEPPER, TO TASTE

CASHEW SOUP

YIELD: 4 SERVINGS / ACTIVE TIME: 25 MINUTES / TOTAL TIME: 1 HOUR AND 15 MINUTES

This very hearty, appetizing soup is an outstanding use of the cashews' rich flavor profile.

1. In a large saucepan, add the butter and cook over medium heat until melted. Add the celery, leeks, and shallot and cook for 5 minutes, or until soft.

2. Sprinkle in the flour and cook for 5 minutes.

3. Add the cashew butter, toasted cashews, and chicken stock. Bring to a boil, while stirring constantly, then reduce heat so that the soup simmers and cook for 15 minutes.

4. Whisk in the cream and season with salt and pepper.

5. Ladle into warmed bowls, serve with Crispy Leeks, Chicken Skin Butter, and crusty bread and garnish with toasted, chopped cashews and celery leaves.

CRISPY LEEKS

1. Add the oil to a large saucepan and cook over medium-high heat until it reaches 350°F.

2. Bring water to boil in a medium saucepan. Add the leeks, cook for 2 minutes, remove, and submerge in ice water.

3. Remove the leeks from the ice water and dry completely.

4. Place the leeks in the oil and, while stirring constantly, cook until golden brown.

5. Remove the leeks with a slotted spoon or large tweezers. Set on paper towels to drain, and season with salt and pepper.

CASHEW BUTTER

If you don't have time to whip this up, don't worry; purchased cashew butter will work just fine.

1. Preheat oven to 350°F.

2. Place the cashews on a baking tray and place the tray into the oven. Cook for 10 minutes, while stirring occasionally, until golden brown. Remove the tray and let the cashews cool.

Continued . . .

INGREDIENTS:

2 TABLESPOONS BUTTER

½ CUP CELERY, CHOPPED, LEAVES RESERVED FOR GARNISH

⅛ CUP LEEKS, WHITE PART ONLY, CHOPPED

1 TABLESPOON SHALLOTS, CHOPPED

1 TABLESPOON ALL-PURPOSE FLOUR

½ CUP CASHEW BUTTER (SEE RECIPE)

¼ CUP CASHEWS, LIGHTLY TOASTED AND CHOPPED, PLUS MORE FOR GARNISH

3 CUPS CHICKEN STOCK

1 CUP HEAVY CREAM

SALT AND PEPPER, TO TASTE

TO SERVE:
CRISPY LEEKS

CHICKEN SKIN BUTTER

CRISPY LEEKS:

1 CUP OIL

¼ LEEK, WHITE PART ONLY, JULIENNED

SALT AND PEPPER, TO TASTE

CASHEW BUTTER:

2 CUPS UNSALTED RAW CASHEWS

½ CUP VEGETABLE OIL

½ TEASPOON SALT

3. In a food processor, add the toasted cashews, vegetable oil, and salt. Puree until smooth, adding more oil if necessary.

CHICKEN SKIN BUTTER

Once you try this, you're certain to think up 100 other uses for it!

1. Preheat the oven to 400°F.

2. Lay the chicken skin on a cutting board, skin-side down, and use a small, sharp knife to scrape off any excess fat and meat.

3. Stretch the skins out on a parchment-lined baking tray and sprinkle with a pinch of flaky sea salt.

4. Lay a second sheet of parchment paper over the skins and then place another tray on top. Place the trays in the oven for 10 minutes, until the skins are golden and crisp. Remove and let the skins cool.

5. Chop the cool, crisp skin into small, fine pieces. Add the butter and the pieces of skin to a bowl and whisk until combined. Fold in the chives and serve with crusty bread.

INGREDIENTS (CONTINUED):

CHICKEN SKIN BUTTER

SKIN FROM 2 LARGE CHICKEN THIGHS

FLAKY SEA SALT

½ CUP BUTTER, SOFTENED

½ TEASPOON CHIVES, CHOPPED

DRIED FAVA SOUP *with* GRILLED HALLOUMI CHEESE *and* PARSLEY LEMON OIL

YIELD: 4 SERVINGS / ACTIVE TIME: 30 MINUTES / TOTAL TIME: 9 HOURS AND 30 MINUTES

This soup is based on a traditional Greek dish that a friend of mine once prepared for me. That flavor has remained with me ever since, which inspired me to create this soup.

1. In a medium saucepan, add the fava beans, veal stock, and garlic and bring to a boil. Reduce the heat so that the soup simmers, cover, and cook for 1 hour, or until the beans are so soft that they fall apart. Add water while cooking, if necessary.

2. Transfer the soup to a food processor and puree until smooth.

3. Return the soup to a clean pan, season with salt and pepper, and serve with lemon wedges, Parsley Lemon Oil, and Grilled Halloumi Cheese.

PARSLEY LEMON OIL

1. In a small saucepan, add oil and cook over medium heat until warm. Add the shallot and cook for 5 minutes, or until soft.

2. Remove the pan from heat and add lemon zest. Let stand for 1 hour.

3. When completely cooled, whisk in the lemon juice and then fold in the parsley. Reserve until ready to serve.

GRILLED HALLOUMI CHEESE

I chose to serve this soup with Grilled Halloumi Cheese, since it is very waxy and grills wonderfully.

1. Preheat your gas or charcoal grill to 350°F. If cooking indoors, warm a grill or sauté pan.

2. Place the olive oil in a small bowl and then add the cheese. Toss until the cheese is coated.

3. Place the cheese on your cooking surface and cook for 2 minutes on each side, or until golden brown.

INGREDIENTS:

1½ CUPS DRIED FAVA BEANS, SOAKED OVERNIGHT

6 CUPS VEAL STOCK

4 GARLIC CLOVES, MINCED

SALT AND PEPPER, TO TASTE

LEMON WEDGES, FOR GARNISH

TO SERVE:

PARSLEY LEMON OIL

GRILLED HALLOUMI CHEESE

PARSLEY LEMON OIL

¼ CUP EXTRA VIRGIN OLIVE OIL

1 SHALLOT, MINCED

ZEST AND JUICE OF 1 LEMON

2 TABLESPOONS PARSLEY, LEAVES REMOVED AND CHOPPED

GRILLED HALLOUMI CHEESE

1 TABLESPOON EXTRA VIRGIN OLIVE OIL

8 OZ. HALLOUMI, SLICED INTO 4 PIECES

FRENCH LENTIL SOUP

YIELD: 4 TO 6 SERVINGS / ACTIVE TIME: 25 MINUTES / TOTAL TIME: 1 HOUR AND 15 MINUTES

This traditional French soup is sure to warm the bones.

1. In a medium saucepan, add the oil and warm over medium heat. Add the onion and garlic and cook for 5 minutes, or until the onion is soft.

2. Add the carrot, leek, and celery, and cook for 5 minutes, or until soft.

3. Add the tomato paste and cook, while stirring, for 2 minutes.

4. Add the lentils, stock, sachet d'epices, bay leaf, thyme, caraway seeds, and lemon slices. Bring to a boil, reduce heat so that the soup simmers, and cook for 30 minutes, or until the lentils are tender.

5. Remove the sachet d'epices and lemon slices.

6. Add the vinegar and Riesling and season with salt and pepper. Serve in warmed bowls with Caraway Water Biscuits.

CARAWAY WATER BISCUITS

This biscuit brings out the caraway flavor in the soup and provides a nice texture.

1. Preheat oven to 350°F.

2. Add the flour and water to a mixing bowl and whisk until combined. Add the salt.

3. On a parchment-lined baking tray, use a pastry brush to transfer the batter to the tray, taking care to make nice, long crackers.

4. Sprinkle with caraway seeds and place in the oven. Bake for 8 minutes, or until golden brown, then remove the tray and let crackers cool.

INGREDIENTS:

2   TABLESPOONS VEGETABLE OIL

1   ONION, PEELED AND CHOPPED

1   GARLIC CLOVE, MINCED

1   CARROT, PEELED AND FINELY DICED

1   LEEK, WHITE PART ONLY, FINELY DICED

1   CELERY STALK, FINELY DICED

1   TABLESPOON TOMATO PASTE

1½ CUPS FRENCH LENTILS

6   CUPS CHICKEN STOCK

1   SACHET D'EPICES (SEE PAGE 90)

1   BAY LEAF

2   THYME SPRIGS, LEAVES REMOVED AND CHOPPED

¼   TEASPOON CARAWAY SEEDS

½   LEMON, SLICED

½   OUNCE APPLE CIDER VINEGAR

¼   CUP RIESLING

    SALT AND PEPPER, TO TASTE

TO SERVE:
CARAWAY WATER BISCUITS

CARAWAY WATER BISCUITS
½   CUP ALL-PURPOSE FLOUR

10 TABLESPOONS WATER

⅛   TEASPOON SALT

2   TABLESPOONS CARAWAY SEEDS

LAMB LEG *and* LENTIL SOUP

YIELD: 4 SERVINGS / ACTIVE TIME: 20 MINUTES / TOTAL TIME: 1 HOUR AND 30 MINUTES

I'm almost certain that lamb and lentils were created for each other. After you try this quick, easy, and delicious soup, I'm certain you'll feel the same way.

1. In a large saucepan, add the stock, lamb, onion, garlic, bay leaves, cloves, and thyme. Bring to a boil, then reduce the heat so that the soup simmers. Cook for 45 minutes, or until the lamb is tender.

2. Remove the thyme sprigs and the cloves, add the potato and lentils, cover, and cook for 15 minutes, or until the lentils and potatoes are cooked.

3. Adjust the seasoning to taste, add the parsley, and serve.

INGREDIENTS:

4   CUPS VEGETABLE STOCK

1   POUND BUTTERFLIED LEG OF LAMB, CUT INTO 1-INCH PIECES

1   ONION, PEELED AND FINELY CHOPPED

2   GARLIC CLOVES, MINCED

2   BAY LEAVES

4   CLOVES

4   THYME SPRIGS

1   POTATO, PEELED AND CUT INTO ½-INCH PIECES

½   CUP RED LENTILS

    SALT AND PEPPER, TO TASTE

2   TABLESPOONS PARSLEY, CHOPPED

OAXACAN BLACK BEAN SOUP

YIELD: 4 TO 6 SERVINGS / ACTIVE TIME: 30 MINUTES / TOTAL TIME: 1 HOUR AND 30 MINUTES

The seafood, fennel, and sausage round out this Mexican classic, but the black beans are the star of the show.

1. Combine the water and beans in a large saucepan and bring to a simmer. Add the fennel, sausage, and onion and cook for approximately 1 hour, until the beans are tender.

2. Transfer the soup to a food processor and puree to a fine consistency, adding more water if necessary.

3. Return the soup to a clean pan and bring to a simmer.

4. Meanwhile in a small saucepan, add the oil and cook over medium-high heat until it is 350°F. Add the tortilla strips, turning frequently until they are crisp. Remove with a slotted spoon and set on paper towels to drain.

5. Once the soup is simmering, add the shrimp and crab and cook for 4 minutes, or until the shrimp are cooked.

6. Ladle into warmed bowls and garnish with cheese, Roasted Chipotle Chili Puree, tortilla crisps, and cilantro.

ROASTED CHIPOTLE CHILI PUREE

1. Preheat oven to 350°F.

2. Place the chipotles and tomatillos on a baking tray and put the tray in the oven. Bake for 5 minutes, remove tray, and turn chipotles and tomatillos over. Return the tray to the oven and cook for an additional 5 minutes. Remove tray and set aside chipotles. Return the tomatillos to the oven and cook for 5 more minutes, or until the skin blisters. Remove and allow to cool.

3. Transfer the chipotles to a bowl and cover with hot water. Let stand for 30 minutes.

4. Place the garlic on an ungreased, nonstick sauté pan and cook, while turning occasionally, over medium heat for 15 minutes, or until the skin is blackened. Remove, allow to cool, and then peel the roasted cloves.

5. Combine all the ingredients in a food processor and puree until a smooth paste forms.

INGREDIENTS:

10	CUPS WATER
1½	CUPS DRIED BLACK BEANS, RINSED
½	CUP FENNEL, CHOPPED
½	CUP ANDOUILLE SAUSAGE, CHOPPED
1	ONION, CHOPPED
2	CUPS VEGETABLE OIL
6	CORN TORTILLAS, CUT INTO ⅛-INCH STRIPS
24	MEDIUM SHRIMP, PEELED AND CLEANED
8	OZ. CRAB MEAT, COOKED
	CILANTRO, CHOPPED, FOR GARNISH
	QUESO FRESCO OR FETA, FOR GARNISH

TO SERVE:
ROASTED CHIPOTLE CHILI PUREE

ROASTED CHIPOTLE CHILI PUREE

1	OZ. CHIPOTLE CHILIES
8	OZ. TOMATILLOS, SHUCKED AND RINSED
3	LARGE GARLIC CLOVES, UNPEELED
½	TEASPOON SALT
¼	TEASPOON SUGAR

POTAGE OF LENTILS
with CONFIT LEMON RINDS

YIELD: 4 TO 6 SERVINGS / ACTIVE TIME: 30 MINUTES / TOTAL TIME: 1 HOUR

Lentils scream winter. But this soup can work in the summer, either hot or cold.

1. In a medium saucepan, add the lemon oil and cook over medium heat until warm. Add the onion and cook for 4 to 5 minutes, or until soft.

2. Add the celery, carrots, garlic, and potato, and continue until the vegetables begin to soften.

3. Add the lentils, 4 cups of the stock, bay leaf, lemon juice, cumin, and Tabasco™ and bring to a boil. Reduce the heat and simmer for 10 minutes, or until the potato and lentils are tender.

4. Remove the bay leaf and use a slotted spoon to remove ½ cup of the solids from the soup. Set aside and use for garnish. Transfer the rest of the soup to a food processor and puree until smooth.

5. Return to the pan, add the remaining stock, and season with salt and pepper. Ladle into bowls, garnish with parsley and reserved lentils and vegetables, and serve with Confit Lemon Rinds.

CONFIT LEMON RINDS

1. Add the lemon peel and oil to a small saucepan, bring to a simmer, and cook for 10 minutes.

2. Turn off the heat and let cool. Strain oil and use in the soup. Reserve lemon rind until ready to serve.

INGREDIENTS:

- ¼ CUP LEMON OIL (SEE CONFIT LEMON RINDS RECIPE)
- 1 ONION, FINELY CHOPPED
- 2 CELERY STALKS, FINELY CHOPPED
- 2 CARROTS, PEELED AND FINELY CHOPPED
- 4 GARLIC CLOVES, MINCED
- 1 POTATO, PEELED AND DICED
- 1 CUP RED LENTILS, RINSED
- 6 CUPS VEGETABLE STOCK
- 1 BAY LEAF
- 2 TABLESPOONS LEMON JUICE
- ½ TEASPOON CUMIN
- ½ TEASPOON TABASCO™

  SALT AND PEPPER, TO TASTE

  PARSLEY, CHOPPED, FOR GARNISH

TO SERVE:
CONFIT LEMON RINDS

CONFIT LEMON RINDS

- 1 LEMON, PEELED AND THINLY SLICED, JUICE RESERVED FOR SOUP
- ½ CUP EXTRA VIRGIN OLIVE OIL

MOROCCAN LEGUME SOUP
with HONEY BUNS

YIELD: 4 SERVINGS / ACTIVE TIME: 45 MINUTES / TOTAL TIME: 13 HOURS

This very healthy, authentic Moroccan soup showcases all the flavors of North African cuisine.

1. In a medium saucepan, add the oil and cook over medium heat until warm. Add the onions and cook for 5 minutes, or until soft.

2. Add the ginger, turmeric, cinnamon, saffron threads, tomatoes, and sugar. Stir in the chickpeas and the stock and bring to a boil. Reduce heat so that the soup simmers, cover, and cook for 10 minutes.

3. Add the lentils and fava beans and continue to cook for 15 minutes, or until all the legumes are tender. Add the cilantro and parsley, season with salt and pepper, and serve in warmed bowls with Honey Buns.

INGREDIENTS:

- 1½ TABLESPOONS EXTRA VIRGIN OLIVE OIL
- 1 ONION, PEELED, HALVED, AND SLICED
- ¼ TEASPOON GROUND GINGER
- ¼ TEASPOON TURMERIC
- ½ TEASPOON CINNAMON
- ⅛ TEASPOON SAFFRON THREADS
- 1 14 OZ. CAN DICED TOMATOES
- 1 TEASPOON SUGAR
- ½ CUP CHICKPEAS, SOAKED OVERNIGHT AND STRAINED
- 4 CUPS VEAL STOCK
- ⅓ CUP BROWN LENTILS, SOAKED OVERNIGHT AND STRAINED
- ½ CUP DRIED FAVA BEANS, SOAKED OVERNIGHT AND STRAINED
- 1 TABLESPOON CILANTRO, LEAVES REMOVED AND CHOPPED
- 1 TABLESPOON PARSLEY, LEAVES REMOVED AND CHOPPED
- SALT AND PEPPER, TO TASTE

TO SERVE:
HONEY BUNS

Continued . . .

HONEY BUNS

1. Combine the yeast and approximately 1 tablespoon of lukewarm water in a bowl and let stand until yeast is dissolved.

2. Sieve the flour and salt into a mixing bowl. Add the dissolved yeast, honey, and fennel seeds, then slowly add 1 cup of the milk. Stir until well-combined.

3. Place the dough on a floured work surface and knead for 5 minutes, until it is smooth and elastic.

4. Cover the dough with a damp cloth and let stand until it has doubled in size.

5. Preheat the oven to 450°F.

6. Divide the dough into 12 pieces and shape each piece into a ball.

7. Place on a baking tray and let stand for 10 minutes.

8. Combine the egg yolk and 1 tablespoon of milk in a small bowl. Brush the top of each bun with the egg mixture, sprinkle on the poppy seeds, if using, and place in the oven. Bake for 15 minutes, or until golden brown on top and bottom.

9. Remove the buns from the tray and place on a wire rack to cool.

INGREDIENTS (CONTINUED):

HONEY BUNS

½ TEASPOON DRIED YEAST

1¾ CUPS BREAD FLOUR

½ TEASPOON SALT

2 TABLESPOONS HONEY

1 TEASPOON FENNEL SEEDS

1 CUP MILK, PLUS 1 TABLESPOON

1 EGG YOLK

1 TEASPOON POPPY SEEDS, OPTIONAL

CURRIED CARROT, SPINACH,
and TOFU BROTH

YIELD: 4 SERVINGS / ACTIVE TIME: 20 MINUTES / TOTAL TIME: 45 MINUTES

A very simple, and very soothing, soup that is both sweet and spicy. If you use vegetable stock, this is a perfect vegan soup.

1. In a medium saucepan, add the oil and cook over medium heat until warm.

2. Add the onion, garlic, and curry powder and cook for 5 minutes.

3. Add the stock, Thai chili, lime zest, lime juice, soy sauce, jaggery, and lime leaves. Bring to a boil, reduce the heat so that the soup simmers, and cook for 10 minutes.

4. Add the carrots and continue to simmer for 5 minutes.

5. Just before serving, add the spinach and tofu. Season with salt and pepper and serve in warm bowls.

INGREDIENTS:

1   TABLESPOON VEGETABLE OIL

1   ONION, CHOPPED

1   GARLIC CLOVE, MINCED

2   TABLESPOONS CURRY POWDER

6   CUPS CHICKEN OR VEGETABLE STOCK

1   THAI CHILI, SEEDS REMOVED, SLICED

    ZEST AND JUICE OF 1 LIME

2   TABLESPOONS SOY SAUCE

4   TABLESPOONS JAGGERY

2   LIME LEAVES

1   CARROT, PEELED AND CUT INTO MATCHSTICKS

2   CUPS SPINACH

12   OZ. TOFU, CUT INTO ½-INCH CUBES

SPICY BABY SPINACH *and* RICE SOUP

YIELD: 4 SERVINGS / ACTIVE TIME: 15 MINUTES / TOTAL TIME: 45 MINUTES

This is a vegetarian delicacy, perfect for a spring or summer day. Feel free to toss in whatever vegetables you like.

1. In a large saucepan, add the water and the spinach and cook over medium-high heat for 5 minutes, or until the spinach is wilted. Remove the spinach, allow to cool, and then finely chop.

2. Add the oil to a large saucepan and cook over medium heat until warm. Add the onion, garlic, and chili and cook for 3 to 4 minutes, or until the onions are soft.

3. Add the stock and then stir in the rice. Bring to a boil, reduce the heat so that the soup simmers, and cook for 15 minutes.

4. Add the spinach and cook for an additional 5 minutes, or until the rice is tender. Serve in warmed bowls garnished with Romano cheese.

INGREDIENTS:

- 2 TABLESPOONS WATER
- 12 CUPS BABY SPINACH
- 3 TABLESPOONS EXTRA VIRGIN OLIVE OIL
- 1 SMALL ONION, FINELY CHOPPED
- 2 GARLIC CLOVES, MINCED
- 1 SMALL RED CHILI, SEEDED AND FINELY CHOPPED
- 4 CUPS VEGETABLE STOCK
- ⅓ CUP ARBORIO RICE

  SALT AND PEPPER, TO TASTE

  ROMANO CHEESE, GRATED, FOR GARNISH

SPLIT PEA SOUP *with* SMOKED HAM

YIELD: 4 SERVINGS / **ACTIVE TIME:** 30 MINUTES / **TOTAL TIME:** 1 HOUR AND 15 MINUTES TO 2 HOURS

This Greek soup is traditionally cooked longer, but I like the peas to be *al dente*. If you prefer to cook them for longer, add a little more stock and cook for an additional 20 to 30 minutes.

1. In a medium saucepan, add the butter and cook over medium heat until melted. Add the onion, carrot, and celery and cook for 5 minutes, or until soft.

2. Add the stock, peas, ham, parsley, bay leaf, and thyme. Bring to a boil, then reduce heat so that the soup simmers. Cook for 45 minutes, or until peas are cooked through. Stir occasionally as the soup cooks and add more stock if it gets too thick.

3. Discard bay leaf and parsley sprigs. Season with salt and pepper and ladle into warm bowls. Garnish with chopped parsley and serve with lemon wedges.

INGREDIENTS:

2	TABLESPOONS BUTTER
1	ONION, FINELY CHOPPED
1	CARROT, PEELED AND FINELY CHOPPED
1	CELERY STALK, FINELY CHOPPED
5	CUPS CHICKEN STOCK
1	CUP SPLIT PEAS
6	OZ. SMOKED HAM, CUT INTO BITE-SIZED PIECES
2	PARSLEY SPRIGS
1	BAY LEAF
1	TEASPOON THYME, CHOPPED
	SALT AND PEPPER, TO TASTE
	PARSLEY, LEAVES REMOVED AND CHOPPED, FOR GARNISH
	LEMON WEDGES, FOR GARNISH

TUSCAN CANNELLINI BEAN SOUP
with CABBAGE *and* CARAWAY EMULSION

YIELD: 4 TO 6 SERVINGS / ACTIVE TIME: 30 MINUTES / TOTAL TIME: 1 HOUR

This hearty Italian soup is sure to warm up your insides!

1. In a medium saucepan, add the oil and cook over medium heat until warm.

2. Add the sausage and cook for 5 minutes, turning often, until it is browned on all sides. Remove and set aside.

3. Add the onions, leeks, carrot, celery, and garlic and cook for 5 minutes, or until vegetables are soft.

4. Add the tomatoes, chicken stock, and Mediterranean herbs and bring to a boil.

5. Reduce heat so that the soup simmers. Add the savoy cabbage and cook for 15 minutes, or until the cabbage is tender.

6. Meanwhile, cut the sausage into ¼-inch thick slices.

7. Add the cannellini beans and the sausage to the saucepan. Season with salt and pepper and simmer for 5 more minutes. Serve in warm bowls with the Cabbage And Caraway Emulsion.

MEDITERRANEAN HERBS

Mix all ingredients together in a bowl. Store in an airtight container until ready to use.

CABBAGE AND CARAWAY EMULSION

1. In a small saucepan, bring 4 cups of water to a boil.

2. Add the cabbage and boil for 3 minutes. Remove and submerge in ice water.

3. Remove cabbage from the ice water and squeeze to remove excess water.

4. Transfer the cabbage to a food processor. Add the oil and caraway seeds and blend for 3 to 4 minutes.

5. Strain through a fine sieve, season with salt and pepper, and reserve until ready to use.

INGREDIENTS:

1	TABLESPOON EXTRA VIRGIN OLIVE OIL
2	ITALIAN SAUSAGES
1	ONION, CHOPPED
¼	CUP LEEKS, CHOPPED
1	CARROT, PEELED AND CHOPPED
1	CELERY STALK, CHOPPED
1	GARLIC CLOVE, MINCED
1	14 OZ. CAN DICED TOMATOES
4	CUPS CHICKEN STOCK
2	TABLESPOONS MEDITERRANEAN HERBS (SEE RECIPE)
2	CUPS SAVOY CABBAGE, FINELY SLICED
1	14 OZ. CAN CANNELLINI BEANS, DRAINED AND RINSED
	SALT AND PEPPER, TO TASTE

TO SERVE:
CABBAGE AND CARAWAY EMULSION

MEDITERRANEAN HERBS

1	TABLESPOON DRIED ROSEMARY
2	TEASPOONS CUMIN
2	TEASPOONS CORIANDER
1	TEASPOON OREGANO
⅛	TEASPOON SALT

CABBAGE AND CARAWAY EMULSION

2	CUPS SAVOY CABBAGE, CHOPPED
1	CUP VEGETABLE OIL
1	TABLESPOON CARAWAY SEEDS
	SALT AND PEPPER, TO TASTE

VEGETARIAN WHITE BEAN SOUP
with PAN-SEARED RICE CAKE

YIELD: 4 SERVINGS / ACTIVE TIME: 30 MINUTES / TOTAL TIME: 1 HOUR AND 30 MINUTES

To take this soup a step further, puree it. Just be aware that this might require a bit more vegetable stock. If you do puree it, it could also be used as a wonderful garnish for a main course.

1. In a medium saucepan, add the butter and cook over medium heat until melted. Add the onion, garlic, carrot, and celery and cook for 5 minutes, or until the vegetables are soft.

2. Drain the beans and add to the saucepan. Add the stock, tomatoes, rosemary, thyme, and bay leaf. Bring to a boil, reduce heat so that the soup simmers, and cook for approximately 1 hour, or until the beans are tender.

3. Season with salt and pepper and ladle into warm bowls. Garnish with oregano and serve with Pan-Seared Rice Cake.

PAN-SEARED RICE CAKE

1. In a small saucepan, add the rice and water and bring to a boil. Cover, reduce heat to low, and simmer for 10 minutes. Remove lid and stir frequently.

2. Add the oregano, Tabasco™, and salt.

3. Lay down a sheet of plastic wrap on a cutting board. Spoon the rice onto the plastic and then roll into a 12-inch log. Cut this into 6-inch logs, transfer to the refrigerator, and chill for an hour.

4. Remove from the refrigerator and cut the logs into 8 slices. In a non-stick pan, add the butter and cook over medium heat until melted. Add the rice cakes and cook for 2 to 3 minutes on each side, or until golden brown.

INGREDIENTS:

2	TABLESPOONS BUTTER
1	ONION, CHOPPED
1	GARLIC CLOVE, MINCED
1	CARROT, PEELED AND CHOPPED
1	CELERY STALK, CHOPPED
½	CUP DRIED WHITE BEANS, SOAKED OVERNIGHT
2½	CUPS VEGETABLE STOCK
2	14 OZ. CANS TOMATOES, FINELY CHOPPED, JUICE RESERVED
½	TEASPOON ROSEMARY, LEAVES REMOVED AND CHOPPED
½	TEASPOON THYME, LEAVES REMOVED AND CHOPPED
1	BAY LEAF
	SALT AND PEPPER, TO TASTE
	OREGANO, CHOPPED, FOR GARNISH

TO SERVE:
PAN-SEARED RICE CAKE

PAN-SEARED RICE CAKE

1	CUP WATER
½	CUP ARBORIO RICE
1	TEASPOON OREGANO, CHOPPED
¼	TEASPOON TABASCO™
	SALT, TO TASTE
4	TABLESPOONS BUTTER, MELTED

RUSSIAN PEA *and* BARLEY SOUP
with SIMPLE COUNTRY-STYLE BREAD

YIELD: 4 SERVINGS / ACTIVE TIME: 45 MINUTES / TOTAL TIME: 21 HOURS

A typical Russian meal starts with appetizers, moves on to a rich bowl of soup, proceeds to an equally hearty main course, and finishes with a not-too-sweet dessert.

1. Add the split peas, barley, and stock to a large saucepan and bring to a boil. Reduce the heat so that the mixture simmers.

2. In a sauté pan, add the bacon and cook over medium heat for 5 minutes, or until crispy. Remove the bacon from the pan and set aside. Leave the bacon fat in the pan.

3. Add the butter to the pan. When it is melted, add the onion and garlic and cook for 5 minutes. Add the parsnip and cook for another 5 minutes, or until the onion is slightly golden brown.

4. Add the bacon and the parsnip mixture to the saucepan and simmer for 20 minutes, or until the peas and barley are tender.

5. Stir in the oregano and season with salt and pepper. Serve in bowls with Simple Country-Style Bread.

SIMPLE COUNTRY-STYLE BREAD

This bread needs some time, but it's very simple to produce.

1. Add all the ingredients to a large bowl and mix by hand until well-combined.

2. Cover the bowl with plastic wrap and keep in a warm place for 18 hours, allowing the flavor to develop.

3. Remove the dough from the bowl, place on a floured surface, and knead it.

4. Sprinkle a cotton towel with cornmeal and place the dough, seam-side down, on the towel.

5. Dust the dough with a bit more cornmeal and cover with another cotton kitchen towel. Let stand for 2 hours.

6. When the dough has rested for 1 hour and 30 minutes, place a cast-iron pot with a lid in a cold oven. Heat the oven to 450°F.

INGREDIENTS:

½   CUP YELLOW SPLIT PEAS, SOAKED OVERNIGHT

¼   CUP PEARL BARLEY, SOAKED OVERNIGHT

6   CUPS HAM STOCK

4   OZ. THICK-CUT BACON, CUBED

2   TABLESPOONS BUTTER

1   ONION, CHOPPED

1   GARLIC CLOVE, MINCED

1½   CUPS PARSNIP, PEELED AND CHOPPED

1   TABLESPOON OREGANO, LEAVES REMOVED AND CHOPPED

SALT AND PEPPER, TO TASTE

TO SERVE:
SIMPLE COUNTRY-STYLE BREAD

SIMPLE COUNTRY-STYLE BREAD
3   CUPS BREAD FLOUR

1¼   TEASPOONS SALT

¼   TEASPOON INSTANT YEAST

1⅓   CUPS WATER, LUKEWARM

7. Remove the pot from the oven and place dough into it. Cover the pot and bake for 30 minutes.

8. Remove the lid and cook for another 15 minutes.

9. Carefully remove the bread from pot and transfer to a wire rack. Let stand for 30 minutes before serving.

BARLEY, DILL, *and* PORK SOUP

YIELD: 4 TO 6 SERVINGS / ACTIVE TIME: 20 MINUTES / TOTAL TIME: 2 HOURS

While traveling through Central Europe, I developed a fondness for dill in meat preparations. In the United States, it's often associated with fish, but it also goes well with meat.

1. In a large saucepan, add the oil and cook over medium-high heat until warm. Add the pork and cook, while turning, for 5 minutes, or until evenly browned. Remove with a slotted spoon and set aside.

2. Add the onion, celery, and carrots, and cook for 5 minutes, or until soft.

3. Add the Pernod, garlic, and thyme and cook until the Pernod has been reduced by half.

4. Return the pork to the saucepan. Add the stock and the barley and bring to a boil.

5. Reduce heat so that the soup simmers. Cover and cook over low heat for 1 hour and 30 minutes, or until pork is very tender.

6. Add the dill, season with salt and pepper, and serve in warm bowls.

INGREDIENTS:

1 TABLESPOON VEGETABLE OIL

1¾ POUNDS PORK SHOULDER, CUT INTO ½-INCH PIECES

1 ONION, CHOPPED

2 CELERY STALKS, CHOPPED

2 CARROTS, PEELED AND CHOPPED

¼ CUP PERNOD

1 GARLIC CLOVE, MINCED

2 SPRIGS THYME, LEAVES REMOVED AND CHOPPED

8 CUPS BEEF OR VEAL STOCK

8 OUNCES PEARL BARLEY

½ CUP DILL, CHOPPED

SALT AND PEPPER, TO TASTE

CAULIFLOWER *and* QUINOA SOUP
with CRISPY CAULIFLOWER

YIELD: 4 SERVINGS / ACTIVE TIME: 30 MINUTES / TOTAL TIME: 1 HOUR

The crunch of the cauliflower, the chewiness of the quinoa, and the creamy broth give this soup a great texture.

1. In a medium saucepan, add the oil and cook over medium heat until warm. Add the onion and cook for 5 minutes, or until soft.

2. Add the garlic and cook for 2 minutes. Add the cauliflower, chicken stock, quinoa, and thyme and bring to a boil. Reduce heat so that the soup simmers, cover, and cook for 15 minutes, or until the cauliflower and quinoa are soft.

3. Stir in the heavy cream, season with salt and pepper, and ladle into warm bowls. Serve with the Crispy Cauliflower and garnish with chives.

CRISPY CAULIFLOWER

1. In a Dutch oven, add oil and cook over medium-high heat until it reaches 350°F.

2. Add the water and salt to a small saucepan and bring to a boil. Add the cauliflower and cook for 3 minutes. Remove and submerge in ice water. Set to dry on a paper towel.

3. In a mixing bowl, combine ½ cup of the flour, the cornstarch, and baking powder. Pass through a sieve. Add the soda water and whisk until smooth.

4. In a small bowl, add the remaining flour and the cauliflower. Mix until the florets are coated.

5. Dip each piece of cauliflower in the batter and then place them in the oil. Fry until golden brown, remove with a slotted spoon, and set on a paper towel to drain. Season with salt and pepper and serve immediately.

INGREDIENTS:

2 TABLESPOONS EXTRA VIRGIN OLIVE OIL

1 ONION, DICED

2 GARLIC CLOVES, MINCED

1 CAULIFLOWER, CHOPPED

4 CUPS CHICKEN STOCK

¾ CUP QUINOA

2 SPRIGS THYME, LEAVES REMOVED AND CHOPPED

½ CUP HEAVY CREAM

SALT AND PEPPER, TO TASTE

CHIVES, CHOPPED, FOR GARNISH

TO SERVE:

CRISPY CAULIFLOWER

CRISPY CAULIFLOWER

1 CUP OIL

4 CUPS WATER

1 TEASPOON SALT

12 SMALL CAULIFLOWER FLORETS

¾ CUP ALL-PURPOSE FLOUR

¼ CUP CORNSTARCH

½ TEASPOON BAKING POWDER

1 CUP SODA WATER

SALT AND PEPPER, TO TASTE

AFRICAN PEANUT SOUP

YIELD: 4 SERVINGS / ACTIVE TIME: 20 MINUTES / TOTAL TIME: 1 HOUR

A traditional African peanut soup. It gets a bit of a kick from the cayenne and the ginger, but the sweetness of the yam keeps it mellow.

1. In a medium saucepan, add the peanut butter and tomato paste. Slowly add the chicken stock, whisking constantly to keep lumps from forming.

2. Add the onion, ginger, thyme, bay leaf, and cayenne pepper.

3. Cook over medium heat and bring to a simmer. Cook for 30 minutes, stirring often.

4. Add the sweet potato and cook for 10 minutes. Add the okra and cook for an additional 5 minutes, or until the okra and sweet potato are tender.

5. Season with salt and pepper and serve warmed bowls with edible flowers.

INGREDIENTS:

½ CUP NATURAL PEANUT BUTTER

2 TABLESPOONS TOMATO PASTE

6 CUPS CHICKEN STOCK

1 ONION, CHOPPED

1-INCH PIECE OF GINGER, PEELED AND MINCED

2 SPRIGS OF THYME, LEAVES REMOVED AND CHOPPED

1 BAY LEAF

⅛ TEASPOON CAYENNE PEPPER, OR TO TASTE

1 SWEET POTATO, PEELED AND CHOPPED

6 FRESH OKRA, SLICED

SALT AND PEPPER, TO TASTE

EDIBLE FLOWERS, FOR GARNISH

AFRICAN PEANUT *and* QUINOA SOUP

YIELD: 4 SERVINGS / ACTIVE TIME: 20 MINUTES / TOTAL TIME: 45 MINUTES

The unique flavor of this soup makes it an intriguing take on the traditional African peanut soup.

1. In a medium saucepan, add the oil and butter and cook over medium heat until warm. Add the red onion, sweet potato, bell pepper, celery, zucchini, jalapeño, and garlic and cook for 10 minutes, or until the vegetables are soft.

2. Add the stock and bring to a boil. Reduce heat so that the soup simmers, add the quinoa and cumin, cover, and simmer for 15 minutes, or until quinoa is tender.

3. Stir in the peanut butter and season with salt and pepper. Ladle into warm bowls sprinkled with toasted peanuts and oregano.

TOASTED PEANUTS

1. Preheat oven to 375°F.

2. In a bowl, combine the vegetable oil and peanuts and gently mix together.

3. On a baking tray, add oiled nuts and sprinkle with salt to taste.

4. Cook for 5-10 minutes or until slightly browned stirring often.

INGREDIENTS:

- 1 TABLESPOON EXTRA VIRGIN OLIVE OIL
- 1 TABLESPOON BUTTER
- 1 RED ONION, CHOPPED
- 1 CUP SWEET POTATO, CHOPPED
- 1 GREEN BELL PEPPER, CHOPPED
- 2 CELERY STALKS, CHOPPED
- 1 ZUCCHINI, QUARTERED AND CHOPPED
- 1 JALAPEÑO PEPPER, SEEDS REMOVED AND FINELY CHOPPED
- 1 GARLIC CLOVE, MINCED
- 6 CUPS CHICKEN STOCK
- ¾ CUP QUINOA
- 1 TEASPOON CUMIN
- ½ CUP PEANUT BUTTER
- SALT AND PEPPER, TO TASTE
- OREGANO, CHOPPED, FOR GARNISH
- PEANUTS, TOASTED AND SALTED, FOR GARNISH

TO SERVE
TOASTED PEANUTS

TOASTED PEANUTS

- 1 TEASPOON VEGETABLE OIL
- ½ CUP SHELLED PEANUTS
- SALT

IRANIAN BARLEY SOUP

YIELD: 4 SERVINGS / ACTIVE TIME: 20 MINUTES / TOTAL TIME: 1 HOUR AND 30 MINUTES

Here is a thick, delicious soup that gets its beautiful color from tomato paste and turmeric. Replace the chicken stock with vegetable if you prefer to make it vegetarian.

1. In a large saucepan, add the oil and cook over medium heat until warm. Add the onions and cook for 5 minutes, or until soft. Add the carrots, barley, tomato paste, and turmeric and cook for 2 minutes.

2. Add the chicken stock and bring to a boil. Reduce heat so that the soup simmers and cook for 1 hour, or until the barley is tender.

3. Remove from heat. Add the sour cream and parsley, season with salt and pepper, and serve in warm bowls with the lime wedges.

INGREDIENTS:

2   TABLESPOONS VEGETABLE OIL

2   ONIONS, CHOPPED

2   CARROTS, PEELED AND CHOPPED

1   CUP PEARL BARLEY

3   TABLESPOONS TOMATO PASTE

1   TEASPOON TURMERIC

8   CUPS CHICKEN STOCK

½   CUP SOUR CREAM

⅓   CUP PARSLEY, LEAVES REMOVED AND CHOPPED

    SALT AND PEPPER, TO TASTE

8   LIME WEDGES

PARSNIP *and* BARLEY SOUP

YIELD: 6 SERVINGS / ACTIVE TIME: 20 MINUTES / TOTAL TIME: 1 HOUR

The barley contributes a lovely texture to this creamy soup.

1. In a medium saucepan, add the butter and cook over medium heat until melted. Add the onion, leek, and parsnips and cook for 5 minutes, or until vegetables are tender.

2. Add the bay leaf and potato, cook for 5 minutes, then add the stock, cinnamon stick, and barley.

3. Bring to a boil, reduce heat so that the soup simmers, and cook for 20 minutes, or until the barley is soft.

4. Remove the cinnamon stick and transfer the soup to a food processor. Puree until creamy and pass through a fine sieve.

5. Return the soup to the pan and bring to a simmer. Add the cream and season with salt and pepper. Serve in warm bowls and garnish with celery hearts and ground nutmeg.

INGREDIENTS:

¼ CUP BUTTER

1 SMALL ONION, CHOPPED

½ LEEK, WHITE PART ONLY, CUT IN ¾-INCH PIECES

6 PARSNIPS, PEELED AND CHOPPED

1 BAY LEAF

1 MEDIUM POTATO, PEELED AND CHOPPED

6 CUPS CHICKEN STOCK

1 CINNAMON STICK

½ CUP BARLEY

½ CUP HEAVY CREAM

SALT AND PEPPER, TO TASTE

GROUND NUTMEG, FOR GARNISH

CELERY HEARTS, FOR GARNISH

ROCKY MOUNTAIN CHILI

YIELD: 4 TO 6 SERVINGS / ACTIVE TIME: 30 MINUTES / TOTAL TIME: 1 HOUR AND 30 MINUTES

This is a great recipe to warm up with on a snowy winter day. Feel free to adjust the chili powder according to your spice threshold.

1. In a large saucepan, add the vegetable oil and cook over medium-high heat until warm.

2. Add the onion and ground turkey and cook for 5 minutes, or until meat has been browned.

3. Add the garlic and cook for 2 minutes, then add the chili powder, bouquet garni, tomatoes, tomato sauce, tomato paste, and beans. Bring to a boil, reduce heat so that the soup simmers and cook for 20 minutes, or until the meat is cooked through.

4. Season with salt and pepper and ladle into warmed bowls. Serve with cornbread, shredded cheddar cheese, sour cream, and chopped chives.

INGREDIENTS:

1   TABLESPOON VEGETABLE OIL

1   ONION, CHOPPED

1   POUND GROUND TURKEY

2   GARLIC CLOVES, MINCED

1   TABLESPOON CHILI POWDER

1   BOUQUET GARNI (SEE PAGE 88)

4   TOMATOES, DICED

1   14 OZ. CAN TOMATO SAUCE

8   TABLESPOONS TOMATO PASTE

1   14 OZ. CAN KIDNEY BEANS

1   14 OZ. CAN WHITE BEANS

1   14 OZ. CAN BLACK BEANS

     SALT AND PEPPER, TO TASTE

     CHEDDAR CHEESE, SHREDDED, FOR GARNISH

     SOUR CREAM, FOR GARNISH

     CHIVES, CHOPPED, FOR GARNISH

TO SERVE:
CORNBREAD (SEE RECIPE ON PAGE 367)

SPICED QUINOA *and* BLACK BEAN SOUP

YIELD: 4 SERVINGS / ACTIVE TIME: 20 MINUTES / TOTAL TIME: 1 HOUR

The bit of spice in this robust soup is sure to take the sting out of a freezing day.

1. In a medium saucepan, add the olive oil and cook over medium heat until warm.

2. Add the onion, celery, and carrots and cook for 5 minutes, or until soft.

3. Add the garlic, paprika, and red pepper flakes and cook for 2 minutes.

4. Add the chicken stock and quinoa, and bring to a boil. Reduce heat so that the soup simmers and cook for 15 minutes, or until the quinoa is tender.

5. Add the tomatoes, black beans, and corn and cook for 10 minutes.

6. Season with salt and pepper and serve in warmed bowls.

INGREDIENTS:

1   TABLESPOON EXTRA VIRGIN OLIVE OIL

1   ONION, CHOPPED

2   CELERY STALKS, CHOPPED

2   CARROTS, PEELED AND CHOPPED

2   GARLIC CLOVES, MINCED

1   TEASPOON PAPRIKA

1   TEASPOON RED PEPPER FLAKES

6   CUPS CHICKEN STOCK

¾   CUP QUINOA

1   14 OZ. CAN STEWED TOMATOES, CHOPPED

1   14 OZ. CAN BLACK BEANS, RINSED AND DRAINED

1   CUP CORN

    SALT AND PEPPER, TO TASTE

TOFU, SHIITAKE MUSHROOM, *and* GINGER BROTH

YIELD: 4 SERVINGS / ACTIVE TIME: 20 MINUTES / TOTAL TIME: 1 HOUR AND 30 MINUTES

This is a great, well-balanced clear broth that is a great starter if you're having a heavier main course.

1. In a large saucepan, add 4 cups of the chicken stock, dried squid, ginger, fish sauce, peppercorns, star anise, cloves, cardamom, cinnamon sticks, and cilantro stalks. Bring to a boil, reduce heat so that the soup simmers, and cook for 20 minutes.

2. Shut off the heat and let stand for 30 minutes. After 30 minutes, strain through a fine sieve.

3. In a medium saucepan, add the vegetable oil and cook over medium heat until warm. Add the shallot and cook for 5 minutes, or until soft.

4. Add the Thai chilies and the remaining stock and bring to a simmer.

5. Add the mushrooms, tofu, and tomatoes and cook for 10 minutes.

6. Season with salt and pepper and serve in warm bowls garnished with cilantro.

INGREDIENTS:

- 6 CUPS CHICKEN STOCK
- 1 OZ. DRIED SQUID, SOAKED FOR 20 MINUTES
- 3-INCH PIECE OF GINGER, PEELED AND CHOPPED
- 4 TABLESPOONS FISH SAUCE
- 10 BLACK PEPPERCORNS
- 2 STAR ANISE
- 6 CLOVES
- 2 CARDAMOM PODS, SEEDS REMOVED
- 2 CINNAMON STICKS
- 6 CILANTRO STALKS, LEAVES REMOVED, CHOPPED, AND RESERVED FOR GARNISH
- 1 TABLESPOON VEGETABLE OIL
- 1 SHALLOT, FINELY CHOPPED
- 2 THAI CHILIES, SEEDS REMOVED AND SLICED
- 4 CUPS SHIITAKE MUSHROOMS, SLICED
- 12 OZ. TOFU, CUT INTO ½-INCH CUBES
- 1 14 OZ. CAN STEWED TOMATOES, CHOPPED
- SALT AND PEPPER, TO TASTE

VEGAN CAULIFLOWER BLACK BEAN CHILI

YIELD: 4 TO 6 SERVINGS / ACTIVE TIME: 15 MINUTES / TOTAL TIME: 45 MINUTES

This recipe is vegan, but it's sure to be a hit with everyone, especially if you dress it up with guacamole and tortilla chips.

1. In a large saucepan, add the olive oil and cook over medium heat until warm.

2. Add the onions, peppers, and garlic. Cook for 7 minutes, or until soft.

3. Add the cauliflower and cook for 5 minutes, or until the florets are lightly browned.

4. Add the tomatoes, stock, and chili powder and bring to a boil. Reduce heat so that the soup simmers, cover, and cook for 15 minutes.

5. Remove the cover and cook for an additional 15 minutes, or until the chili starts to thicken and the cauliflower is tender.

6. Add the beans, cook for another 3 minutes, and season with salt and pepper. Serve in warm bowls and garnish with a sprinkle of parsley.

INGREDIENTS:

- 2 TABLESPOONS EXTRA VIRGIN OLIVE OIL
- 2 RED ONIONS, FINELY CHOPPED
- 1 RED BELL PEPPER, FINELY CHOPPED
- 1 YELLOW BELL PEPPER, FINELY CHOPPED
- 2 GARLIC CLOVES, MINCED
- 2 HEADS CAULIFLOWER, FLORETS REMOVED AND FINELY CHOPPED
- 4 14 OZ. CANS STEWED TOMATOES
- 2 CUPS VEGETABLE STOCK
- 1 TABLESPOON CHILI POWDER, OR TO TASTE
- 2 14 OZ. CANS BLACK BEANS, RINSED AND DRAINED

SALT AND PEPPER, TO TASTE

PARSLEY, CHOPPED, FOR GARNISH

VEGAN CURRIED LAKSA SOUP

YIELD: 4 TO 6 SERVINGS / ACTIVE TIME: 20 MINUTES / TOTAL TIME: 45 MINUTES

You don't have to be a vegan to enjoy this soup. It is packed with plenty of flavor and, if, using as an appetizer, a perfect choice to cleanse your palate.

1. In a medium saucepan, add the oil and cook over medium heat until warm. Add the Laksa Curry Paste and cook for 3 minutes, while stirring constantly.

2. Add the mushrooms and cook for 2 minutes.

3. Add the carrots, bell peppers, zucchini, and summer squash and cook for 5 minutes, or until soft.

4. Add the vegetable stock and coconut milk and bring to a boil. Reduce heat so that the soup simmers, add the noodles, and cook for 10 minutes.

5. Fold in the kale and tofu, simmer for 2 minutes, and then season with soy sauce, lime juice, sugar, salt, and pepper.

6. Serve in warmed bowls with the Thai chilies and cilantro.

LAKSA CURRY PASTE

1. In a small nonstick pan, add the coriander and fennel seeds and cook for 2 minutes over medium heat, or until they become fragrant.

2. Combine the toasted seeds and remaining ingredients in a food processor and puree until smooth.

INGREDIENTS:

1	TABLESPOON VEGETABLE OIL
	LAKSA CURRY PASTE
2	CUPS SHIITAKE MUSHROOMS, SLICED
1	CUP CARROTS, SLICED
¼	CUP RED BELL PEPPERS, CHOPPED
¼	CUP GREEN BELL PEPPERS, CHOPPED
¼	CUP GREEN ZUCCHINI, CHOPPED
¼	CUP YELLOW SUMMER SQUASH, CHOPPED
4	CUPS VEGETABLE STOCK
1	14 OZ. CAN COCONUT MILK
8	OZ. OF RICE NOODLES
1	CUP KALE, CHOPPED
8	OZ. TOFU, CUT INTO ½-INCH CUBES
1	TABLESPOON SOY SAUCE
1	TABLESPOON LIME JUICE
1	TEASPOON SUGAR
	SALT AND PEPPER, TO TASTE
	THAI CHILIES, SEEDS REMOVED, SLICED, FOR GARNISH
	CILANTRO, CHOPPED, FOR GARNISH

LAKSA CURRY PASTE

2	TEASPOONS CORIANDER SEEDS
½	TEASPOON FENNEL SEEDS
1	TEASPOON TURMERIC
	1-INCH PIECE OF GINGER, PEELED AND MINCED
1	GREEN CHILI, SEEDED AND CHOPPED
½	TEASPOON CAYENNE PEPPER
1	STALK OF LEMONGRASS
2	GARLIC CLOVES
2	TABLESPOONS CASHEWS, SOAKED IN WARM WATER FOR 10 MINUTES
½	CUP CILANTRO, LEAVES REMOVED AND CHOPPED
1	TEASPOON LIME JUICE
2	TABLESPOONS WATER
	SALT AND PEPPER, TO TASTE

VEGETABLE QUINOA SOUP

YIELD: 4 SERVINGS / ACTIVE TIME: 20 MINUTES / TOTAL TIME: 1 HOUR

Here is a hearty soup that's still very healthy. And, if you opt to skip the parmesan as a garnish, vegan.

1. In a medium saucepan, add the oil and cook over medium heat until warm.

2. Add the onion, carrots, celery, corn, zucchini, and peppers and cook for 8 minutes, or until soft.

3. Add the garlic and thyme and cook for 2 minutes. Add the tomatoes, quinoa, stock, bay leaf, and red pepper flakes and bring to a boil. Reduce the heat so that the soup simmers, cover, and cook for 25 minutes.

4. Remove the lid, add the chickpeas and kale, and cook for 5 minutes.

5. Season with the lemon juice, salt, and pepper. Serve in warm bowls and garnish with parmesan cheese.

INGREDIENTS:

2 TABLESPOONS EXTRA VIRGIN OLIVE OIL

1 ONION, CHOPPED

2 CARROTS, PEELED AND CHOPPED

2 CELERY STALKS, CHOPPED

½ CUP CORN KERNELS

½ CUP ZUCCHINI, CHOPPED

½ CUP RED BELL PEPPER

½ CUP GREEN BELL PEPPER

4 GARLIC CLOVES, MINCED

2 SPRIGS OF THYME, LEAVES REMOVED AND CHOPPED

2 14 OZ. CANS STEWED TOMATOES

1 CUP QUINOA

6 CUPS VEGETABLE STOCK

1 BAY LEAF

PINCH OF RED PEPPER FLAKES

1 14 OZ. CAN CHICKPEAS, DRAINED AND RINSED

1½ CUP KALE, RIBS REMOVED AND FINELY CHOPPED

JUICE OF ½ LEMON

SALT AND PEPPER, TO TASTE

PARMESAN CHEESE, GRATED, FOR GARNISH

CHICKEN *and* CORN SUCCOTASH SOUP

YIELD: 4 SERVINGS / ACTIVE TIME: 20 MINUTES / TOTAL TIME: 1 HOUR

This soup is based on a classic Southern recipe. The addition of chicken makes this one sing, as it complements the sweetness of the corn nicely.

1. In a medium saucepan, add the butter and cook over medium heat until melted. Add the bacon, onions, and garlic and cook for 5 minutes. Add the chicken breasts and cook for 5 minutes.

2. Add the flour and cook, while stirring constantly, for 5 minutes.

3. Add the chicken stock slowly, whisking constantly to prevent lumps from forming.

4. Bring to a boil. Reduce heat so that the soup simmers. Add the corn kernels and kidney beans and simmer for 5 minutes.

5. Add the cream and return to a simmer. Add chopped parsley, season with salt and pepper, and serve in warm bowls.

INGREDIENTS:

- ¼ CUP BUTTER
- 4 SLICES OF THICK-CUT BACON, CUT INTO ¼-INCH PIECES
- 2 ONIONS, CHOPPED
- 2 GARLIC CLOVES, MINCED
- 2 CHICKEN BREASTS, SKIN REMOVED AND CHOPPED INTO ½-INCH PIECES
- ¼ CUP ALL-PURPOSE FLOUR
- 4 CUPS CHICKEN STOCK
- 4 EARS OF CORN, KERNELS REMOVED
- 1 14 OZ. CAN KIDNEY BEANS, RINSED AND DRAINED
- 1 CUP HEAVY CREAM
- 3 TABLESPOONS PARSLEY, LEAVES REMOVED AND CHOPPED

    SALT AND PEPPER, TO TASTE

CHICKEN CHILI

YIELD: 4 TO 6 SERVINGS / ACTIVE TIME: 15 MINUTES / TOTAL TIME: 45 MINUTES

Typically, chili is made with ground beef or pork, but this is a lovely version made with chicken. It's a little bit lighter but still plenty hearty.

1. In a large saucepan, add the oil and cook over medium-high heat until warm.

2. Add the chicken and onion and cook for 5 minutes, or until the chicken is evenly browned.

3. Add the garlic and cook for 2 minutes. Add the chicken stock, chilies, cumin, oregano, and cayenne. Bring to a boil, reduce heat so that the soup simmers, and then add 2 cans of kidney beans.

4. Place the remaining can of kidney beans in a small bowl. Use a potato masher to mash the beans and then add this to the soup to help thicken it.

5. Simmer for 15 to 20 minutes, or until the chicken is cooked through.

6. Meanwhile, preheat your oven to the broiler setting.

7. Once the chili is cooked, sprinkle Monterey Jack cheese and the jalapeño slices on top. Place saucepan under the broiler and melt the cheese. Serve in warm bowls.

INGREDIENTS:

2	TABLESPOONS VEGETABLE OIL
1	POUND CHICKEN BREASTS, SKIN REMOVED AND CUT INTO ½-INCH PIECES
1	ONION, CHOPPED
2	GARLIC CLOVES, MINCED
4	CUPS CHICKEN STOCK
1	4 OZ. CAN GREEN CHILIES, CHOPPED
2	TEASPOONS CUMIN
1	TABLESPOON OREGANO, LEAVES REMOVED AND CHOPPED
1	TEASPOON CAYENNE PEPPER
3	14 OZ. CANS KIDNEY BEANS
	SALT AND PEPPER, TO TASTE
	MONTEREY JACK CHEESE, SHREDDED, FOR GARNISH
	JALAPEÑO, SLICED, FOR GARNISH

RABBIT *and* LENTIL STEW

YIELD: 4 SERVINGS / ACTIVE TIME: 20 MINUTES / TOTAL TIME: 1 HOUR

Rabbit is a great, flavorful meat. Cooked in this way, it becomes very tender, and makes the soup very hearty.

1. Place the flour in a mixing bowl and dredge the pieces of rabbit meat in the flour until evenly coated.

2. Warm a medium saucepan over medium heat. Add the bacon and cook for 5 minutes, or until bacon is crispy.

3. Use a slotted spoon to remove the bacon and set aside.

4. Add the rabbit and cook for 5 minutes, or until browned. Use a slotted spoon to remove rabbit and add to bacon.

5. Add the onion and garlic to the saucepan. Cook for 5 minutes, or until soft.

6. Add the red wine and cook for 5 minutes, or until it has been reduced by half.

7. Add the stock, lentils, bay leaf, and rosemary, and bring to a boil. Reduce heat so that the soup simmers, return the bacon and rabbit to the saucepan, and cook for 30 minutes, or until the lentils are tender.

8. Season with lemon juice, salt, and pepper. Serve in warmed bowls with crusty bread.

INGREDIENTS:

¼ CUP FLOUR

2 WHOLE RABBITS, TENDERLOINS AND THIGHS REMOVED, AND CUT INTO ½-INCH PIECES

6 PIECES OF THICK-CUT BACON, CHOPPED

1 ONION, CHOPPED

1 GARLIC CLOVE, MINCED

1 CUP RED WINE

4 CUPS CHICKEN STOCK

1 CUP LE PUY LENTILS

1 BAY LEAF

1 TEASPOON ROSEMARY, LEAVES REMOVED AND CHOPPED

1 TABLESPOON LEMON JUICE

SALT AND PEPPER, TO TASTE

WALNUT SOUP *with* CHIVE *and* SHALLOT OIL

YIELD: 4 SERVINGS / ACTIVE TIME: 20 MINUTES / TOTAL TIME: 1 HOUR AND 15 MINUTES

One of the great things about soup is that you can make one out of practically anything. This soup certainly doesn't fall into a classic category, but it's delicious. If available, make this with black walnuts.

1. In a large saucepan, add the butter, shallot, and celery and cook over medium heat for 3 minutes, or until soft.

2. Sprinkle in the flour and cook for 3 minutes.

3. Add the chicken stock, bay leaf, salt, pepper, and the toasted walnuts and bring to a boil.

4. Reduce heat so that the soup simmers. Add 2 cups of the cream and simmer for 30 minutes.

5. Remove the bay leaf. Transfer the soup to a food processor, puree until smooth, and then strain through a fine sieve.

6. Return the soup to the pan, bring to a simmer, and adjust the seasoning.

7. Serve in warm bowls and garnish with the Chive and Shallot Oil and walnuts.

CHIVE AND SHALLOT OIL

1. In a small saucepan, add the oil and cook over medium heat until warm.

2. Add the shallot and cook for 5 minutes, or until soft.

3. Remove from heat and add chives. Transfer to a container until ready to serve.

INGREDIENTS:

- 3   TABLESPOONS BUTTER
- 1   TABLESPOON SHALLOT, MINCED
- 1   CELERY STALK, FINELY CHOPPED
- 3   TABLESPOONS ALL-PURPOSE FLOUR
- 6   CUPS CHICKEN STOCK
- 1   BAY LEAF
- 1   TABLESPOON SALT
-    PINCH OF BLACK PEPPER
- 1   CUP WALNUTS, TOASTED
- 2   CUPS HEAVY CREAM
-    GRATED WALNUTS, FOR GARNISH
-    CHIVE AND SHALLOT OIL, FOR GARNISH

CHIVE AND SHALLOT OIL

- ½   CUPS VEGETABLE OIL
- 1   SHALLOT, MINCED
- 1   TABLESPOON CHIVES, CHOPPED

BUTTERNUT SQUASH, QUINOA, *and* CHICKEN SOUP

YIELD: 4 SERVINGS / ACTIVE TIME: 20 MINUTES / TOTAL TIME: 1 HOUR AND 15 MINUTES

This is a great post-workout meal, thanks to the healthy carbs from the sweet potato, the superfood quinoa, and protein from the chicken. And, it tastes good. Beats any protein shake!

1. Preheat oven to 375°F.

2. Place butternut squash on baking tray, sprinkle with oil and place in oven flesh side down for 30 minutes, or until the flesh is very tender.

3. Meanwhile, in a heavy-bottom pan warm the remaining oil over medium heat.

4. Add the chicken breast and cook for 5 minutes, or until evenly browned. Remove with a slotted spoon, and set aside.

5. Add the onion and cook for 5 minutes or until soft.

6. Add the garlic and cook for an additional 2 minutes.

7. Add 3 cups of the stock, stewed tomatoes, and oregano and bring to a boil, then reduce to a simmer.

8. Scoop the cooked flesh from the baked butternut squash, add to a food processor with the remaining chicken stock, and puree. and add with the remaining chicken stock in food processor and puree.

9. Add the butternut squash puree, chicken, and quinoa to the simmering broth and simmer for 15 minutes or until the quinoa is tender.

10. Season with salt and pepper and serve in warmed bowls.

INGREDIENTS:

1	BUTTERNUT SQUASH, HALVED AND SEEDED
3	TABLESPOONS EXTRA VIRGIN OLIVE OIL
2	CHICKEN BREASTS, CUT INTO ½ INCH CUBES
1	ONION, CHOPPED
2	GARLIC CLOVES, MINCED
4	CUPS CHICKEN STOCK
1	14 OUNCE CAN CHOPPED STEWED TOMATOES
1	OREGANO SPRIG, LEAVES REMOVED AND CHOPPED
⅔	CUP QUINOA
	SALT AND PEPPER

BEEF

Beef is a magical protein that adds a lot of depth to the flavor profile of whatever soup it appears in. As the cuts are typically of lesser quality, they require long cooking to become tender. But these lesser quality cuts are your friend—not only are they less expensive, the requisite cook time adds a ton of flavor to the dish. This boost makes beef a popular ingredient in soups around the world—whether it be the various chilis of America, or Pho from Vietnam.

CHILI CON CARNE

YIELD: 4 TO 6 SERVINGS / ACTIVE TIME: 20 MINUTES / TOTAL TIME: 2 HOURS

This lovely chili is great with the melted mozzarella on top and tortilla chips on the side. If you don't want chips, you can also serve with rice.

1. In a large saucepan, add the oil and cook over medium heat until warm.

2. Add the green bell pepper and onion, and cook for 5 minutes, or until soft.

3. Add the ground beef and cook for 10 minutes, or until nicely browned.

4. Add the bouillon cubes and red wine, and cook for 2 minutes.

5. Add the stewed tomatoes, garlic, tomato paste, paprika, chili powder, cayenne pepper, basil, oregano, parsley, and Tabasco™ and bring to a boil.

6. Reduce heat to the lowest setting, cover, and cook for 1 hour, stirring occasionally.

7. Add the kidney beans and cook for an additional 15 minutes.

8. In a mixing bowl, combine the flour, cornmeal, and water. Add this mixture to the chili and cook for an additional 10 minutes. The chili should be nice and thick at this point.

9. Preheat your oven to the broiler setting.

10. Once chili is cooked, sprinkle a healthy amount of mozzarella on top and place the saucepan under the broiler until the cheese is melted. Serve in warmed bowls with tortilla chips.

INGREDIENTS:

- ¼ CUP VEGETABLE OIL
- 1 GREEN BELL PEPPER, CHOPPED
- 1 ONION, PEELED AND CHOPPED
- 2 POUNDS GROUND BEEF
- 2 BEEF BOUILLON CUBES, CRUSHED
- 1 CUP RED WINE
- 2 14 OZ. CANS STEWED TOMATOES, CHOPPED
- 2 GARLIC CLOVES, MINCED
- 6 TABLESPOONS TOMATO PASTE
- 1 TEASPOON PAPRIKA
- 2 TEASPOONS CHILI POWDER
- 1 TEASPOON CAYENNE POWDER
- 2 TEASPOONS BASIL, LEAVES REMOVED AND CHOPPED
- 1 TEASPOON OREGANO, LEAVES REMOVED AND CHOPPED
- 2 TABLESPOONS PARSLEY, LEAVES REMOVED AND CHOPPED
- ½ TEASPOON TABASCO™
- 1 14 OZ. CAN KIDNEY BEANS
- 3 TABLESPOONS ALL-PURPOSE FLOUR
- 2 TABLESPOONS CORNMEAL
- ½ CUP WATER
- SALT AND PEPPER, TO TASTE
- MOZZARELLA, SHREDDED, FOR GARNISH

HONEY, HUCKLEBERRY, *and* VEAL SOUP

YIELD: 4 SERVINGS / ACTIVE TIME: 20 MINUTES / TOTAL TIME: 45 MINUTES

This sweet-and-sour soup is lovely and is both comforting and restorative.

1. In a medium saucepan, add the oil and cook over medium heat until warm.

2. Add the veal and cook for 5 minutes, or until nicely browned. Remove the veal from the pan and set aside.

3. Reduce the heat to low and add the onion and butter. Cook for 5 minutes, or until the onions are soft.

4. Add the veal stock and huckleberries. Bring to a boil, then reduce the heat so that the soup simmers. Cook for 20 minutes.

5. Return the veal to the pan and add the honey. Cook for 3 minutes, season with salt and pepper, and add more honey, if necessary. Serve in warmed bowls.

INGREDIENTS:

2   TABLESPOONS VEGETABLE OIL

1   POUND VEAL BUTT TENDERS, CUT INTO ½-INCH PIECES

1   LARGE ONION, PEELED AND THINLY SLICED

1   TABLESPOON BUTTER

4   CUPS VEAL STOCK

1   CUP FRESH HUCKLEBERRIES

4   TEASPOONS HONEY

    SALT AND PEPPER, TO TASTE

VENISON *and* BARLEY SOUP

YIELD: 4 TO 6 SERVINGS / ACTIVE TIME: 20 MINUTES / TOTAL TIME: 2 HOURS

Venison and vegetables cooked in a beef stock, alongside the chewy barley, make this soup perfect for a cold winter's day.

1. In a large saucepan, add the oil and cook over medium-high heat until warm. Add the venison and cook for 5 minutes, or until evenly browned. Remove the venison with a slotted spoon and set aside.

2. Add the onion, celery, and carrots and cook for 5 minutes, or until soft.

3. Add the red wine, garlic, chili powder, and cumin and cook until the wine is reduced by half.

4. Return the venison to the pan. Add the thyme, stock, and barley and bring to a boil.

5. Reduce heat so that the soup simmers. Cover and cook over low heat for 1 hour and 30 minutes, or until the venison is very tender.

6. Season with salt and pepper and serve in warmed bowls.

INGREDIENTS:

1   TABLESPOON VEGETABLE OIL

1¾ POUND VENISON SHOULDER, CUT INTO ½-INCH PIECES

1   ONION, PEELED AND CHOPPED

2   CELERY STALKS, CHOPPED

2   CARROTS, PEELED AND CHOPPED

½   CUP RED WINE

1   CLOVE OF GARLIC, MINCED

1   TEASPOON CHILI POWDER

1   TEASPOON CUMIN

2   SPRIGS OF THYME, LEAVES REMOVED AND CHOPPED

8   CUPS BEEF OR VEAL STOCK

8   OZ. PEARL BARLEY

    SALT AND PEPPER, TO TASTE

SANTA FE CHILI *with* CORNBREAD

YIELD: 4 SERVINGS / ACTIVE TIME: 45 MINUTES / TOTAL TIME: 2 HOURS AND 30 MINUTES

This is the perfect dish for a get-together. The cornbread recipe is adapted from a corn muffin we made at the Culinary Institute of America. It's nice and moist, to match my personal preference.

1. In a large saucepan, add the oil and beef shanks and cook over medium heat for 5 minutes on each side, or until lightly browned.

2. Remove the beef shanks from the pan and set aside. Add the onion and cook for 3 minutes.

3. Add the corn kernels, bell pepper, cumin, and garlic and cook for 3 minutes, or until the vegetables are soft.

4. Reduce heat and return the beef shanks to the pan. Add the tomato paste and stock and allow soup to simmer for 2 hours, or until the meat is tender.

5. Remove the beef shanks. Cut the meat from the bone and chop into ½-inch pieces. Return meat to the soup.

6. Add tomato and simmer for 10 minutes.

7. Skim any fat off the top of the soup. Add the red pepper flakes, Tabasco™, salt, and pepper and serve in bowls with the Cornbread and Spiced Butter.

CORNBREAD

1. Preheat oven to 375°F.

2. In a mixer, combine the egg, milk, and oil and mix on low speed.

3. Meanwhile, sieve your dry ingredients together.

4. Slowly incorporate the dry mixture into the egg mixture.

5. Pour the batter into a buttered and floured 8" cast-iron pan. Place in oven and cook for 30 minutes, or until a cake tester or toothpick comes out clean.

INGREDIENTS:

- 1 TABLESPOON VEGETABLE OIL
- 1 POUND BEEF SHANKS, BONE-IN
- 1 ONION, PEELED AND CHOPPED
- 1 CUP CORN KERNELS
- ½ CUP GREEN BELL PEPPER, CHOPPED
- ½ TEASPOON GROUND CUMIN
- 2 GARLIC CLOVES, MINCED
- 1 TABLESPOON TOMATO PASTE
- 6 CUPS BEEF OR VEAL STOCK
- 1 TOMATO, CONCASSE (SEE PAGE 89)
- ⅛ TEASPOON RED PEPPER FLAKES
- ⅛ TEASPOON TABASCO™

  SALT AND PEPPER, TO TASTE

TO SERVE:
CORNBREAD

SPICED BUTTER

CORNBREAD

- 1 LARGE EGG
- ¾ CUP MILK
- ½ CUP VEGETABLE OIL
- ½ CUP SUGAR, PLUS 3 TABLESPOONS
- 1 CUP ALL-PURPOSE FLOUR
- ⅓ CUP CORNMEAL, PLUS 2 TABLESPOONS
- 1 TEASPOON SALT
- 1 TEASPOON BAKING POWDER

SPICED BUTTER

1. Combine butter and spices in the bowl of a standing mixer and whip for 5 minutes.

2. Season to taste with salt and serve.

SPICED BUTTER

1	CUP BUTTER, SOFTENED
1	TEASPOON CINNAMON
½	TEASPOON GROUND GINGER
¼	TEASPOON GROUND CLOVES
¼	TEASPOON NUTMEG
	SALT, TO TASTE

CINCINNATI CHILI

YIELD: 4 TO 6 SERVINGS / ACTIVE TIME: 15 MINUTES / TOTAL TIME: 1 HOUR AND 30 MINUTES

The chocolate works as a seasoning here, rounding out the flavor rather than taking over.

1. In a medium saucepan, add the vegetable oil and cook over medium heat until warm.

2. Add the onion and cook for 5 minutes, or until soft.

3. Add the beef and use a wooden spoon to break it up as it cooks. Cook for 5 minutes, or until evenly browned.

4. Add the chili powder, cinnamon, cumin, allspice, cloves, bay leaves, beef stock, tomato sauce, vinegar, and cayenne pepper and bring to a boil.

5. Reduce heat to low, cover, and cook for 1 hour, stirring occasionally.

6. Right before serving, remove from heat, add the chocolate, and season with salt and pepper.

7. Place a bed of spaghetti in a bowl. Pour chili on top, garnish with cheddar cheese, additional spaghetti, and parsley and serve.

INGREDIENTS:

2 TABLESPOONS VEGETABLE OIL

1 ONION, PEELED AND CHOPPED

1½ POUNDS GROUND BEEF

2 TABLESPOONS CHILI POWDER, OR TO TASTE

1 TEASPOON CINNAMON

1 TEASPOON CUMIN

¼ TEASPOON ALLSPICE

¼ TEASPOON GROUND CLOVES

2 BAY LEAVES

2 CUPS BEEF STOCK

1 CUP TOMATO SAUCE

2 TABLESPOONS APPLE CIDER VINEGAR

¼ TEASPOON CAYENNE PEPPER

1 OZ. UNSWEETENED CHOCOLATE

SALT AND PEPPER, TO TASTE

CHEDDAR CHEESE, SHREDDED, FOR GARNISH

PARSLEY, CHOPPED, FOR GARNISH

TO SERVE:
SPAGHETTI, COOKED ACCORDING TO MANUFACTURER'S INSTRUCTIONS

BEEF *and* BRAISED CABBAGE SOUP
with HORSERADISH CREAM

D: 6 SERVINGS / ACTIVE TIME: 30 MINUTES / TOTAL TIME: 2 HOURS AND 20 MINUTES

Consider bringing this to your next pot luck dinner, as it's great with or without the steak. It also pairs well with game meats.

1. Preheat oven to 300°F.

2. In a mixing bowl, add the cabbage, onions, apple, brown sugar, garlic, nutmeg, caraway seeds, and vinegar with a ½ cup of the stock. Mix until well-combined.

3. Season with salt and pepper and transfer to a large, buttered casserole dish. Cover the pan and place it in the oven. Cook for 1 hour and 30 minutes, removing to stir the contents of the casserole dish.

4. Turn off the oven and open the oven door slightly.

5. When the dish has cooled slightly, remove it from the oven and set aside. Preheat oven to 450°F.

6. In a medium sauté pan, add the olive oil and warm over medium heat. Season the sirloin with salt and pepper and then add to pan. Cook until golden brown on both sides. Remove sirloin from the pan and set aside.

7. Spoon the cabbage dish into a large saucepan. Add the remaining stock and bring to a boil. Reduce heat so that the soup simmers.

8. Place the sirloin in the oven and cook until it is the desired level of doneness.

9. Remove the sirloin from the oven and let it stand for 5 minutes. Ladle the soup into serving bowls. Thinly slice the steak and place it on top of the soup. Serve with Horseradish Cream and watercress.

HORSERADISH CREAM

1. Combine the horseradish, vinegar, mustard, and 4 tablespoons of the cream in a mixing bowl.

2. Lightly whip the remaining cream and then fold this into the horseradish mixture. Season to taste and refrigerate until ready to serve.

INGREDIENTS:

- 2 POUNDS RED CABBAGE, CORE REMOVED, SHREDDED
- 2 ONIONS, PEELED AND FINELY SLICED
- 1 LARGE APPLE, PEELED, CORED, AND CHOPPED
- 3 TABLESPOONS SOFT BROWN SUGAR
- 2 GARLIC CLOVES, MINCED
- ¼ TEASPOON GRATED NUTMEG
- ½ TEASPOON CARAWAY SEEDS
- 3 TABLESPOONS APPLE CIDER VINEGAR
- 4 CUPS VEAL STOCK
- SALT AND PEPPER, TO TASTE
- 2 TABLESPOONS EXTRA VIRGIN OLIVE OIL
- 1½ POUNDS SIRLOIN STEAK, FAT REMOVED
- WATERCRESS, FOR GARNISH

TO SERVE:
HORSERADISH CREAM

HORSERADISH CREAM
- 2 TABLESPOONS FRESH HORSERADISH, PEELED AND GRATED
- 2 TEASPOONS WHITE WINE VINEGAR
- ½ TEASPOON DIJON MUSTARD
- 1 CUP HEAVY CREAM
- SALT AND PEPPER, TO TASTE

MEXICAN BEEF CHILI
with NACHOS

YIELD: 4 SERVINGS / ACTIVE TIME: 20 MINUTES / TOTAL TIME: 1 HOUR AND 15 MINUTES

Filled with beans, beef, and Mexican flavors, whip this up, open a couple of Coronas, and enjoy the game with your friends and family.

1. In a large pan, add the oil and the meat and cook over medium-high heat until the meat is golden-brown.

2. Reduce the heat. Add the onions, garlic, and chilies and cook for 5 minutes, or until soft.

3. Add the cayenne pepper and cumin, cook for 2 minutes, and then add the beef stock, bay leaves, and tomato paste.

4. Bring to a boil, reduce heat so that the soup simmers, and cook for 30 to 40 minutes, or until the meat is tender.

5. Meanwhile, preheat oven to 350°F.

6. Place ⅓ of the cannellini beans and black beans in a bowl and mash them with a fork.

7. Once the meat is tender, add the mashed beans, which will help thicken the soup.

8. On a baking tray, lay out the tortilla chips. Sprinkle with cheese and jalapeño slices, and place in the oven. Cook for 5 minutes, or until cheese is melted. Remove from oven and top with sour cream and cilantro.

9. Add the remaining beans to the soup. Adjust seasoning to taste and then serve in warmed bowls with the nachos.

INGREDIENTS:

- 3 TABLESPOONS EXTRA VIRGIN OLIVE OIL
- 16 OZ. BEEF ROUND ROAST, CUT INTO PIECES
- 3 ONIONS, PEELED AND CHOPPED
- 3 GARLIC CLOVES, MINCED
- 2 RED CHILIES, SEEDED AND FINELY CHOPPED
- 1 TEASPOON CAYENNE PEPPER
- 1 TEASPOON GROUND CUMIN
- 6 CUPS BEEF OR VEAL STOCK
- 2 BAY LEAVES
- 3 TABLESPOONS TOMATO PASTE
- 1 14 OZ. CAN CANNELLINI BEANS, DRAINED AND RINSED
- 1 14 OZ. CAN BLACK BEANS, DRAINED AND RINSED
- 1 BAG TORTILLA CHIPS
- 8 OZ. MONTEREY JACK CHEESE, GRATED
- 1 JALAPEÑO, SLICED
- CILANTRO, CHOPPED
- SOUR CREAM
- SALT AND PEPPER, TO TASTE

TOMATO *and* BEEF SOUP

YIELD: 4 SERVINGS / ACTIVE TIME: 20 MINUTES / TOTAL TIME: 45 MINUTES

A great soup for your kids. To me, it could be called hamburger soup, as this is what it tastes like. However, Tomato and Beef sounds just a bit more elegant.

1. Preheat oven to 350°F.

2. In a medium saucepan, add 1 tablespoon of the oil and the 8 ounces of chopped steak. Cook over medium heat, turning quickly to brown all sides. Remove from the pan and set aside.

3. Add the stock and bring to a boil.

4. Meanwhile, in a sauté pan, add the other tablespoon of oil and the whole piece of sirloin. Cook over medium heat, while turning once, until both sides are golden brown. Place the sirloin in the oven and cook to desired level of doneness. Remove from oven and let stand.

5. Add the tomato paste, tomatoes, and sugar to the stock. Add the sautéed pieces of sirloin, bring the soup to a boil and then reduce heat so that the soup simmers. Cook for 2 minutes.

6. In a mixing bowl, combine the cornstarch and the cold water and mix until they form a paste.

7. Slowly add the cornstarch paste to the soup, stirring constantly until the soup thickens.

8. Transfer the soup to a food processor. Add the Worcestershire sauce and the Dijon mustard. Puree the soup and then strain through a fine sieve.

9. Season the soup with cayenne pepper, salt, and pepper. Pour into warmed bowls.

10. Drizzle sesame oil over each portion. Garnish with scallions and toasted sesame seeds, and serve with the piece of sirloin.

INGREDIENTS:

- 2 TABLESPOONS VEGETABLE OIL
- 16 OZ. SIRLOIN STEAK, HALF CUT INTO ¼-INCH PIECES, THE OTHER HALF LEFT WHOLE
- 4 CUPS VEAL STOCK
- 2 TABLESPOONS TOMATO PASTE
- 6 TOMATOES, CONCASSE (SEE PAGE 89) AND CHOPPED
- 2 TEASPOONS SUGAR
- 1 TABLESPOON CORNSTARCH
- 1 TABLESPOON COLD WATER
- 1 TABLESPOON WORCESTERSHIRE SAUCE
- 1 TABLESPOON DIJON MUSTARD
- ⅛ TEASPOON CAYENNE PEPPER, OR TO TASTE

SALT AND PEPPER, TO TASTE

SESAME OIL, FOR GARNISH

SCALLIONS, WHITE PART, THINLY SLICED, FOR GARNISH

TO SERVE:
TOASTED SESAME SEEDS

TOASTED SESAME SEEDS
- 1 TEASPOON VEGETABLE OIL
- ¼ CUP SESAME SEEDS

SALT AND PEPPER

TOASTED SESAME SEEDS

1. In a nonstick pan, add the oil and cook over medium heat until warm.

2. Add the sesame seeds to the pan and cook, while stirring constantly, until golden-brown.

3. Remove seeds from the pan and set to drain on a paper towel.

4. Season with salt and pepper, and serve.

SPICY EGGPLANT
and BEEF SOUP

YIELD: 4 SERVINGS / ACTIVE TIME: 45 MINUTES / TOTAL TIME: 2 HOURS AND 30 MINUTES

This is a Khmer dish, and its sweet, spicy, and tangy flavor comes from the Tuk Trey and the jaggery.

1. Soak the dried chilies in water for 30 minutes.

2. In a large saucepan, add the stock, ginger, cinnamon, star anise, peppercorns, cardamom, lime leaf, lemongrass, and galangal root. Bring to a boil, add the brisket, cover, and reduce heat so that the soup simmers. Cook for 1 hour.

3. Remove the lid and add the soy sauce and Tuk Trey.

4. Simmer for 45 minutes, uncovered, until the stock is reduced by half.

5. Remove the brisket. Skim any fat from the top, strain the stock through a fine sieve, and set aside.

6. Tear or cut the brisket into thin strips.

7. Drain the soaked chilies and finely chop, removing any seeds.

8. In a medium saucepan, add the oil and cook over medium heat until warm. Add the shallot and chopped chilies and cook for 5 minutes.

9. Add the strained broth to the saucepan and bring to a simmer.

10. Add the tamarind extract, jaggery, brisket, and eggplant. Cook for an additional 20 minutes.

11. Season the soup to taste. Stir in the curry leaves and watercress and cook for an additional 2 minutes.

12. Pour into warmed bowls, garnish with the curry leaves, chopped red chilies, and toasted peanuts, and serve.

INGREDIENTS:

2	DRIED NEW MEXICO CHILIES
8	CUPS VEAL OR BEEF STOCK
	3-INCH PIECE OF GINGER, SLICED
1	CINNAMON STICK
2	STAR ANISE
½	TEASPOON BLACK PEPPERCORNS
4	CARDAMOM PODS, SEEDS REMOVED AND CHOPPED
1	LIME LEAF
1	STALK OF LEMONGRASS, BRUISED
	1-INCH PIECE OF GALANGAL ROOT, CHOPPED
1	POUND BRISKET
1	TABLESPOON SOY SAUCE
3	TABLESPOONS TUK TREY (SEE RECIPE ON NEXT PAGE)
1	TABLESPOON VEGETABLE OIL
1	SHALLOT, FINELY CHOPPED
2	TABLESPOONS TAMARIND EXTRACT
1	TABLESPOON JAGGERY
8	THAI EGGPLANTS, STEMS REMOVED, CUT INTO ¼-INCH SLICES
1	TEASPOON CURRY LEAVES, CHOPPED
½	BUNCH OF WATERCRESS
	SALT AND PEPPER, TO TASTE
	CURRY LEAVES, CHOPPED, FOR GARNISH
	RED CHILIES, SEEDS REMOVED, SLICED, FOR GARNISH
	TOASTED PEANUTS, FOR GARNISH

Continued . . .

TUK TREY

Add all the ingredients to a mixing bowl and stir until well-combined. Place in refrigerator until ready to use.

TUK TREY

1	TEASPOON SUGAR
1½	TABLESPOONS FISH SAUCE
	JUICE OF ½ LIME
2	TABLESPOONS WATER
1	GARLIC CLOVE, MINCED
¼	CUP ROASTED PEANUTS, CHOPPED
½	RED CHILI, SEEDS REMOVED, FINELY CHOPPED

MOROCCAN BEEF *and* BEAN STEW
with HONEY-GLAZED MOROCCAN CARROTS

YIELD: 4 SERVINGS / ACTIVE TIME: 45 MINUTES / TOTAL TIME: 14 HOURS

Also known as harira, the smell of this soup permeates the streets of Morocco and Algeria during the holy month of Ramadan. It cooks throughout the day until the cannon fires at sunset, signaling the fast is over for the day.

1. In a large saucepan, bring 6 cups of the water to a boil. Place the marrow bone in the pan and cook for 5 minutes. Remove the marrow bone and discard the water. Run the marrow bone under cold water and then return to the pan.

2. Add the sirloin, onion, kidney beans, and remaining water to the pan. Bring to a boil, then reduce heat and simmer for 1 hour.

3. Add the drained lentils, tomato, celery, tomato paste, ginger, and saffron threads. Simmer for an additional 15 minutes, adding water if necessary, or until the lentils start to soften.

4. In a small bowl, add your flour. While whisking continuously, slowly add ½ cup of the broth slowly, taking care not to create any lumps.

5. Add another ½ cup of simmering broth to the flour mixture and then set aside.

6. Add the rice to the broth and cook for 20 minutes, or until rice is cooked.

7. Just before serving, add the flour mixture to the soup, stirring vigorously until well-combined.

8. Add the cilantro and parsley and cook for 3 minutes.

9. Remove marrow bone and ladle into warmed bowls. Serve with Honey-Glazed Moroccan Carrots and Charred Lemon Wedges.

INGREDIENTS:

- 12 CUPS WATER
- 1 MARROW BONE
- 12 OZ. BEEF SIRLOIN, CUT INTO ½-INCH PIECES
- 1 LARGE ONION, CHOPPED
- ¼ CUP DRIED KIDNEY BEANS, SOAKED IN WATER OVERNIGHT
- 4 TABLESPOONS BROWN LENTILS, RINSED
- 2 TOMATOES, CHOPPED
- 1 CELERY STALK, CHOPPED
- 2 TEASPOONS TOMATO PASTE
- ⅛ TEASPOON GROUND GINGER
- ⅛ TEASPOON SAFFRON THREADS
- 3 TABLESPOONS ALL-PURPOSE FLOUR
- 4 TABLESPOONS LONG GRAIN RICE
- 4 TABLESPOONS CILANTRO, CHOPPED
- 2 TABLESPOONS PARSLEY, CHOPPED
- SALT AND PEPPER, TO TASTE

TO SERVE:
HONEY-GLAZED MOROCCAN CARROTS

CHARRED LEMON WEDGES

HONEY-GLAZED MOROCCAN CARROTS

1. Preheat oven to 400°F.

2. In a bowl, add the olive oil, honey, cumin, ginger, and cinnamon and stir until combined.

3. Add the carrots and toss to coat.

4. Place the carrots on a baking tray lined with parchment. Season with salt and pepper, place in the oven, and roast for 15 minutes, or until tender and lightly golden-brown. Remove from the oven and serve.

CHARRED LEMON WEDGES

In a dry, non-stick pan, add the lemons and cook over medium heat on each open side for 3 minutes, or until charred. Remove, let cool, and serve.

INGREDIENTS (CONTINUED):

HONEY-GLAZED MOROCCAN CARROTS

1	TABLESPOON EXTRA VIRGIN OLIVE OIL
2	TEASPOONS HONEY
½	TEASPOON CUMIN
¼	TEASPOON GROUND GINGER
¼	TEASPOON CINNAMON
2	CARROTS, PEELED AND CHOPPED
	SALT AND PEPPER, TO TASTE

CHARRED LEMON WEDGES

2	LEMONS, CUT INTO 8 PIECES

CLEAR OXTAIL SOUP

YIELD: 4 SERVINGS / ACTIVE TIME: 25 MINUTES / TOTAL TIME: 3 HOURS AND 45 MINUTES

I'm thrilled to share this recipe with you, since there's a certain joy that serving a clear consommé can provide. I love most slow-cooking meats, but the oxtail is such a delicacy if cooked properly. Ask your butcher about it—if they don't stock it, they can certainly get it.

1. In a large saucepan, add the oil and cook over medium heat until warm. Add the oxtail and cook for 5 minutes, or until brown.

2. Add the carrots, onions, and chopped celery and cook for 5 minutes, or until soft.

3. Add the stock, tomato, and sachet d'epices. Bring to a boil, reduce the heat so that the soup simmers, and cook for 2 hours, or until the oxtail is tender.

4. Pour the soup through a fine sieve. Set the solids aside and let the stock cool in the refrigerator.

5. Meanwhile, bring 8 cups of water to boil. Add the finely diced celery, carrots, celery root, and parsnip, and cook for 5 minutes, or until tender. Remove from the pan and submerge in an ice bath.

6. Remove the meat from the oxtail and chop finely.

7. Prepare the raft: in a bowl add the egg whites, remaining water, white wine vinegar, ground beef, and salt, and whisk until combined.

8. When the stock is completely cold, skim the fat from the top.

9. In a stockpot, add the chilled stock and the egg white mixture. Whisk until combined and then slowly bring it to a simmer, with the egg white mixture creating a raft that will clarify the stock. Simmer on the lowest possible heat for 45 minutes.

10. Ladle the stock through a cheesecloth. Return to a clean pan, add the finely diced vegetables and oxtail, and season with salt and pepper. Return to a boil, add the sherry, serve immediately in warmed bowls and garnish with chives and Horseradish Oil (see next page).

INGREDIENTS:

2 TABLESPOONS VEGETABLE OIL

2½ POUNDS OXTAIL, DISJOINTED

2 CARROTS, PEELED AND CHOPPED

1 ONION, PEELED AND CHOPPED

2 CELERY STALKS, CHOPPED, PLUS 1 CUP, FINELY DICED

6 CUPS VEAL OR BEEF STOCK

1 TOMATO, CHOPPED

1 SACHET D'EPICES (SEE PAGE 90)

10 CUPS WATER

1 CUP CARROTS, FINELY DICED

1 CUP CELERY ROOT, FINELY DICED

1 CUP PARSNIPS, FINELY DICED

3 EGG WHITES

⅛ CUP WHITE WINE VINEGAR

4 OZ. GROUND BEEF

SALT AND PEPPER, TO TASTE

1 OZ. SHERRY

FRESH CHIVES, CHOPPED, FOR GARNISH

HORSERADISH OIL, FOR GARNISH

Continued . . .

HORSERADISH OIL

1. In a small saucepan, add the horseradish, lemon, and oil. Cook over medium heat for 5 minutes.

2. Turn off the heat and let stand for at least an hour.

3. Strain through a fine sieve and reserve the oil until ready to serve.

INGREDIENTS (CONTINUED):

HORSERADISH OIL

½   CUP FRESH HORSERADISH, PEELED AND GRATED

ZEST OF ½ A LEMON

1   CUP EXTRA VIRGIN OLIVE OIL

HUNGARIAN GOULASH
with CUCUMBER SALAD

YIELD: 4 SERVINGS / ACTIVE TIME: 30 MINUTES / TOTAL TIME

Goulash is a soup of meat and vegetables, seasoned with paprika a
ing in medieval Hungary, Goulash is an extremely popular meal

1. Preheat oven to 350°F.

2. Pour the flour into a bowl and then dredge the pieces of meat in the flour until coated.

3. In a large saucepan, add the oil and cook over medium heat until warm. Add the onion, pepper, carrots, and celery and cook for 5 minutes, or until soft.

4. Add the meat and cook until browned.

5. Add the red wine and cook for 5 minutes.

6. Add the paprika, tomato paste, thyme, and parsley and cook for 2 minutes.

7. Add the stock, diced tomatoes, and Worcestershire sauce. Bring soup to a simmer, cover, and place the saucepan in the oven. Cook for 45 minutes.

8. Remove cover, stir, and cook for an additional 45 minutes, or until the steak is tender.

9. Season with salt, pepper, and cayenne pepper, ladle into bowls and serve with Cucumber Salad, sour cream, and crusty bread.

CUCUMBER SALAD

1. Slice cucumber into half-moons and place into a mixing bowl with the salt. Stir until combined and then let stand for 1 hour.

2. Transfer cucumbers in a colander and press with a paper towel to remove any excess water.

3. Transfer the cucumbers into a mixing bowl. Add the sour cream, vinegar, and garlic, stir to combine, and place in refrigerator for 1 hour.

4. Before serving, adjust seasoning and then add dill and paprika.

INGREDIENTS:

- ¼   **CUP FLOUR**
- 1   **POUND BEEF CHUCK ROAST, CUBED**
- 2   **TABLESPOONS VEGETABLE OIL**
- 1   **LARGE ONION, PEELED AND CHOPPED**
- 1   **GREEN BELL PEPPER, SEEDS REMOVED, CHOPPED**
- 2   **CARROTS, PEELED AND CHOPPED**
- 1   **CELERY STALK, CHOPPED**
- 1   **CUP RED WINE**
- 2   **TEASPOONS PAPRIKA**
- 3   **TABLESPOONS TOMATO PASTE**
- 1   **TEASPOON THYME, LEAVES REMOVED AND CHOPPED**
- 1   **TEASPOON PARSLEY, LEAVES REMOVED AND CHOPPED**
- 4   **CUPS BEEF STOCK**
- 1   **14 OZ. CAN DICED TOMATOES**
- 1   **TABLESPOON WORCESTERSHIRE SAUCE**
-   **SALT AND PEPPER, TO TASTE**
- ¼   **TEASPOON CAYENNE PEPPER**

TO SERVE:
CUCUMBER SALAD

SOUR CREAM

CUCUMBER SALAD
- 1   **MEDIUM CUCUMBER, PEELED, HALVED, AND SEEDED**
- ½   **TEASPOON SALT**
- 2   **TABLESPOONS SOUR CREAM**
- 1   **TEASPOON WHITE VINEGAR**
- ⅛   **TEASPOON GARLIC, MINCED**
-   **SALT AND PEPPER, TO TASTE**
- 1   **TABLESPOON DILL, FINELY CHOPPED**
- ½   **TEASPOON PAPRIKA**

BEEF *and* LAMB STEW

YIELD: 4 SERVINGS / ACTIVE TIME: 30 MINUTES / TOTAL TIME: 14 HOURS AND 30 MINUTES

This stew is a traditional Jewish chamin, a stew-like dish served at the Shabbat morning meal in Sephardi homes. This recipe combines meats and chickpeas and cooks slowly in the oven for over an hour, in order to get every ounce of flavor into the soup.

1. Preheat oven to 250°F.

2. Drain the chickpeas. Place the oil in a Dutch oven and cook over medium heat until warm.

3. Add the onion, garlic, parsnip, carrots, cumin, turmeric, and ginger and cook for 2 minutes.

4. Add the brisket and lamb and cook for 5 minutes, or until all sides are browned.

5. Add the stock and bring to a simmer.

6. Add the chickpeas, potato, zucchini, tomatoes, lentils, bay leaf, and cilantro.

7. Cover, place in the oven, and cook for 1 hour and 15 minutes, or until the meat is tender.

8. Begin cooking the Long-Grain Rice (recipe below) 30 minutes before serving.

9. Once the stew is ready, remove the lid and skim the fat from the top of the soup. Season with salt and pepper and ladle into warmed bowls with the rice. Serve with lemon wedges and garnish with the chilies.

LONG-GRAIN RICE

1. In a medium saucepan, bring the water and salt to a boil.

2. Add the rice, reduce heat to low, cover, and cook for 15 minutes while stirring occasionally.

3. Turn off flame, and let stand for 5 minutes before serving.

INGREDIENTS:

½	CUP CHICKPEAS, SOAKED OVERNIGHT
1½	TABLESPOONS EXTRA VIRGIN OLIVE OIL
1	SMALL ONION, PEELED AND CHOPPED
5	GARLIC CLOVES, MINCED
¾	CUP PARSNIP, SLICED
¾	CUP CARROTS, SLICED
1	TEASPOON CUMIN
¼	TEASPOON TURMERIC
1½	TABLESPOONS FRESH GINGER ROOT, PEELED AND MINCED
5	OZ. BRISKET, CLEANED AND CUT INTO ¼-INCH CUBES
5	OZ. LAMB SHOULDER, CLEANED AND CUT INTO ¼-INCH CUBES
4	CUPS BEEF OR VEAL STOCK
1	SMALL POTATO, PEELED AND CUT INTO CHUNKS
1	SMALL ZUCCHINI, SLICED
8	OZ. FRESH TOMATO, DICED
2	TABLESPOONS BROWN LENTILS
1	BAY LEAF
½	BUNCH OF FRESH CILANTRO, CHOPPED
	SALT AND PEPPER, TO TASTE
	LEMON WEDGES, FOR GARNISH
	FRESH CHILIES, CHOPPED, FOR GARNISH

TO SERVE:
LONG-GRAIN RICE

LONG-GRAIN RICE

2	CUPS WATER
1	TEASPOON SALT
1	CUP LONG-GRAIN RICE

BEEF, BARLEY, *and* PORTOBELLO MUSHROOM SOUP

YIELD: 4 TO 6 SERVINGS / ACTIVE TIME: 20 MINUTES / TOTAL TIME: 2 HOURS

This simple and easy soup is even better the next day, so be sure to make enough. I like to enjoy it with a serving of warmed cheesy polenta.

1. In a large sauce pan, warm oil on medium-high heat.

2. Add the beef and cook for 5 minutes, or until evenly browned, remove with a slotted spoon and reserve.

3. Add the onion, celery, and carrots and cook for 5 minutes or until soft.

4. Add the red wine, garlic, and thyme and reduce by half.

5. Add the seared beef, the stock, and the barley and bring to a boil.

6. Reduce to a simmer, cover, and cook on low heat for 1 hour and 30 minutes.

7. Add the mushrooms and cook for 10 minutes or until the beef is very tender.

8. Season with salt and pepper and serve in warmed bowls.

INGREDIENTS:

1 TABLESPOON VEGETABLE OIL

1¾ POUND BEEF STEW MEAT, CUT INTO 1 INCH PIECES

1 ONION, CHOPPED

2 CELERY STALKS, CHOPPED

2 CARROTS, PEELED AND CHOPPED

½ CUP RED WINE

1 GARLIC CLOVE, MINCED

2 SPRIGS THYME, LEAVES REMOVED AND CHOPPED

8 CUPS BEEF OR VEAL STOCK

¾ CUP PEARL BARLEY

1 POUND PORTOBELLO MUSHROOMS, SLICED

SALT AND PEPPER, TO TASTE

CORNED BEEF *and* BARLEY SOUP
with HORSERADISH CRÈME FRAICHE

YIELD: 4 SERVINGS / ACTIVE TIME: 20 MINUTES / TOTAL TIME: 1 HOUR AND 30 MINUTES

Corned beef is a salt-cured beef product that is typically from the beef round primal cut, and it is positively delicious in this soup.

1. In a medium saucepan, add 2 tablespoons of the oil and cook over medium heat until warmed. Add the corned beef and cook, while turning, until it is nice and brown all over.

2. Add stock, salt and pepper, and sachet d'epices and allow the soup to simmer for 1 hour, skimming any impurities from the top while cooking.

3. Remove the corned beef, strain the broth through a fine sieve, and set both aside.

4. In a separate saucepan, add the remaining oil and cook over medium heat until warm. Add the onion and celery and cook for 5 minutes, or until soft.

5. While the onion and celery is cooking, chop the beef into ½-inch pieces.

6. Add the broth, corned beef, and barley and bring to a boil. Reduce heat so that the soup simmers and cook for 15 minutes, or until the lentils are tender.

7. Add the tomato and cook for 10 more minutes. Season with salt and pepper, add the parsley, and then serve in warmed bowls with the Horseradish Crème Fraiche.

HORSERADISH CRÈME FRAICHE

In a mixing bowl, add the crème fraiche and use a whisk to whip it until soft peaks begin to form. Add the horseradish and gently stir until combined. Season with salt and pepper and serve.

INGREDIENTS:

3	TABLESPOONS VEGETABLE OIL
1	POUND CORNED BEEF
4	CUPS VEAL STOCK
	SALT AND PEPPER, TO TASTE
1	SACHET D'EPICES (SEE PAGE 90)
1	ONION, PEELED AND FINELY CHOPPED
1	CELERY STALK, FINELY CHOPPED
½	CUP BARLEY
1	TOMATO, CONCASSE (SEE PAGE 89)
2	TABLESPOONS PARSLEY, CHOPPED

TO SERVE:
HORSERADISH CRÈME FRAICHE

HORSERADISH CRÈME FRAICHE

1	CUP CRÈME FRAICHE
2	TABLESPOONS HORSERADISH, FINELY GRATED
	SALT AND PEPPER, TO TASTE

PORK

ork has a very neutral flavor, which makes it a perfect companion for the variety of ingredients used to make quality soup. A favorite all over the world, you'll find a number of preparations from around the globe in this chapter.

And while we search far and wide for quality recipes, you don't have to do the same to procure your pork. Chances are there's a great pig farmer right around your town, who treats their pigs well and provides them with quality feed needed to maximize the flavor of the pork. So when you feel inspired to try out one of these soups, head down to the farmers market and purchase some of the fresh, local pork available there.

PORK SINIGANG

YIELD: 4 SERVINGS / ACTIVE TIME: 15 MINUTES / TOTAL TIME: 1 HOUR

This Filipino soup is great for an appetizer, or you can add rice and serve it as a hearty main course. It has a nice sweet and salty taste thanks to the tamarind and the soy sauce.

1. In a medium saucepan, add the oil and cook over medium-high heat until warm. Add the pork chops and cook for 5 minutes, or until nicely browned. Add the onion and cook for 5 minutes, or until soft.

2. Add the ginger, tomatoes, stock, and tamarind extract and bring to a boil.

3. Reduce heat so that the soup simmers and cook for 30 minutes, or until the pork is tender and cooked through.

4. Add the soy sauce, fish sauce, and green beans and cook for 5 minutes.

5. Season with salt and pepper and serve in warm bowls.

INGREDIENTS:

1 TABLESPOON VEGETABLE OIL

1½ POUNDS PORK CHOPS, CUT INTO ½-INCH PIECES

1 ONION, CHOPPED

1-INCH PIECE OF GINGER, MINCED

2 PLUM TOMATOES, CUT INTO ½-INCH PIECES

6 CUPS HAM STOCK

1 TABLESPOON TAMARIND EXTRACT

1 TABLESPOON SOY SAUCE

2 TABLESPOONS FISH SAUCE

2 CUPS GREEN BEANS, EDGES TRIMMED, CUT INTO 1-INCH PIECES

SALT AND PEPPER, TO TASTE

TANUKI JIRU

YIELD: 4 SERVINGS / ACTIVE TIME: 20 MINUTES / TOTAL TIME: 40 MINUTES

This soup was traditionally made with raccoon in Japan, but nowadays pork is the go-to protein.

1. Trim the pork loin into thin slices. Cut those slices into 1-inch pieces.

2. Place the sesame oil in a medium saucepan and cook over medium heat until it starts to smoke.

3. Add the pork, burdock root/parsnips, daikon, and shiittake mushrooms. Cook for 5 minutes.

4. Once the pork is cooked through, add the fish stock and tofu.

5. Bring to a boil. Reduce heat so that the soup simmers and cook for 10 minutes.

6. Place the miso in a bowl. Add 4 tablespoons of the broth and stir to make a smooth paste.

7. Stir ⅓ of the miso mixture into the soup. Taste and add more if desired.

8. Ladle into bowls, garnish with scallions, and serve with Daikon Salad.

DAIKON SALAD

1. Place all of the ingredients in a mixing bowl and stir until combined.

2. Place in the refrigerator for at least 10 minutes before serving.

INGREDIENTS:

8	OZ. BONELESS PORK LOIN
2	TABLESPOONS SESAME OIL
	6-INCH PIECE OF BURDOCK ROOT, IF UNAVAILABLE USE PARSNIPS, PEELED AND SLICED
½	CUP DAIKON, CHOPPED
4	SHIITAKE MUSHROOMS, STALKS REMOVED AND SLICED
2½	CUPS FISH STOCK
¾	CUP TOFU, CHOPPED
4	TABLESPOONS MISO
	SALT AND PEPPER, TO TASTE
	SCALLIONS, CHOPPED, FOR GARNISH

TO SERVE:
DAIKON SALAD

DAIKON SALAD

	3-INCH PIECE DAIKON
1	TABLESPOON SESAME SEEDS, TOASTED
2	TABLESPOONS SCALLION GREENS, CHOPPED
1	TEASPOON SESAME OIL
1	TEASPOON SOY SAUCE

HAM *and* VEGETABLE SOUP
with LEEK OIL

YIELD: 4 SERVINGS / ACTIVE TIME: 35 MINUTES / TOTAL TIME: 1 HOUR AND 5 MINUTES

A soup for when you're sick of winter and ready for it to be over.

1. In a medium saucepan, add the olive oil and cook over medium heat until warm. Add the onion, pepper, zucchini, carrot, leeks, celery, potatoes, garlic, and thyme and cook for 10 minutes, or until soft.

2. Add the V8™ and cook for 5 minutes. Add the ham stock and simmer for 15 minutes. Season to taste with salt and pepper, garnish with the Leek Oil, and serve. For my preparation, although optional, I cloched the soup prior to serving and smoked it with hickory wood chips

LEEK OIL

1. In a medium saucepan, bring 4 cups of water to boil. Add the leeks and cook for 2 minutes. Add the spinach and cook for 2 minutes. Remove the leeks and spinach and submerge in ice water.

2. Remove the leeks and spinach, drain, and place in a food processor. Add the oil and puree for 3 minutes. Strain through a cheesecloth and reserve until ready to serve.

INGREDIENTS:

1   TABLESPOON EXTRA VIRGIN OLIVE OIL

1   ONION, DICED

½   CUP GREEN BELL PEPPER, SEEDS REMOVED AND DICED

½   CUP ZUCCHINI, DICED

½   CUP CARROT, PEELED AND DICED

½   CUP LEEKS, DICED, WHITE PART ONLY

½   CUP CELERY, DICED

½   CUP POTATOES, PEELED AND DICED

1   GARLIC CLOVE, MINCED

1   THYME SPRIG, LEAVES REMOVED AND CHOPPED

1   CUP V8™

4   CUPS HAM STOCK

    SALT AND PEPPER, TO TASTE

TO SERVE:
LEEK OIL

LEEK OIL

1   CUP LEEKS, GREENS ONLY, CHOPPED

1   CUP SPINACH

1   CUP VEGETABLE OIL

CARNE ADOVADA

YIELD: 4 TO 6 SERVINGS / ACTIVE TIME: 30 MINUTES / TOTAL TIME: 16 HOURS AND 30 MINUTES

This is a great chili that can serve a number of purposes. Serve with rice and beans or place it in tortillas and top with your favorites.

1. In a medium saucepan, add oil and cook over medium heat until warm.

2. Add the flour and cook for 5 minutes, or until a light golden brown

3. Stir in the chili powder and then slowly add the ham stock, stirring to prevent any lumps from forming.

4. Add the garlic, oregano, cumin, salt, and pepper and cook for 2 minutes. Remove from heat and let cool.

5. Place the pork in a large casserole pan. Pour the contents of the saucepan over it and stir until combined. Place in refrigerator to marinate overnight.

6. Preheat oven to 300°F. Place pork in the oven and cook for at least 4 hours, removing to stir occasionally. When the sauce has thickened and the meat is very tender, serve in warm bowls with rice, or place in tortillas and serve with your favorite taco toppings.

INGREDIENTS:

- 2 TABLESPOONS VEGETABLE OIL
- 3 TABLESPOONS ALL-PURPOSE FLOUR
- ¼ CUP NEW MEXICO CHILI POWDER
- 6 CUPS HAM STOCK
- 4 GARLIC CLOVES, MINCED
- 1 TABLESPOON OREGANO, LEAVES REMOVED AND CHOPPED
- ½ TEASPOON CUMIN
- SALT AND PEPPER, TO TASTE
- 2½ POUNDS PORK STEW MEAT, CUBED

POZOLE

YIELD: 8 SERVINGS / ACTIVE TIME: 30 MINUTES / TOTAL TIME: 14 HOURS AND 15 MINUTES

Pozole means "hominy," which is a key ingredient in this rich stew. This traditional Mexican soup once had ritual significance, in part because it is divine. When you're soaking the hominy, make sure you change the water a few times.

1. Place oil in a large saucepan and cook over medium-high heat until warm. Add pork and onion and season with salt and pepper. Cook, while stirring occasionally, for 15 minutes or until pork and onion are browned.

2. Add chipotles, hominy, thyme, and cumin.

3. Add water to cover everything by about an inch. Bring to a boil and then reduce heat so that the soup simmers.

4. Cook, while stirring occasionally, until the pork and hominy are tender, at least 1½ hours. Add more water if necessary.

5. Stir in the garlic and cook for a few more minutes. Adjust seasoning, ladle into bowls, and garnish with cilantro and lime wedges.

INGREDIENTS:

2 TABLESPOONS VEGETABLE OIL

2 POUNDS PORK BUTT, CUT INTO 1-INCH CHUNKS

1 LARGE ONION, CHOPPED

SALT AND PEPPER, TO TASTE

4 DRIED CHIPOTLE PEPPERS, HALVED, SEEDS REMOVED, CUT INTO ½-INCH PIECES

2 CUPS DRIED HOMINY, SOAKED FOR 12 HOURS

2 TABLESPOONS THYME, LEAVES REMOVED AND CHOPPED

2 TABLESPOONS CUMIN

2 TABLESPOONS GARLIC, MINCED

CILANTRO, CHOPPED, FOR GARNISH

LIME WEDGES, FOR GARNISH

HAM HOCK *and* COLLARD GREEN SOUP

YIELD: 4 SERVINGS / **ACTIVE TIME:** 30 MINUTES / **TOTAL TIME:** 1 HOUR AND 35 MINUTES

This is a filling soup. Here in Maine, collard greens are not that easy to come by, so for my preparation I used kale, and it came out delicious. When choosing ham hocks, ask your butcher for nice, meaty ones.

1. In a medium saucepan, add the water and salt and bring to a boil. Add your greens and cook for 4 minutes, or until soft. Remove with a slotted spoon and submerge in ice water. Set aside to dry.

2. In a large saucepan, add the oil and then the salt pork. Cook over medium heat until the salt pork is melted.

3. Add the onions and celery and cook for 5 minutes, or until soft.

4. Add the flour slowly, while stirring constantly, and cook for 4 minutes.

5. Gradually add the chicken stock while whisking constantly to prevent any lumps from forming. Bring to a boil, reduce heat so that the soup simmers, and add the ham hocks and sachet d'epices. Cook for 1 hour.

6. Remove ham hocks and sachet d'epices and add the collard greens to the saucepan.

7. Remove meat from the ham hocks, finely dice, and return to soup.

8. Add the heavy cream, season to taste, and serve in warm bowls.

INGREDIENTS:

4	QUARTS WATER
1	TEASPOON SALT
1	POUND COLLARD GREENS OR KALE, CHOPPED
1	TABLESPOON VEGETABLE OIL
2	OZ. SALT PORK
½	CUP ONIONS, FINELY DICED
¼	CUP CELERY, FINELY DICED
½	CUP FLOUR
8	CUPS CHICKEN STOCK
2	SMOKED HAM HOCKS
	SACHET D'EPICES (SEE PAGE 90)
½	CUP HEAVY CREAM

SWEET *and* SOUR PORK SOUP

YIELD: 4 SERVINGS / ACTIVE TIME: 30 MINUTES / TOTAL TIME: 50 MINUTES

The sour comes from the tamarind and lime and the sweet comes from the honey—this is a perfect flavor profile for pork.

1. In a food processor, add the shallots, garlic, peppercorns, shrimp paste, ginger, water, sugar, and tamarind concentrate. Blend until a smooth paste.

2. Place the oil in a medium saucepan and cook over medium heat until warm. Add the paste and cook for 2 minutes. Add the stock and bring to a boil.

3. Reduce the heat so that the soup simmers. Add the pork and papaya and simmer for 7 to 8 minutes, until the pork is tender.

4. Add the honey, lime juice, Thai chili, and the scallions. Season with salt and pepper, ladle into warm bowls, and garnish with Thai chili and scallion.

INGREDIENTS:

2 SHALLOTS, FINELY CHOPPED

2 GARLIC CLOVES, MINCED

½ TEASPOON BLACK PEPPERCORNS

2 TEASPOONS SHRIMP PASTE

1-INCH PIECE OF GINGER, PEELED AND MINCED

½ CUP WATER

1 TEASPOON SUGAR

1 TEASPOON TAMARIND CONCENTRATE

1 TABLESPOON VEGETABLE OIL

4 CUPS CHICKEN STOCK

1 POUND PORK TENDERLOIN, CUT INTO FINE, 2-INCH-LONG STRIPS

3 CUPS RIPE PAPAYA, HALVED, SEEDED, PEELED, AND CHOPPED

1 TEASPOON HONEY

JUICE OF 1 LIME

1 SMALL THAI CHILI, SEEDED AND SLICED, PLUS MORE FOR GARNISH

2 SCALLIONS, WHITE PART SLICED, PLUS MORE FOR GARNISH

SALT AND PEPPER, TO TASTE

APPLE *and* PORK STEW

YIELD: SERVES 4 TO 6 / **ACTIVE TIME:** 20 MINUTES / **TOTAL TIME:** 1 HOUR AND 15 MINUTES

This stew is a hearty blend of vegetables, pork, apples, and wine. The apples provide a slight sweetness that you and your guests will treasure.

1. In a mixing bowl, add the pork and flour and toss until the pork is coated.

2. In a large saucepan, add the oil and cook over medium-high heat until warm. Add the pork and cook for 5 minutes, or until evenly browned.

3. Remove the meat from the pan and set aside.

4. Reduce the heat to medium and add the butter. Add the onions and garlic and cook for 5 minutes, or until soft. Add the herbs and potatoes and cook for 5 minutes.

5. Add the red wine and cook for 5 minutes, or until reduced by half.

6. Add the veal stock and bring to a boil. Reduce heat so that the soup simmers, return the pork to the pan, cover, and cook for 20 minutes.

7. Add the apples and cook for 15 minutes.

8. Once the pork, apples, and potatoes are tender, season with salt and pepper and serve in warm bowls.

INGREDIENTS:

1½ POUNDS PORK SHOULDER, CUBED

⅓ CUP ALL-PURPOSE FLOUR

2 TABLESPOONS VEGETABLE OIL

2 TABLESPOONS BUTTER

2 ONIONS, DICED

4 GARLIC CLOVES, MINCED

1 TABLESPOON THYME, LEAVES REMOVED AND CHOPPED

1 TABLESPOON ROSEMARY, LEAVES REMOVED AND CHOPPED

2 POTATOES, PEELED AND CHOPPED INTO ½-INCH CUBES

1 CUP RED WINE

6 CUPS VEAL STOCK

2 GRANNY SMITH APPLES, PEELED, CORED, AND CHOPPED

SALT AND PEPPER, TO TASTE

LOTUS ROOT *and* PORK RIB BROTH

YIELD: 4 SERVINGS / ACTIVE TIME: 20 MINUTES / TOTAL TIME: 2 HOURS AND 20 MINUTES

Lotus root, which is native to Central Vietnam and has a flavor similar to coconut, is celebrated in this delicate and spicy soup.

1. In a large saucepan, add the stock, pork ribs, dried squid, fish sauce, and soy sauce. Bring to a boil, reduce heat so that the soup simmers, cover, and cook for 1 hour and 30 minutes.

2. Remove the pork ribs and set aside. Strain the stock through a fine sieve, while skimming any impurities or fat from the top.

3. Remove the meat from the pork ribs and shred.

4. Return the strained broth to a clean pan and bring to a simmer. Add the lotus root and cook for 30 minutes, or until tender.

5. Return the shredded meat to the pan. Season with salt and pepper, ladle into bowls, and garnish with Thai chili and Thai basil.

INGREDIENTS:

12 CUPS HAM STOCK

1½ POUNDS PORK RIBS

1 OZ. DRIED SQUID, SOAKED FOR 30 MINUTES

4 TABLESPOONS FISH SAUCE

1 TABLESPOON SOY SAUCE

12 OZ. FRESH LOTUS ROOT, PEELED AND THINLY SLICED

SALT AND PEPPER, TO TASTE

THAI CHILI, SEEDS REMOVED, THINLY SLICED, FOR GARNISH

THAI BASIL, FOR GARNISH

CHILI VERDE

YIELD: 4 SERVINGS / ACTIVE TIME: 20 MINUTES / TOTAL TIME: 1 HOUR AND 15 MINUTES

This great green chili is also known as a Colorado Chili. The jalapeño provides a nice heat and the tomatillos provide a refreshing finish.

1. Over an open flame, char the jalapeño. Place in a bowl, cover, and let stand for 5 minutes.

2. Cut jalapeño into 8 slices and reserve for garnish. Remove seeds and finely chop the remaining pepper.

3. In a medium saucepan, add the olive oil and cook over medium-high heat until warm.

4. Add the pork and cook for 5 minutes.

5. Add the onions and garlic and cook for 5 minutes, or until the pork is nicely browned.

6. Add the tomatoes, tomatillos, chicken stock, oregano, and cloves.

7. Bring to a boil, reduce the heat to low, cover, and cook for 20 minutes, while stirring occasionally.

8. Remove 2 cups of the broth, taking care not to remove any of the pork, and place it in a food processor. Puree until smooth.

9. Return the puree to the saucepan and cook for 25 minutes, while stirring occasionally, until the pork is tender.

10. Ladle into warm bowls, serve with long-grain rice, and garnish with reserved jalapeño.

INGREDIENTS:

- 1 JALAPEÑO
- 1 TABLESPOON EXTRA VIRGIN OLIVE OIL
- 1 POUND PORK STEW MEAT, CUT INTO ½-INCH PIECES
- 1 ONION, CHOPPED
- 2 GARLIC CLOVES, MINCED
- 1 14 OZ. CAN DICED STEWED TOMATOES
- 2 TOMATILLOS, HUSKED AND CHOPPED
- 4 CUPS CHICKEN STOCK
- 1 TEASPOON OREGANO, LEAVES REMOVED AND CHOPPED
- PINCH OF GROUND CLOVES
- SALT AND PEPPER, TO TASTE

TO SERVE:
LONG-GRAIN RICE

LONG-GRAIN RICE
- 1 CUP LONG-GRAIN RICE
- 2 CUPS WATER
- 1 TEASPOON SALT

LONG-GRAIN RICE

1. In a medium saucepan, bring the water and salt to a boil.

2. Add the rice, reduce heat to low, cover, and cook for 15 minutes while stirring occasionally.

3. Turn off flame, and let stand for 5 minutes before serving.

HAM HOCK SOUP

YIELD: 4 TO 6 SERVINGS / ACTIVE TIME: 30 MINUTES / TOTAL TIME: 2 HOURS AND 45 MINUTES

The meat, fat, and bone of the ham hock all contribute heavily to the flavor of this soup.

1. In a large saucepan, add the oil and cook over medium-high heat until warm.

2. Add the ham hocks and cook for 5 minutes, or until evenly browned.

3. Remove the ham hocks and set aside. Add the onion, carrots, celery, green bell pepper, and thyme. Cook for 5 minutes, or until the onion is soft.

4. Return the ham hocks to the pan and add the stock.

5. Bring to a boil, reduce heat so that the soup simmers, cover, and cook for 2 hours. If necessary, add more water to make sure that the ham hocks are always covered.

6. When the meat on the ham hocks is tender and falling off the bone, remove from stock and set aside.

7. Add the potatoes and simmer for 15 minutes, or until tender.

8. Meanwhile, remove the skin and fat from the ham hocks. Remove the meat and dice.

9. Add the diced meat, tomatoes, and kidney beans to the pan and cook for 5 minutes.

10. Season with salt and pepper and serve with crusty bread.

INGREDIENTS:

2   TABLESPOONS VEGETABLE OIL

4   HAM HOCKS

1   ONION, CHOPPED

2   CARROTS, FINELY CHOPPED

2   CELERY STALKS, FINELY CHOPPED

1   GREEN BELL PEPPER, FINELY CHOPPED

4   THYME SPRIGS, LEAVES REMOVED AND CHOPPED

8   CUPS HAM STOCK

2   POTATOES, PEELED AND CHOPPED INTO ½-INCH CUBES

1   14 OZ. CAN STEWED TOMATOES, CHOPPED

1   14 OZ. CAN KIDNEY BEANS

    SALT AND PEPPER, TO TASTE

ITALIAN SAUSAGE SOUP

YIELD: 4 SERVINGS / ACTIVE TIME: 20 MINUTES / TOTAL TIME: 1 HOUR

This winter favorite is very easy to prepare and makes for a beautiful, filling main course.

1. In a medium saucepan, add the olive oil and cook over medium heat until warm.

2. Add the sausage and cook for 5 minutes, or until evenly browned.

3. Use a slotted spoon to remove the sausage. Set aside.

4. Add the onion, carrots, celery, and garlic to the pan and cook for 5 minutes, or until soft.

5. Add the stock and bring to a boil. Reduce heat so that the soup simmers and cook for 10 minutes.

6. Add the zucchini, tomatoes, and beans and cook for 15 minutes.

7. Cut the cooked sausage into ¼-inch slices. Add sausage and spinach to the saucepan and simmer for 5 minutes.

8. Season with salt and pepper and serve in warm bowls.

INGREDIENTS:

2 TABLESPOONS EXTRA VIRGIN OLIVE OIL

1 POUND HOT ITALIAN SAUSAGE

1 ONION, CHOPPED

2 CARROTS, CHOPPED

1 CELERY STALK, CHOPPED

2 GARLIC CLOVES, MINCED

6 CUPS BEEF STOCK

1 ZUCCHINI, QUARTERED, SEEDS REMOVED, CHOPPED

1 14 OZ. CAN STEWED TOMATOES

1 14 OZ. CAN CANNELLINI BEANS

2 CUPS SPINACH

SALT AND PEPPER, TO TASTE

PIGS' TROTTER STEW

YIELD: 4 SERVINGS / ACTIVE TIME: 20 MINUTES / TOTAL TIME: 1 HOUR AND 20 MINUTES

In many cultures it is imperative to use all the meat from an animal. Pigs' feet are tiny, but the meat has great flavor and gets very tender when cooked nice and slow. Don't be scared, if you prepare this right, you won't think about what you're eating.

1. In a large saucepan, add the oil and cook over medium heat until warm. Add the onion, carrots, and celery and cook for 5 minutes. Add the ginger and the garlic and cook for 2 minutes.

2. Add the remaining ingredients and bring to a boil.

3. Reduce heat so that the soup simmers and cook for 1 hour, until the meat can be easily pulled from the bones and the broth has thickened.

4. Use a slotted spoon to remove the trotters.

5. Remove the meat from the bone and dice.

6. Return the meat to the soup, remove the sachet d'epices and season with salt and pepper.

7. Serve over long-grain rice and garnish with chives.

LONG-GRAIN RICE

1. In a medium saucepan, bring the water and salt to a boil.

2. Add the rice, reduce heat to low, cover, and cook for 15 minutes while stirring occasionally.

3. Turn off flame, and let stand for 5 minutes before serving.

INGREDIENTS:

- 2 TABLESPOONS VEGETABLE OIL
- 1 ONION, CHOPPED
- 2 CARROTS, FINELY CHOPPED
- 2 CELERY STALKS, FINELY CHOPPED
- 1-INCH PIECE OF GINGER, MINCED
- 2 GARLIC CLOVES, MINCED
- 3 POUNDS PIG TROTTERS, RINSED
- 4 CUPS HAM STOCK
- 1 CUP WHITE WINE VINEGAR
- ⅓ CUP SOY SAUCE
- SACHET D'EPICES (SEE PAGE 90)
- SALT AND PEPPER, TO TASTE
- CHIVES, CHOPPED, FOR GARNISH

TO SERVE
LONG -GRAIN RICE

LONG-GRAIN RICE
- 1 CUP LONG-GRAIN RICE
- 2 CUPS WATER
- 1 TEASPOON SALT

PROSCIUTTO DI PARMA
and ONION SOUP

YIELD: 4 SERVINGS / ACTIVE TIME: 20 MINUTES / TOTAL TIME: 1 HOUR

On a snowy day you won't mind being cooped up once this sweet, luxuriant soup is ready.

1. In a medium saucepan, add the chopped prosciutto and cook over low heat for 5 minutes. Add the olive oil, butter, and onions, cover, and cook, while stirring occasionally for 20 minutes.

2. Add the maple syrup, stock, and tomatoes. Cook for 15 additional minutes.

3. Season with salt and pepper, serve, and garnish with pecorino and basil.

INGREDIENTS:

6 OZ. PROSCIUTTO DI PARMA, CHOPPED

1 TABLESPOON EXTRA VIRGIN OLIVE OIL

2 TABLESPOONS BUTTER

2 ONIONS, THINLY SLICED

1 TABLESPOON MAPLE SYRUP

6 CUPS HAM STOCK

1 14 OZ. CAN DICED, STEWED TOMATOES

SALT AND PEPPER, TO TASTE

PECORINO CHEESE, GRATED, FOR GARNISH

BASIL, FINELY CHOPPED, FOR GARNISH

SWEDISH MEATBALL SOUP

YIELD: 4 TO 6 SERVINGS / ACTIVE TIME: 30 MINUTES / TOTAL TIME: 1 HOUR AND 15 MINUTES

Swedish meatballs are a meal on their own. Cook them in a nice seasoned broth and they become an ideal dinner option.

SWEDISH MEATBALLS

1. In a mixing bowl, add the bread crumbs and cream. Let bread soak for 10 minutes.

2. In a small sauté pan, add 1 tablespoon of the oil and warm over medium heat. Add the onion and cook for 5 minutes, or until soft. Turn off the heat and let onion cool.

3. Once cool, add the cooked onion to the mixing bowl. Add the remaining ingredients and stir until well-combined.

4. Place a small amount of the mixture in the microwave or cook a small amount on the stove. Taste and adjust seasoning accordingly.

5. Divide the mixture into 24 piles and roll each one into a nice, round ball.

6. In a large saucepan, add the remaining oil and cook over medium-high heat until warm.

7. Add the meatballs to the pan and cook for 5 minutes, while stirring constantly. When they are golden brown all over, remove and set aside.

SOUP

1. In a large saucepan, add the butter and cook over medium heat until warm.

2. Add the carrots and celery and cook for 3 minutes. Add the mushrooms and garlic and cook for 3 more minutes, or until the celery and carrots are soft.

3. Add the flour and cook for 3 minutes. Slowly add the beef stock to the pan, stirring constantly to prevent any lumps from forming.

4. Bring to a boil. Reduce heat so that the soup simmers, add the Swedish Meatballs, and cook for 15 minutes, or until meatballs are cooked through.

5. Add the cream, Worcestershire sauce, paprika, and red pepper flakes. Cook for 5 minutes, season with salt and pepper, ladle into bowls, and garnish with parsley.

INGREDIENTS:

SWEDISH MEATBALLS

1	CUP PANKO BREAD CRUMBS
½	CUP HEAVY CREAM
2	TABLESPOONS EXTRA VIRGIN OLIVE OIL
1	ONION, CHOPPED
8	OZ. GROUND BEEF
8	OZ. GROUND PORK
1	EGG
⅛	TEASPOON ALLSPICE
	SALT AND PEPPER, TO TASTE

SOUP

¼	CUP BUTTER
2	CARROTS, PEELED AND CHOPPED
2	CELERY STALKS, CHOPPED
2	CUPS BUTTON MUSHROOMS, THINLY SLICED
2	GARLIC CLOVES, MINCED
⅓	CUP FLOUR
6	CUPS BEEF STOCK
¾	CUP HEAVY CREAM
1	TEASPOON WORCESTERSHIRE SAUCE
½	TEASPOON PAPRIKA
½	TEASPOON RED PEPPER FLAKES
	SALT AND PEPPER, TO TASTE
	PARSLEY, CHOPPED, FOR GARNISH

CHINESE SPICY HOT *and* SOUR SOUP

YIELD: 4 SERVINGS / ACTIVE TIME: 20 MINUTES / TOTAL TIME: 45 MINUTES

This traditional Chinese soup is transformed by the addition of tiger lily buds and wood ear mushrooms.

1. Soak the dried mushrooms and tiger lily buds in a bowl of warm water for 15 minutes.

2. Remove from water, squeeze to remove any excess moisture, and tear the tiger lily buds into small pieces. Slice the mushrooms.

3. In a medium saucepan, add the mushrooms, tiger lily buds, stock, bamboo shoots, and ground pork and bring to a boil. Reduce heat so that the soup simmers and cook for 10 minutes.

4. Combine the soy sauce, sugar, vinegar, cornstarch, and water in a small mixing bowl.

5. Introduce a small amount of the hot broth to the cornstarch mixture. Stir until combined, then add the mixture to the saucepan. Return to a simmer.

6. Add the tofu and cook for 2 minutes.

7. Turn off the heat and gradually stir in the egg.

8. Ladle into warm bowls and garnish with scallions and a drizzle of sesame oil.

INGREDIENTS:

- 6 DRIED WOOD EAR MUSHROOMS
- 6 DRIED SHIITAKE MUSHROOMS
- 6 DRIED TIGER LILY BUDS
- 4 CUPS CHICKEN STOCK
- ¼ CUP BAMBOO SHOOTS, DICED
- ½ CUP GROUND PORK
- 1 TEASPOON SOY SAUCE
- ½ TEASPOON SUGAR
- 2 TABLESPOONS RED WINE VINEGAR
- 2 TABLESPOONS CORNSTARCH
- ¼ CUP WATER
- 8 OZ. TOFU, CHOPPED INTO ½-INCH PIECES
- 1 EGG, BEATEN
- SALT AND PEPPER, TO TASTE
- 2 SCALLIONS, SLICED, FOR GARNISH
- 1 TEASPOON SESAME OIL, FOR GARNISH

PORK *and* ZUCCHINI SOUP

YIELD: 4 SERVINGS / ACTIVE TIME: 20 MINUTES / TOTAL TIME: 45 MINUTES

This is a very healthy and inexpensive meal to whip up for the family.

1. Place the pork and flour in a mixing bowl and gently toss until the pork is coated.

2. In a medium saucepan, add the oil and warm over medium-high heat. Add the onion, garlic, and pork and cook for 5 minutes, or until the pork is nicely browned. Add the peppers, zucchini, tomatoes, and mushrooms and cook for 5 minutes. Slowly add the stock, while stirring, and bring to a boil.

3. Reduce heat so that the soup simmers. Add the oyster sauce and simmer for 15 minutes.

4. Add the basil, oregano, salt, and pepper. Ladle into warm bowls and garnish with a sprinkle of parmesan.

INGREDIENTS:

1½ POUNDS PORK TENDERLOIN, CUT INTO ½-INCH PIECES

⅓ CUP ALL-PURPOSE FLOUR

2 TABLESPOONS VEGETABLE OIL

1 ONION, CHOPPED

2 GARLIC CLOVES, MINCED

½ CUP RED BELL PEPPER, CHOPPED

½ CUP GREEN BELL PEPPER, CHOPPED

2 ZUCCHINI, QUARTERED AND SLICED

1 14 OZ. CAN DICED TOMATOES

⅛ CUP SUN-DRIED TOMATOES, CHOPPED

2 CUPS BUTTON MUSHROOMS, SLICED

4 CUPS CHICKEN STOCK

2 TABLESPOONS OYSTER SAUCE

1 TABLESPOON BASIL, LEAVES REMOVED AND CHOPPED

1 TEASPOON OREGANO, LEAVES REMOVED AND CHOPPED

SALT AND PEPPER, TO TASTE

PARMESAN CHEESE, GRATED, FOR GARNISH

LIVER *and* BACON SOUP

YIELD: 4 SERVINGS / ACTIVE TIME: 30 MINUTES / TOTAL TIME: 1 HOUR

Based on the traditional liver-and-onions of Ireland, I added bacon to this soup to add a bit more depth. Dip the sliced baguette with melted Gruyère into the soup—it's absolutely decadent.

1. Pat the livers dry with a paper towel. Cut into ½-inch pieces and set aside.

2. In a large saucepan, add 1 tablespoon of the oil and the bacon. Cook over medium heat for a few minutes. Stir in the onion and garlic and cook until the onion is soft.

3. Add 1 tablespoon of flour and cook for 2 minutes.

4. Gradually add the water, while stirring constantly. Add the Worcestershire sauce, soy sauce, and thyme and bring to a boil.

5. Reduce heat and simmer for 30 minutes.

6. Once soup is almost ready, dredge the livers in the remaining flour until coated. Place remaining vegetable oil in a sauté pan and warm over medium-high heat. Add the liver and cook until golden brown. Remove liver from sauté pan and add to the soup.

7. Meanwhile, preheat the broiler on your oven. Sprinkle the Gruyère onto the slices of baguette and place the bread onto a baking tray. Place tray in oven and cook until cheese has melted.

8. Ladle soup into warm bowls and serve with the baguette.

INGREDIENTS:

8 OZ. CHICKEN OR DUCK LIVERS

2 TABLESPOONS VEGETABLE OIL

4 STRIPS THICK-CUT BACON, CHOPPED

1 ONION, CHOPPED

2 GARLIC CLOVES, MINCED

2 TABLESPOONS ALL-PURPOSE FLOUR

6 CUPS WATER

2 TABLESPOONS WORCESTERSHIRE SAUCE, OR TO TASTE

2 TABLESPOONS SOY SAUCE, OR TO TASTE

1 TABLESPOON THYME, LEAVES REMOVED AND CHOPPED

1 CUP GRUYÈRE, GRATED

4 SLICES OF BAGUETTE

SALT AND PEPPER, TO TASTE

SAUERKRAUT *and* CHORIZO SOUP

4 SERVINGS / ACTIVE TIME: 25 MINUTES / TOTAL TIME: 1 HOUR AND 10 MINUTES

This soup comes to us from Slovakia, where many of the households make and smoke their own chorizo. Another way to enjoy these flavors is to remove the potato from the soup and serve it with a baked potato.

1. In a large saucepan, add the oil and warm over medium heat. Add the potato and onion and cook for 5 minutes, or until the potato and onion are soft.

2. Add the dried chorizo and garlic and cook for 3 minutes. Add the bay leaf and caraway seeds and cook for 2 minutes.

3. Add the paprika, cayenne pepper, water, and sauerkraut. Cover and simmer for 45 minutes.

4. Season with salt and pepper, ladle into warm bowls, and garnish with a spoonful of sour cream.

INGREDIENTS:

1 TABLESPOON EXTRA VIRGIN OLIVE OIL

1 LARGE POTATO, PEELED AND CHOPPED

1 SMALL ONION, FINELY CHOPPED

8 OZ. DRIED CHORIZO SAUSAGES, CUT INTO ¼-INCH SLICES

3 GARLIC CLOVES, MINCED

1 BAY LEAF

1 TEASPOON CARAWAY SEEDS

2 TABLESPOONS SWEET PAPRIKA

   LARGE PINCH OF CAYENNE PEPPER

4 CUPS WATER

1 POUND SAUERKRAUT

   SALT AND PEPPER, TO TASTE

   SOUR CREAM, FOR GARNISH

LAMB

*L*amb is one of those proteins that people either love or hate. For me, it's love, particularly since I was very fortunate to live in Great Britain, where I enjoyed some of the world's greatest lamb and mutton. Some people are thrown off even by the smell, which, admittedly, is pungent.

But lamb is a meat rich in color and flavor, and a great vehicle for exotic spices and light broths. It also has a tendency to dry out, making it perfect for the slow cooking soups require.

INDIAN MULLIGATAWNY LAMB SOUP

YIELD: 4 SERVINGS / ACTIVE TIME: 20 MINUTES / TOTAL TIME: 1 HOUR

The tenderness of the lamb and the incredible aroma of this soup make this classic Indian dish a surefire hit.

1. In a small nonstick sauté pan, add the poppy seeds, cumin seeds, and coriander seeds and toast for 30 seconds over medium heat.

2. In a food processor, add the toasted seeds, turmeric, onion, garlic, ginger, and 2 tablespoons of the oil. Blend into a paste.

3. In a medium saucepan, add the remaining oil and cook over medium-high heat until warm. Add the lamb and cook for 5 minutes, or until the lamb is evenly browned.

4. Add the paste and cook for 2 minutes, while stirring constantly.

5. Add the cayenne pepper and stocks and bring to a boil. Reduce the heat so that the soup simmers, add the rice, and cook for 20 minutes, or until rice is cooked.

6. Season with the lemon juice, coconut milk, salt, and pepper. Serve in warmed bowls garnished with the coconut and cilantro.

INGREDIENTS:

4 TEASPOONS POPPY SEEDS

½ TEASPOON CUMIN SEEDS

1 TEASPOON CORIANDER SEEDS

¼ TEASPOON TURMERIC

1 ONION, PEELED AND CHOPPED

4 GARLIC CLOVES, PEELED AND MINCED

1-INCH PIECE OF GINGER, PEELED AND GRATED

4 TABLESPOONS VEGETABLE OIL

12 OZ. LAMB LOIN, CUT INTO ½-INCH PIECES

⅛ TEASPOON CAYENNE PEPPER

2 CUPS LAMB STOCK

2 CUPS VEAL STOCK

¼ CUP LONG-GRAIN RICE

4 TEASPOONS LEMON JUICE

¼ CUP COCONUT MILK

SALT AND PEPPER, TO TASTE

SHREDDED DRIED COCONUT, FOR GARNISH

CILANTRO, CHOPPED, FOR GARNISH

LAMB *and* BARLEY SOUP

YIELD: 4 TO 6 SERVINGS / ACTIVE TIME: 20 MINUTES / TOTAL TIME: 1 HOUR AND 15 MINUTES

The addition of barley gives this soup an appetizing texture.

1. In a medium saucepan, add the olive oil and cook over medium heat until warm.

2. Add the onion, carrots, and celery and cook for 5 minutes, or until soft.

3. Add the ground lamb and cook for 5 minutes, or until evenly browned.

4. Add the thyme, tomatoes, stocks, barley, cumin, and chili powder and bring to a boil. Reduce heat so that the soup simmers and cook for 30 minutes, or until barley is tender.

5. Fold in the parsley. Season with salt and pepper and serve in warmed bowls.

INGREDIENTS:

2   TABLESPOONS EXTRA VIRGIN OLIVE OIL

1   ONION, PEELED AND CHOPPED

2   CARROTS, PEELED AND CHOPPED

2   CELERY STALKS, CHOPPED

1½ POUNDS GROUND LAMB

2   THYME SPRIGS, LEAVES REMOVED AND CHOPPED

2   14 OZ. CANS OF TOMATOES

3   CUPS LAMB STOCK

3   CUPS VEAL OR BEEF STOCK

½   CUP PEARL BARLEY

½   TEASPOON CUMIN

½   TEASPOON CHILI POWDER

¼   CUP PARSLEY, LEAVES REMOVED AND CHOPPED

SALT AND PEPPER, TO TASTE

LAMB *and* OKRA STEW

YIELD: 4 SERVINGS / ACTIVE TIME: 15 MINUTES / TOTAL TIME: 55 MINUTES

This stew is Iranian in origin; however, if fresh okra is not available, use asparagus in its place.

1. In a medium saucepan, add the oil and cook over medium heat until warm.

2. Add the onions and cook for 5 minutes or until soft.

3. Add the lamb shoulder and turmeric and cook for 5 minutes, or until the lamb is evenly browned.

4. Add the tomato paste, lamb stock, and garlic and bring to a boil. Reduce heat so that the soup simmers and cook for 30 minutes, until the meat is very tender.

5. Add the okra and simmer for 5 more minutes.

6. Season with salt and pepper and serve in warmed bowls.

INGREDIENTS:

2 TABLESPOONS VEGETABLE OIL

2 ONIONS, PEELED AND CHOPPED

1½ POUNDS LAMB SHOULDER, CUT INTO ½-INCH PIECES

2 TABLESPOONS GROUND TURMERIC

½ CUP TOMATO PASTE

4 CUPS LAMB STOCK

2 GARLIC CLOVES

20 FRESH OKRA, CUT IN ¼-INCH SLICES

SALT AND PEPPER, TO TASTE

LAMB *and* CANNELLINI SOUP

YIELD: 4 TO 6 SERVINGS / ACTIVE TIME: 20 MINUTES / TOTAL TIME: 13 HOURS AND 30 MINUTES

The flavors of Greece are showcased in this lively soup.

1. In a large saucepan, add the olive oil and cook over medium heat until warm.

2. Add the onion and cook for 5 minutes, or until soft

3. Add the garlic and cook for an additional 2 minutes.

4. Add the lamb and cook for 3 to 4 minutes. Add the carrots and celery, and cook for an additional 5 minutes.

5. Stir in the tomatoes, herbs, cannellini beans, and chicken stock. Bring to a boil, reduce heat so that the soup simmers, cover, and cook for 1 hour, or until the beans are tender.

6. Add the spinach and olives. Cook for 2 minutes, or until spinach is wilted.

7. Season with salt and pepper and serve in warmed bowls with a sprinkle of feta cheese.

INGREDIENTS:

- 2 TABLESPOONS EXTRA VIRGIN OLIVE OIL
- 1 ONION, CHOPPED
- 2 GARLIC CLOVES, MINCED
- 1½ POUNDS GROUND LAMB
- 3 CARROTS, PEELED AND CHOPPED
- 3 CELERY STALKS, CHOPPED
- 1 14 OZ. CAN STEWED TOMATOES
- ¼ CUP PARSLEY, LEAVES REMOVED AND CHOPPED
- 2 SPRIGS THYME, LEAVES REMOVED AND CHOPPED
- 8 OZ. CANNELLINI BEANS, SOAKED IN WATER OVERNIGHT
- 6 CUPS CHICKEN STOCK
- 8 OUNCES BABY SPINACH
- ¼ CUP KALAMATA OLIVES, SLICED
- SALT AND PEPPER, TO TASTE
- FETA CHEESE, FOR GARNISH

FRESH CUCUMBER *and* LAMB BROTH

YIELD: 4 SERVINGS / ACTIVE TIME: 20 MINUTES / TOTAL TIME: 45 MINUTES

This very quick light and refreshing soup is great for a lunch or appetizer, especially on a hot day.

1. In a small bowl, combine the lamb loin, soy sauce, mirin, and sesame oil and let marinate for 20 minutes.

2. In a medium saucepan, add the chicken stock and lemongrass and bring to a boil.

3. Reduce the heat so that the broth simmers, add the marinated lamb, and cook for 2 minutes.

4. Add the cucumber slices and scallion whites and cook for an additional 2 minutes.

5. Season with the rice wine vinegar, salt, and pepper and serve in warmed bowls with the scallion greens, cilantro, and lime.

INGREDIENTS:

1   POUND LAMB LOIN, CUT INTO ½-INCH PIECES

2   TABLESPOONS SOY SAUCE

2   TABLESPOONS MIRIN

1   TEASPOON SESAME OIL

4   CUPS CHICKEN STOCK

1   PIECE LEMONGRASS, BRUISED

    6-INCH PIECE OF CUCUMBER, HALVED AND CUT INTO ⅛-INCH SLICES

4   SCALLIONS, SLICED, GREEN PIECES RESERVED FOR GARNISH

4   TEASPOONS RICE WINE VINEGAR

    SALT AND PEPPER, TO TASTE

    CILANTRO, CHOPPED, FOR GARNISH

1   LIME, QUARTERED, FOR GARNISH

ITALIAN LAMB STEW

YIELD: 4 TO 6 SERVINGS / ACTIVE TIME: 30 MINUTES / TOTAL TIME: 1 HOUR AND 30 MINUTES

The aromatics in this stew, and some crusty bread, guarantee you a cozy evening.

1. In a large saucepan, add the oil and cook over medium-high heat until warm.

2. Add the lamb and cook for 5 minutes, or until evenly browned.

3. Add the garlic and cook for 2 minutes.

4. Add the wine and cook until it is reduced by half.

5. Add the stock, tomatoes, oregano, and bay leaves and reduce the heat so that the soup simmers. Cook for 45 minutes, or until the lamb is tender.

6. Raise the heat to medium-high and add the potatoes, green beans, peppers, and zucchini. Cook for 15 minutes, or until the vegetables are tender.

7. Remove the bay leaves, add the parsley, and season with salt and pepper. Serve in warmed bowls with crusty bread.

INGREDIENTS:

- 2 TABLESPOONS EXTRA VIRGIN OLIVE OIL
- 2 POUNDS LEG OF LAMB, CUT INTO 1-INCH PIECES
- 4 GARLIC CLOVES, MINCED
- ¾ CUP RED WINE
- 2 CUPS CHICKEN STOCK
- 3 14 OZ. CANS STEWED TOMATOES, CHOPPED
- 2 TEASPOONS DRIED OREGANO
- 2 BAY LEAVES
- 6 POTATOES, PEELED AND CUT INTO ½-INCH PIECES
- 2 CUPS GREEN BEANS, CUT INTO 1-INCH PIECES
- 2 RED BELL PEPPERS, SEEDS REMOVED AND CUT INTO 1-INCH PIECES
- 2 ZUCCHINI, HALVED AND SLICED
- ¼ CUP PARSLEY, LEAVES REMOVED AND CHOPPED
- SALT AND PEPPER, TO TASTE

MEDITERRANEAN LAMB *and* LENTIL STEW

YIELD: 4 TO 6 SERVINGS / ACTIVE TIME: 20 MINUTES / TOTAL TIME: 45 MINUTES

The ricotta cheese adds a creamy depth to this tasty stew.

1. In a medium saucepan, add the olive oil and cook over medium heat until warm.

2. Add the lamb and cook for 5 minutes, or until evenly browned.

3. Add the onions, carrots, and garlic, and cook for 5 minutes, or until soft.

4. Add the lentils, stock, tomatoes, and herbs and bring to a boil. Reduce the heat so that the soup simmers and cook for 20 minutes, or until the lentils are tender.

5. Add the spinach, lemon zest, and lemon juice and season with salt and pepper.

6. Serve in warmed bowls with a sprinkle of ricotta cheese.

INGREDIENTS:

2 TABLESPOONS EXTRA VIRGIN OLIVE OIL

2 POUNDS LAMB SHOULDER, CUT INTO ½-INCH PIECES

2 ONIONS, PEELED AND CHOPPED

4 CARROTS, PEELED AND CHOPPED

4 CLOVES GARLIC, MINCED

1½ CUPS RED LENTILS

6 CUPS CHICKEN STOCK

2 14 OZ. CANS STEWED TOMATOES, DICED

2 TEASPOONS THYME, LEAVES REMOVED AND CHOPPED

1 TEASPOONS SAGE, LEAVES REMOVED AND CHOPPED

4 CUPS BABY SPINACH, CHOPPED

ZEST AND JUICE OF 2 LEMONS

SALT AND PEPPER, TO TASTE

RICOTTA CHEESE, FOR GARNISH

MUTTON BROTH

YIELD: 6 SERVINGS / ACTIVE TIME: 20 MINUTES / TOTAL TIME: 2 HOURS AND 15 MINUTES

This spectacular, simple soup is prepared using traditional methods employed in both Ireland and Australia. It pairs well with roasted or boiled potatoes.

1. In a large saucepan, add all of the ingredients and bring to a boil.

2. Reduce heat so that the soup simmers, cover, and cook for 1 to 2 hours or until the mutton is tender.

3. Season with salt and pepper and serve in bowls sprinkled with the parsley.

INGREDIENTS:

2 POUNDS MUTTON LEG, CUT INTO ½-INCH PIECES

2 CARROTS, PEELED AND CHOPPED

1 ONION, PEELED AND CHOPPED

2 LEEKS, CHOPPED

1 TABLESPOON PEARL BARLEY

8 CUPS WATER

SALT AND PEPPER, TO TASTE

PARSLEY, CHOPPED, FOR GARNISH

SOUTH INDIAN-STYLE MUTTON SOUP

YIELD: 4 TO 6 SERVINGS / ACTIVE TIME: 30 MINUTES / TOTAL TIME: 1 HOUR AND 15 MINUTES

Packed with spices, this soup is a delicious way to enjoy mutton.

1. In a large saucepan, add 2 tablespoons of the vegetable oil and cook over medium heat until warm.

2. Add the mutton and cook for 5 minutes, or until evenly browned.

3. Add the curry leaves, peppercorns, cumin seeds, fennel seeds, cinnamon sticks, cloves, cardamom seeds, and bay leaves and cook for 3 minutes, or until fragrant.

4. Add the stock and bring to a boil.

5. Reduce the heat so that the soup simmers and cook for 10 minutes.

6. Meanwhile, in a medium saucepan, add the remaining oil and cook over medium heat until warm.

7. Add the shallots, garlic, and ginger and cook for 3 minutes, or until fragrant.

8. Add the tomatoes, turmeric, ground cumin, and paprika, reduce the flame to low, and cook for 10 minutes, or until tomatoes are mushy.

9. Add the contents of the medium saucepan to the mutton broth and bring to a boil.

10. Reduce the heat so that the soup simmers and cook for 15 minutes. Add the potatoes and cook for 20 minutes, or until the potatoes and mutton are tender.

11. Season with salt and pepper. Serve in warmed bowls, with crusty bread, and garnish with cilantro leaves.

INGREDIENTS:

- 4 TABLESPOONS VEGETABLE OIL
- 1½ POUNDS MUTTON SHOULDER, CUT INTO ½-INCH PIECES
- 2 CURRY LEAVES
- 2 TEASPOONS BLACK PEPPERCORNS
- 2 TEASPOONS CUMIN SEEDS
- 2 TABLESPOONS FENNEL SEEDS
- 2 CINNAMON STICKS
- 4 CLOVES
- 4 CARDAMOM PODS, SEEDS REMOVED, SHELLS DISCARDED
- 2 BAY LEAVES
- 8 CUPS LAMB STOCK
- 4 SHALLOTS, PEELED AND MINCED
- 4 GARLIC CLOVES, MINCED
- 1-INCH PIECE OF GINGER, PEELED AND MINCED
- 2 TOMATOES, CHOPPED
- ½ TEASPOON TURMERIC
- 2 TEASPOONS GROUND CUMIN
- 2 TEASPOONS PAPRIKA
- 2 CUPS OF POTATO, PEELED AND CHOPPED
- SALT AND PEPPER, TO TASTE
- CILANTRO, CHOPPED, FOR GARNISH

MANSAF

YIELD: 4 TO 6 SERVINGS / ACTIVE TIME: 30 MINUTES / TOTAL TIME: 1 HOUR AND 30 MINUTES

This stew is the national dish of Jordan, and is traditionally made with Jameed, a heavily churned, yogurt-like substance made from the milk of ewes or goats. As this was not available, I replaced it with Greek yogurt, and was happy to discover that the results remained delicious.

1. In a medium saucepan, add the oil and cook over medium-high heat until warm.

2. Add the onion and cook for 5 minutes, or until soft.

3. Add the lamb and cook for 5 minutes, or until evenly browned.

4. Add the stock and cardamom and bring to a boil. Reduce the heat so that the soup simmers, cover, and cook for 1 hour, or until the lamb is tender.

5. Add the yogurt and season with salt and pepper.

6. Place the Naan in the middle of the bowls and top each with a scoop of rice. Spoon the stew over the rice and garnish with toasted pine nuts and chopped parsley.

LONG-GRAIN RICE

1. In a medium saucepan, bring the water and salt to a boil.

2. Add the rice, reduce heat to low, cover, and cook for 15 minutes while stirring occasionally.

3. Turn off flame, and let stand for 5 minutes before serving.

INGREDIENTS:

2   TABLESPOONS EXTRA VIRGIN OLIVE OIL

1   ONION, PEELED AND CHOPPED

2   POUNDS LAMB SHOULDER, CUT INTO 1-INCH PIECES

6   CUPS LAMB STOCK

2   CARDAMOM PODS, SEEDS REMOVED, SHELLS DISCARDED

1   CUP GREEK YOGURT

    SALT AND PEPPER, TO TASTE

¼   CUP PINE NUTS, TOASTED FOR GARNISH

    PARSLEY, CHOPPED, FOR GARNISH

TO SERVE:

LONG-GRAIN RICE

NAAN

LONG-GRAIN RICE

2   CUPS WATER

1   TEASPOON SALT

1   CUP LONG-GRAIN RICE

NAAN

1. Combine the yeast and warm water in a bowl and let stand for 10 minutes.

2. In a separate bowl, combine the yeast mixture, sugar, milk, egg, salt, and bread flour and mix by hand until it is formed into a ball of dough.

3. On a lightly floured surface, knead the dough for 5 minutes. Place the dough in a bowl, cover it with a towel, and let stand for 30 to 45 minutes in a warm place, until it doubles in size.

4. Cut into 4 pieces and roll on a lightly floured surface. Each piece should be ¼ inch high.

5. Brush both sides with melted butter and cook on a grill until golden brown. Remove from grill and brush the tops with melted butter before serving.

INGREDIENTS:

NAAN

½	TEASPOON YEAST
1	CUP WARM WATER
2	TABLESPOONS SUGAR
1	TABLESPOON MILK
1	EGG
1	TEASPOON SALT
2½	CUPS BREAD FLOUR
½	CUP BUTTER, MELTED

BULGARIAN SOUR LAMB SOUP
with PAPRIKA BUTTER

YIELD: 4 SERVINGS / ACTIVE TIME: 25 MINUTES / TOTAL TIME: 1 HOUR AND 35 MINUTES

This preparation utilizes lamb, but chicken and pork can also be used. I prefer to place the Paprika Butter in the soup cold, as it adds a nice temperature balance, and the butter's fat pairs nicely with the acidity in the soup.

1. In a medium saucepan, add the oil and cook over medium heat until warm. Add the lamb and cook for 5 minutes, or until it is brown on all sides.

2. Add the onion and cook 5 minutes, or until soft.

3. Sprinkle in the flour and the paprika and cook for 2 minutes. Add the stock, while stirring vigorously, and let soup simmer for 10 minutes.

4. Tie the parsley, scallions, and dill together and add to the soup.

5. Add the rice, bring to a boil, and reduce the heat so that the soup simmers. Cook for 30 to 40 minutes, or until the lamb is tender.

6. Remove the pan from heat and stir in the eggs.

7. Add the vinegar, discard the bunch of herbs, and season to taste.

8. Serve in a warmed bowl. Place a coin of Paprika Butter on top, allow it to melt, and then garnish with the dill.

PAPRIKA BUTTER

1. In a bowl, add the butter and paprika and whisk together. Quenelle the butter and roll it into logs in plastic wrap.

2. Chill until ready to serve.

INGREDIENTS:

2	TABLESPOONS VEGETABLE OIL
1	POUND LAMB SHOULDER, TRIMMED AND CUBED
1	ONION, PEELED AND DICED
2	TABLESPOONS ALL-PURPOSE FLOUR
1	TABLESPOON PAPRIKA
4	CUPS LAMB OR VEAL STOCK
3	SPRIGS FRESH PARSLEY
4	SCALLIONS
4	SPRIGS FRESH DILL, PLUS MORE FOR GARNISH
¼	CUP LONG-GRAIN RICE
2	EGGS, BEATEN
2 TO 3	TABLESPOONS DISTILLED VINEGAR
	SALT AND PEPPER, TO TASTE

TO SERVE:
PAPRIKA BUTTER

PAPRIKA BUTTER

4	TABLESPOONS BUTTER, SOFTENED
2	TEASPOONS PAPRIKA

LAMB SHANK *and* BARLEY SOUP
with FONDANT POTATO

YIELD: 4 TO 6 SERVINGS / **ACTIVE TIME:** 30 MINUTES / **TOTAL TIME:** 2 HOURS

This warming soup is packed with slow-cooked lamb, fresh vegetables, and barley, making it more like a stew than a soup.

1. In a large saucepan, add the oil and cook over medium heat until warm. Add the lamb shanks and cook until they are browned evenly. Remove the lamb shanks and set aside.

2. Add the onion, garlic, carrots, celery, and leek and cook for 5 minutes, or until soft.

3. Add the red wine and cook for an additional 5 minutes.

4. Return the lamb shanks to the pan. Add the stock, pearl barley, and 1 tablespoon of the rosemary. Bring to a boil, reduce the heat so that the soup simmers, cover, and cook for 1 hour and 30 minutes, or until the meat is very tender and falling off the bone.

5. Remove the shanks and allow to cool slightly. Remove the meat off the bone and cut into pieces. Return the meat to the soup, add the remaining rosemary, season to taste, and serve with the Fondant Potato.

FONDANT POTATO

1. In a small saucepan, add the butter and cook over low heat until melted. Add the potatoes and cook for 10 minutes on one side, or until golden brown.

2. Turn the potatoes over and cook for another 5 minutes, or until it's golden brown and the butter starts browning and gives off a nutty fragrance. Remove, season with salt and pepper, and serve.

INGREDIENTS:

2	TABLESPOONS VEGETABLE OIL
2	LAMB SHANKS, TRIMMED
1	ONION, PEELED AND CHOPPED
2	GARLIC CLOVES, CRUSHED
2	CARROTS, PEELED AND CHOPPED
2	CELERY STALKS, CHOPPED
1	LEEK, WHITE PART ONLY, SLICED
½	CUP RED WINE
8	CUPS LAMB OR BEEF STOCK
½	CUP PEARL BARLEY
1½	TABLESPOONS ROSEMARY, CHOPPED

TO SERVE:
FONDANT POTATO

FONDANT POTATO

¼	CUP BUTTER
2	POTATOES, SLICED INTO 1-INCH THICK PIECES AND CUT WITH A RING CUTTER
	SALT AND PEPPER, TO TASTE

LAMB STEW *with* CANDIED CARROTS *and* GARLIC ROASTED LITTLE CREAMER POTATOES

YIELD: 4 TO 6 SERVINGS / ACTIVE TIME: 30 MINUTES / TOTAL TIME: 2 HOURS

An ideal, flavorful family meal.

1. Preheat oven to 250°F.

2. In a mixing bowl, add flour and then the lamb pieces. Toss until each piece is evenly coated.

3. In a Dutch oven, add the butter and cook over medium heat until melted.

4. Add the lamb and any additional flour. Cook for 5 minutes, or until the lamb is nicely browned.

5. Add the onion, carrot, leek, and garlic and cook for 5 minutes, or until soft.

6. Add the wine and cook for 5 minutes.

7. Add the stock, bay leaves, and thyme, raise heat to medium-high, and bring to a boil.

8. Cover Dutch oven and place it in the oven for 1 hour, remove every 15 minutes to stir the contents.

9. While the stew is cooking, warm the oil in a small sauté pan and then add the sausage. Cook for 5 minutes, or until nicely browned

10. Increase the oven temperature to 325°F. Remove cover, add sausage, olives, and sherry vinegar. Cook for an additional 20 minutes, or until lamb is tender.

11. Skim any fat off the top and season with salt and pepper.

12. Remove the thyme and bay leaves and serve in bowls with Candied Carrots and Garlic Roasted Little Creamer Potatoes.

INGREDIENTS:

⅓	CUP ALL-PURPOSE FLOUR
2	POUNDS BUTTERFLIED LEG OF LAMB, FAT AND SILVER SKIN REMOVED, CUT INTO 1-INCH PIECES
4	TABLESPOONS BUTTER
1	ONION, PEELED AND CHOPPED
1	CARROT, PEELED AND CHOPPED
½	LEEK, WHITE PART ONLY, CHOPPED
5	GARLIC CLOVES, MINCED
1	CUP RED WINE
2	CUPS LAMB OR BEEF STOCK
2	BAY LEAVES
6	SPRIGS OF THYME
1	TABLESPOON VEGETABLE OIL
8	OZ. LAMB OR PORK SAUSAGE, THICKLY SLICED
1	TABLESPOON SHERRY VINEGAR
½	CUP KALAMATA OLIVES, PITTED AND SLICED
	SALT AND PEPPER, TO TASTE

TO SERVE:

CANDIED CARROTS

GARLIC ROASTED LITTLE CREAMER POTATOES

CANDIED CARROTS

1. In a medium saucepan, bring 6 cups of water to boil. Add the carrots and cook for 8 minutes, or until tender.

2. Drain the carrots. Reduce the heat to the lowest possible setting and return the carrots to the pan. Stir in butter, brown sugar, salt, and pepper. Cook for 3 to 5 minutes, while stirring, until the carrots are evenly coated.

GARLIC ROASTED LITTLE CREAMER POTATOES

1. Preheat oven to 350°F.

2. Place the potatoes on a baking tray, drizzle with the olive oil, and season with salt and pepper.

3. Place in oven and cook for 10 minutes.

4. Remove the tray from oven and sprinkle the garlic over the potatoes. Return to the oven and cook for an additional 20 minutes, or until the potatoes are cooked through

5. Remove from pan, toss with the chopped parsley, and serve.

INGREDIENTS:

CANDIED CARROTS

1   POUND BABY CREAMER POTATOES

2   TABLESPOONS EXTRA VIRGIN OLIVE OIL

    SALT AND PEPPER, TO TASTE

6   CLOVES GARLIC, MINCED

    PARSLEY, CHOPPED

GARLIC ROASTED LITTLE CREAMER POTATOES

5   CARROTS, PEELED AND CUT INTO 1-INCH PIECES

2   TABLESPOONS BUTTER

¼   CUP LIGHT BROWN SUGAR

    SALT AND PEPPER, TO TASTE

BREAD SOUP *with* PITA BREAD

YIELD: 6 SERVINGS / ACTIVE TIME: 30 MINUTES / TOTAL TIME: 2 HOURS 30 MINUTES

This soup is traditionally called shorbet el fata. It is an Egyptian soup, employed on a feast day 72 days after Ramadan, and made from the meat and bones of a sacrificial lamb.

1. In a large stockpot, add the bones and enough water to cover them by one inch. Bring to a boil and cook the marrow bones for 5 minutes. Remove the bones, submerge them in cold water, and discard the cooking water.

2. Return the blanched bones to the stockpot and cover with the same amount of fresh water. Bring to a boil, then reduce the heat so that the water simmers.

3. Add the lamb shoulder and cook for 2 hours, or until the meat is tender. Add water if necessary, as the bones and meat should always be submerged.

4. Remove the marrow bones 20 minutes before serving and add the rice. Simmer for 10 minutes, or until the rice is cooked.

5. Split open the pita bread and toast under a broiler, turning once, until both sides are crispy and lightly browned.

6. Place the pita on the bottom of warmed soup bowls.

7. In a small saucepan, cook the garlic and butter over low heat until fragrant. Add the white wine vinegar and bring to a boil.

8. Pour the garlic-and-vinegar mixture over the pita bread. Adjust the seasoning of the soup, pour it into the serving bowls, and garnish with parsley.

PITA BREAD

1. Preheat oven to 500°F.

2. Combine all the ingredients in a mixing bowl and mix to form a dough.

3. Place the dough on a lightly floured surface and knead with your hands until smooth.

4. Place the dough in a lightly greased bowl and cover it with a towel. Let it stand until it nearly doubles in size and is quite puffy.

Continued . . .

INGREDIENTS:

2 MARROW BONES

1 POUND LAMB SHOULDER, CLEANED AND CUBED

4 CUPS WATER

⅓ CUP LONG-GRAIN RICE, RINSED

SALT AND PEPPER, TO TASTE

3 GARLIC CLOVES, MINCED

3 TABLESPOONS BUTTER

3 TABLESPOONS WHITE WINE VINEGAR

3 TABLESPOONS PARSLEY, CHOPPED, FOR GARNISH

TO SERVE:
PITA BREAD

PITA BREAD

1½ CUPS BREAD FLOUR

1 TEASPOON INSTANT YEAST

½ TEASPOON SUGAR

¾ TEASPOON SALT

¾ CUP WATER

1 TABLESPOON VEGETABLE OIL

5. Place the dough on a lightly oiled work surface and divide into 4 pieces.

6. Roll the pieces into 6" circles and place them on a lightly greased baking tray. Allow them to stand for 15 minutes.

7. Place the baking tray on the lowest rack in your oven and bake for 5 minutes, or until the bread has puffed up.

8. Move the tray to a higher rack and bake for an additional 5 minutes, or until the bread is golden brown on top.

9. Remove from the oven and serve.

MUTTON LEG *and* BARLEY STEW

YIELD: 4 SERVINGS / ACTIVE TIME: 20 MINUTES / TOTAL TIME: 1 HOUR AND 30 MINUTES

Mutton is meat from a sheep that is older than 1 year, and typically harvested at 3 years of age. It has an intense red color and contains a considerable amount of fat. Its flavor is considerably stronger than lamb, making this stew a very filling dinner.

1. In a large saucepan, add the stock, mutton, onion, garlic, bay leaves, cloves, and thyme and bring to a boil. Reduce heat so that the soup simmers and cook for 45 minutes, or until the mutton is tender.

2. Remove the bay leaves, thyme sprigs, and cloves.

3. Add the potato and barley, cover, and let simmer for 15 minutes, or until the barley and potatoes are cooked through.

4. Adjust seasonings to taste, add chopped parsley, and serve.

INGREDIENTS:

4   CUPS LAMB STOCK

1   POUND BUTTERFLIED MUTTON LEG, CUT INTO 1-INCH PIECES

1   ONION, PEELED AND FINELY CHOPPED

2   GARLIC CLOVES, MINCED

2   BAY LEAVES

4   CLOVES

4   SPRIGS OF THYME

1   POTATO, PEELED AND CUT INTO ½-INCH PIECES

½   CUP BARLEY

    SALT AND PEPPER, TO TASTE

2   TABLESPOONS PARSLEY, CHOPPED

IRISH COUNTRY SOUP *with* SODA BREAD

YIELD: 4 SERVINGS / ACTIVE TIME: 30 MINUTES / TOTAL TIME: 1 HOUR AND 15 MINUTES

Traveling around Ireland, I have noticed that there are quite a few variations of this soup. This is my favorite and, as is true for most soups, this one is certainly better the day after you make it. Irish Soda Bread is often served with dried currants, but as a garnish for a soup, it's more appropriate to omit them.

1. In a medium saucepan, add the oil and lamb and cook over medium-high heat for 5 minutes, or until the lamb is evenly browned.

2. Add the onion, leeks, and carrots and cook for 5 minutes, or until soft.

3. Add the stock and bring to a boil. Reduce heat so that the soup simmers, and cook for 45 minutes.

4. Add the potatoes and thyme, and cook for 10 minutes, or until the potatoes are tender.

5. Remove the soup from heat and let stand for 5 minutes. Skim any fat off, strain the stock into a fresh pan, and whisk in the butter.

6. Adjust the seasoning to taste. Return the meat and vegetables back to the soup.

7. Ladle soup into warm bowls, garnish with parsley leaves, and serve with a piece of Irish soda bread.

IRISH SODA BREAD

1. Preheat oven to 425°F.

2. Grease and flour a 9" round cake pan.

3. In a large bowl, combine the flour, baking soda, and salt. Gradually stir in the buttermilk until a slightly sticky ball of dough forms.

4. Place the dough onto a lightly floured surface and knead gently for a few minutes. Form the dough into a ball and then press into the prepared cake pan so that the dough resembles a large disk. The dough should reach the edges of the pan, but may spring back slightly.

5. Cut an X into the top of the dough with a sharp knife, about a ¼ inch deep. Cover the pan with another round cake pan turned upside down.

6. Place in the oven and bake for 30 minutes. Remove the top pan and bake uncovered for approximately 10 minutes, or until the crust is a dark golden brown. Remove from oven, and serve.

INGREDIENTS:

1 TABLESPOON VEGETABLE OIL

1 POUND BONELESS LAMB LOIN, TRIMMED AND CUBED

1 ONION, PEELED AND CHOPPED

2 LEEKS, WHITE PART ONLY, THINLY SLICED

2 CARROTS, PEELED AND THICKLY SLICED

4 CUPS VEAL STOCK

2 POTATOES, PEELED AND CUT INTO CHUNKS

4 SPRIGS OF THYME, LEAVES REMOVED AND CHOPPED

1 TABLESPOON BUTTER

SALT AND PEPPER, TO TASTE

PARSLEY, CHOPPED, FOR GARNISH

TO SERVE:
IRISH SODA BREAD

IRISH SODA BREAD

4 CUPS ALL-PURPOSE FLOUR

2 TEASPOONS BAKING SODA

1 TEASPOON SALT

1¾ CUPS BUTTERMILK

POULTRY

*C*hicken seems to be made for soup, to the point that chicken soup is synonymous with comfort, and is still our best answer for the common cold. However, there are a number of other fowl that are wonderful in soups, such as guinea hen, quail, and turkey. This chapter includes recipes that feature the lean, flavorful meat of all these winged creatures.

Some of these birds might not be common at your local butcher, but there are some great distributors that will deliver these animals to your door—professionally, and personally, I use D'artagnan to get specific game birds. Their main office is in New Jersey, but they have regional offices all around the country.

CHICKEN CONSOMMÉ

YIELD: 4 SERVINGS / ACTIVE TIME: 30 MINUTES / TOTAL TIME: 1 HOUR AND 30 MINUTES

Consommé is a clear soup made from richly flavored stock or bouillon that has been clarified. Although the process appears to be intimidating, it's actually very easy—and very satisfying.

1. In a medium saucepan, bring 8 cups of water to boil. Add the celery, celery root, parsnips, carrots, and onion and cook for 5 minutes, or until tender. Remove from pan and submerge in ice water. Dry and set aside.

2. In a large stockpot, add the remaining ingredients stir until combined. Slowly bring to a simmer. The egg white will rise to form a raft and clarify the stock. Simmer for 45 minutes, or until the correct flavor and clarity has been achieved

3. Ladle the stock through a cheese cloth. Return the stock to a clean pan, add the cooked vegetables, and bring to a boil. Season with salt and pepper, ladle into warm bowls, and garnish with chives.

INGREDIENTS:

1 CUP PARSNIPS, FINELY DICED

1 CUP CARROTS, FINELY DICED

2 CARROTS, PEELED AND CHOPPED

1 ONION, CHOPPED

2 CELERY STALKS, CHOPPED

8 OZ. GROUND CHICKEN MEAT, LEAN

1 TOMATO, CHOPPED

6 CUPS CHICKEN STOCK, COLD

SACHET D'EPICES, WITH 1 WHOLE CLOVE AND 1 ALLSPICE BERRY ADDED (SEE PAGE 90)

5 EGG WHITES, BEATEN

SALT, TO TASTE

CHIVES, CHOPPED, FOR GARNISH

CHICKEN *and* SHRIMP GUMBO

YIELD: 4 SERVINGS / ACTIVE TIME: 30 MINUTES / TOTAL TIME: 1 HOUR

Gumbo is traditionally served over rice. However, to make this a one-pot soup, I elected to cook the rice with the gumbo. If you prefer the traditional way, feel free to cook the rice separately.

1. Preheat oven to 375°F.

2. In a medium saucepan, add the oil, sausage, and chicken and cook over medium heat for 5 minutes.

3. Meanwhile, place the flour on a baking tray, place tray in the oven, and cook until the flour is dark brown, 5 to 8 minutes.

4. Add the onion, green bell pepper, celery, jalapeño, scallions, garlic, okra, and tomato and cook for 8 minutes, or until vegetables are soft.

5. Add the browned flour to the pan and cook, while stirring, for 4 minutes.

6. Add the stock and stir to prevent any lumps from forming. Bring to a boil, reduce heat so that soup simmers, and add the rice, bay leaf, oregano, onion powder, thyme, and basil. Cook for 25 minutes, or until the rice is tender.

7. Add the shrimp and simmer for 3 minutes, or until the shrimp is cooked through

8. Season with salt and pepper and ladle into bowls.

INGREDIENTS:

1	TABLESPOON VEGETABLE OIL
6	OZ. ANDOUILLE SAUSAGE, CHOPPED
8	OZ. CHICKEN BREASTS, SKIN REMOVED, CHOPPED
⅓	CUP ALL-PURPOSE FLOUR
1	ONION, CHOPPED
¾	CUP GREEN BELL PEPPERS, SEEDS REMOVED, CHOPPED
¾	CUP CELERY, CHOPPED
½	TABLESPOON JALAPEÑO, FINELY CHOPPED
2	SCALLIONS, SPLIT AND CUT ON A BIAS
2	GARLIC CLOVES, MINCED
½	CUP OKRA, SLICED
1	TOMATO, CONCASSE (SEE PAGE 89)
6	CUPS CHICKEN STOCK
½	CUP LONG-GRAIN RICE
1	BAY LEAF
¼	TEASPOON DRIED OREGANO
¼	TEASPOON ONION POWDER
⅛	TEASPOON DRIED THYME
⅛	TEASPOON DRIED BASIL
12	OZ. SHRIMP, PEELED, DEVEINED, CHOPPED
	SALT AND PEPPER, TO TASTE

MULLIGATAWNY CHICKEN CURRY SOUP
with CURRIED CASHEWS

YIELD: 4 SERVINGS / ACTIVE TIME: 20 MINUTES / TOTAL TIME: 45 MINUTES

When Anglicized, the Tamil words for "pepper water" become the name of this soup. This soup was so popular with the English living in India during the colonial era that it was one of the few Indian dishes mentioned in the literature of the period.

1. In a large stockpot, add the onion, carrots, celery, and butter and cook over medium heat for 5 minutes, or until soft.

2. Stir in the flour, curry, poppy seeds, and cumin and cook for 3 minutes. Pour in the chicken stock and bring to a boil.

3. Add the rice, reduce heat so that the soup simmers, and cook for 15 minutes.

4. Add in the apple, chicken, and thyme and simmer for 10 more minutes.

5. Add the cream, return to a simmer, season with salt and pepper, garnish with cilantro, and serve with Curried Cashews.

CURRIED CASHEWS

1. In a small sauté pan, add the butter and cook over medium heat until melted.

2. Add the cashews and cook for 4 minutes, while stirring constantly.

3. Add the curry powder and cook until the cashews are golden brown.

4. Remove, set on a paper towel, season with salt, and reserve until ready to serve.

INGREDIENTS:

1	ONION, CHOPPED
2	CARROTS, PEELED AND CHOPPED
2	CELERY STALKS, CHOPPED
¼	CUP BUTTER
2	TABLESPOONS ALL-PURPOSE FLOUR
1	TABLESPOON CURRY POWDER
1	TABLESPOON POPPY SEEDS
1	TEASPOON CUMIN
4	CUPS CHICKEN STOCK
⅓	CUP LONG-GRAIN RICE
1	APPLE, PEELED, CORED, AND CHOPPED
1	CUP COOKED CHICKEN MEAT FROM THE LEG, CHOPPED
¼	TEASPOON DRIED THYME
½	CUP HEAVY CREAM
	SALT AND PEPPER, TO TASTE
	CILANTRO, FOR GARNISH

TO SERVE:
CURRIED CASHEWS

CURRIED CASHEWS

2	TABLESPOONS BUTTER
½	CUP UNSALTED RAW CASHEWS
1	TEASPOON CURRY POWDER
	SALT, TO TASTE

TOM KHA KAI

YIELD: 4 TO 6 SERVINGS / ACTIVE TIME: 20 MINUTES / TOTAL TIME: 45 MINUTES

This is one of the most popular soups in Thai cuisine. The combination of the spices in this soup makes it sour, sweet, hot, and salty all at the same time.

1. Rinse, dry, and remove the stems from the mushrooms.

2. In a medium saucepan, add the coconut milk and bring to a simmer over medium heat.

3. Add the mushrooms, scallions, lemongrass, galangal root, red chili pepper, lime leaf, and ginger. Cook, while lightly stirring, for about 5 minutes, until the contents of the pan are fragrant.

4. Add fish sauce, lime juice, chicken breast, and sugar. Raise heat to medium-high and cook for 10 minutes, or until the chicken is cooked through.

5. Remove the lemongrass and galangal, ladle into warm bowls, and garnish with bean sprouts.

INGREDIENTS:

- 2 CUPS SHIITAKE MUSHROOMS, SLICED
- 2 14 OZ. CANS OF COCONUT MILK
- 4 SCALLIONS, WHITE PART ONLY, SLICED
- 4-INCH LEMONGRASS STALK, BRUISED WITH THE BACK OF A KNIFE
- 1-INCH PIECE OF GALANGAL ROOT
- 1 SMALL RED CHILI PEPPER, SEEDS REMOVED, FINELY DICED
- 1 LIME LEAF
- 2 TEASPOONS GINGER, FINELY GRATED
- ½ CUP FISH SAUCE, OR TO TASTE
- JUICE OF 2 LIMES
- 1 POUND OF CHICKEN BREAST, CUT INTO 1-INCH CUBES
- 1 TEASPOON SUGAR
- BEAN SPROUTS, FOR GARNISH

CREAMED VEGETABLE SOUP
with TURKEY DUMPLINGS

YIELD: 4 SERVINGS / ACTIVE TIME: 45 MINUTES / TOTAL TIME: 4 HOURS AND 15 MINUTES

Got lots of leftover turkey from your Thanksgiving dinner? Here's a great way to use it up. Feel free to adjust what vegetables are used: this soup is very accommodating.

TURKEY STOCK

1. Place all of the ingredients in a large stockpot. Bring to a boil, reduce heat so that stock simmers, and cook for 3½ hours, or until nice and flavorful.

2. Skim top to remove impurities from the stock. Strain through a fine sieve and set aside.

CREAMED VEGETABLE SOUP

1. In a medium saucepan, warm the oil over medium heat. Add the onion, celery, celeriac, and parsnips and cook for 10 minutes, or until tender.

2. Add the rosemary and cook for 2 minutes. Add the white wine and stock and bring to a boil.

3. Reduce heat so that the soup simmers and cook for 30 minutes, or until the vegetables are very tender.

4. Transfer the soup to a food processor, puree until creamy, and then strain through a fine sieve.

5. Place the soup in a clean pan and bring to a simmer. Add the heavy cream and season with salt and pepper.

6. Serve in warm bowls with the Turkey Dumplings (see next page).

INGREDIENTS:

TURKEY STOCK

1	LEFTOVER TURKEY CARCASS
4	QUARTS WATER
2	CELERY STALKS, CHOPPED
2	CARROTS, PEELED AND CHOPPED
1	ONION, CHOPPED
2	THYME SPRIGS
2	BAY LEAVES
6	BLACK PEPPERCORNS

CREAMED VEGETABLE SOUP

2	TABLESPOONS VEGETABLE OIL
1	ONION, CHOPPED
2	CELERY STALKS, CHOPPED
1	CELERIAC, PEELED AND CHOPPED
2	PARSNIPS, PEELED AND CHOPPED
1	ROSEMARY SPRIG, LEAVES REMOVED AND CHOPPED
½	CUP WHITE WINE
4	CUPS TURKEY STOCK
1	CUP HEAVY CREAM
	SALT AND PEPPER, TO TASTE

TO SERVE:
TURKEY DUMPLINGS

Continued . . .

TURKEY DUMPLINGS

1. Place the bread and parsley in a food processor and pulse until combined. Add the flour and baking powder and blend until combined.

2. Slowly add the milk, egg, and butter to the food processor. Pulse until a paste forms.

3. Fold in the turkey and season with salt and pepper. Refrigerate for 1 hour.

4. Place the turkey stock in a medium saucepan. If there is not enough from the recipe above, top off with chicken stock.

5. Drop tablespoon-sized balls of the turkey mixture into the stock. Cover and cook for 12 minutes. Remove and set aside.

INGREDIENTS (CONTINUED):

DUMPLINGS

4	SLICES OF BREAD, CHOPPED
½	CUP PARSLEY, LEAVES REMOVED AND CHOPPED
1¼	CUP ALL-PURPOSE FLOUR
1	TEASPOON BAKING POWDER
½	CUP MILK
1	EGG
¼	CUP BUTTER, MELTED
1	CUP COOKED TURKEY LEG MEAT, CHOPPED
	SALT AND PEPPER, TO TASTE
4	CUPS TURKEY STOCK

CHICKEN NOODLE SOUP

YIELD: 4 SERVINGS / ACTIVE TIME: 20 MINUTES / TOTAL TIME: 30 MINUTES

A soup cookbook would be incomplete without this classic. It's so simple, so quick, and you probably already have all the ingredients in your house.

1. Place the oil in a medium saucepan and cook over medium heat until warm.

2. Add the onion and cook for 5 minutes, or until soft. Add the remaining vegetables and cook until tender.

3. Add the thyme and chicken stock and bring to a boil. Reduce heat so that the soup simmers and cook for 20 minutes.

4. Season with salt and pepper.

5. Bring to a boil, add the egg noodles, and cook for 7 minutes, or until the noodles reach the desired tenderness.

6. Chop the seared chicken breast into ½-inch pieces and add to the soup.

7. Serve in warm bowls.

INGREDIENTS:

1   TABLESPOON VEGETABLE OIL

½   ONION, FINELY CHOPPED

1   CARROT, PEELED AND FINELY CHOPPED

1   CELERY STALK, FINELY CHOPPED

1   SPRING OF THYME, LEAVES REMOVED AND CHOPPED

4   CUPS CHICKEN STOCK

    SALT AND PEPPER, TO TASTE

1½ CUPS MEDIUM EGG NOODLES

1   CHICKEN BREAST, SEARED AND COOKED THROUGH

CHICKEN SOUP *with* CHICKEN LIVER MATZO BALLS

YIELD: 4 SERVINGS / ACTIVE TIME: 30 MINUTES / TOTAL TIME: 1 HOUR AND 50 MINUTES

Matzo balls are made from a mixture of matzo meal, eggs, water, and a fat, such as oil, margarine, or chicken fat. Typically served in chicken soup, they are a traditional food during Passover.

1. Place the oil in a large saucepan and cook over medium heat until warm. Add the onion and cook for 5 minutes, or until soft. Add the remaining vegetables and cook until tender.

2. Add the thyme and chicken stock, bring to a boil, and then reduce heat so that the soup simmers. Cook for 20 minutes.

3. Season with salt and pepper, bring to a boil, and add the prepared Chicken Liver Matzo Balls. Cook for 12 minutes.

4. Place 2 balls in a bowl and pour the broth over the top. Garnish with parsley and serve.

INGREDIENTS:

1	TABLESPOON VEGETABLE OIL
½	ONION, FINELY CHOPPED
1	CARROT, PEELED AND FINELY CHOPPED
1	CELERY STALK, FINELY CHOPPED
1	SPRING OF THYME, LEAVES REMOVED AND CHOPPED
4	CUPS CHICKEN STOCK
	SALT AND PEPPER, TO TASTE
	PARSLEY, CHOPPED, FOR GARNISH

TO SERVE:
CHICKEN LIVER MATZO BALLS

Continued . . .

CHICKEN LIVER MATZO BALLS

1. In a mixing bowl, add the matzo meal, egg, parsley, and 1 table-spoon of the chicken or duck fat. Stir to combine, add water to form a soft dough, and season with salt and pepper.

2. Cover with plastic wrap and refrigerate for 1 hour.

3. In a sauté pan, add 1 tablespoon of chicken or duck fat and the onion. Cook over medium heat for 5 minutes, or until soft.

4. Season with salt and pepper, add the chicken or duck liver, and cook for another 3 minutes, or until the liver is cooked through.

5. Remove pan from heat and let cool. Once cool, place on a cutting board and finely chop.

6. Spoon into 8 piles, place the piles on a plate, and freeze for 10 minutes. Remove and form into balls. Return to the freezer for 10 minutes.

7. Portion the matzo mix into 8 pieces and wrap them around the liver-and-onion balls.

8. In a medium saucepan, add the remaining chicken or duck fat and warm over medium heat. Add the matzo balls and cook until golden brown. Remove and set aside until ready to add to simmering soup.

INGREDIENTS (CONTINUED):

CHICKEN LIVER MATZO BALLS

- ⅔ CUP MATZO MEAL
- 1 LARGE EGG
- 2 TABLESPOONS PARSLEY, CHOPPED
- 5 TABLESPOONS CHICKEN OR DUCK FAT
- 4 TEASPOONS WATER
  SALT AND PEPPER, TO TASTE
- 1 SMALL ONION, FINELY CHOPPED
- 2 OZ. CHICKEN OR DUCK LIVER, FINELY CHOPPED

WRAPPING THE MATZO BALL AROUND A FILLING

Place the matzo mix in the palm of your non-dominant hand and spread it so it's about a ⅛-inch thick. Place the ball of liver in the middle of the matzo and slowly make your hands into a ball shape, with the fingers intertwined. Seal the edges together with your dominant hand, and then roll the mixture into a ball.

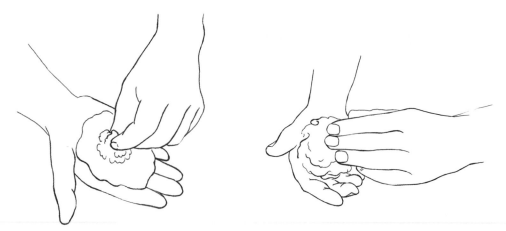

LEMON TURKEY COUSCOUS SOUP

YIELD: 4 SERVINGS / ACTIVE TIME: 20 MINUTES / TOTAL TIME: 1 HOUR

Feeling a bit lethargic after your Thanksgiving meal? Whip up this light, leftover turkey soup for lunch.

1. In a medium saucepan, add the olive oil and cook over medium heat until warm. Add the onion and cook for 5 minutes, or until soft.

2. Add the garlic and cook for 2 minutes. Add the carrots, celery, and bell peppers and cook for 5 minutes, or until tender. Add the stock, lemon zest, and couscous and bring to a boil.

3. Reduce heat so that the soup simmers and cook for 15 minutes.

4. Add the cooked turkey and lemon juice and simmer for 5 minutes.

5. Add the spinach and cook for 2 minutes, or until it wilts. Season with salt and pepper and serve in warm bowls.

INGREDIENTS:

2   TABLESPOONS EXTRA VIRGIN OLIVE OIL

1   ONION, CHOPPED

2   GARLIC CLOVES

2   CARROTS, PEELED AND FINELY CHOPPED

2   CELERY STALKS, FINELY CHOPPED

⅓   CUP RED BELL PEPPER, FINELY CHOPPED

⅓   CUP GREEN BELL PEPPER, FINELY CHOPPED

6   CUPS TURKEY STOCK

    ZEST AND JUICE OF 1 LEMON

½   CUP ISRAELI COUSCOUS

2   CUPS COOKED TURKEY MEAT, CHOPPED

4   CUPS SPINACH

    SALT AND PEPPER, TO TASTE

AROMATIC DUCK BROTH
with HOMEMADE EGG NOODLES

YIELD: 4 SERVINGS / ACTIVE TIME: 45 MINUTES / TOTAL TIME: 1 HOUR AND 30 MINUTES

Make sure you keep an eye on your guests' faces as you pour this aromatic broth over your homemade noodles—they're guaranteed to be impressed.

BROTH

1. Place a large saucepan over low heat.

2. Add the duck breasts, fat side down, and cook for 10 minutes, or until the skin is crispy.

3. Flip the breasts over and cook for 5 minutes.

4. Remove the breasts and set aside

5. Add the ginger and garlic and cook for 3 minutes, while stirring constantly.

6. Add the lemongrass and duck stock. Bring to a boil, add the fish sauce, soy sauce, five-spice powder, sugar, and scallion whites, and reduce heat so that the soup simmers. Cook for 30 minutes, skimming any impurities or fat from the top.

7. Once finished, strain through a fine sieve. Return to the pan and bring to a rolling boil.

8. Meanwhile, bring 8 cups of water to boil in a medium saucepan. Add the bok choy and boil for 3 minutes. Remove and submerge in ice water. Dry and set aside.

9. Place the Egg Noodles in the boiling water and cook for 5 minutes. Remove, drain, and set aside.

10. Slice the cooked duck breast into ¼-inch slices. Place the noodles into each individual bowl. Place the blanched bok choy on top, and then fan the slices of duck breast on top of this. Ladle the very hot broth over the duck breast and garnish with scallion greens and sliced red chilies.

INGREDIENTS:

BROTH

2	DUCK BREASTS
	2-INCH PIECE OF GINGER, PEELED AND THINLY SLICED
2	GARLIC CLOVES, MINCED
2	LEMONGRASS STALKS
8	CUPS DUCK STOCK
2	TABLESPOONS FISH SAUCE
1	TABLESPOON SOY SAUCE
1	TEASPOON FIVE-SPICE POWDER
2	TEASPOONS SUGAR
4	SCALLIONS, SLICED, GREENS RESERVED FOR GARNISH
2	BOK CHOY, HALVED
	EGG NOODLES
	SALT AND PEPPER, TO TASTE
	RED CHILIES, SLICED, FOR GARNISH

EGG NOODLES

2½	CUPS "00" FLOUR
⅛	TEASPOON SALT
2	EGGS, BEATEN
½	CUP MILK
1	TABLESPOON BUTTER, MELTED

EGG NOODLES

1. Place flour and salt on a clean work surface and use your hand to make a well in the center.

2. Place the eggs, milk, and butter in the middle of the well, and use a fork to beat the egg yolks together while drawing the flour in to make a paste.

3. Once the mixture becomes too hard to work with a fork, use your hands to knead the dough. Knead for 5 minutes, or until smooth. Wrap in plastic wrap to keep it from drying out and let stand at room temperature for 30 minutes.

4. Cut the dough into 2 pieces.

5. Use a pasta maker to roll each piece into a long, thin rectangle.

6. Place these rectangles on a floured work surface, and roll into a small, loose log.

7. Starting at the end of the log, slice the noodles to the desired width. Toss them until they uncurl. Set aside until ready to boil.

CREAM OF PHEASANT
and MUSHROOM SOUP

YIELD: 4 SERVINGS / ACTIVE TIME: 30 MINUTES / TOTAL TIME: 3 HOURS AND 15 MINUTES

Pheasants are a large, long-tailed game bird native to Asia. This creamed soup is a beautiful way to prepare them.

1. Preheat oven to 400°F. Remove the breasts of the pheasant. Place the legs and carcass on a baking tray and then place the tray in oven for 45 minutes, or until golden brown. Remove and set aside.

2. Meanwhile, add the butter to a stockpot and cook over medium heat until melted. Add the carrot, onion, celery, herbs, and garlic and cook for 5 minutes, or until soft.

3. Add the white port and cook for 5 minutes.

4. Add the roasted legs and carcass to the stockpot and cover with water. Simmer for 2 hours, or until the stock is nice and flavorful.

5. Strain the pheasant stock through a fine sieve.

6. Place 6 cups of stock and the mushrooms in a food processor and puree until velvety. Add more stock if necessary.

7. Transfer the puree to a pan, bring to a boil, and then reduce heat so that the soup simmers. Cook for 10 minutes, add the cream, and return to a simmer. Season with salt and pepper and ladle into warm bowls. Serve with Grilled Pheasant Breasts and Sautéed Wild Mushrooms and garnish with chives.

INGREDIENTS:

1	2½-POUND PHEASANT
2	TABLESPOONS BUTTER
1	CARROT, DICED
1	ONION, DICED
2	CELERY STALKS, DICED
3	ROSEMARY SPRIGS, LEAVES REMOVED AND CHOPPED
3	THYME SPRIGS, LEAVES REMOVED AND CHOPPED
2	GARLIC CLOVES, CHOPPED
1	CUP WHITE PORT
1	POUND PORTOBELLO MUSHROOMS, CHOPPED
1	CUP HEAVY CREAM
	SALT AND PEPPER, TO TASTE
	CHIVES, CHOPPED, FOR GARNISH

TO SERVE:
GRILLED PHEASANT

SAUTÉED WILD MUSHROOMS

GRILLED PHEASANT

1. Preheat oven to 400°F.

2. Place the oil in a cast-iron skillet or sauté pan and warm over medium-high heat.

3. Once hot, gently place the pheasant breasts skin side down in the pan and lower the flame to medium.

4. Cook for 5 minutes or until the skin is nice and crispy.

5. Flip the breast and cook for an additional 5 minutes.

6. Place the seared breasts on a baking tray and place a piece of the sliced butter on top of each breasts.

7. Place in the oven and cook for 5 to 10 minutes or until cooked to desired temperature.

8. Rest on a cutting board for 5 minutes and thinly slice.

SAUTÉED WILD MUSHROOMS

1. In a medium heavy bottom warm oil on medium high heat.

2. Add the mushrooms and cook for 5 to 10 minutes or until golden brown.

3. Add butter and let melt.

4. Once melted, baste the butter over the mushrooms for 5 minutes or until the butter gets frothy and has the aroma of nuts.

5. Season with salt and pepper.

6. Remove from pan and place on paper towels to absorb excess fat.

INGREDIENTS (CONTINUED):

GRILLED PHEASANT

2 TABLESPOON EXTRA VIRGIN OLIVE OIL

4 PHEASANT BREASTS

SALT AND PEPPER

2 TABLESPOONS BUTTER, SLICED INTO 4 PIECES

SAUTÉED WILD MUSHROOMS

1 TABLESPOON EXTRA VIRGIN OLIVE OIL

1 POUND OF MIXED MUSHROOMS, CUT TO DESIRED SHAPES

2 TABLESPOONS BUTTER

SALT AND PEPPER, TO TASTE

DUCK A L'ORANGE BROTH
with SPICED DUMPLINGS

YIELD: 4 SERVINGS / ACTIVE TIME: 45 MINUTES / TOTAL TIME: 1 HOUR AND 45 MINUTES

A rich soup inspired by the classic French dish.

1. Place a large saucepan over low heat.

2. Add the duck breasts, fat side down, and cook for 10 minutes, or until the skin is crispy.

3. Flip the breast over and cook for 5 minutes.

4. Remove the breast and set aside. Reserve 2 tablespoons of the rendered fat for the dumplings.

5. Raise heat to medium and add the onion, carrots, celery, and garlic. Cook for 5 minutes, or until soft.

6. Add the wine and cook for 5 minutes, or until it has reduced by half.

7. Add the duck stock, orange zest, orange juice, honey, thyme, marjoram, coriander, and cumin and bring to a boil.

8. Add the duck legs, reduce heat so that the soup simmers, and cook for 45 minutes, or until the meat is very tender and falling off the bone.

9. Remove the duck legs and let cool for 5 minutes. Remove the meat from the bones and cut into small pieces.

10. Cut the cooked duck breast into ½-inch pieces. Return both the breast and leg meat to the broth.

11. Simmer for 5 minutes, add the Spiced Dumplings, and season with salt and pepper.

12. Serve in warm bowls and garnish with chives.

INGREDIENTS:

1	4-POUND DUCK, BREASTS AND LEGS REMOVED
1	ONION, FINELY CHOPPED
2	CARROTS, PEELED AND FINELY CHOPPED
2	CELERY STALKS, FINELY CHOPPED
1	GARLIC CLOVE, MINCED
1	CUP WHITE WINE
6	CUPS DUCK STOCK
	ZEST AND JUICE OF 2 ORANGES
1	TABLESPOON HONEY
2	THYME SPRIGS, LEAVES REMOVED AND CHOPPED
2	MARJORAM SPRIGS, LEAVES REMOVED AND CHOPPED
½	TEASPOON GROUND CORIANDER
½	TEASPOON CUMIN
	SALT AND PEPPER, TO TASTE
	CHIVES, CHOPPED, FOR GARNISH

TO SERVE:
SPICED DUMPLINGS

Continued . . .

SPICED DUMPLINGS

1. Place the bread and the milk in a bowl and soak for 10 minutes.

2. Remove the bread and squeeze out any excess milk.

3. Place the bread and the remaining ingredients in a bowl and stir until well-combined.

4. Spoon out 20 piles of the mixture onto a baking tray. Roll into small balls. (Make sure to taste before you commit to all 20. If the mixture is too dry, add a little milk, if too wet, add a little more flour.)

5. Bring water to boil in a small saucepan. Add the dumplings and cook for 5 minutes.

6. Remove and add to the duck broth. The dumplings can also be prepared in advance and left to cool at room temperature.

INGREDIENTS (CONTINUED):

SPICED DUMPLINGS

4   SLICES OF CRUSTY BREAD, CHOPPED

4   TABLESPOONS MILK

2   STRIPS THICK-CUT BACON, CHOPPED

1   SHALLOT, FINELY CHOPPED

1   GARLIC CLOVE, MINCED

2   THYME SPRIGS, LEAVES REMOVED AND CHOPPED

2   TABLESPOONS DUCK FAT

1   EGG YOLK, BEATEN

½   TEASPOON PAPRIKA

½   TEASPOON CUMIN

½   CUP ALL-PURPOSE FLOUR

    SALT AND PEPPER, TO TASTE

CREAM OF DUCK SOUP
with BLACK CURRANT COMPOTE

YIELD: 4 SERVINGS / ACTIVE TIME: 30 MINUTES / TOTAL TIME: 1 HOUR AND 15 MINUTES

The decadence of the duck and the tartness of the black currant balance out nicely, making for an elegant preparation.

1. Place a large saucepan over on low heat. Add the duck breast, fat side down, and cook for 10 minutes, or until the skin is crispy.

2. Flip the breast over and cook for 5 minutes.

3. Remove the breast from the pan and set aside. Add the bacon, onion, garlic, carrots, and celery to the pan and cook for 5 minutes, or until soft.

4. Add the tomato paste and the chopped leg meat. Cook for 5 minutes, then stir in the flour and cook for 2 minutes.

5. Gradually stir in the crème de cassis, red wine, and port. Cook for 5 minutes, or until half of the liquid has evaporated.

6. Add the stock, bay leaf, and thyme. Bring to a boil, reduce heat so that the soup simmers, and cook for 30 minutes.

7. Meanwhile, slice the duck breast into ¼-inch strips.

8. After the soup has cooked for 30 minutes, remove the bay leaf and transfer the soup to a food processor. Puree until smooth and then strain through a fine sieve.

9. Place the soup in a clean pan, add the cream, and bring to a simmer. Season with salt and pepper, add the sliced duck breast, and cook for 2 minutes.

10. Ladle into warm bowls, garnish with the parsley, and serve with the Black Currant Compote.

BLACK CURRANT COMPOTE

1. In a small saucepan, add all of the ingredients and cook over medium heat. Simmer for 5 minutes, while mashing the currants with a fork.

2. Remove the pan from heat and set aside until ready to serve.

INGREDIENTS:

1	4-POUND DUCK, BREAST AND LEGS REMOVED, LEG MEAT SKINNED AND CHOPPED
4	STRIPS OF THICK-CUT BACON, CHOPPED
1	ONION, CHOPPED
2	GARLIC CLOVES, MINCED
2	CARROTS, PEELED AND CHOPPED
2	CELERY STALKS, CHOPPED
1	TABLESPOON TOMATO PASTE
1	TABLESPOON ALL-PURPOSE FLOUR
3	TABLESPOONS CRÈME DE CASSIS
1	CUP RED WINE
½	CUP PORT
4	CUPS DUCK STOCK
1	BAY LEAF
2	THYME SPRIGS, LEAVES REMOVED AND CHOPPED
⅔	CUP HEAVY CREAM
	SALT AND PEPPER, TO TASTE
	PARSLEY, CHOPPED, FOR GARNISH

TO SERVE:
BLACK CURRANT COMPOTE

BLACK CURRANT COMPOTE

1	CUP FRESH BLACK CURRANTS
1	TABLESPOON SUGAR
	ZEST AND JUICE OF 2 LEMONS
1	TABLESPOON PARSLEY, LEAVES REMOVED AND CHOPPED
1	TABLESPOON CRÈME DE CASSIS

GOOSE, DATES, *and* NUT SOUP

YIELD: 4 SERVINGS / ACTIVE TIME: 20 MINUTES / TOTAL TIME: 2 HOURS AND 30 MINUTES

Inspired by a Vietnamese dish, the sweetness of the dates and the richness of the nuts are perfect for the goose meat.

1. In a large saucepan, add the oil and cook over medium-high heat until warm.

2. Add the goose thighs and wings and cook for 5 minutes on each side, until golden brown.

3. Add the chicken stock, coconut milk, fish sauce, and lemongrass.

4. Bring to a simmer, cover, and cook for 2 hours, or until the goose thighs are very tender.

5. Remove the goose and lemongrass.

6. Remove the meat from the bones and return to the soup. Add the nuts and dates, and simmer for 30 minutes.

7. Season with salt and pepper, ladle into warm bowls, and garnish with Thai basil.

INGREDIENTS:

- 2 TABLESPOONS VEGETABLE OIL
- 2 GOOSE THIGHS AND WINGS
- 7 CUPS CHICKEN STOCK
- 1 14 OZ. CAN COCONUT MILK
- 6 TABLESPOONS FISH SAUCE
- 2 LEMONGRASS STALKS, BRUISED WITH THE BACK OF A KNIFE
- 16 CHESTNUTS, PEELED
- ¼ CUP ROASTED CASHEWS
- ¼ CUP ROASTED ALMONDS
- ¼ CUP ROASTED PEANUTS
- 16 DATES, PITTED
- SALT AND PEPPER, TO TASTE
- THAI BASIL, FOR GARNISH

SQUAB *and* ROOT VEGETABLE SOUP

YIELD: 4 SERVINGS / ACTIVE TIME: 30 MINUTES / TOTAL TIME: 2 HOURS

Squabs are young pigeons, typically under 4 weeks old, that have never flown. Their meat is similar to the dark meat of a turkey. Calvados is an apple-flavored brandy that lends its slight sweetness to this soup.

1. In a large saucepan, warm the oil over medium-high heat.

2. Add the squabs and cook, while turning, for 5 minutes, or until browned all over.

3. Remove the squabs and set aside. Reduce heat to medium and add butter.

4. Add the onion, carrots, turnip, parsnips, and celery and cook for 10 minutes, or until soft.

5. Stir in the flour and cook for 2 minutes. Add the tomato paste, stock, cider, Calvados, thyme, and sage and bring to a boil.

6. Reduce heat so that the soup simmers. Return the squabs to the pan, cover, and simmer for 1½ hours.

7. Remove the squabs from the pan and remove the meat from bones. Chop it nice and fine.

8. Return squab meat to the soup. Add the remaining herbs and season with salt and pepper. Serve in warm bowls.

INGREDIENTS:

- 2 TABLESPOONS VEGETABLE OIL
- 2 1-POUND SQUABS
- 2 TABLESPOONS BUTTER
- 1 ONION, FINELY CHOPPED
- 4 CARROTS, PEELED AND FINELY CHOPPED
- 1 TURNIP, PEELED AND FINELY CHOPPED
- 2 PARSNIPS, FINELY CHOPPED
- 4 CELERY STALKS, FINELY CHOPPED
- 2 TABLESPOONS ALL-PURPOSE FLOUR
- 2 TABLESPOONS TOMATO PASTE
- 6 CUPS CHICKEN STOCK
- 1 CUP APPLE CIDER
- 2 TABLESPOONS CALVADOS
- 1 TABLESPOON THYME, LEAVES REMOVED AND CHOPPED
- 1 TABLESPOON SAGE, LEAVES REMOVED AND CHOPPED
- 1 TABLESPOON CHIVES, CHOPPED
- 2 TABLESPOONS PARSLEY, LEAVES REMOVED AND CHOPPED

QUAIL *and* GINSENG ROOT BROTH

YIELD: 4 SERVINGS / ACTIVE TIME: 10 MINUTES / TOTAL TIME: 1 HOUR

Ginseng root is well known for its healing properties, but here it adds a nice touch to this quick, easy broth.

1. In a medium saucepan, add the chicken stock and sherry and bring to a boil.

2. Reduce heat so that the stock simmers and add the quail. Cover and simmer for 15 minutes.

3. Add the ginger, ginseng root, and soy sauce and cook for 30 minutes. Season with salt and pepper, place each quail in a warm bowl, and pour the broth over the quail. Garnish with chives and serve.

INGREDIENTS:

6   CUPS CHICKEN STOCK

½   CUP SHERRY

4   WHOLE QUAIL, DISJOINTED

     1-INCH PIECE OF GINGER, MINCED

⅓   CUP GINSENG ROOT, CUT INTO ⅛-INCH SLICES

1   TABLESPOON SOY SAUCE

     SALT AND PEPPER, TO TASTE

     CHIVES, CHOPPED, FOR GARNISH

PHEASANT CONSOMMÉ

YIELD: 4 SERVINGS / ACTIVE TIME: 30 MINUTES / TOTAL TIME: 1 HOUR AND 30 MINUTES

For the pheasant stock, follow the chicken stock recipe (see page 102) and replace the chicken bones with pheasant bones.

1. In a medium saucepan, bring 8 cups of water to boil. Add the celery, carrots, celery root, and parsnips and cook for 5 minutes, or until tender. Remove from pan and submerge in ice water. Set aside.

2. Place the remaining ingredients in a large stockpot and stir until combined. Slowly bring to a simmer and cook for 45 minutes, or until the correct flavor and clarity have been achieved. The egg whites will create a raft and clarify the stock as it cooks.

3. Ladle the stock through cheesecloth. Place the stock in a clean pan, add the finely diced cooked vegetables, and bring to a boil. Season with salt-and-pepper, ladle into warm bowls, and garnish with the pheasant meat.

INGREDIENTS:

- 1 CUP CELERY, FINELY DICED
- 1 CUP CARROTS, FINELY DICED
- 1 CUP CELERY ROOT, FINELY DICED
- 1 CUP PARSNIPS, FINELY DICED
- 1 ONION, CHOPPED
- 2 WHOLE CARROTS, PEELED AND CHOPPED
- 2 CELERY STALKS, CHOPPED
- 8 OZ. GROUND CHICKEN MEAT, LEAN
- 1 TOMATO, CHOPPED
- 6 CUPS PHEASANT STOCK, COLD
- 1 SACHET D'EPICES, 1 WHOLE CLOVE AND 1 ALLSPICE BERRY ADDED (SEE PAGE 90)
- 5 EGG WHITES, BEATEN

  SALT, TO TASTE

  MEAT OF 1 PHEASANT BREAST OR LEG, COOKED AND CHOPPED, FOR GARNISH

GUINEA HEN *and* WILD RICE SOUP

YIELD: 4 SERVINGS / ACTIVE TIME: 20 MINUTES / TOTAL TIME: 1 HOUR

Guinea Hens are a game bird indigenous to Africa. They are a little smaller than most chickens and the meat is slightly darker. They also happen to be perfect for this particular dish.

1. In a large saucepan, add the butter and cook over medium heat until melted. Add the leeks, carrots, and celery and cook for 5 minutes, or until the vegetables are soft.

2. Add the flour and cook for 3 minutes, while stirring constantly.

3. Add the chicken stock gradually, stirring to prevent lumps from forming.

4. Bring the soup to a boil, reduce heat so that it simmers, and add the wild rice. Cook for 20 minutes, or until the rice is cooked through.

5. Meanwhile, sear the guinea hen breasts. When cooked through, remove from pan and set aside.

6. Add the cream and sherry, season with salt and pepper, and ladle into warm bowls. Serve with guinea hen breasts and garnish with chives.

INGREDIENTS:

¼ CUP BUTTER, CLARIFIED (SEE PAGE 639)

2 CUPS LEEKS, FINELY DICED

1 CUP CARROTS, FINELY DICED

1 CUP CELERY, SLICED

2 TABLESPOONS ALL-PURPOSE FLOUR

8 CUPS CHICKEN STOCK

1 CUP WILD RICE

2 GUINEA HEN BREASTS

1 CUP HEAVY CREAM

2 TABLESPOONS SHERRY

SALT AND PEPPER, TO TASTE

CHIVES, CHOPPED, FOR GARNISH

GUINEA HEN *and* ROASTED GRAPE STEW

YIELD: 4 SERVINGS / **ACTIVE TIME:** 20 MINUTES / **TOTAL TIME:** 1 HOUR AND 15 MINUTES

I n this stew, the meat becomes very tender, paring perfectly with the mushrooms and roasted grapes.

1. Preheat oven to 350°F.

2. In a mixing bowl, add the flour and pieces of guinea hen. Gently toss until the meat is coated.

3. Warm a cast-iron pan over medium heat. Add the bacon, cook until bacon is crispy, remove with a slotted spoon, and set aside.

4. Add the pieces of guinea hen and cook for 5 minutes, or until evenly browned.

5. Remove with a slotted spoon and set aside with the bacon.

6. Add the grapes, white wine, and Riesling and cook for 5 minutes, or until reduced by half.

7. Remove the grapes and set aside with the bacon and guinea hen.

8. Add the remaining ingredients, bring to a simmer, and then place in the oven. Bake for 20 minutes.

9. Return the bacon, guinea hen, and grapes to the pan and continue to cook for 30 minutes, or until the guinea hen is cooked and the vegetables are tender.

10. Season with salt and pepper and serve with Long-Grain Rice.

LONG-GRAIN RICE

1. In a medium saucepan, bring the water and salt to a boil.

2. Add the rice, reduce heat to low, cover, and cook for 15 minutes while stirring occasionally.

3. Turn off flame, and let stand for 5 minutes before serving.

INGREDIENTS:

⅓ CUP ALL-PURPOSE FLOUR

2 GUINEA HENS, BREASTS AND LEGS REMOVED

6 STRIPS THICK-CUT BACON, CUT INTO 1-INCH CUBES

2 CUPS RED GRAPES

1 CUP WHITE WINE

1 CUP RIESLING

1 CUP WILD MUSHROOMS, SLICED

1 ONION, CHOPPED

2 CARROTS, PEELED AND CHOPPED

1 CUP ORANGE JUICE

2 CUPS CHICKEN STOCK

SALT AND PEPPER, TO TASTE

TO SERVE:
LONG-GRAIN RICE

LONG-GRAIN RICE
1 CUP LONG-GRAIN RICE

2 CUPS WATER

1 TEASPOON SALT

PHEASANT, MOREL MUSHROOM, *and* OLIVE BROTH

YIELD: 4 SERVINGS / ACTIVE TIME: 20 MINUTES / TOTAL TIME: 45 MINUTES

This stew helps keep the pheasant moist, tender, and delicious.

1. Place the flour and the pheasant in a bowl and gently toss until the pheasant is coated.

2. In a large saucepan, warm the vegetable oil over medium-high heat. Add the pheasant breast, skin side down, and cook for 5 minutes, or until evenly browned.

3. Add the onion, mushrooms, and garlic and cook for 5 minutes, or until soft.

4. Add the white wine and cook until reduced by half.

5. Add the stock and bring to a boil. Reduce heat so that the soup simmers and cook for 20 minutes, or until the pheasant is cooked through.

6. Add the olives and simmer for 3 minutes. Season with salt and pepper and serve in warm bowls.

INGREDIENTS:

½ CUP FLOUR

4 PHEASANT BREASTS

2 TABLESPOONS VEGETABLE OIL

1 ONION, CHOPPED

1½ CUPS MOREL MUSHROOMS, STEMS REMOVED, HALVED

3 GARLIC CLOVES, MINCED

1 CUP WHITE WINE

4 CUPS CHICKEN STOCK

½ CUP BLACK OLIVES, SLICED

SALT AND PEPPER, TO TASTE

PRESERVED LIME *and* DUCK LEG BROTH

YIELD: 4 SERVINGS / ACTIVE TIME: 20 MINUTES / TOTAL TIME: 1 HOUR AND 15 MINUTES

This dish was inspired by a Colombian soup, samlaw tiah. Preserved limes can be purchased, but there is a certain magic about making this simple delicacy yourself.

PRESERVED LIMES

1. Place 1 tablespoon of salt in the bottom of a mason jar. Place a few layers of the lime quarters in the jar, pressing down on the limes to release their juice. Add the spices, another tablespoon of salt, and another layer of lime quarters.

2. Continue with the remaining limes and salt, remembering to push down on the limes to release as much juice as possible. The limes need to be covered with the salty brine. If not, squeeze a bit more lime juice into the mason jar to cover.

3. Seal the jars and leave them in a cool, dark place for 8 weeks.

4. Open and place in the refrigerator until ready to use.

BROTH

1. In a large saucepan, add the oil and cook over medium-high heat until warm. Add the duck legs and cook for 5 minutes on each side until golden brown.

2. Remove the legs from the pan and set aside.

3. Add the ginger and garlic and cook for 3 minutes, while stirring constantly.

4. Add the duck stock and bring to a boil.

5. Reduce heat so that the soup simmers. Add the cooked duck legs and the preserved limes.

6. Simmer for 45 minutes or until the duck meat is tender and almost falling off the bone.

7. Add scallion whites and cook for 5 minutes.

8. Season with salt and pepper. Place each leg in a bowl and then pour the broth over it. Garnish with scallion greens and serve.

INGREDIENTS:

PRESERVED LIMES

- ¼ CUP SALT
- 2 POUNDS FRESH LIMES, CUT INTO QUARTERS
- 1 BAY LEAF
- 6 BLACK PEPPERCORNS
- ½ TEASPOON CORIANDER SEEDS

BROTH

- 1 TABLESPOON VEGETABLE OIL
- 4 DUCK LEGS
- 2-INCH PIECE OF GINGER, PEELED AND THINLY SLICED
- 2 GARLIC CLOVES, MINCED
- 8 CUPS DUCK STOCK
- 8 PRESERVED LIME QUARTERS
- 4 SCALLIONS, SLICED, GREENS RESERVED FOR GARNISH

SALT AND PEPPER, TO TASTE

SOUTHWESTERN CHICKEN SOUP

YIELD: 4 SERVINGS / ACTIVE TIME: 15 MINUTES / TOTAL TIME: 45 MINUTES

Rich and creamy avocados are the key to this soup. I like to serve it with cornbread.

1. In a large saucepan, add the chicken, stock, stewed tomatoes, jalapeño, plum tomatoes, onion, garlic, lime juice, cayenne pepper, and cumin and bring to a boil.

2. Reduce heat so that the soup simmers and cook for 25 minutes.

3. Stir in the avocado and simmer for 10 minutes, or until the soup thickens slightly.

4. Season with salt and pepper, ladle into warm bowls, and garnish with sour cream, cilantro, and Monterey Jack cheese.

CORNBREAD

1. Preheat oven to 375°F.

2. In a mixer, combine the egg, milk, and oil and mix on low speed.

3. Meanwhile, sieve your dry ingredients together.

4. Slowly incorporate the dry mixture into the egg mixture.

5. Pour the batter into a buttered and floured 8" cast iron pan. Place in oven and cook for 30 minutes, or until a cake tester or toothpick comes out clean.

INGREDIENTS:

- 2 CUPS COOKED CHICKEN MEAT, FINELY CHOPPED
- 4 CUPS CHICKEN STOCK
- 2 14 OZ. CANS STEWED TOMATOES
- ½ JALAPEÑO, SEEDS REMOVED AND CHOPPED
- 2 PLUM TOMATOES, CHOPPED
- 1 ONION, CHOPPED
- 2 GARLIC CLOVES, MINCED
- JUICE OF 1 LIME
- ½ TEASPOON CAYENNE PEPPER
- ½ TEASPOON GROUND CUMIN
- 2 RIPE AVOCADOS, PEELED AND CHOPPED
- SALT AND PEPPER, TO TASTE
- SOUR CREAM, FOR GARNISH
- CILANTRO, CHOPPED, FOR GARNISH
- 1 CUP MONTEREY JACK CHEESE, SHREDDED, FOR GARNISH

TO SERVE
CORNBREAD

CORNBREAD

- 1 LARGE EGG
- ¾ CUP MILK
- ½ CUP VEGETABLE OIL
- ½ CUP SUGAR, PLUS 3 TABLESPOONS
- 1 CUP ALL-PURPOSE FLOUR
- ⅓ CUP CORNMEAL, PLUS 2 TABLESPOONS
- 1 TEASPOON SALT
- 1 TEASPOON BAKING POWDER

TURKEY *and* WILD RICE SOUP

YIELD: 4 SERVINGS / ACTIVE TIME: 20 MINUTES / TOTAL TIME: 1 HOUR

Flavored with aromatics and turkey, this is a great cold weather soup.

1. Place the stock, scallions, wild rice, and thyme in a medium saucepan. Bring to a boil, reduce heat so that the soup simmers, and cook for 35 minutes, or until the rice is tender.

2. Meanwhile, in a large saucepan, add the bacon and cook over medium heat until crispy. Remove and set aside.

3. Place the butter in the large saucepan and melt. Sprinkle the flour into the pan and cook for 2 minutes. Slowly add the milk and heavy cream, stirring to prevent any lumps from forming. Cook for 2 minutes.

4. Add the milk-and-heavy cream mixture to the rice broth and bring to a boil.

5. Reduce heat so that the soup simmers and cook for 5 minutes, or until it has thickened.

6. Add the turkey meat, sherry, salt, and pepper. Serve in warm bowls and garnish with reserved bacon and edible flowers.

INGREDIENTS:

- 6 CUPS TURKEY STOCK
- 8 SCALLIONS, SLICED
- ½ CUP WILD RICE
- 4 THYME SPRIGS, LEAVES REMOVED AND CHOPPED
- 8 SLICES THICK-CUT BACON, CHOPPED
- ¼ CUP BUTTER
- ½ CUP ALL-PURPOSE FLOUR
- 1 CUP MILK
- 1 CUP HEAVY CREAM
- 2 CUPS TURKEY MEAT, COOKED AND CHOPPED
- 2 TABLESPOONS SHERRY
- SALT AND PEPPER, TO TASTE
- EDIBLE FLOWERS, FOR GARNISH

VELVETY CHICKEN *and* CHESTNUT SOUP

YIELD: 4 SERVINGS / ACTIVE TIME: 45 MINUTES / TOTAL TIME: 27 HOURS AND 45 MINUTES

Refine your Christmas Day offerings by preparing this soup, which works with chicken, pheasant, or guinea hen. The time required is mainly spent on the stock and drying out the chestnuts, so if you prepare those in advance it's a fast soup. Perhaps you could roast some chestnuts over an open fire on Christmas Eve, and use what remains for this soup the following day.

1. Roast the chestnuts (see recipe). Cool, peel, and reserve.

2. Preheat the oven to 400°F. Remove the breasts of the chicken and set aside. Place the legs and the carcass on a baking tray and bake for 45 minutes, or until golden brown. Remove and set aside.

3. Meanwhile, add the butter to a stockpot and cook over medium heat until melted. Add the carrot, onion, celery stalks, herbs, and garlic and cook for 5 minutes, or until soft.

4. Add the Riesling and cook for 5 minutes.

5. Add the roasted legs and carcass to the saucepan, cover with water, and simmer for 2 hours, or until the stock is nice and flavorful.

6. Strain the chicken stock through a fine sieve.

7. Place 4 cups of stock and three quarters of the peeled chestnuts in a food processor and puree until velvety. Add more chicken stock, if necessary. Chop the remaining chestnuts and reserve.

8. Place the soup in a pan, bring to a boil, and add the heavy cream.

9. Season with salt and pepper and ladle into bowls. Garnish with the reserved chestnuts and serve with Chicken Breasts.

INGREDIENTS:

1	POUND CHESTNUTS, ROASTED
1	WHOLE CHICKEN, 3½ POUNDS
2	TABLESPOONS BUTTER
1	CARROT, DICED
1	ONION, DICED
2	CELERY STALKS, DICED
3	ROSEMARY SPRIGS, LEAVES REMOVED AND CHOPPED
3	THYME SPRIGS, LEAVES REMOVED AND CHOPPED
2	GARLIC CLOVES, CHOPPED
1	CUP RIESLING
1	CUP HEAVY CREAM
	SALT AND PEPPER, TO TASTE

Continued . . .

ROASTED CHESTNUTS

1. Score the top of each chestnut, place on a baking tray, and leave out for 1 day to dry.

2. Preheat oven to 400°F.

3. Cook chestnuts for 45 minutes or until nice and fragrant. Remove from oven and let cool.

4. When cool, peel chestnuts and set aside.

CHICKEN BREASTS

1. Preheat oven to 400°F.

2. Warm the oil in a heavy bottom grill pan or saute pan on medium high heat.

3. Once hot, gently place the chicken breasts skin side down in the pan and lower the heat to medium.

4. Cook for 5 minutes or until the skin is nice and crispy.

5. Flip the breast and cook for an additional 5 minutes.

6. Place the seared breasts on a baking tray and place two pieces of the sliced butter on top of each breast.

7. Place in the oven and cook for 5 to 10 minutes or until cooked to desired temperature.

8. Rest on a cutting board for 5 minutes and thinly slice.

INGREDIENTS (CONTINUED):

ROASTED CHESTNUTS
1 POUND CHESTNUTS

CHICKEN BREASTS
1 TABLESPOON EXTRA VIRGIN OLIVE OIL

2 CHICKEN BREASTS

   SALT AND PEPPER

2 TABLESPOONS BUTTER, SLICED INTO 4 PIECES

COCONUT *and* CHICKEN CURRY SOUP
with NAAN

YIELD: 4 SERVINGS / ACTIVE TIME: 45 MINUTES / TOTAL TIME: 1 HOUR AND 30 MINUTES

Here we take a traditional Indian curry and turn it into a soup. If you're worried about the level of spice, or you want more, adjust the amount of jalapeño.

1. In a medium saucepan, add the oil and cook over medium heat until it is nice and hot.

2. Add the chicken breasts, skin side down, and cook for 5 minutes, or until golden brown.

3. Flip the breasts and cook for an additional 5 minutes. Remove and set aside.

4. Add the onion, carrot, and garlic to the pan and cook for 5 minutes, or until soft.

5. Add the chicken stock and coconut milk and bring to a boil.

6. Add the cilantro, lime leaves, curry powder, and jalapeño. Reduce heat so that the soup simmers and cook for 15 minutes.

7. Meanwhile, remove the skin from the chicken breasts and discard. Cut the breasts into 1-inch cubes. (Note: the inside should still be raw.)

8. After the soup has cooked for 15 minutes, remove the lime leaves and transfer the soup to a food processor. Puree until smooth, return to the pan, and bring to a simmer. Add the chicken and lime juice, and simmer for 10 minutes, or until the chicken is cooked through.

9. Season with salt and pepper and ladle into warm bowls. Garnish with cilantro, scallion greens, and bamboo shoots, and serve with Long-Grain Rice and Naan.

INGREDIENTS:

- 2 TABLESPOONS VEGETABLE OIL
- 2 CHICKEN BREASTS, SKIN-ON
- 1 ONION, CHOPPED
- 1 CARROT, PEELED AND CHOPPED
- 1 GARLIC CLOVE, MINCED
- 2 CUPS CHICKEN STOCK
- 1 14 OZ. CAN COCONUT MILK
- ½ CUP CILANTRO, STEMS AND LEAVES CHOPPED, PLUS MORE FOR GARNISH
- 2 LIME LEAVES
- 1 TABLESPOON CURRY POWDER
- ½ JALAPEÑO, SEEDS REMOVED, CHOPPED
- JUICE OF ½ LIME
- SALT AND PEPPER, TO TASTE
- SCALLION GREENS, FOR GARNISH
- BAMBOO SHOOTS, CHOPPED, FOR GARNISH

TO SERVE:
LONG-GRAIN RICE

NAAN

Continued . . .

LONG-GRAIN RICE

1. In a medium saucepan, bring the water and salt to a boil.

2. Add the rice, reduce heat to low, cover, and cook for 15 minutes while stirring occasionally.

3. Turn off flame, and let stand for 5 minutes before serving.

NAAN

1. Combine the yeast and warm water in a bowl and let stand for 10 minutes.

2. In a separate bowl, combine the yeast mixture, sugar, milk, egg, salt, and bread flour and mix by hand until it is formed into a ball of dough.

3. On a lightly floured surface, knead the dough for 5 minutes. Place the dough in a bowl, cover it with a towel, and let stand for 30 to 45 minutes in a warm place, until it doubles in size.

4. Cut into 4 pieces and roll on a lightly floured surface. Each piece should be ¼ inch high.

5. Brush both sides with melted butter and cook on a grill until golden brown. Remove from grill and brush the tops with melted butter before serving.

INGREDIENTS (CONTINUED):

LONG-GRAIN RICE

1	CUP LONG-GRAIN RICE
2	CUPS WATER
1	TEASPOON SALT

NAAN

½	TEASPOON YEAST
1	CUP WARM WATER
2	TABLESPOONS SUGAR
1	TABLESPOON MILK
1	EGG
1	TEASPOON SALT
2.	CUPS BREAD FLOUR
½	CUP BUTTER, MELTED

SQUAB MULLIGATAWNY SOUP

YIELD: 4 SERVINGS / ACTIVE TIME: 30 MINUTES / TOTAL TIME: 1 HOUR AND 30 MINUTES

As you'll see in this dish, Indian spices do wonders for squab meat.

1. Preheat oven to 375°F.

2. Place the squabs on a baking tray and sprinkle with 1 tablespoon of the olive oil.

3. Sprinkle the garam masala on the squabs and rub to evenly disperse.

4. Place in oven and cook for 20 minutes. Remove and let stand for 10 minutes.

5. Meanwhile, place a small, dry sauté pan over low heat. Add the coriander and cumin seeds and cook until fragrant.

6. Remove from pan, cool, and grind to a powder with a pestle and mortar.

7. Cook the rice per manufacturer's instructions, and then set aside.

8. Place the remaining olive oil in a medium saucepan and warm over medium heat.

9. Add the onion and garlic and cook for 5 minutes, or until tender.

10. Add the ground toasted seeds, chili, turmeric, bay leaf, lentils, and stock and bring to a boil.

11. Reduce heat so that the soup simmers and cook for 20 minutes, or until the lentils have been softened.

12. Add the coconut milk and simmer for an additional 5 minutes. Remove the meat from the squab carcasses and chop.

13. Add the meat and the resting juices to the soup.

14. Season with lemon juice, salt, and pepper. Place a spoonful of rice in each bowl, ladle the soup over it, and garnish with yogurt and cilantro.

GARAM MASALA

Place all ingredients in a small bowl and whisk until well-combined. Store in an airtight container.

INGREDIENTS:

2	1-POUND SQUABS
2	TABLESPOONS EXTRA VIRGIN OLIVE OIL
2	TEASPOONS GARAM MASALA (SEE RECIPE)
1	TEASPOON CORIANDER SEEDS
1	TEASPOON CUMIN SEEDS
4	OZ. BASMATI RICE
1	ONION, CHOPPED
2	GARLIC CLOVES, MINCED
1	THAI CHILI, SEEDS REMOVED AND SLICED
1	TEASPOON TURMERIC
1	BAY LEAF
4	OZ. RED LENTILS
4	CUPS CHICKEN STOCK
1	14 OZ. CAN COCONUT MILK
	JUICE OF 1 LEMON
	SALT AND PEPPER, TO TASTE
	YOGURT, FOR GARNISH
	CILANTRO, CHOPPED, FOR GARNISH

GARAM MASALA

1½	TABLESPOONS CUMIN
¾	TEASPOON GROUND CORIANDER
¾	TEASPOON CARDAMOM
¾	TEASPOON GROUND BLACK PEPPER
½	TEASPOON CINNAMON
¼	TEASPOON GROUND CLOVES
¼	TEASPOON NUTMEG

TRUFFLED WHITE BEAN *and* CHICKEN SOUP

YIELD: 4 TO 6 SERVINGS / ACTIVE TIME: 20 MINUTES / TOTAL TIME: 12 HOURS AND 45 MINUTES

This combination of chicken, root vegetables, and white beans is very filling. If you want to speed up the preparation, replace the dried beans with a 14 oz. can of beans.

1. In a medium saucepan, add the oil and warm over medium heat. Add the chicken thighs and cook for 3 minutes on each side, or until golden brown.

2. Add the chicken stock and bring to a boil. Reduce heat so that the soup simmers and add the white beans. Cook for 15 minutes, add the remaining vegetables, and cook for 15 more minutes, until the beans and vegetables are tender.

3. Remove the chicken thighs and set aside. Transfer the soup to a food processor, puree, and then strain through a fine sieve.

4. Remove the meat from the cooked chicken thighs, chop, and set aside.

5. Return the soup to the pan and gently bring it to a simmer. Add the truffle paste and truffle oil, season with salt and pepper, and ladle into bowls. Garnish with truffle oil, alfalfa sprouts, paprika, and the chopped chicken.

INGREDIENTS:

¼ CUP VEGETABLE OIL

2 CHICKEN THIGHS

8 CUPS CHICKEN STOCK

¾ CUP DRIED WHITE BEANS, SOAKED OVERNIGHT

2 ONIONS, CHOPPED

4 CELERY STALKS, CHOPPED

2 PARSNIPS, PEELED AND CHOPPED

2 TABLESPOONS TRUFFLE PASTE

2 TABLESPOONS TRUFFLE OIL, PLUS MORE FOR GARNISH

SALT AND PEPPER, TO TASTE

ALFALFA SPROUTS, FOR GARNISH

PAPRIKA, FOR GARNISH

AROMATIC CHICKEN STEW
with SWEET *and* HOT PEPPERS *with* KATSAMAKI

YIELD: 4 SERVINGS / ACTIVE TIME: 30 MINUTES / TOTAL TIME: 2 HOUR AND 40 MINUTES

This recipe was originally a Greek staple that I incorporated into a stew. Mixing the Katsamaki into the stew gives a great texture and mouthfeel from the cheese. It is very similar to polenta and the cheese can be replaced with any hard sheep cheese.

1. Heat 1 tablespoon of the butter in a large heavy bottom pan over medium heat and sear the chicken pieces for 8 minutes or until lightly browned on all sides.

2. With a slotted spoon, remove and set aside.

3. Add another tablespoon of butter to the pan and cook the onions, garlic, and bell peppers for 8 minutes or until soft.

4. Place the chicken back in the pot and add the allspice, cloves, cinnamon, thyme, and Thai chili. Stir for 2 minutes.

5. Add the olives and chicken stock, reduce the flame to low, and simmer for 40 minutes or until the chicken is tender.

6. Add the tomatoes and season with salt and pepper, swirl in the remaining butter.

7. Make a circle with the Katsamaki creating a bowl for the soup. Pour the soup in the middle, garnish with thyme leaves, and sprinkle with feta cheese.

KATSAMAKI

1. In a medium, heavy bottom pan, boil the stock.

2. On a low flame slowly add the corn meal, whisk nicely and cook for 4 to 5 minutes or until corn meal is cooked.

3. Remove from heat, add the cheese.

4. Season with salt and pepper and serve.

INGREDIENTS:

3	TABLESPOONS BUTTER
1	CHICKEN BREAST, SKIN REMOVED AND CUT INTO ½ INCH PIECES
1	LARGE ONION, CHOPPED
1	GARLIC CLOVE, MINCED
2	GREEN BELL PEPPERS, SEEDS REMOVED AND CHOPPED
¼	TEASPOON GROUND ALLSPICE
½	TEASPOON GROUND CLOVES
½	TEASPOON GROUND CINNAMON
¼	TEASPOON THYME, LEAVES REMOVED AND CHOPPED
½	THAI CHILI, SEEDS REMOVED, FINELY CHOPPED
¼	CUP KALAMATA OLIVES, SLICED
4	CUPS CHICKEN STOCK
1½	CUPS TOMATOES, CONCASSE (SEE PAGE 89) AND CHOPPED
	SALT AND PEPPER
	FETA CHEESE, FOR GARNISH
	THYME LEAVES, FOR GARNISH

TO SERVE:
KATSAMAKI

KATSAMAKI

1¼	CUPS OF VEGETABLE STOCK
½	CUP CORN MEAL
1	CUP GRATED KEFALOTYRI CHEESE (HARD GREEK SHEEP'S MILK CHEESE)
	SALT AND PEPPER

LEMONGRASS-SCENTED CHICKEN
and RICE SOUP

YIELD: 4 PORTIONS / ACTIVE TIME: 30 MINUTES / TOTAL TIME: 2 HOURS AND 30 MINUTES

Also known as Chnor Chrook, this soup is Cambodia's version of chicken noodle soup. It is light and refreshing. This soup awakens the senses with the chili and the citrus aroma. It is a bit spicy, so adjust to your personal taste.

1. In a large saucepan add the chicken thighs, chicken stock, ginger, lemongrass, Thai chilis, and fish sauce.

2. Bring to a boil and simmer for 2 hours or until the chicken legs are tender.

3. Skim off any fat.

4. Remove the chicken legs and pick apart the meat. Discard the skin and bones.

5. Strain the stock through a fine sieve.

6. Reboil stock, stir in the rice, and simmer for 30 minutes, or until rice is cooked.

7. Remove chili, add chicken leg meat until hot and serve.

8. Garnish with thinly sliced chili, chopped cilantro, and lime wedges and serve with Naan.

NAAN

1. Combine the yeast and warm water in a bowl and let stand for 10 minutes.

2. In a separate bowl, combine the yeast mixture, sugar, milk, egg, salt, and bread flour and mix by hand until it is formed into a ball of dough.

3. On a lightly floured surface, knead the dough for 5 minutes. Place the dough in a bowl, cover it with a towel, and let stand for 30 to 45 minutes in a warm place, until it doubles in size.

4. Cut into 4 pieces and roll on a lightly floured surface. Each piece should be ¼ inch high.

5. Brush both sides with melted butter and cook on a grill until golden brown. Remove from grill and brush the tops with melted butter before serving.

INGREDIENTS:

2	CHICKEN THIGHS
8	CUPS CHICKEN STOCK
	1-INCH PIECE OF GINGER, SLICED
3	LEMONGRASS STALKS, CUT IN HALF AND BRUISED WITH THE BACK SIDE OF A KNIFE
1	THAI CHILI WITH SEEDS
3	TABLESPOONS FISH SAUCE
½	CUP LONG-GRAIN RICE, RINSED
	CHILI, CUT INTO THIN STRIPS, FOR GARNISH
	CHOPPED CILANTRO, FOR GARNISH
	LIME WEDGES, FOR GARNISH

TO SERVE:
NAAN

NAAN

½	TEASPOON YEAST
1	CUP WARM WATER
2	TABLESPOONS SUGAR
1	TABLESPOON MILK
1	EGG
1	TEASPOON SALT
2.	CUPS BREAD FLOUR
½	CUP BUTTER, MELTED

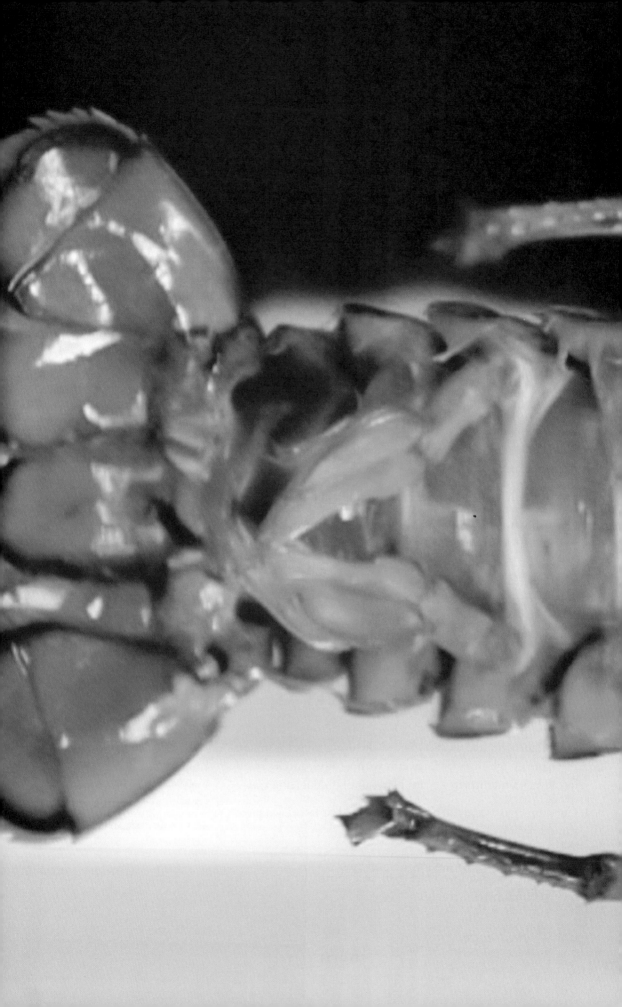

SEAFOOD

The fun thing about this chapter is that the recipes take you on an international journey, inviting you to employ techniques and ingredients from around the globe. While it is easy to get fresh seafood from far-flung bodies of water into your home, that doesn't mean you need to look beyond what is local, as most of the proteins in these recipes are easily interchangeable with what is available in your neighborhood.

In this day and age, it's crucial that seafood be sourced sustainably and locally—it not only supports your community; it also keeps fish populations from diminishing to dangerous levels. So please, use the recipes here as guidelines rather than hard and fast rules. You, and your cooking, will benefit from such an approach.

FIVE-SPICE-DUSTED MUSSEL CAPPUCCINO
with SHRIMP CRACKERS

YIELD: 4 SERVINGS / ACTIVE TIME: 30 MINUTES / TOTAL TIME: 12 HOURS AND 30 MINUTES

This is a soup presented in the fashion of a cappuccino, so even though your mouth is screaming cappuccino, your tongue is out to sea. This is a great amuse-bouche or intermezzo, so if you want to impress some folks, make a smaller batch to add another layer to your dinner party.

1. In a medium saucepan, add the butter and cook over medium heat until melted. Add the shallots and garlic and cook for 3 minutes, or until soft.

2. Add the white wine and cilantro, and bring to a simmer.

3. Add your mussels, cover the pan, and cook for 4 minutes, or until all mussels have opened. Remove pan from heat, remove mussels with a slotted spoon, and let cool. Once cool, remove the meat.

4. Transfer the contents of the saucepan, the mussel meat, the heavy cream, and ½ cup of the milk to a food processor and puree until smooth.

5. Strain through a fine sieve and transfer to a clean pan. Bring to a simmer and season with salt and pepper.

6. Add the remaining milk, and then use a milk frother or a hand blender to froth the soup.

7. Ladle into warm cups, top with a spoonful of milk froth, sprinkle with five–spice, and serve with Shrimp Crackers.

SHRIMP CRACKERS

1. In a medium saucepan, add the water and bring it to a simmer.

2. Meanwhile, place the shrimp in a food processor and blend until smooth.

3. Add the salt, sugar, pepper, and baking powder to the food processor and mix for 2 minutes.

4. Add the tapioca starch and blend until the batter starts to form into a ball.

5. Place the batter on a clean surface and knead with your hands for 5 minutes, or until it is a smooth paste.

Continued . . .

INGREDIENTS:

- 2 TABLESPOONS BUTTER
- 2 SHALLOTS, CHOPPED
- 1 GARLIC CLOVE, MINCED
- ½ CUP WHITE WINE
- 2 SPRIGS CILANTRO
- 2 POUNDS MUSSELS
- ½ CUP HEAVY CREAM
- 1½ CUPS MILK
  SALT AND PEPPER, TO TASTE
  FIVE-SPICE, FOR GARNISH

TO SERVE:
SHRIMP CRACKERS

SHRIMP CRACKERS
- 4 CUPS WATER
- 8 OZ. RAW SHRIMP, SHELLS REMOVED AND DEVEINED
- 1 TEASPOON SALT
- 1 TEASPOON SUGAR
- ¼ TEASPOON GROUND BLACK PEPPER
- ½ TEASPOON BAKING POWDER
- 2 CUPS TAPIOCA STARCH
- 2 CUPS VEGETABLE OIL
  SALT, PEPPER, AND PAPRIKA, TO TASTE

6. Separate into 2 balls and roll each into a 1-inch log.

7. Wrap each log in plastic wrap, nice and tight, and tie a knot at each end.

8. Gently place the logs in the simmering water and reduce the heat to the lowest temperature. Cook for 20 minutes.

9. Remove and submerge in ice water until cool.

10. Once the logs have cooled, remove from plastic wrap and place on paper towels to dry. When they are dry, chill in refrigerator overnight.

11. When ready to serve, place the vegetable oil in a Dutch oven and cook over medium-high heat until it is 375°F.

12. Cut the logs into ⅛-inch slices and drop into the hot oil until crispy.

13. Remove with tongs or a slotted spoon and transfer to a paper towel to drain. Season with salt, pepper, and paprika, and serve.

WRAPPING THE SHRIMP CRACKER LOGS IN PLASTIC WRAP

Plastic wrap is a great way to shape your preparations, acting as intestines do for sausage.

Place one layer of plastic wrap on the table. Using a towel, flatten it down smoothly on the table. Place one more layer of plastic wrap on top and smooth again with a towel. Place the mix in a tube-like shape, ½ the size you want the final tube to be. Roll up the log with the plastic wrap, so it's completely covered. Grab each end of the plastic wrap and tighten. Tie a knot at each end of log and follow the instructions for the recipe.

SEAFOOD *and* SAUSAGE GUMBO

YIELD: 4 TO 6 SERVINGS / ACTIVE TIME: 30 MINUTES / TOTAL TIME: 1 HOUR

This gumbo takes some time, but trust me, it's well worth the investment.

1. To make a Cajun roux, heat the oil in a medium saucepan. Once the oil is hot, add the flour a little at a time and blend until it is a smooth paste.

2. Cook for about 5 to 10 minutes, while stirring constantly, until the roux is the color of peanut butter. Remove pan from heat and set aside to cool.

3. In a medium saucepan, add the butter and cook over medium heat until melted. Add the onion, peppers, and celery. Cook for 5 minutes, or until the onions have softened.

4. Add the sausage and garlic and cook for 5 minutes.

5. Add the bay leaf, thyme, and cayenne. Stir in the stock, tomatoes, and okra. Bring to a boil, reduce heat so that the soup simmers, and cook for 10 minutes.

6. Meanwhile, cook the rice according to the manufacturer's instructions.

7. Whisk the roux into the soup and return to a boil, while whisking constantly. Lower the heat and simmer for 5 minutes.

8. Add the shrimp, crab, and calamari. Cook for 3 to 4 minutes, or until the shrimp turns pink and the calamari bodies begin to curl.

9. Season with salt, pepper, and, if using, the Tabasco™.

10. To serve, put a scoop of rice in the middle of a warm bowl and ladle the gumbo around it.

INGREDIENTS:

½ CUP VEGETABLE OIL

½ CUP ALL-PURPOSE FLOUR

4 TABLESPOONS BUTTER

1 ONION, FINELY CHOPPED

1 CUP GREEN BELL PEPPER, SEEDED AND CHOPPED

1 CUP RED BELL PEPPER, SEEDED AND CHOPPED

2 CELERY STALKS, CHOPPED

1 POUND ANDOUILLE SAUSAGE, CUT INTO ½-INCH SLICES

2 GARLIC CLOVES, MINCED

1 BAY LEAF

¼ TEASPOON THYME, LEAVES REMOVED AND CHOPPED

½ TEASPOON CAYENNE PEPPER

3 CUPS LOBSTER OR CRAB STOCK

1 CUP TOMATO, CONCASSE AND CHOPPED (SEE PAGE 89)

1 CUP CANNED, CUT OKRA

1½ CUPS LONG-GRAIN RICE

1½ POUNDS RAW SHRIMP, PEELED AND DEVEINED

8 OZ. CRAB MEAT, COOKED AND CLEANED

8 OZ. CALAMARI, TENTACLES WHOLE, BODIES HALVED AND SCORED

SALT AND PEPPER, TO TASTE

TABASCO™

SCORING CALAMARI

Separate the squid's body from the tentacles. Cut the body in half and separate the two halves. Flip them over so that the skin is right-side up and gently cut crisscross patterns into them with a sharp knife, being careful not to cut into the flesh.

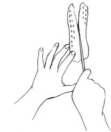
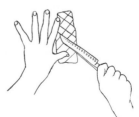

CREAMY HADDOCK CHOWDER

YIELD: 4 SERVINGS / ACTIVE TIME: 30 MINUTES / TOTAL TIME: 1 HOUR

This thick, satisfying soup is packed with fish and potatoes, making it perfect for the winter.

1. In a medium saucepan, add the bacon and cook over low heat until crispy.

2. Add the onion and potatoes and cook for 10 minutes.

3. Add fish stock and bring to a boil.

4. Reduce the heat so that the soup simmers and cook for 10 minutes, or until the potatoes are soft.

5. Add the haddock and the herbs and simmer for 10 minutes.

6. Add the cream and slowly return to a simmer. Season with salt and pepper, ladle into warm bowls, garnish with chives, and serve with Chowder Crackers.

CHOWDER CRACKERS

1. Preheat oven to 375°F.

2. Add the flour, salt, sugar, and baking powder to a mixing bowl and whisk until combined. Add butter and mix with your hands until the mixture resembles a coarse meal.

3. Add the water and mix until it forms a dough. Be careful not to overmix.

4. Place the dough in a lightly floured bowl and chill in the refrigerator for 15 to 20 minutes.

5. Remove the dough from the refrigerator and place on a well-floured surface. Roll out to a ¼-inch thickness, cut dough into ½-inch diamonds, and transfer to a parchment-lined baking tray.

6. Place the tray in the oven and bake for 20 minutes, or until there is just a little color around the edges. Remove and let cool on a wire rack.

INGREDIENTS:

- 4 PIECES THICK-CUT BACON, CUT INTO SMALL PIECES
- 1 LARGE ONION, CHOPPED
- 4 CUPS POTATOES, CUT INTO ¼-INCH CUBES
- 4 CUPS FISH STOCK
- 1½ POUNDS HADDOCK, SKIN REMOVED, CUT INTO ½-INCH CUBES
- 2 TABLESPOONS PARSLEY, LEAVES REMOVED AND CHOPPED
- 1 TABLESPOON CHIVES, CHOPPED, PLUS MORE FOR GARNISH
- 1 TABLESPOON TARRAGON, LEAVES REMOVED AND CHOPPED
- 2 CUPS HEAVY CREAM
  SALT AND PEPPER, TO TASTE

TO SERVE:
CHOWDER CRACKERS

CHOWDER CRACKERS
- 1 CUP ALL-PURPOSE FLOUR
- 1 TEASPOON SALT
- 1 TEASPOON SUGAR
- 1 TEASPOON BAKING POWDER
- 2 TABLESPOONS BUTTER, CUT INTO ¼-INCH CUBES
- ¼ CUP COLD WATER, PLUS 3 TABLESPOONS

CHILLED TUNA NIÇOISE SOUP

YIELD: 4 SERVINGS / ACTIVE TIME: 25 MINUTES / TOTAL TIME: 1 HOUR

This famous salad from Nice shouldn't work as a soup, but the garlic-olive broth comes to the rescue.

1. Bring 4 cups of salted water to a boil. Add the green beans and cook for 2 to 3 minutes. Remove and submerge in ice water. Once cool, cut in half, lengthwise.

2. Add the potatoes to the boiling water and cook for 10 minutes, or until a toothpick can be inserted smoothly. Remove and submerge in ice water. Once cool, cut in half.

3. In a medium saucepan, add the stock, garlic, red wine vinegar, Dijon mustard, olive brine, lemon juice, and Worcestershire sauce. Bring to a simmer and cook for 10 minutes. Remove from heat and let cool.

4. Once cool, strain the soup through a fine sieve, season with salt and pepper, and refrigerate until ready to use.

5. Meanwhile, season the tuna pieces with salt and pepper. Add 1 tablespoon of the olive oil to a non-stick pan and cook over medium-high heat. When the oil is warm, add the pieces of tuna and cook for 30 seconds on each side.

6. Remove tuna from pan, set to drain on a paper towel, and refrigerate immediately.

7. Add the green beans, potatoes, tomato, anchovies, black olives, and microgreens to a bowl with the remaining olive oil and toss gently. Season with salt and pepper and place on chilled plate with the tuna. Right before serving, add Poached Egg to the plate (see next page). Pour the soup tableside in front of your guests, and serve with crusty bread.

INGREDIENTS:

16   **GREEN BEANS**

8   **SMALL CREAMER OR FINGERLING POTATOES**

4   **CUPS VEGETABLE STOCK**

3   **GARLIC CLOVES, MINCED**

2   **TEASPOONS RED WINE VINEGAR**

2   **TEASPOONS DIJON MUSTARD**

2   **TABLESPOONS KALAMATA OLIVE BRINE**

2   **TEASPOONS LEMON JUICE**

    DASH OF WORCESTERSHIRE SAUCE

8   **OZ. YELLOWFIN TUNA, CUT INTO 4 PIECES**

    SALT AND PEPPER, TO TASTE

2   **TABLESPOONS EXTRA VIRGIN OLIVE OIL**

1   **PLUM TOMATO, CONCASSE (SEE PAGE 89) AND CUT INTO THIN STRIPS**

8   **ANCHOVY FILLETS, DRAINED**

8   **BLACK OLIVES, PITTED AND CUT INTO QUARTERS**

    MICROGREENS

TO SERVE:
POACHED EGGS

Continued . . .

POACHED EGGS

1. Crack each egg into a small, individual bowl.

2. In a medium saucepan, add 3 cups water and 2 tablespoons white and bring to a boil.

3. Reduce the heat so that the water simmers and gently add the eggs to the water one at a time.

4. Cook for 3 minutes, gently basting the eggs with the poaching water as they cook.

5. Gently remove the eggs with a slotted spoon and place on a paper towel to dry.

6. Season each egg with salt and pepper and serve immediately.

SPICY CLAM BROTH

YIELD: 6 SERVINGS / ACTIVE TIME: 30 MINUTES / TOTAL TIME: 1 HOUR

This broth comes to us by way of Cambodia—and when you see how packed with clams it is, you'll be glad that it did.

1. In a medium saucepan, add the oil and cook over medium heat until warm. Add the onion and cook for 5 minutes, or until soft.

2. Add the garlic, Thai chilies, and chorizo. Cook for 2 minutes and then add the wine.

3. Bring to a boil, reduce the heat so that the soup simmers, and cook for 2 minutes.

4. Add the tomatoes, diced potato, and stock. Return to a boil, reduce heat so that the soup simmers, cover, and cook until the broth has thickened and the potatoes are beginning to break apart.

5. Add the clams, cover, and cook for 5 to 6 minutes, or until the clams have opened.

6. Stir in the cilantro and parsley and season with salt.

7. Ladle the soup into warm bowls and serve with a lemon wedges, Chorizo Oil, parsley, and toasted bread rubbed with garlic.

CHORIZO OIL

1. In a small pan, add the oil and cook over low heat until warm. Add the chorizo and garlic and bring to a simmer.

2. Remove from heat and let stand until cool. Strain to remove the solids and serve.

INGREDIENTS:

- 2 TABLESPOONS EXTRA VIRGIN OLIVE OIL
- 1 ONION, FINELY CHOPPED
- 2 GARLIC CLOVES, MINCED
- 2 THAI CHILIES, SEEDED AND FINELY CHOPPED
- ⅔ CUP SPICY DRIED CHORIZO, FINELY CHOPPED
- 1 CUP WHITE WINE
- 1 14 OZ. CAN OF STEWED TOMATOES
- 1½ CUPS POTATO, PEELED AND DICED
- 2 CUPS CRAB STOCK
- 4 POUNDS LITTLE NECK CLAMS, SCRUBBED AND RINSED UNDER COLD WATER
- 1 TABLESPOON CILANTRO, CHOPPED
- 1 TABLESPOON PARSLEY, CHOPPED, PLUS MORE FOR GARNISH
- SALT, TO TASTE
- LEMON WEDGES, FOR GARNISH

TO SERVE:
CHORIZO OIL

CHORIZO OIL
- 4 TABLESPOONS VEGETABLE OIL
- 2 TABLESPOONS CHORIZO, CHOPPED
- 1 GARLIC CLOVE, CHOPPED

CULLEN SKINK

YIELD: 4 SERVINGS / ACTIVE TIME: 30 MINUTES / TOTAL TIME: 25 HOURS

This soup comes courtesy of Chef Chris McCall, who hails from Scotland. Chris claims the name of this soup originates from the town of Cullen in Northeast Scotland, a major white-fish port back in its day.

As I do not have an outdoor smoker at my house, I used a smoking gun to cold smoke the fish indoors. If you want, you can purchase the fish already smoked.

1. In a bowl, add the haddock, water, and salt and let stand for 10 minutes.

2. Remove the haddock and rinse under cold water.

3. Place the haddock on a cooking rack with a tray underneath it. Lightly cover the tray and then place it in the refrigerator overnight.

4. Remove the haddock from the refrigerator and cold smoke for 12 hours.

5. When the haddock has finished smoking, place it in a medium saucepan. Cover with the milk and simmer for 10 minutes, or until the fish becomes flaky. Remove the fish from the pan and reserve the poaching milk.

6. Meanwhile, in a medium saucepan, add the butter and cook over low heat until melted. Add the onion and cook for 5 minutes, or until soft.

7. Add the leeks, the potato, and the poaching milk to the saucepan and cook for 5 minutes, or until the potato is tender.

8. Use a fork to flake the haddock. Add flakes to the soup.

9. Season with salt and pepper and ladle into warmed bowls. Serve with Bacon Jam (see next page), crusty bread, and garnish with chives.

INGREDIENTS:

9   OZ. HADDOCK FILLET, SKIN ON

1½ CUPS WATER

1   CUP SALT

4   CUPS MILK, OR ENOUGH TO COVER THE HADDOCK

4   TABLESPOONS BUTTER

1   ONION, CHOPPED

1   CUP LEEKS, SLICED

1   CUP POTATO, PEELED AND CHOPPED

    SALT AND PEPPER, TO TASTE

    CHIVES, CHOPPED, FOR GARNISH

TO SERVE:
BACON JAM

BACON JAM

8   OZ. THICK-CUT BACON

2   SHALLOTS, FINELY CHOPPED

1   GARLIC CLOVE, MINCED

2   TABLESPOONS APPLE CIDER VINEGAR

2   TABLESPOONS BROWN SUGAR

1   TABLESPOON MAPLE SYRUP

Continued . . .

BACON JAM

This is not a traditional side for this soup, but the smokiness and the sweetness work well together.

1. Preheat oven to 350°F.

2. Place the bacon in the oven and cook for 20 minutes, or until crispy. Reserve rendered fat.

3. Finely chop the cooked bacon.

4. Place the reserved bacon fat in a medium saucepan and cook over medium heat until warm. Add shallots and garlic and cook for 5 minutes, or until translucent.

5. Add the apple cider vinegar, brown sugar, and maple syrup and simmer for 5 minutes.

6. Add the chopped crispy bacon and let cool. Transfer to a container until ready to serve.

CANH CHUA CÁ

YIELD: 4 SERVINGS / ACTIVE TIME: 30 MINUTES / TOTAL TIME: 45 MINUTES

This beautiful, flavorful, hot-and-sour soup is perfect for a summertime lunch.

1. Season the catfish with salt, pepper, and chili powder.

2. In a medium saucepan, add the vegetable oil and cook over medium heat until warm. Add the minced garlic and cook for 5 minutes. Transfer the garlic and the oil to a small bowl. Add the Thai chili and reserve for garnish.

3. Add the chopped tomato to the saucepan and cook for 3 minutes. Add the stock and bring to a boil.

4. Reduce heat so that the soup simmers. Add the tamarind extract, sugar, fish sauce, pineapple, and okra, and cook for 2 minutes.

5. Add the catfish and cook for 3 minutes. Add the bean sprouts and cook for an additional 2 minutes. Add the basil and spring onions. Season to taste with fish sauce, salt, and pepper and serve in warm bowls garnished with tomato wedges and a splash of the garlic-and-chili oil.

INGREDIENTS:

1	POUND CATFISH, CUT INTO ½-INCH PIECES
	SALT AND PEPPER, TO TASTE
	CHILI POWDER, TO TASTE
2	TABLESPOONS VEGETABLE OIL
2	TABLESPOONS GARLIC, MINCED
1	THAI CHILI, SEEDS REMOVED AND SLICED
3	TOMATOES, 1 CHOPPED, THE OTHER 2 CUT INTO WEDGES
6	CUPS VEGETABLE STOCK
1	TABLESPOON TAMARIND EXTRACT
¼	CUP SUGAR
¼	CUP FISH SAUCE
1	CUP PINEAPPLE, THINLY SLICED
6	OKRA, THINLY SLICED
2	OZ. BEAN SPROUTS
1	BUNCH THAI BASIL, LEAVES REMOVED AND CHOPPED
2	SPRING ONIONS, FINELY SLICED

LEEK *and* FISH SOUP

YIELD: 4 TO 6 SERVINGS / ACTIVE TIME: 30 MINUTES / TOTAL TIME: 1 HOUR

A soup so filling, it's nearly a stew. A perfect *fruits de mer.*

1. Add the oil to a medium saucepan and cook over medium heat until warm. Add the leeks, crushed coriander seeds, and chili flakes and cook for 5 minutes.

2. Add potatoes and tomatoes. Pour in the stock and the wine, add the bay leaves, star anise, orange zest, and saffron and bring to a boil. Reduce heat so that the soup simmers and cook for 15 minutes, or until the potatoes are tender.

3. Taste and adjust the seasoning. Add the fish and the squid to the soup and cook for 3 to 4 minutes. Add the shrimp and cook for 2 minutes.

4. Serve in warm bowls with Parsley Grilled Baguette, Garlic Mayonnaise, and microgreens.

GARLIC MAYONNAISE

1. Combine the egg yolk, garlic, vinegar, water, and mustard in a stainless steel bowl. Whisk until foamy.

2. Gradually add the oils in a thin stream, constantly whisking until all of the oils have been incorporated and the mayonnaise is thick.

3. Season with lemon juice, salt, and pepper. Refrigerate immediately.

INGREDIENTS:

2	TABLESPOONS EXTRA VIRGIN OLIVE OIL
2	LEEKS, WHITE PART ONLY, CUT INTO ⅛-INCH SLICES
2	TEASPOONS CORIANDER SEEDS, CRUSHED
⅛	TEASPOON CHILI FLAKES
3	CUPS MULTI-COLORED LITTLE CREAMER POTATOES, CUT INTO ¼-INCH SLICES
1	14 OZ. CAN DICED TOMATOES
4	CUPS FISH STOCK
1	CUP WHITE WINE
2	BAY LEAVES
1	STAR ANISE
	ZEST OF 1 ORANGE
⅛	TEASPOON SAFFRON
1	POUND COD FILLET, CUT INTO ½-INCH PIECES
1	POUND SMALL SQUID, BODIES HALVED AND SCORED, TENTACLES LEFT WHOLE
10	OZ. SHRIMP, PEELED AND DEVEINED
	SALT AND PEPPER, TO TASTE

TO SERVE:

GARLIC MAYONNAISE

PARSLEY GRILLED BAGUETTE

PARSLEY GRILLED BAGUETTE

1. In a large sauté pan, add 2 tablespoons of the butter and cook over medium heat until melted.

2. Add 4 slices of the baguette and cook for 1 minute, flip, sprinkle half of the chopped parsley on and cook for another minute.

3. Flip the pieces of bread and cook the side with the parsley on it for 30 seconds.

4. Repeat with the remaining 4 slices of baguette.

GARLIC MAYONNAISE

1	EGG YOLK
4	GARLIC CLOVES, MASHED TO A PASTE
1	TABLESPOON WHITE VINEGAR
1	TABLESPOON WATER
½	TEASPOON DRY MUSTARD
1	CUP VEGETABLE OIL
½	CUP EXTRA VIRGIN OLIVE OIL
1	TEASPOON LEMON JUICE
	SALT AND PEPPER, TO TASTE

PARSLEY GRILLED BAGUETTE

4	TABLESPOONS BUTTER
8	SLICES BAGUETTE
1	TABLESPOON PARSLEY, LEAVES REMOVED AND CHOPPED

SEAFARERS' STEW

YIELD: 4 SERVINGS / ACTIVE TIME: 30 MINUTES / TOTAL TIME: 13 HOURS

Feel free to be creative with the seafood you use in this stew. However, make sure to use a smoked fish, as its flavor is crucial to the dish.

1. In a large saucepan over medium heat, add the mackerel, swordfish, shrimp, lobster stock, and fish stock. Bring to a simmer and cook for 5 minutes.

2. Add the clams, cover the pan, and cook for 3 minutes.

3. Add the mussels and cook for an additional 3 minutes, or until the mussels and clams have opened. Remove any that don't open.

4. Strain the soup through a fine sieve and reserve the broth and the solids.

5. In a large saucepan, add the oil and cook over medium-high heat until warm. Add the shallots and bacon and cook until the bacon is browned.

6. Add the broth and bring to a boil. Reduce heat so that the soup simmers, add the carrots, and cook for 5 minutes.

7. Add the cream and the reserved solids. Continue to simmer.

8. Ladle into warmed bowls and garnish with Crispy Calamari and parsley.

CRISPY CALAMARI

1. Add the oil to a Dutch oven and cook over medium-high heat until oil reaches 375°F.

2. Place the calamari and the buttermilk in a bowl. Marinate for 15 minutes.

3. Combine the flour, cornmeal, and Old Bay seasoning in a bowl. Dredge the calamari in the mixture until evenly coated.

4. Using tongs, gently place the calamari into the oil. Cook until golden brown, remove with a slotted spoon, and set on a paper towel to drain. Season with salt and pepper and serve.

INGREDIENTS:

- 8 OZ. SMOKED MACKEREL, SKIN REMOVED, CUT INTO ¼-INCH PIECES
- 8 OZ. SWORDFISH, CUT INTO 1-INCH CUBES
- 4 OZ. SMALL SHRIMP, SKINS REMOVED AND DEVEINED
- 3 CUPS LOBSTER STOCK
- 3 CUPS FISH STOCK
- 8 CLAMS, CLEANED
- 8 MUSSELS, CLEANED
- 1 TABLESPOON EXTRA VIRGIN OLIVE OIL
- 2 SHALLOTS, MINCED
- 4 PIECES THICK-CUT BACON, CUT INTO 1-INCH PIECES
- 3 CUPS CARROTS, PEELED AND GRATED
- ¾ CUP HEAVY CREAM
- SALT AND PEPPER, TO TASTE
- PARSLEY, CHOPPED, FOR GARNISH

TO SERVE:
CRISPY CALAMARI

CRISPY CALAMARI

- 1 CUP VEGETABLE OIL
- 6 CALAMARI TENTACLES
- 2 CALAMARI BODIES, SLICED INTO ¼-INCH RINGS
- 1 CUP BUTTERMILK
- ½ CUP ALL-PURPOSE FLOUR
- ½ CUP CORNMEAL
- 1 TEASPOON OLD BAY SEASONING
- SALT AND PEPPER, TO TASTE

SMOKED MACKEREL *and* TOMATO SOUP

YIELD: 4 SERVINGS / ACTIVE TIME: 25 MINUTES / TOTAL TIME: 12 HOURS AND 45 MINUTES

Sadly, mackerel is an overlooked fish. It's very flavorful and very oily. I grew up on the coast catching them, so personally I love them. This soup is quick, easy to prepare, and easy to clean up.

1. In a medium saucepan, add the stock, lemongrass, galangal root, shallots, and garlic. Bring to a boil and then reduce the heat so that the broth simmers. Cook for 10 minutes.

2. Add the fish, tomatoes, red chili flakes, fish sauce, brown sugar, and tamarind extract. Cook for 5 minutes.

3. Meanwhile, add the scallions to the broth and cook for 2 minutes. Remove and submerge in ice water. When cool, tie the scallions into knots.

4. Remove the galangal root and lemongrass. Season with salt and pepper and serve in warm bowls with the scallion knots and Crispy Mackerel Skin.

CRISPY MACKEREL SKIN

1. Remove any excess meat from the skin with the back of a knife. Gently lay the skin on a lined baking tray.

2. Let dry in a warm place overnight.

3. When ready to serve, add the vegetable oil to a Dutch oven and cook over medium-high heat until it is 375°F.

4. When the skin is dry, place it in the oil and fry until it is crispy and golden brown.

5. Remove with tongs or a slotted spoon and set on a paper towel to drain. Season with salt and pepper, and serve.

INGREDIENTS:

6 CUPS VEGETABLE STOCK

1 STALK LEMONGRASS, BRUISED WITH THE BACK OF A KNIFE

2-INCH PIECE OF GALANGAL ROOT

4 SHALLOTS, FINELY CHOPPED

2 GARLIC CLOVES, MINCED

12 OZ. SMOKED MACKEREL FILLETS, SKIN REMOVED AND RESERVED FOR GARNISH, MEAT CUT INTO 1-INCH PIECES

4 TOMATOES, SEEDS REMOVED, FINELY CHOPPED

½ TEASPOON RED CHILI FLAKES

2 TABLESPOONS FISH SAUCE

2 TEASPOONS LIGHT BROWN SUGAR

2 TABLESPOONS TAMARIND EXTRACT

8 SCALLIONS

SALT AND PEPPER, TO TASTE

TO SERVE:

CRISPY MACKEREL SKIN, OPTIONAL

CRISPY MACKEREL SKIN

RESERVED MACKEREL SKIN

SALT AND PEPPER, TO TASTE

1 CUP VEGETABLE OIL

SOLE *and* PASTA SOUP

YIELD: 4 SERVINGS / ACTIVE TIME: 30 MINUTES / TOTAL TIME: 1 HOUR AND 30 MINUTES

This beautiful and light Mediterranean soup is perfect for lunch, so make a little extra and bring it to work tomorrow.

1. Over an open flame, char the red pepper on all sides. Place in a bowl, cover with plastic wrap, and let stand for 10 minutes. Remove the skin and seeds and chop the pepper into small pieces. Reserve ¼ for the Rouille.

2. In a large saucepan, add the oil and cook over medium heat until warm. Add the onion, garlic, and leek and cook for 5 minutes, or until soft.

3. Add vegetable stock, tomatoes, Mediterranean Herbs, and saffron and bring to a boil. Add the pasta and cook for 15 minutes.

4. Add the fish and roasted red pepper. Add the mussels, reduce heat so that the soup simmers, and cook for 5 to 10 minutes, or until the mussels open and the fish is cooked. Discard any mussels that do not open.

5. Season with salt and pepper and serve in warm bowls with toasted French bread and the Rouille.

ROUILLE

1. Combine the egg yolk, garlic, vinegar, water, and dry mustard in a stainless-steel bowl. Whisk until foamy.

2. Gradually add the oil in a thin stream, constantly whisking until the oil has been incorporated and the mixture is thick.

3. Add the lemon juice, chili powder, and finely chopped roasted red pepper.

4. Season with salt and pepper and refrigerate immediately.

INGREDIENTS:

1	RED BELL PEPPER
2	TABLESPOONS EXTRA VIRGIN OLIVE OIL
1	ONION, SLICED
1	GARLIC CLOVE, MINCED
½	LEEK, WHITE PART ONLY, SLICED
4	CUPS VEGETABLE STOCK
1	14 OZ. CAN DICED TOMATOES
1	TEASPOON MEDITERRANEAN HERBS (SEE RECIPE ON PAGE 325)
⅛	TEASPOON SAFFRON
2	CUPS FARFALLE PASTA
1½	POUNDS SOLE FILLETS, CLEANED AND HALVED LENGTHWISE
16	MUSSELS
	SALT AND PEPPER, TO TASTE

TO SERVE:
TOASTED FRENCH BREAD WITH ROUILLE

ROUILLE

1	EGG YOLK
4	GARLIC CLOVES, MASHED
1	TABLESPOON WHITE WINE VINEGAR
1½	TEASPOONS WATER
½	TEASPOON DRY MUSTARD
1	CUP VEGETABLE OIL
1	TEASPOON LEMON JUICE
⅛	TEASPOON CHILI POWDER
	RESERVED ROASTED RED PEPPER FROM SOUP, FINELY CHOPPED
	SALT AND PEPPER, TO TASTE

SMOKED TROUT *with* TOMATOES *and* PICKLED ENOKI MUSHROOMS

YIELD: 6 SERVINGS / ACTIVE TIME: 30 MINUTES / TOTAL TIME: 1 HOUR

This is a very quick and simple soup that celebrates the wonderful flavors of various mushrooms. Feel free to use whatever mushrooms are available, and don't hesitate to replace the trout with smoked salmon for a different take.

1. In a medium saucepan, add the butter, onion, and garlic and cook over medium heat for 5 minutes, or until soft.

2. Add the bell peppers and Tabasco™ and cook for 2 minutes. Sprinkle the flour over this mixture and cook for 3 minutes, while stirring gently.

3. Add the stock, tomatoes, mushrooms, and milk. Bring to a boil and then reduce heat so that the soup simmers. Cook for 5 minutes, or until the vegetables have softened.

4. Add the haddock and the smoked trout. Cook for 2 to 3 minutes, add the mussels, and cook for 5 minutes. Discard any mussels that do not open.

5. Season with salt and pepper and ladle into warmed bowls. Garnish with parsley and gruyere and serve with a sliced baguette, Rouille, and Pickled Enoki Mushrooms.

PICKLED ENOKI MUSHROOMS

1. In a small saucepan, add the water, rice wine vinegar, and sugar. Bring to a boil, add the chives, and cook for 30 seconds.

2. Use tongs to remove the chives. Submerge in ice water and set aside. Remove the saucepan from heat and let cool; this is the pickling liquid.

3. Wrap the bunches of mushrooms with 2 pieces of chive and tie to hold them together.

4. Pour the pickling liquid over the enoki mushrooms and marinate for 30 minutes.

INGREDIENTS:

2	TABLESPOONS BUTTER
1	ONION, FINELY CHOPPED
1	GARLIC CLOVE, MINCED
½	CUP RED BELL PEPPER, FINELY CHOPPED
½	CUP GREEN BELL PEPPER, FINELY CHOPPED
½	TEASPOON TABASCO™
¼	CUP ALL-PURPOSE FLOUR
3	CUPS FISH STOCK
1	14 OZ. CAN DICED TOMATOES
¾	CUPS BEECH MUSHROOMS
¾	CUPS BABY BROWN PEARL MUSHROOMS, SLICED
1	CUP MILK
12	OZ. HADDOCK, CUT INTO 1/2-INCH PIECES
4	OZ. SMOKED TROUT, CUT INTO ¼-INCH PIECES
12	MUSSELS, CLEANED
	SALT AND PEPPER, TO TASTE
	PARSLEY, CHOPPED, FOR GARNISH
	GRUYERE CHEESE, GRATED, FOR GARNISH

TO SERVE:
SLICED BAGUETTE
ROUILLE (SEE RECIPE ON PAGE 570)
PICKLED ENOKI MUSHROOMS

PICKLED ENOKI MUSHROOMS

¼	CUP WATER
¼	CUP RICE WINE VINEGAR
¼	CUP SUGAR
12	CHIVES
6	BUNCHES OF ENOKI MUSHROOMS

BOUILLABAISSE

YIELD: 6 SERVINGS / ACTIVE TIME: 25 MINUTES / TOTAL TIME: 1 HOUR

This is one of the most popular dishes in the Mediterranean region. Originally a stew made by Marseille fishermen to use up the bony rockfish which they were unable to sell, it is now a treasure on menus worldwide.

1. In a medium saucepan, warm 4 tablespoons of the olive oil over medium heat. Add the onion, leek, celery, and fennel and cook for 10 minutes, or until soft.

2. Add the garlic, bouquet garni, orange zest, and chopped tomato. Stir in the saffron and then add the fish stock, lobster stock, Pernod, and tomato paste. Season with salt and pepper and bring to a boil. Reduce heat so that the soup simmers and cook for 20 minutes.

3. Meanwhile, in a separate pan add the remaining oil and warm it over medium heat. Season the fish and shrimp with salt and pepper and cook for 2 minutes on each side. Remove both from the pan and set aside.

4. Add the clams to the broth and cook for 3 minutes. Add the mussels and cook for an additional 3 to 4 minutes. Discard any mussels that don't open.

5. Add the fish and shrimp to the broth and warm through.

6. Season with salt and pepper and ladle the soup into warm bowls. Serve with toasted baguette and Garlic Butter and garnish with parsley.

GARLIC BUTTER

Place the butter in a bowl and whisk for 2 minutes. Add the remaining ingredients, season with salt and pepper, and serve.

INGREDIENTS:

6	TABLESPOONS EXTRA VIRGIN OLIVE OIL
1	ONION, CHOPPED
1	CUP LEEK, WHITE PART ONLY, SLICED
½	CUP CELERY, SLICED
1	CUP FENNEL, CHOPPED
2	GARLIC CLOVES, MINCED
	BOUQUET GARNI (SEE PAGE 88)
	ZEST OF 1 ORANGE
1	TOMATO, CONCASSE (SEE PAGE 89) AND CHOPPED
	PINCH OF SAFFRON
3	CUPS FISH STOCK
3	CUPS LOBSTER STOCK
2	TEASPOONS PERNOD
1	TABLESPOON TOMATO PASTE
	SALT AND PEPPER, TO TASTE
1	POUND MONKFISH, CUT INTO 1-INCH PIECES
12	SMALL SHRIMP, SHELLED AND DEVEINED
12	STEAMER CLAMS
24	MUSSELS
	PARSLEY, CHOPPED, FOR GARNISH

TO SERVE:
BAGUETTE, SLICED AND TOASTED
GARLIC BUTTER, AT ROOM TEMPERATURE

GARLIC BUTTER

1	CUP BUTTER, SOFTENED
1½	TEASPOONS LEMON JUICE
2	GARLIC CLOVES, MINCED
3	TABLESPOONS PARSLEY, CHOPPED
	SALT AND PEPPER, TO TASTE

CARIBBEAN RICE STEW
with SALT COD BRANDADE EN CROUTE

YIELD: 4 SERVINGS / ACTIVE TIME: 45 MINUTES / TOTAL TIME: 26 HOURS

Based on a classic Caribbean dish, this soup fuses the cuisines of multiple continents.

1. In a medium saucepan, add the oil and butter and cook over medium heat until warm. Add the bacon and cook until crispy. Add the onion, garlic, and red chili and cook for 3 to 4 minutes.

2. Add the rice and cook for 2 minutes. Add the thyme, cinnamon stick, and black-eyed peas and cook for 2 minutes.

3. Add the water and bring to a boil. Reduce heat to low and cook for 20 minutes, or until the rice is cooked.

4. Meanwhile, dredge the pieces of salt cod in the flour.

5. Stir the coconut milk into the saucepan. Bring to a simmer, add the Salt Cod, and cook for 5 minutes.

6. Stir in the baby spinach and remove cinnamon stick. Cook for an additional 3 minutes, season with salt and pepper, and serve in warm bowls with Salt Cod Brandade en Croute.

SALT COD

1. Place half of the salt on a baking tray.

2. Lay the pieces of cod on top of the salt bed. Sprinkle the remaining salt over the fish.

3. Cover and leave in the refrigerator for 12 hours.

4. Remove from the refrigerator and rinse under cold water.

5. Place the fish on a clean baking tray, cover with water, and cover the tray with plastic wrap. Place in refrigerator for 24 hours, changing the water every 6 hours.

6. Drain liquid, pat dry, and refrigerate until needed.

INGREDIENTS:

2	TEASPOONS VEGETABLE OIL
4	TABLESPOONS BUTTER
3	OZ. THICK-CUT BACON, CUT INTO THIN STRIPS
1	ONION, CHOPPED
1	GARLIC CLOVE, MINCED
1	RED CHILI, SEEDED AND CHOPPED
¾	CUP LONG-GRAIN RICE
2	SPRIGS OF THYME, LEAVES REMOVED AND CHOPPED
1	CINNAMON STICK
14	OZ. CAN BLACK-EYED PEAS
4	CUPS WATER
8	OZ. SALT COD, CUT INTO ½-INCH PIECES
1½	TABLESPOONS ALL-PURPOSE FLOUR
1	CUP COCONUT MILK
4	CUPS BABY SPINACH
	SALT AND PEPPER, TO TASTE

TO SERVE:
SALT COD BRANDADE EN CROUTE

SALT COD

12	OZ. COD FILLET, SKIN REMOVED, HALVED
¾	CUP SALT

Continued . . .

SALT COD BRANDADE EN CROUTE

Brandade is an emulsion of salt cod and olive oil that is eaten in France and Spain during the winter.

1. Preheat oven to 375°F.

2. Place potato in the oven and bake for 45 minutes.

3. Meanwhile, in a small saucepan add the salt cod, milk, garlic, and onion and bring to a simmer. Cook for 10 minutes, or until the fish is flaky.

4. Strain through a fine sieve. Reserve both the fish and the milk.

5. Remove the potato from the oven, cut in half, remove the meat, and discard the skin.

6. Place the potato in a small bowl and use a fork to mash it.

7. Add the butter, capers, dill, parsley, lemon juice, and Tabasco™ to the bowl. Mix until combined. Add 2 to 3 tablespoons of the reserved milk, or enough to make it nice and creamy.

8. Season with salt and pepper and serve on the toasted brioche.

INGREDIENTS (CONTINUED):

SALT COD BRANDADE EN CROUTE

1	SMALL POTATO
4	OZ. SALT COD
½	CUP MILK
1	GARLIC CLOVE, MINCED
½	ONION, CHOPPED
2	TEASPOONS BUTTER
2	TEASPOONS CAPERS, CHOPPED
2	TEASPOONS DILL, CHOPPED
2	TEASPOONS PARSLEY, CHOPPED
1	TEASPOON LEMON JUICE
¼	TEASPOON TABASCO™
	SALT AND PEPPER, TO TASTE
4	SLICES BRIOCHE, HALVED AND TOASTED

THAI FISH BROTH

YIELD: 4 SERVINGS / ACTIVE TIME: 20 MINUTES / TOTAL TIME: 45 MINUTES

This is a very fragrant broth thanks to the lemongrass, chilies, galangal root, lime juice, and lime leaf. It's meant to be very sour, which makes it perfect as a palate cleanser.

1. In a medium saucepan, add the fish stock, lemongrass, lime zest, galangal root, cilantro stalks, and lime leaf and bring to a boil. Reduce the heat so that the broth simmers and cook for 5 minutes.

2. Turn off heat and let stand for 15 minutes.

3. Strain the broth through a fine sieve. Return to a cleaned pan and bring to a boil.

4. Reduce heat so that the broth simmers. Add the lime juice, monkfish, shrimp, Thai chilies, rice vinegar, and fish sauce. Simmer for 3 to 4 minutes, or until the fish is cooked.

5. Ladle into warmed bowls and garnish with cilantro leaves, bean sprouts, toasted sesame seeds, and sesame oil.

INGREDIENTS:

- 4 CUPS FISH STOCK
- 2 STALKS OF LEMONGRASS, BRUISED WITH THE BACK OF A KNIFE
- ZEST AND JUICE OF 2 LIMES
- 1-INCH PIECE OF GALANGAL ROOT, PEELED AND THINLY SLICED
- 6 STALKS CILANTRO
- 1 KAFFIR LIME LEAF
- 2 MONKFISH FILLETS, SKINNED AND CUT INTO 1-INCH PIECES
- 12 SMALL SHRIMP
- 2 THAI CHILIES, SEEDED AND THINLY SLICED
- 1 TABLESPOON RICE WINE VINEGAR
- 4 TABLESPOONS FISH SAUCE
- CILANTRO LEAVES, CHOPPED, FOR GARNISH
- BEAN SPROUTS, FOR GARNISH
- TOASTED SESAME SEEDS, FOR GARNISH
- SESAME OIL, FOR GARNISH

NEW ENGLAND CLAM CHOWDER

YIELD: 4 TO 6 SERVINGS / ACTIVE TIME: 45 MINUTES / TOTAL TIME: 1 HOUR AND 30 MINUTES

Chopped clams, potatoes, and cream combine to make this famously rich stew.

1. In a medium saucepan add the clams, wine, and half of the chopped onions. Cover and cook over medium-high heat for 5 minutes, or until all the clams have opened.

2. Strain through a fine sieve. Set the clams aside and reserve the cooking liquid.

3. In a clean medium saucepan, add the butter and cook over medium heat until melted. Add the remaining onions and cook for 5 minutes, or until soft.

4. Add the reserved cooking liquid and thyme and bring to a simmer. Cook for 5 minutes, or until the liquid has been reduced by half.

5. Meanwhile, remove the meat from the clams. Separate the bellies and reserve. Peel the outer membrane from the clam and discard. Roughly chop the clam.

6. Add the potatoes and heavy cream to the saucepan and cook for 5 minutes, or until the potatoes are tender.

7. Add the chopped clams and clam bellies. Season with salt and pepper, and ladle into warm bowls. Garnish with parsley and serve with Oyster Crackers.

OYSTER CRACKERS

1. Preheat oven to 375°F.

2. Add the flour, salt, sugar, and baking powder to a mixing bowl and whisk until combined. Add the butter and mix with your hands until the mixture resembles a coarse meal.

3. Add the water and mix until it a dough forms. Be careful not to overmix.

4. Place the dough in a lightly floured bowl and chill in the refrigerator for 15 to 20 minutes.

5. Remove the bowl from the refrigerator and place on a well-floured surface. Roll to a ¼-inch thickness, cut into small circles with a ring cutter, and transfer to a parchment-lined baking tray.

6. Bake for 20 minutes, or until there is a little color around the bottom edges of the crackers. Remove and let cool on a wire rack before serving.

INGREDIENTS:

- 4 POUNDS STEAMER CLAMS
- 2 CUPS WHITE WINE
- 2 CUPS ONIONS, CHOPPED
- 4 TABLESPOONS BUTTER
- 1 TEASPOON THYME, LEAVES REMOVED AND CHOPPED
- 2 CUPS YUKON GOLD POTATOES, PEELED AND CHOPPED
- 4 CUPS HEAVY CREAM
- SALT AND PEPPER, TO TASTE
- PARSLEY, CHOPPED, FOR GARNISH

TO SERVE:
OYSTER CRACKERS

OYSTER CRACKERS

- 1 CUP ALL-PURPOSE FLOUR
- 1 TEASPOON SALT
- 1 TEASPOON SUGAR
- 1 TEASPOON BAKING POWDER
- 2 TABLESPOONS BUTTER, CUT INTO 1/4-INCH CUBES
- ¼ CUP COLD WATER, PLUS 3 TABLESPOONS

MANHATTAN CLAM CHOWDER
with SALTINES

YIELD: 4 SERVINGS / ACTIVE TIME: 45 MINUTES / TOTAL TIME: 1 HOUR AND 30 MINUTES

This is the "red one," which James Beard famously called "horrendous." But this version has its diehard fans. Try it and you'll see why.

1. In a medium saucepan, add the clams and water. Cover and cook over medium-high heat for 5 minutes, or until all the clams have opened.

2. Use a fine sieve to strain the clams from the water. Reserve the cooking liquid.

3. In a clean medium saucepan, add the salt pork and cook over medium heat until melted. Add the onion, carrots, leeks, green pepper, and garlic and cook for 5 minutes, or until soft.

4. Add the reserved cooking liquid, tomato juice, tomato, bay leaf, thyme, and oregano. Bring to a simmer and cook for 10 minutes.

5. Meanwhile, remove the meat from the clams. Separate the bellies and reserve. Peel the outer membrane from the clam and discard. Roughly chop the clam and set aside.

6. Add the potato to the saucepan and cook for 5 minutes, or until tender.

7. Remove the bay leaf, thyme, and oregano. Add the chopped clams and the clam bellies. Season with Tabasco™, Worcestershire sauce, and Old Bay, ladle into warm bowls, and serve with Saltines (see next page).

INGREDIENTS:

- 15 STEAMER CLAMS, SCRUBBED AND CLEANED
- 2 CUPS WATER
- ⅓ CUP SALT PORK, CHOPPED
- ¾ CUP ONION, CHOPPED
- ⅓ CUP CARROTS, FINELY CHOPPED
- 1 CUP LEEKS, WHITE PART ONLY, FINELY CHOPPED
- ⅓ CUP GREEN BELL PEPPER, FINELY CHOPPED
- 1 GARLIC CLOVE, MINCED
- 1 CUP TOMATO JUICE
- ½ CUP TOMATO, CONCASSE (SEE PAGE 89) AND CHOPPED
- 1 BAY LEAF
- 1 SPRIG THYME
- ½ SPRIG OREGANO
- 1 CUP POTATO, PEELED AND CHOPPED
- ⅛ TEASPOON TABASCO™
- ⅛ TEASPOON WORCESTERSHIRE SAUCE
- ⅛ TEASPOON OLD BAY

TO SERVE:
SALTINES

Continued . . .

SALTINES

This is a classic from your cupboard, but try making my homemade version.

1. Preheat oven to 325°F.

2. In a mixing bowl, add the flour and baking powder and whisk until combined. Add the butter and knead with your hands until the mixture resembles a coarse meal.

3. Add the milk and mix until a dough forms. Be careful not to overmix.

4. Place the dough in a lightly floured bowl and chill in the refrigerator for 15 to 20 minutes.

5. Remove the bowl from the refrigerator and place dough on a well-floured surface. Roll out to ⅛-inch thickness. Cut dough into 2½-inch squares and transfer them to a parchment-lined baking tray.

6. Using a fork to prick holes in the squares.

7. In a small bowl, add the egg yolk and the water, and whisk until combined. Use a pastry brush to apply a very thin layer of the egg wash on each cracker.

8. Sprinkle with a small amount of coarse salt, place the tray in the oven, and bake for 20 minutes, or until there is a little color around the bottom edges. Remove and let cool on a wire rack before serving.

INGREDIENTS (CONTINUED):

SALTINES

2 CUPS ALL-PURPOSE FLOUR

1½ TEASPOONS BAKING POWDER

2 TABLESPOONS BUTTER

¾ CUP MILK

1 EGG YOLK

1 TEASPOON WATER

COARSE SALT, TO TASTE

CORN *and* SEAFOOD CHOWDER
with SALT COD BEIGNETS

YIELD: 4 TO 6 SERVINGS / ACTIVE TIME: 1 HOUR / TOTAL TIME: 36 HOURS

For something utilizing the famously light fruits of the sea, this is a very rich dish.

1. In a blender, add the corn kernels and milk and puree until creamy.

2. In a medium saucepan, add the butter and cook over medium heat until melted. Add the garlic and bacon and cook for 5 minutes. Add the green pepper and celery and sweat for 4 minutes, or until soft.

3. Add the rice and cook for 4 minutes. Add the flour and cook for 2 minutes, while stirring constantly.

4. Gradually add the pureed corn and stock to the saucepan. Bring to a simmer and cook for 20 minutes, or until the rice is tender.

5. Stir in the scallops, haddock, and lobster. Cook for 4 minutes and then add the parsley, cayenne pepper, and tomatoes. Cook for a few more minutes, adjust the seasoning, and ladle into warm bowls. Serve with Salt Cod Beignets and garnish with parsley.

SALT COD BEIGNETS

Placing salt cod in a light, delicious beignet is a lovely vehicle for this old favorite.

1. In a small saucepan, add the milk and butter and bring to a boil.

2. Add the flour, and stir until it forms a ball of dough.

3. Remove the saucepan from heat and let stand for 10 minutes.

4. Add the egg slowly and whisk until well-combined. Add the salt cod and cilantro, roll into a log, wrap with plastic wrap, and place in the freezer for 2 hours.

5. Place the oil in a Dutch oven and cook over medium-high heat until 375°F.

6. Remove the log from the freezer and cut into ½-inch thick slices.

7. Gently place each slice in the oil and fry until golden brown.

8. Use a slotted spoon to remove from oil and set on a paper towel to drain.

9. Season to taste with salt and pepper, and serve.

INGREDIENTS:

- 1½ CUPS CORN KERNELS
- 2 CUPS MILK
- 2 TABLESPOONS BUTTER
- 1 GARLIC CLOVE, MINCED
- 4 STRIPS THICK-CUT BACON, CHOPPED
- 1 GREEN BELL PEPPER, SEEDED AND CHOPPED
- ¾ CUPS CELERY, CHOPPED
- ½ CUP LONG-GRAIN RICE
- 1 TABLESPOON ALL-PURPOSE FLOUR
- 2 CUPS CRAB STOCK
- 4 SCALLOPS, CUT INTO ¼-INCH THICK SLICES
- 4 OZ. HADDOCK, CUT INTO ½-INCH PIECES
- 3 OZ. LOBSTER, CUT INTO ¼-INCH PIECES
- 2 TABLESPOONS PARSLEY, CHOPPED, PLUS MORE FOR GARNISH
- ⅛ TEASPOON CAYENNE PEPPER
- 1½ CUPS TOMATOES, CONCASSE (SEE PAGE 89) AND CHOPPED
- SALT AND PEPPER, TO TASTE

TO SERVE:
SALT COD BEIGNETS

SALT COD BEIGNETS
- ½ CUP MILK
- 3 TABLESPOONS BUTTER
- ¼ CUP ALL-PURPOSE FLOUR
- 1 EGG
- 4 OZ. SALT COD, CHOPPED
- 1 TABLESPOON CILANTRO, CHOPPED
- 2 CUPS VEGETABLE OIL

CRAB BISQUE
with CAVIAR CRÈME FRAICHE

YIELD: 4 SERVINGS / ACTIVE TIME: 20 MINUTES / TOTAL TIME: 1 HOUR

For this preparation, I used Peekytoe crabs, which are very plentiful here in Maine. Remember, it is important to fish sustainably and source locally.

1. In a medium saucepan, add the butter and cook over medium heat until melted. Add the leek, carrot, and fennel and cook for 5 minutes, or until soft.

2. Deglaze the pan with the Riesling. Add the tomatoes, tomato paste, white wine, crab stock, and tarragon. Bring to a boil, reduce heat so that the soup simmers, and cook for 30 minutes.

3. Transfer the soup to a blender, puree, and then strain through a fine sieve.

4. Return the broth to a clean pan and bring to a simmer. Add the heavy cream and crab meat and season with salt and pepper.

5. Ladle into warm bowls and serve with a scoop of the Caviar Crème Fraiche.

CAVIAR CRÈME FRAICHE

In a mixing bowl, combine all of the ingredients and mix until well-combined. Serve immediately.

INGREDIENTS:

¼ CUP BUTTER

1 CUP LEEK, CHOPPED

1 CUP CARROT, PEELED AND CHOPPED

¾ CUP FENNEL, CHOPPED

2 TABLESPOONS RIESLING

1 CUP TOMATO, CHOPPED

1 TABLESPOON TOMATO PASTE

½ CUP WHITE WINE

6 CUPS CRAB STOCK

1 SPRIG TARRAGON

½ CUP HEAVY CREAM

1½ CUPS CRAB MEAT

TO SERVE:

CAVIAR CRÈME FRAICHE

CAVIAR CRÈME FRAICHE

½ CUP CRÈME FRAICHE

1 TABLESPOON CAVIAR

½ TEASPOON LEMON JUICE

SALT AND PEPPER, TO TASTE

FINNISH SALMON SOUP

YIELD: 4 SERVINGS / ACTIVE TIME: 20 MINUTES / TOTAL TIME: 50 MINUTES

This is known as Lohikeitto in Finland, and it is to die for. Creamy and hearty, it is guaranteed to warm your soul on a cold winter day.

1. In a large saucepan, add the butter and cook over medium heat until melted. Add the onion and cook for 5 minutes, or until soft.

2. Add the stock and bring to a boil. Reduce heat so that the soup simmers, add the potato, and cook for 10 minutes, or until tender.

3. Add the salmon and cook for 3 minutes, or until the salmon is cooked through.

4. Add the heavy cream, season with salt and pepper, and ladle into warm bowls. Garnish with the fennel fronds, fennel pollen, salmon roe, and crème fraiche, and serve with Melba Toast.

MELBA TOAST

1. Preheat oven to 350°F.

2. Remove the crusts and use a rolling pin to get the bread as thin as possible.

3. Cut bread into the desired shape and place on a lined baking tray.

4. Bake for 5 minutes, or until the edges are browned and the bread is crispy. Remove from oven and serve.

INGREDIENTS:

- 2 TABLESPOONS BUTTER
- 1 ONION, DICED
- 4 CUPS FISH STOCK
- 1 MEDIUM POTATO, PEELED AND DICED
- 12 OZ. SALMON FILLET, SKIN REMOVED, CUT INTO ½-INCH CUBES
- 1 CUP HEAVY CREAM
- SALT AND PEPPER, TO TASTE
- FENNEL FRONDS, FOR GARNISH
- FENNEL POLLEN, FOR GARNISH
- SALMON ROE, FOR GARNISH
- CRÈME FRAICHE, FOR GARNISH

TO SERVE:
MELBA TOAST

MELBA TOAST
- 2 SLICES OF BREAD

MAINE LOBSTER BISQUE

YIELD: 4 TO 6 SERVINGS / ACTIVE TIME: 25 MINUTES / TOTAL TIME: 1 HOUR AND 15 MINUTES

If you have dined at The White Barn Inn, you have either tasted this or seen it at your table. This recipe is a tried-and-true crowd-pleaser.

1. Preheat oven to 400°F.

2. Place your lobsters on a baking tray. Place in the oven, and roast for 15 minutes. Remove and set aside.

3. Meanwhile, in a large stockpot, add the butter and cook over medium heat until melted. Add the onion, garlic, tomatoes, fennel, and herbs and cook for 10 minutes, or until the onion is soft.

4. Add the Riesling and brandy and cook until the liquid is reduced by half.

5. Add the lobsters, stock, and heavy cream. Bring to a boil, reduce heat so that the soup simmers, and cook for 45 minutes.

6. Remove the lobsters with tongs, squeeze as much liquid as possible into the soup, and then discard.

7. Transfer the soup to a food processor, puree until creamy, and then strain through a fine sieve.

8. Return the soup to a clean pot and bring to a simmer. Season with cayenne pepper, lemon juice, salt, and pepper and then place the lobster meat into the soup. Cook until warmed through, approximately 2 minutes.

9. Ladle the soup into warmed bowls, garnish with fennel fronds, and serve with Pernod Cream.

PERNOD CREAM

1. Add the cream to a mixing bowl and whip until soft peaks begin to form.

2. Add the Pernod and whip until medium peaks begin to form. Fold in the fennel fronds and toasted fennel seeds. Season with salt and pepper and serve.

INGREDIENTS:

- 6 LOBSTERS
- 4 TABLESPOONS BUTTER
- 1 ONION, DICED
- 1 GARLIC CLOVE, MINCED
- 4 CUPS TOMATOES, CHOPPED
- ½ CUP FENNEL, CHOPPED
- ⅛ TEASPOON THYME, LEAVES REMOVED AND CHOPPED
- 2 TEASPOONS PARSLEY, LEAVES REMOVED AND CHOPPED
- 2 TEASPOONS TARRAGON, LEAVES REMOVED AND CHOPPED
- ½ CUP RIESLING
- 1 CUP BRANDY
- 4 CUPS LOBSTER STOCK
- 4 CUPS HEAVY CREAM
- ¼ TEASPOON CAYENNE PEPPER
- 1 TABLESPOON LEMON JUICE
- SALT AND PEPPER, TO TASTE
- 1 CUP LOBSTER MEAT, COOKED
- FENNEL FRONDS, FOR GARNISH

TO SERVE:
PERNOD CREAM

PERNOD CREAM
- ½ CUP HEAVY CREAM
- 1 TABLESPOON PERNOD
- 2 TEASPOONS FENNEL FRONDS, CHOPPED
- 1 TEASPOON FENNEL SEEDS, TOASTED
- SALT AND PEPPER, TO TASTE

SEAFOOD MINESTRONE
with BASIL PESTO

YIELD: 4 TO 6 SERVINGS / **ACTIVE TIME:** 45 MINUTES / **TOTAL TIME:** 1 HOUR AND 30 MINUTES

This version of the classic Italian soup uses mussels, shrimp, and oysters to take it up a notch.

1. In a large saucepan, add the wine and the mussels, cover, and cook over medium heat until the mussels open. Discard any that do not.

2. Strain through a cheesecloth. Set the mussels aside and reserve the cooking liquid.

3. Remove the mussels from their shells. Reserve a few shells for garnish.

4. In a medium saucepan, add the oil and warm over medium heat. Add the bacon and cook for 4 minutes. Add the garlic, onion, and celery and cook for 5 minutes, or until the vegetables are tender.

5. Add the tomato paste, rosemary, thyme, bay leaf, lemon juice, kidney beans, rice, and tomato and cook for 2 minutes.

6. Add the fish stock and the reserved mussel liquid and bring to a boil. Reduce heat so that the soup simmers and cook for 12 minutes, or until the beans and rice are tender.

7. Add the mussels, shrimp, and oysters. Season to taste and simmer for 4 minutes, or until the shrimp and oysters are cooked.

8. Ladle into warm bowls and garnish with reserved mussel shells, Basil Pesto, basil leaves, and parmesan.

INGREDIENTS:

½   CUP WHITE WINE

30 MUSSELS, RINSED AND SCRUBBED

1   TABLESPOON EXTRA VIRGIN OLIVE OIL

4   STRIPS THICK-CUT BACON, CHOPPED

1   GARLIC CLOVE, MINCED

1   ONION, CHOPPED

2   CELERY STALKS, CHOPPED

1   TABLESPOON TOMATO PASTE

1   TEASPOON ROSEMARY, LEAVES REMOVED AND CHOPPED

1   TEASPOON THYME, LEAVES REMOVED AND CHOPPED

1   BAY LEAF

1   TEASPOON LEMON JUICE

6   TABLESPOONS DRIED KIDNEY BEANS, SOAKED IN COLD WATER OVERNIGHT

6   TABLESPOONS ARBORIO RICE

⅔   CUP TOMATO, CONCASSE (SEE PAGE 89) AND CHOPPED

6   CUPS FISH STOCK

6   OZ. SHRIMP, PEELED AND DEVEINED

12 OYSTERS, REMOVED FROM SHELL, JUICES RESERVED

    SALT AND PEPPER, TO TASTE

    BASIL LEAVES, FOR GARNISH

    PARMESAN CHEESE, SHAVED, FOR GARNISH

TO SERVE:
BASIL PESTO

BASIL PESTO

I add spinach to my pesto, as it has a neutral flavor and the chlorophyll in it provides a beautiful burst of green.

1. Bring to 2 cups of water to boil in a medium saucepan. Add the basil and spinach and cook for 1 minute. Remove and submerge in ice water. Drain any excess water and set aside.

2. Place basil, spinach, garlic, pine nuts, parmesan, and olive oil into a food processor and puree until the mixture is the desired consistency. Season with salt and pepper. Serve immediately or refrigerate.

INGREDIENTS:

BASIL PESTO

1   OZ. BASIL

2   OZ. SPINACH

1   GARLIC CLOVE, MINCED

2   TABLESPOONS PINE NUTS

¼   CUP PARMESAN, GRATED

6   TABLESPOONS EXTRA VIRGIN OLIVE OIL

     SALT AND PEPPER, TO TASTE

OYSTER STEW
with HERB BUTTER

YIELD: 4 TO 6 SERVINGS / ACTIVE TIME: 45 MINUTES / TOTAL TIME: 1 HOUR AND 30 MINUTES

Oysters make for a very special soup. This one is great for Valentine's Day or another special occasion.

1. Add the milk, cream, green bell pepper, onion, garlic, and oyster liquid to a medium saucepan. Cook over low heat for 10 minutes, or until the pepper is tender.

2. Meanwhile, bring water to boil in a saucepan. Add the potatoes and cook for 5 minutes, or until soft. Remove and add to the other saucepan.

3. Add the oysters and cook for 3 to 4 minutes, while stirring occasionally, until the oysters are plump.

4. Add the paprika, tomato, lemon juice, and capers. Season to taste with salt and pepper, ladle into bowls, place a small ring of the Herb Butter in the center, and garnish with parsley and paprika.

HERB BUTTER

1. Place the butter in a bowl and whisk until it is nice and creamy.

2. Place the oil in a sauté pan and cook over medium heat until warm. Add the shallot and cook 2 to 3 minutes, or until soft.

3. Add the lemon juice, remove the pan from heat, and set aside to cool.

4. When cool, transfer the contents of the pan to the butter. Add the chopped herbs and mix to combine. Season with salt and pepper and roll into thin logs. Cover with plastic wrap and refrigerate until ready to use.

INGREDIENTS:

2	CUPS MILK
2	CUPS HEAVY CREAM
1	CUP GREEN BELL PEPPER, SEEDED AND CHOPPED
1	CUP ONION, CHOPPED
1	GARLIC CLOVE, MINCED
25	OYSTERS, RINSED, SHUCKED, AND MEAT REMOVED, LIQUID RESERVED
1½	CUPS SMALL CREAMER OR FINGERLING POTATOES, QUARTERED
1	TEASPOON PAPRIKA, PLUS MORE FOR GARNISH
2	TOMATOES, CONCASSE (SEE PAGE 89)
1	TEASPOON LEMON JUICE
1	TABLESPOON CAPERS, CHOPPED
	SALT AND PEPPER, TO TASTE
	PARSLEY, CHOPPED, FOR GARNISH

TO SERVE:
HERB BUTTER

HERB BUTTER

½	CUP BUTTER, BROUGHT TO ROOM TEMPERATURE
1	TABLESPOON VEGETABLE OIL
1	SMALL SHALLOT, FINELY CHOPPED
1	TEASPOON LEMON JUICE
2	TEASPOONS PARSLEY, CHOPPED
1	TEASPOON TARRAGON, CHOPPED
1	TEASPOON CHIVES, CHOPPED
1	TEASPOON MARJORAM, CHOPPED
	SALT AND PEPPER, TO TASTE

SAFFRON-INFUSED SUNCHOKE
and SCALLOP SOUP *with* CAVIAR

YIELD: 4 SERVINGS / ACTIVE TIME: 30 MINUTES / TOTAL TIME: 1 HOUR

When you need to pull out all the stops, make this soup. It'll impress even the most skeptical dinner guest. After preparing the sunchokes, store them in a bowl with enough water to cover and a squeeze of lemon juice.

1. Add the butter to a medium saucepan and cook over medium heat until melted. Add the onions and cook for 5 minutes, or until soft.

2. Drain the sunchokes and add to the pan. Cook for 5 minutes, add the stock, milk, and saffron, and bring to a boil.

3. Reduce heat so that the soup simmers and cook for 10 minutes, or until the sunchokes are tender.

4. Meanwhile, in a sauté pan, heat the oil. Add the scallops and cook for 2 minutes on each side. Remove and set aside.

5. Transfer the soup to a food processor, add half of the scallops, and blend until smooth. Strain through a fine sieve and return the soup to a clean pan.

6. Bring to a simmer and stir in the cream and the remaining scallops. Season with salt and pepper and ladle into bowls. Garnish with tarragon leaves and serve with Saffron Confit Sunchokes and caviar.

SAFFRON CONFIT SUNCHOKES

Place all of the ingredients in a small saucepan and cook over the lowest-possible heat. Cook for 10 minutes, remove pan from heat, and let the sunchoke cool in the oil. When cool, serve immediately.

INGREDIENTS:

- ½ CUP BUTTER
- 2 ONIONS, FINELY CHOPPED
- 2 POUNDS SUNCHOKES, PEELED AND CHOPPED
- 2 CUPS FISH STOCK
- 2 CUPS MILK
- ¼ TEASPOON SAFFRON
- 1½ TABLESPOONS VEGETABLE OIL
- 12 MEDIUM SCALLOPS, CUT INTO ½-INCH PIECES
- 1 CUP HEAVY CREAM
- SALT AND PEPPER, TO TASTE
- TARRAGON LEAVES, FOR GARNISH
- CAVIAR, FOR GARNISH

TO SERVE:
SAFFRON CONFIT SUNCHOKES

SAFFRON CONFIT SUNCHOKES
- 1 LARGE SUNCHOKE, PEELED AND SLICED INTO ¼-INCH PIECES
- ½ CUP EXTRA VIRGIN OLIVE OIL
- ⅛ TEASPOON SAFFRON

CREAM OF LANGOUSTINE SOUP

YIELD: 4 SERVINGS / ACTIVE TIME: 25 MINUTES / TOTAL TIME: 50 MINUTES

Langoustines, also known as scampi, are a slimy, pink-orange lobster that grow up to 10 inches long and reside in the Atlantic Ocean and Mediterranean Sea. Commercially, they are the most important European crustacean.

1. In a medium saucepan, add the oil and cook over medium-high heat until warm. Add the langoustine tails and cook for 1 minute on each side, or until cooked through. Remove langoustine tails and set aside to cool.

2. Reduce heat to medium, add the onion, carrot, and celery and cook for 5 minutes, or until the vegetables are soft.

3. Add the brandy and Riesling and cook for 2 minutes. Add the lobster stock, lemon juice, tomato paste, and bouquet garni and bring to a boil.

4. Reduce heat so that the soup simmers and cook for 10 minutes.

5. Transfer the soup to a food processor. Add half of the langoustine tails, puree until creamy, and then strain through a fine sieve.

6. Return the soup to a clean pan and add the cream. Bring to a simmer, cook for 3 minutes, and then add the remaining langoustine tails.

7. Season with salt and pepper, ladle into warmed bowls, and garnish with chives. Serve with grilled bread.

INGREDIENTS:

1　TABLESPOON VEGETABLE OIL

1½　POUNDS LANGOUSTINE TAILS, PEELED

1　ONION, CHOPPED

1　CARROT, PEELED AND CHOPPED

1　CELERY STALK, CHOPPED

2　TABLESPOONS BRANDY

2　TABLESPOONS RIESLING

5　CUPS LOBSTER STOCK

⅛　TEASPOON LEMON JUICE

1　TABLESPOON TOMATO PASTE

　BOUQUET GARNI (SEE PAGE 88)

½　CUP HEAVY CREAM

　SALT AND PEPPER, TO TASTE

　CHIVES, CHOPPED, FOR GARNISH

OYSTER BISQUE
with BEER-BATTERED OYSTERS

YIELD: 4 TO 6 SERVINGS / ACTIVE TIME: 45 MINUTES / TOTAL TIME: 1 HOUR AND 30 MINUTES

Chef Jonathan Cartwright taught me that "The flavor of an oyster is in the brine." So make sure you reserve it!

1. In a large saucepan, add the water and oysters. Cover and cook over medium heat for 7 minutes, or until all the oysters open.

2. Strain through a fine sieve. Set the oysters aside and let cool. Reserve the cooking liquid.

3. When cool, remove the oyster meat from the shell and set aside.

4. In a medium saucepan, melt the butter over medium heat. Add the onion and cook for 5 minutes, or until soft.

5. Add the stock, reserved cooking liquid, and rice. Bring to a boil, reduce heat so that the soup simmers, and cook for 25 minutes, or until the rice is soft.

6. Transfer the soup to a food processor, puree until smooth, and then strain through a fine sieve.

7. Return the soup to the pan and bring to a simmer. Add the cream and season with Tabasco™, Worcestershire sauce, salt, and pepper. Ladle into warm bowls, garnish with parsley, and serve with Beer-Battered Oysters.

BEER-BATTERED OYSTERS

Make sure you rinse your oysters thoroughly, as you'll want to remove every last grain of grit.

1. Place the oil in a Dutch oven and cook over medium-high heat until the oil is 350°F.

2. Place ½ cup of the flour, cornstarch, and baking powder in a bowl and mix until combined. Run the mixture through a sieve.

3. Add the ale to the bowl and whisk until smooth.

4. In a small bowl, add the remaining flour and the oysters. Mix gently until the oysters are coated.

5. Dip each oyster in the batter and then place into the oil. Fry until golden brown.

6. Use a slotted spoon to remove the oysters from the oil and set on a paper towel to dry. Season with salt and pepper and serve immediately.

INGREDIENTS:

1½	CUPS WATER
24	OYSTERS, WASHED AND SCRUBBED
6	TABLESPOONS BUTTER
1½	CUPS ONION, CHOPPED
6	CUPS FISH OR CRAB STOCK
¾	CUP LONG-GRAIN RICE
3	CUPS CREAM
¼	TEASPOON TABASCO™
¼	TEASPOON WORCESTERSHIRE SAUCE
	SALT AND PEPPER, TO TASTE
	PARSLEY, CHOPPED, FOR GARNISH

TO SERVE:
BEER-BATTERED OYSTERS

BEER-BATTERED OYSTERS

2	CUPS VEGETABLE OIL
¾	CUP ALL-PURPOSE FLOUR
¼	CUP CORNSTARCH
½	TEASPOON BAKING POWDER
½	CUP ALE, PLUS 2 TABLESPOONS
6–12	OYSTERS, SHUCKED, MEAT REMOVED
	SALT AND PEPPER, TO TASTE

PUMPKIN SOUP *with* SEARED DIVER SCALLOPS *and* CHINESE FIVE-SPICE CREAM

YIELD: 4 SERVINGS / ACTIVE TIME: 25 MINUTES / TOTAL TIME: 1 HOUR AND 15 MINUTES

Want to spice up your traditional Thanksgiving? Try this soup with scallops. You can also use it to get through your leftovers.

1. In a medium saucepan, add the butter and cook over low heat until melted. Add the pumpkin, onion, carrot, apple, garlic, and thyme and cook for about 10 minutes, stirring often.

2. Increase the heat to medium and add the white wine. Cook until the wine is nearly evaporated. Add the chicken stock and reduce heat so that the soup simmers. Cook for 30 minutes, while stirring occasionally, or until all the vegetables are tender.

3. Transfer the soup to a food processor, puree, and then strain through a fine sieve. Stir in the cream and season with the nutmeg, cinnamon, salt, and pepper.

4. Place a Pan-Seared Scallop in the center of each bowl and cover with the soup. Garnish with a dollop of the Crispy Pumpkin Strips, Chinese Five-Spice Cream, and a sprig of rosemary.

PAN-SEARED SCALLOPS

1. Place the olive oil in a medium nonstick pan and cook over high heat until warm.

2. Season the scallops with salt and pepper and place in the pan.

3. Cook for approximately 2 minutes, turn, and cook for 2 more minutes. The scallops should be golden brown on each side.

4. Remove the scallops from the pan and place on a paper towel to drain.

INGREDIENTS:

2	TABLESPOONS BUTTER
3	CUPS PUMPKIN, PEELED AND DICED
1	ONION, DICED
1	CARROT, PEELED AND DICED
1	SMALL APPLE, PEELED AND DICED
½	GARLIC CLOVE, MINCED
1	SPRIG OF THYME, LEAVES REMOVED AND CHOPPED
¼	CUP WHITE WINE
2	CUPS CHICKEN STOCK
1	CUP HEAVY CREAM
⅛	TEASPOON NUTMEG
	PINCH OF CINNAMON
	SALT AND PEPPER, TO TASTE
	ROSEMARY SPRIGS, FOR GARNISH

TO SERVE:
PAN-SEARED SCALLOPS

CRISPY PUMPKIN STRIPS

CHINESE FIVE-SPICE CREAM

PAN-SEARED SCALLOPS

1	TEASPOON OLIVE OIL
8	MEDIUM SCALLOPS
	SALT AND PEPPER, TO TASTE

Continued . . .

CRISPY PUMPKIN STRIPS

1. Place the oil in a Dutch oven and cook over medium-high heat until it is 375°F.

2. Use a peeler to cut the pumpkin into long ribbons.

3. In a small saucepan, bring the water to boil. Add the pumpkin ribbons and cook for 1 minute. Remove and submerge in ice water. Dry the pumpkin thoroughly and then place into the hot oil. Fry until golden brown, remove, and set on a paper towel to drain. Season with salt and serve.

CHINESE FIVE-SPICE CREAM

1. Place the cream in a bowl and whisk until medium peaks begin to form.

2. Add the Chinese five-spice and the salt. Mix until combined and refrigerate until ready to use.

INGREDIENTS:

CRISPY PUMPKIN STRIPS
2   CUPS VEGETABLE OIL
1   CUP PUMPKIN, PEELED
2   CUPS WATER
     SALT, TO TASTE

CHINESE FIVE-SPICE CREAM
½   CUP HEAVY CREAM
½   TEASPOON CHINESE FIVE-SPICE
     PINCH OF SALT

HATTERAS CLAM CHOWDER

YIELD: 4 TO 6 SERVINGS / ACTIVE TIME: 20 MINUTES / TOTAL TIME: 45 MINUTES

This broth-based clam chowder comes to us from The Outer Banks of North Carolina. It's a very healthy chowder, but still certain to be liked by seafood lovers.

1. In a large saucepan, add the bacon and cook over medium heat for 5 minutes. Add the onions, celery and carrots and cook for 5 minutes. Add half of the clam juice, increase heat to medium-high, and bring to a boil.

2. Reduce heat so that the chowder simmers, add the clams, cover, and cook for 5 minutes, or until the clams have opened. Remove the clams and set aside.

3. Add the remaining clam juice, potatoes, and thyme. Simmer for 10 minutes, or until the potatoes are tender.

4. Meanwhile, shuck the cooked clams.

5. When the potatoes are cooked, return the shucked clams to the pan and cook for 2 minutes.

6. Season with salt and pepper, ladle into bowls, and garnish with parsley.

INGREDIENTS:

8 STRIPS OF THICK-CUT BACON, CHOPPED

2 ONIONS, CHOPPED

2 CELERY STALKS, CHOPPED

2 CARROTS, PEELED AND CHOPPED

8 CUPS CLAM JUICE

2 POUNDS LITTLE NECK CLAMS

2 CUPS POTATOES, PEELED AND CHOPPED

4 SPRIGS THYME, LEAVES REMOVED AND CHOPPED

SALT AND PEPPER, TO TASTE

¼ CUP PARSLEY, LEAVES REMOVED AND CHOPPED, FOR GARNISH

SAFFRON *and* MUSSEL BROTH

YIELD: 4–6 SERVINGS / ACTIVE TIME: 20 MINUTES / TOTAL TIME: 45 MINUTES

Never been to Spain? This soup will take you there.

1. Place the mussels and the wine in a large saucepan, cover, and cook, while shaking the pan occasionally, over medium heat for 4 to 5 minutes, or until all the mussels are open. Discard any unopened mussels.

2. Strain, set the mussels aside, and reserve the cooking liquid.

3. Remove the meat from the mussels. Keep 18 mussels in the shell and reserve for garnish.

4. Add the butter to a large saucepan and cook over medium heat until melted. Add the leeks, celery, fennel, carrot, and garlic and cook for 5 minutes, or until soft.

5. Strain the reserved liquid through a fine sieve, cheesecloth, or coffee filter.

6. Add the reserved liquid to the saucepan with the vegetables. Reduce the heat and cook for 10 minutes to reduce the liquid.

7. Add the saffron and the cream and bring to a boil.

8. Season with salt and pepper. Add the mussels, tomatoes, and chopped parsley and cook gently until heated through.

9. Ladle into bowls and garnish with microgreens, radish, and the reserved mussels.

INGREDIENTS:

- 3 POUNDS MUSSELS, RINSED AND SCRUBBED
- 3 CUPS WHITE WINE
- ¼ CUP BUTTER
- 4 CUPS LEEKS, CHOPPED
- 2 CELERY STALKS, CHOPPED
- ¾ CUP FENNEL, CHOPPED
- 1 CARROT, FINELY CHOPPED
- 2 GARLIC CLOVES, MINCED
- ⅛ TEASPOON SAFFRON
- 2 CUPS HEAVY CREAM
- SALT AND PEPPER, TO TASTE
- ¼ CUP PARSLEY, LEAVES REMOVED AND CHOPPED, FOR GARNISH
- 3 TOMATOES, CONCASSE (SEE PAGE 89) AND CHOPPED
- MICROGREENS, FOR GARNISH
- RADISH, SHAVED, DRESSED WITH OLIVE OIL AND A SQUEEZE OF LEMON JUICE, FOR GARNISH

SEAFOOD WONTON SOUP

YIELD: 4 SERVINGS / ACTIVE TIME: 40 MINUTES / TOTAL TIME: 1 HOUR

Wonton soup is probably one of the most popular Chinese soups. The mere mention of it sets my mouth watering.

1. In a medium saucepan, add the sesame oil and cook over medium heat until warm.

2. Add the onion and carrots and cook for 5 minutes, or until soft. Add the garlic, cook for 2 minutes, and then add the sake, fish stock, lemongrass, soy sauce, and fish sauce.

3. Simmer for 10 minutes, then remove the lemongrass and season with salt and pepper.

4. Bring the soup to a boil and add the wontons. Reduce heat so that the soup simmers and cook for 5 minutes, or until the wontons float to the top.

5. Place 3 wontons in each bowl. Ladle the broth over the wontons, and garnish with romaine lettuce, toasted sesame seeds, cilantro, and shaved radish.

SEAFOOD WONTONS

1. Combine all ingredients, save the wonton wrappers, in a bowl and mix until combined.

2. Place 2 teaspoons of the mixture into the center of a wonton wrapper.

3. Dip your finger into cold water and rub a small amount around the edge of the wonton wrapper. Bring each corner together to make a purse and seal.

4. Repeat with remaining wonton wrappers and refrigerate until ready to use.

INGREDIENTS:

1	TABLESPOON SESAME OIL
1	ONION, FINELY CHOPPED
2	CARROTS, FINELY CHOPPED
2	GARLIC CLOVES, FINELY CHOPPED
1	CUP SAKE
4	CUPS FISH STOCK
1	STALK LEMONGRASS, SMASHED WITH THE BACK OF A KNIFE
1	TABLESPOON SOY SAUCE
1	TABLESPOON FISH SAUCE
12	SEAFOOD WONTONS (SEE RECIPE)
	SALT AND PEPPER, TO TASTE
1	ROMAINE LETTUCE LEAF, SHREDDED, FOR GARNISH
	TOASTED SESAME SEEDS, FOR GARNISH
	CILANTRO, CHOPPED, FOR GARNISH
	RADISH, SHAVED, FOR GARNISH

SEAFOOD WONTONS

4	OZ. RAW SHRIMP, PEELED, DEVEINED, AND FINELY CHOPPED
4	OZ. COOKED CRAB, CLEANED AND FINELY CHOPPED
1	TABLESPOON SHALLOTS, MINCED
1	TABLESPOON CHIVES, CHOPPED
1	TABLESPOON FISH SAUCE
2	TABLESPOONS MISO
1	TABLESPOON SHRIMP PASTE
2	TABLESPOONS RADISH, CHOPPED
1	TABLESPOON SESAME SEEDS, TOASTED
1	TEASPOON SESAME OIL
1	TEASPOON SHERRY
12	WONTON WRAPPERS

SHRIMP BISQUE
with BRANDY-SCENTED CREAM

YIELD: 4 SERVINGS / ACTIVE TIME: 30 MINUTES / TOTAL TIME: 1 HOUR

This flavorful soup, once garnished with the brandied cream, makes for a good introduction to any meal.

1. In a medium saucepan, add the oil and cook over medium-high heat until warm. Add the shrimp and cook for 1 minute on each side, or until cooked through.

2. Remove the shrimp from the pan and set aside.

3. Reduce the heat to medium, add the onion, carrot, and celery and cook for 5 minutes, or until the vegetables are soft.

4. Add the brandy and Riesling and cook for 2 minutes.

5. Add the stocks, lemon juice, tomato paste, and bouquet garni. Bring to a boil, reduce heat so that the soup simmers, and cook for 10 minutes.

6. Transfer the soup to a food processor, add half of the shrimp, and puree until creamy. Strain the soup through a fine sieve and return to a clean pan.

7. Bring to a simmer and add the cream. Simmer for 3 minutes and then add the remaining shrimp.

8. Season with salt and pepper, ladle into warm bowls, and serve with the Brandy-Scented Cream.

BRANDY-SCENTED CREAM

1. Place the cream in a bowl and whip until soft peaks form.

2. Add the brandy and whip until medium peaks form. Season with salt and pepper and refrigerate until ready to use.

INGREDIENTS:

1   TABLESPOON VEGETABLE OIL

1½ POUNDS SHRIMP, PEELED AND DEVEINED

1   ONION, CHOPPED

1   CARROT, PEELED AND CHOPPED

1   CELERY STALK, CHOPPED

2   TABLESPOONS BRANDY

2   TABLESPOONS RIESLING

2   CUPS CRAB STOCK

3   CUPS LOBSTER STOCK

⅛   TEASPOON LEMON JUICE

1   TABLESPOON TOMATO PASTE

    BOUQUET GARNI (SEE PAGE 88)

½   CUP HEAVY CREAM

    SALT AND PEPPER, TO TASTE

TO SERVE:
BRANDY-SCENTED CREAM

BRANDY-SCENTED CREAM

1   CUP HEAVY CREAM

1   TABLESPOON BRANDY

    SALT AND PEPPER, TO TASTE

SMOKED HADDOCK
and LOBSTER CHOWDER

YIELD: 4 SERVINGS / ACTIVE TIME: 30 MINUTES / TOTAL TIME: 25 HOURS

The sweet potato helps bind the plethora of seafood together.

1. In a bowl, add the haddock, water, and salt. Let stand for 10 minutes. Remove the haddock and rinse under cold water. Place the haddock on a cooking rack with a tray underneath it, lightly cover, and place in the refrigerator overnight.

2. The following morning, remove the haddock from the refrigerator and cold smoke for 12 hours.

3. In a medium saucepan, bring water to boil and add the sweet potato. Cook for 5 minutes, or until soft, remove with a slotted spoon, and set aside. Place the butternut squash in the boiling water and cook for 3 to 5 minutes, until it is tender. Remove the squash and submerge in ice water. Remove, dry, and set aside.

4. Place the sweet potato, 2 tablespoons of the butter, and 1 cup of the milk in a food processor. Puree until smooth and then set aside.

5. Place the remaining butter in a clean medium saucepan and cook over medium heat until melted. Add the onion and chorizo and cook for 5 minutes, or until the onion is soft.

6. Add the smoked haddock, lobster stock, and remaining milk. Bring to a boil, reduce heat so that the soup simmers, and cook for 10 minutes, or until the fish is flaky.

7. Use a slotted spoon to remove the haddock from the pan and set aside to cool. When cool, use a fork to flake the meat from the skin.

8. Whisk the pureed sweet potato into the soup and return to a boil. Reduce heat so that the soup simmers, stir in the butternut squash lobster, and haddock and simmer for 2 minutes.

9. Season with salt and pepper, ladle into warm bowls, and garnish with basil.

INGREDIENTS:

- 9 OZ. HADDOCK FILLET, SKIN ON
- 1½ CUPS WATER
- 1 CUP SALT
- 2 CUPS SWEET POTATO, PEELED AND FINELY CHOPPED
- 1 CUP BUTTERNUT SQUASH, PEELED AND FINELY CHOPPED
- 4 TABLESPOONS BUTTER
- 2 CUPS MILK
- 1 ONION, CHOPPED
- ¼ CUP DRIED CHORIZO, FINELY CHOPPED
- 1 CUP LOBSTER STOCK
- 1 CUP LOBSTER MEAT, COOKED
- SALT AND PEPPER, TO TASTE
- BASIL, CHIFFONADE, FOR GARNISH

SPICY AND SOUR FISH SOUP

YIELD: 4 SERVINGS / ACTIVE TIME: 40 MINUTES / TOTAL TIME: 1 HOUR AND 30 MINUTES

This is based on Canh Chua Cá, a very popular soup in Southeast Asia. It is tart, sweet, and spicy—a real roller coaster for your taste buds.

1. Place the swordfish, 2 tablespoons of the fish sauce, and the garlic in a bowl. Toss until the swordfish is coated and set aside.

2. Drain and rinse dried squid.

3. In a medium saucepan, add the oil and warm over medium heat. Add the dried squid, scallions, shallots, ginger, and lemongrass and cook for 2 minutes. Add the fish stock, bring to a boil, and then reduce heat so that the soup simmers. Cook for 10 minutes and then strain through a fine sieve.

4. Return the stock to a clean pan and bring to a boil. Stir in the remaining fish sauce, tamarind concentrate, and chilies and simmer for 3 minutes.

5. Add the pineapple, tomatoes, bamboo shoots, and calamari and cook for 3 minutes. Stir in the marinated swordfish and the cilantro and cook for 3 minutes, or until the swordfish is cooked through.

6. Place the rice noodles into a bowl and cover with boiling water. Leave to soak for 4 minutes, or follow the manufacturer's instructions.

7. Season the soup to taste and place the noodles in a warm bowl or hollowed pineapple shell. Ladle the soup over the noodles and garnish with bean sprouts, alfalfa sprouts, lime wedges, and cilantro.

INGREDIENTS:

12   OZ. SWORDFISH, CUT INTO ½-INCH CUBES

8   TABLESPOONS FISH SAUCE

2   GARLIC CLOVES, MINCED

1   OZ. DRIED SQUID, SOAKED FOR 30 MINUTES

1   TABLESPOON VEGETABLE OIL

4   SCALLIONS, SLICED

2   SHALLOTS, FINELY CHOPPED

2   TABLESPOONS GINGER ROOT, PEELED AND MINCED

2   STALKS LEMONGRASS, BRUISED WITH THE BACK OF A KNIFE

4   CUPS FISH STOCK

2   TABLESPOONS TAMARIND CONCENTRATE

2   THAI CHILIES, SEEDED AND SLICED

12   OZ. PINEAPPLE, DICED

4   PLUM TOMATOES, CONCASSE (SEE PAGE 89) AND CUT INTO ¼-INCH PIECES

3   OZ. CANNED SLICED BAMBOO SHOOTS, DRAINED

8   OZ. CALAMARI, BODIES SLICED INTO ¼-INCH THICK PIECES, TENTACLES LEFT WHOLE

2   TABLESPOONS CILANTRO, LEAVES REMOVED AND FINELY CHOPPED, PLUS MORE FOR GARNISH

3   OZ. RICE NOODLES

SALT AND PEPPER, TO TASTE

BEAN SPROUTS, FOR GARNISH

ALFALFA SPROUTS, FOR GARNISH

LIME WEDGES, FOR GARNISH

SPICY MUSSEL BROTH

YIELD: 6 SERVINGS / ACTIVE TIME: 45 MINUTES / TOTAL TIME: 1 HOUR AND 30 MINUTES

The heat in this soup is provided by the Harissa Sauce. Harissa is a hot red chili pepper paste closely associated with North African cuisine. Feel free to use store-bought harissa, but I have provided a recipe using ingredients I sourced locally.

1. Add the wine to large saucepan and bring to a boil. Add the mussels, cover, and cook for 5 minutes, or until the mussels open. Discard any unopened mussels.

2. Strain, set the mussels aside to cool, and reserve the cooking liquid.

3. Once cool, remove the meat from the mussels, reserving a few in the shell.

4. In a medium saucepan, add the butter and cook over medium heat until melted. Add the onion, garlic, celery, and scallion, and cook for 5 minutes.

5. Add the mussels that have been removed from their shells, the reserved cooking liquid, the V8™, potato, Harissa Sauce, and tomato. Bring to a boil, reduce heat so that the soup simmers, and cook until the potatoes are cooked through.

6. Stir in the parsley and the remaining mussels. Season with salt and pepper, ladle into warm bowls, and serve with Herbed Yogurt and celery leaves.

HERBED YOGURT

Combine all the ingredients in a bowl, mix, and serve.

INGREDIENTS:

- 1½ CUPS WHITE WINE
- 3 POUNDS FRESH MUSSELS, RINSED, SCRUBBED, AND CLEANED
- 2 TABLESPOONS BUTTER
- 1 ONION, CHOPPED
- 2 GARLIC CLOVES, MINCED
- 2 CELERY STALKS, CHOPPED, LEAVES RESERVED FOR GARNISH
- 6 SCALLIONS, WHITE PART ONLY, FINELY SLICED
- 1 CUP V8™
- 1 CUP POTATO, PEELED AND DICED
- 1 TABLESPOON HARISSA SAUCE (SEE RECIPE)
- 1½ CUPS TOMATO, CONCASSE (SEE PAGE 89) AND DICED
- ½ CUP PARSLEY, CHOPPED
- SALT AND PEPPER, TO TASTE

TO SERVE:
HERBED YOGURT

HERBED YOGURT
- 1 CUP GREEK YOGURT
- 1 TEASPOON CILANTRO, LEAVES REMOVED AND CHOPPED
- 1 TEASPOON MINT, LEAVES REMOVED AND CHOPPED
- 1 TEASPOON PARSLEY, LEAVES REMOVED AND CHOPPED
- 1 TEASPOON CHIVES, CHOPPED
- SALT AND PEPPER, TO TASTE

Continued . . .

HARISSA SAUCE

YIELD: ½ CUP

1. Place the habanero over an open flame on your stove. Turn until all sides of the pepper are charred.

2. Remove from heat, place in a bowl, cover with plastic wrap, and set aside for 10 minutes.

3. Remove the peel and seeds from the pepper. Gloves are recommended while handling the habanero.

4. In a nonstick pan, add the caraway seeds, coriander seeds, and cumin seeds and cook over medium heat, while stirring, until the seeds begin to release their aroma.

5. Remove the pan and let cool. When cool, grind into a fine powder, using either a coffee grinder or a mortar and pestle.

6. Place all of the ingredients in a blender and mix until it is a smooth paste.

INGREDIENTS (CONTINUED):

HARISSA SAUCE

1	HABANERO PEPPER
¾	TEASPOON CARAWAY SEEDS
¾	TEASPOON CORIANDER SEEDS
1½	TEASPOONS CUMIN SEEDS
1½	TEASPOONS DRIED MINT
3	TEASPOONS SALT
12	GARLIC CLOVES, PEELED
3	LEMONS, JUICED
3	TABLESPOONS EXTRA VIRGIN OLIVE OIL
1	CUP GREEK YOGURT
1	TEASPOON CILANTRO, LEAVES REMOVED AND CHOPPED
1	TEASPOON MINT, LEAVES REMOVED AND CHOPPED
1	TEASPOON PARSLEY, LEAVES REMOVED AND CHOPPED
1	TEASPOON CHIVES, CHOPPED
	SALT AND PEPPER, TO TASTE

HUMARSUPA

YIELD: 4 SERVINGS / ACTIVE TIME: 20 MINUTES / TOTAL TIME: 45 MINUTES

This is an Icelandic-style langoustine soup. The sweetness of the coconut milk complements the langoustine and the curry powder provides a touch of heat. If langoustines are unavailable, replace with lobster.

1. In a medium saucepan, add the oil and cook over medium heat until warm. Add the onion and garlic, and cook for 5 minutes, or until soft. Add the carrots, celery, and potatoes. Cook for 5 minutes, add the paprika, curry, and crab stock, and bring to a boil.

2. Reduce heat so that the soup simmers and cook for 10 minutes, or until the potatoes are tender.

3. Add the langoustine tails and coconut milk and cook for 5 minutes.

4. Season with salt and pepper and ladle into warm bowls. Garnish with chives and serve with crusty bread.

INGREDIENTS:

2   TABLESPOONS VEGETABLE OIL

1   ONION, CHOPPED

2   GARLIC CLOVES, MINCED

2   CARROTS, PEELED AND CHOPPED

2   CELERY STALKS, CHOPPED

2   POTATOES, PEELED AND CHOPPED

1   TABLESPOON PAPRIKA

1   TABLESPOON CURRY POWDER

6   CUPS CRAB STOCK

1   POUND LANGOUSTINE TAILS, PEELED AND COOKED

1   14 OZ. CAN COCONUT MILK

SALT AND PEPPER, TO TASTE

CHIVES, CHOPPED, FOR GARNISH

CRAB VELOUTE

YIELD: 4 SERVINGS / ACTIVE TIME: 30 MINUTES / TOTAL TIME: 1 HOUR

If this soup doesn't draw you in, perhaps the bruschetta will, as it's delicious in its own right. The traditional technique for veloutes works perfectly with crab.

1. In a medium saucepan, add the butter and cook over medium heat until melted. Add the shallots and cook for 3 minutes, or until soft.

2. Add the flour and cook for 3 minutes while stirring constantly. Add the stock, brandy, and tomato paste and stir until well-combined. Bring to a boil, reduce heat, and simmer for 10 minutes, or until the broth starts to thicken.

3. Remove the soup from heat and strain through a fine sieve.

4. In a bowl, add the egg yolks and the cream and whisk until smooth.

5. Return the soup to the pan and bring to a simmer. Add ⅓ cup of the hot soup to the egg-and-cream mixture, which will help introduce heat to the eggs without scrambling them. Whisk until combined and then add the egg mixture to the saucepan. Reduce heat to low and whisk constantly for 3 minutes.

6. Add the crab meat, lemon juice, cayenne pepper, salt, and pepper. Ladle into bowls and serve with Crab Bruschetta and Crispy Shallot Rings.

CRAB BRUSCHETTA

1. Add the garlic, mayonnaise, anchovy, crab, and tarragon to a bowl and stir until well-combined. Season with salt and pepper.

2. Spoon this mixture onto the bread, place on top of the soup, and garnish with a sprig of tarragon.

INGREDIENTS:

- 2 TABLESPOONS BUTTER
- 2 SHALLOTS, CHOPPED
- 2 TABLESPOONS ALL-PURPOSE FLOUR
- 4 CUPS CRAB STOCK
- ⅛ CUP BRANDY
- 2 TABLESPOONS TOMATO PASTE
- 4 EGG YOLKS
- 2 CUPS CREAM
- 2 CUPS CRAB MEAT, COOKED, CLEANED, AND CHOPPED
- 1 TEASPOON LEMON JUICE
- PINCH OF CAYENNE PEPPER
- SALT AND PEPPER, TO TASTE

TO SERVE:

CRAB BRUSCHETTA

CRISPY SHALLOT RINGS

CRAB BRUSCHETTA

- ½ GARLIC CLOVE, MINCED
- 4 TABLESPOONS MAYONNAISE
- 1 ANCHOVY FILLET, FINELY CHOPPED
- 3 TABLESPOONS CRAB MEAT, COOKED
- ½ TEASPOON TARRAGON, LEAVES REMOVED AND CHOPPED, PLUS MORE FOR GARNISH
- SALT AND PEPPER, TO TASTE
- 4 SLICES OF SEEDED BREAD, TOASTED

CRISPY SHALLOT RINGS

1. In a bowl, add the shallots and the buttermilk and let stand for 30 minutes.

2. Place the oil in a Dutch oven and cook over medium heat until it is 350°F.

3. Combine the flour and cornstarch in a bowl and run through a fine sieve.

4. Dredge marinated shallots in the flour-and-cornstarch mixture. Drop each ring individually into the hot oil and fry until golden brown. Remove from oil with tongs or a slotted spoon and set to drain on a paper towel.

5. Season with salt and pepper and serve.

INGREDIENTS:

CRISPY SHALLOT RINGS

2   SHALLOTS, FINELY SLICED

⅓   CUP BUTTERMILK

2   CUPS VEGETABLE OIL

¼   CUP FLOUR

¼   CUP CORNSTARCH

     SALT AND PEPPER, TO TASTE

MINORCAN CLAM CHOWDER

YIELD: 4 SERVINGS / ACTIVE TIME: 20 MINUTES / TOTAL TIME: 45 MINUTES

This is a tomato-based clam chowder from St. Augustine, Florida. Traditionally, datil chili is used for this dish, but since this was not available, I chose a habanero.

1. In a medium saucepan, add the clam juice and warm over medium heat. Add the clams, cover, and cook for 5 minutes, or until all the clams have opened.

2. Remove clams and set aside. Reserve clam juice.

3. In a clean medium saucepan, add the salt pork and oil and cook over medium-high heat until the salt pork is crispy. Add the thyme, basil, oregano, garlic, bay leaf, chili, green pepper, and onion and cook for 5 minutes, or until the vegetables are soft.

4. Add the reserved clam juice, plum tomatoes, stewed tomatoes, and stock and bring to a boil.

5. Reduce heat so that the soup simmers, add the potato, and cook for 15 minutes, or until tender.

6. Meanwhile, shuck the cooked clams.

7. When potatoes are ready, stir in the shucked clams, season with salt and pepper, and serve.

INGREDIENTS:

- ½ CUP CLAM JUICE
- 1 POUND LITTLE NECK CLAMS
- 1 OZ. SALT PORK
- 1 TABLESPOON EXTRA VIRGIN OLIVE OIL
- 1 TEASPOON THYME, LEAVES REMOVED AND CHOPPED
- 1 TEASPOON BASIL, LEAVES REMOVED AND CHOPPED
- 1 TEASPOON OREGANO, LEAVES REMOVED AND CHOPPED
- 2 GARLIC CLOVES, MINCED
- 1 BAY LEAF
- ½ HABANERO CHILI, FINELY CHOPPED
- ½ GREEN BELL PEPPER, CHOPPED
- 1 ONION, CHOPPED
- 2 PLUM TOMATOES, CHOPPED
- 1 14 OZ. CAN OF STEWED TOMATOES, CHOPPED
- 2 CUPS FISH STOCK
- 1 POTATO, PEELED AND CUT INTO ½-INCH PIECES
- SALT AND PEPPER, TO TASTE

CURRY VELOUTE
with FENNEL-DUSTED HALIBUT

YIELD: 4 SERVINGS / ACTIVE TIME: 45 MINUTES / TOTAL TIME: 1 HOUR AND 30 MINUTES

I chose halibut for this soup because it's local to Maine and one of my favorite fish—it can easily be replaced by another fish of your preference.

1. In a large saucepan, add the butter and cook over medium heat until melted. Add the onion, leek, fennel, celery, carrot, and garlic and cook for 5 minutes, or until soft.

2. Add 1 tablespoon of the curry powder and cook for 5 minutes. Remove a third of the cooked vegetables and reserve for garnish.

3. Add the remaining curry powder, cinnamon, chicken stock, 1½ cups of the heavy cream, and the white wine. Bring to a boil, reduce heat so that the soup simmers, and cook for 20 minutes.

4. Transfer the soup to a food processor, puree until creamy, and then strain through a fine sieve.

5. Return to the pan and bring to a simmer. Add the Pernod and season with salt and pepper.

6. Place the remaining cream and the egg yolks in a bowl and whisk until combined. Introduce ⅓ cup of the simmering soup into the mixture and vigorously whisk until combined. Add the warmed eggs to the soup and cook on the lowest possible heat for 2 minutes.

7. Meanwhile, prepare your Fennel-Dusted Halibut.

8. Ladle the soup into warm bowls, place the halibut in the center, and garnish with the reserved vegetables and Marinated Fennel.

INGREDIENTS:

¼	CUP BUTTER
½	CUP RED ONION, CHOPPED
½	CUP LEEK, WHITE PART ONLY, FINELY DICED
½	CUP FENNEL, FINELY DICED
½	CUP CELERY, FINELY DICED
½	CUP CARROTS, PEELED AND FINELY DICED
1	GARLIC CLOVE, MINCED
2	TABLESPOONS CURRY POWDER
½	TEASPOON CINNAMON
4	CUPS CHICKEN STOCK
2	CUPS HEAVY CREAM
½	CUP WHITE WINE
1	TABLESPOON PERNOD
	SALT AND PEPPER, TO TASTE
4	EGG YOLKS

TO SERVE:
FENNEL-DUSTED HALIBUT

MARINATED FENNEL

Continued . . .

FENNEL-DUSTED HALIBUT

Fennel pollen has a unique flavor and is great in salads and pastries, as well as on roasted vegetables and various proteins.

1. Place the halibut and the olive oil in a bowl and let stand for 30 minutes.

2. In a small bowl, add the fennel pollen, salt, and pepper and stir to combine.

3. Remove the halibut from the olive oil and dredge in the seasoned fennel pollen until covered. Set halibut aside and reserve the olive oil.

4. In a medium sauté pan, add 1 tablespoon of the reserved olive oil and cook over medium heat. Add the halibut and cook for 1 to 2 minutes on each side. Gently remove the halibut from the pan and serve immediately.

MARINATED FENNEL

1. Using a very sharp knife or a mandolin, slice the fennel very thin.

2. In a small bowl, combine the olive oil and lemon juice. Add the salt and pepper and stir to combine. Lay the sliced fennel in the oil and let marinate for 30 minutes before serving.

INGREDIENTS (CONTINUED):

FENNEL-DUSTED HALIBUT

- 8 OZ. CENTER-CUT HALIBUT, CUT INTO 8 PIECES
- 4 TABLESPOONS EXTRA VIRGIN OLIVE OIL
- 3 TABLESPOONS FENNEL POLLEN

  SALT AND PEPPER, TO TASTE

MARINATED FENNEL

- ½ BULB OF FENNEL
- 4 TABLESPOONS EXTRA VIRGIN OLIVE OIL
- 1 TEASPOON LEMON JUICE

  SALT AND PEPPER, TO TASTE

PRINCE EDWARD ISLAND MUSSEL SOUP

YIELD: 4 TO 6 SERVINGS / ACTIVE TIME: 20 MINUTES / TOTAL TIME: 45 MINUTES

Some of my favorite mussels come from Prince Edward Island, and this is a simple and fast way to celebrate them.

1. In a medium saucepan, add the oil and cook over medium heat until warm. Add the bacon and cook for 5 minutes, or until crispy.

2. Add the shallots, fennel, and garlic and cook for 5 minutes. Add the white wine and cook until reduced by half. Add the potatoes, heavy cream, and cilantro and bring to a boil.

3. Add the mussels, cover, and cook for 5 minutes, or until they open. Discard any mussels that do not open.

4. Season with salt and pepper, ladle into warm bowls, and serve with slices of grilled sourdough.

INGREDIENTS:

2 TABLESPOONS EXTRA VIRGIN OLIVE OIL

8 STRIPS THICK-CUT BACON, CHOPPED

2 SHALLOTS, FINELY CHOPPED

1 FENNEL BULB, FINELY CHOPPED

2 GARLIC CLOVES, MINCED

1 CUP WHITE WINE

1 CUP POTATOES, PEELED, CHOPPED, AND BLANCHED

2 CUPS HEAVY CREAM

1 TABLESPOON CILANTRO, LEAVES REMOVED AND CHOPPED

2 POUNDS PEI MUSSELS, WASHED, SCRUBBED, AND BEARDS REMOVED

SALT AND PEPPER, TO TASTE

CRAB *and* OYSTER GUMBO

YIELD: 4 TO 6 SERVINGS / ACTIVE TIME: 30 MINUTES / TOTAL TIME: 1 HOUR

This is a very fun take on traditional gumbo. I decided to substitute orzo for the traditional rice. I was pleased that I did, as I expect you will be.

1. *To make a Cajun Roux:* In a medium saucepan, add the oil and warm over medium heat. Add the flour and whisk vigorously until combined. Cook, while stirring constantly, for 8 minutes, or until the roux resembles peanut butter.

2. Add the bell peppers, onion, celery, garlic, and sausage and cook for 4 minutes. Add the stock 1 cup at a time, while stirring constantly. Bring to a boil, reduce heat so that the soup simmers, and cook for 10 minutes. Add the orzo and simmer for an additional 10 minutes.

3. Add the oysters, the reserved liquid, the crab meat, and the scallions. Cook for 3 minutes, add the Tabasco™, salt, and pepper, and then serve in warm bowls garnished with the scallion greens.

INGREDIENTS:

⅓ CUP VEGETABLE OIL

½ CUP ALL-PURPOSE FLOUR

½ CUP GREEN BELL PEPPER, CHOPPED

½ CUP RED BELL PEPPER, CHOPPED

1 ONION, CHOPPED

1 CELERY STALK, CHOPPED

1 GARLIC CLOVE, MINCED

4 OZ. ANDOUILLE SAUSAGE, CUT IN ⅛-INCH SLICES

3 CUPS CRAB STOCK

2 CUPS LOBSTER STOCK

¾ CUP ORZO

30 OYSTERS, SHUCKED AND RINSED, LIQUID RESERVED

½ POUND CRAB MEAT, CLEANED AND COOKED

4 SCALLIONS, WHITE PART CHOPPED, GREENS RESERVED FOR GARNISH

1 TEASPOON TABASCO™

SALT AND PEPPER, TO TASTE

RHODE ISLAND CLAM CHOWDER

YIELD: 4 TO 6 SERVINGS / ACTIVE TIME: 20 MINUTES / TOTAL TIME: 45 MINUTES

Quahogs are hard-shell bivalves that are native to Eastern North America. They are distinctively larger than other bivalves and usually not as tender. For this reason they are not eaten raw and are typically used in stews and chowders. This soup is intended to be a bit spicy, so season to taste with the Tabasco™ and cayenne pepper.

1. In a large saucepan, add the butter and cook over medium heat until melted.

2. Add the onions and celery and cook for 5 minutes. Add the clam juice and chicken stock, increase heat to medium-high, and bring to a boil.

3. Reduce the heat so that the soup simmers, add the quahogs and potatoes, cover, and cook for 5 minutes, or until the quahogs have opened.

4. Remove the quahogs and set aside. Continue to simmer for 10 minutes, or until the potatoes are tender.

5. Meanwhile, shuck the cooked quahogs.

6. When the potatoes are cooked, return the shucked quahogs to the saucepan and simmer for 2 minutes. Add the dill, cayenne pepper, Tabasco™, salt, and pepper. Ladle into bowls and garnish with the parsley.

INGREDIENTS:

⅓ CUP BUTTER

2 ONIONS, CHOPPED

2 CELERY STALKS, CHOPPED

4 CUPS CLAM JUICE

4 CUPS CHICKEN STOCK

2 POUNDS QUAHOGS

1 POUND FINGERLING POTATOES, QUARTERED

3 TABLESPOONS DILL, CHOPPED

PINCH OF CAYENNE PEPPER

TABASCO™, TO TASTE

SALT AND PEPPER, TO TASTE

¼ CUP PARSLEY, CHOPPED, FOR GARNISH

WILD RICE SOUP *with* CRAB SALAD

YIELD: 4 SERVINGS / ACTIVE TIME: 30 MINUTES / TOTAL TIME: 1 HOUR

This is a delicious combination of crab and wild rice. The rice is cooked with clarified butter, which stabilizes the butter and makes it less likely to burn.

1. In a large saucepan, add the butter, leeks, carrots, and celery and cook over medium heat for 5 minutes, or until the vegetables are soft.

2. Add the flour and cook for 3 minutes, stirring constantly. Add the crab stock gradually, stirring to prevent lumps from forming.

3. Bring the soup to a boil, reduce heat so that it simmers, and add the wild rice. Cook for 20 minutes, or until the rice is tender.

4. Add the heavy cream and sherry, season with salt and pepper, and ladle into warm bowls. Serve with Crab Salad and garnish with the chives.

CLARIFIED BUTTER

1. In a small saucepan, add the butter and melt over medium heat.

2. Reduce heat to the lowest-possible setting. Cook until the butter fat is very clear, and the milk solids drop to the bottom of the pan.

3. Skim the foam from the surface and discard. Transfer the butter to a container and refrigerate until ready to use.

CRAB SALAD

1. In a mixing bowl, add the crab, shallots, crème fraiche, mayonnaise, and lemon juice and stir until combined.

2. Gently fold in the chives and salmon roe. Season with salt and pepper, and serve.

INGREDIENTS:

- ¼ CUP BUTTER, CLARIFIED
- 2 CUPS LEEKS, FINELY DICED
- 1 CUP CARROTS, FINELY DICED
- 1 CUP CELERY, SLICED
- 2 TABLESPOONS ALL-PURPOSE FLOUR
- 8 CUPS CRAB STOCK
- 1 CUP WILD RICE
- 1 CUP HEAVY CREAM
- 2 TABLESPOONS SHERRY
  SALT AND PEPPER, TO TASTE
  CHIVES, CHOPPED, FOR GARNISH

TO SERVE:
CRAB SALAD

CLARIFIED BUTTER
- 1 CUP BUTTER

CRAB SALAD
- 6 OZ. CRAB MEAT, CLEANED AND COOKED
- 1 TABLESPOON SHALLOTS, CHOPPED
- 1 TABLESPOON CRÈME FRAICHE
- 1 TABLESPOON MAYONNAISE
- ¼ TEASPOON LEMON JUICE
- 2 TABLESPOONS CHIVES, CHOPPED
- 2 TABLESPOONS SALMON ROE
  SALT AND PEPPER, TO TASTE

CHILLED & DESSERT SOUPS

When most people think of soup, this category doesn't pop into their heads. Sure, there are the classics like Vichyssoise, Gazpacho, and Borscht, but there are a lot of other great options out there. On a warm summer's day, a chilled soup is a perfect appetizer or a hearty lunch. They are also perfect as a small amuse-bouche during a multi-course meal, teasing the palate before the real journey begins.

This chapter also contains one of my favorite recipes in the entire book: the Golden Gazpacho. Using unripe tomatoes and yellow vegetables, it has a sharper, tarter flavor than its forerunner. Dessert soups are also lovely, and often healthier than the standard dessert options.

CHILLED SAFFRON *and* ALMOND SOUP

YIELD: 4 SERVINGS / ACTIVE TIME: 30 MINUTES / TOTAL TIME: 3 HOURS

This beautiful Spanish soup is a perfect start to a meal intended to impress your friends. If you feel like taking it to the next level, pair with ceviche.

1. In a medium saucepan, add the olive oil and cook over low heat until warm.

2. Add the onion and garlic and cook for 15 minutes, stirring often.

3. Add the saffron and almonds, cook for 5 minutes, and add the vermouth. Cook for 5 minutes, or until half of the vermouth has evaporated.

4. Add the stock and bring to a boil. Reduce heat so that the soup simmers and cook for 10 minutes.

5. Season with salt and pepper, transfer to a food processor, puree until smooth, and strain through a fine sieve.

6. Place in the refrigerator and chill for at least 2 hours.

7. Pour into chilled bowls and garnish with toasted almonds and parsley.

INGREDIENTS:

2 TABLESPOONS EXTRA VIRGIN OLIVE OIL

2 ONIONS, CHOPPED

1 GARLIC CLOVE, MINCED

¼ TEASPOON SAFFRON

¼ CUP ALMONDS, SLIVERED

¼ CUP DRY VERMOUTH

4 CUPS VEGETABLE STOCK

SALT AND PEPPER, TO TASTE

ALMONDS, TOASTED AND SLIVERED, FOR GARNISH

PARSLEY, CHOPPED, FOR GARNISH

CHILLED CANTALOUPE *and* GINGER SOUP
with CHAMPAGNE ESPUMA

YIELD: 4 SERVINGS / ACTIVE TIME: 25 MINUTES / TOTAL TIME: 2 HOURS AND 25 MINUTES

Make sure you use ripe melons, and, if you have the time, carve a nice bowl out of the shell. I also froze some of the soup in ice cube trays to add before serving so that it would remain chilled but not become watered down.

1. Puree the melon, ginger, and lemon juice in a food processor and then pass through a fine sieve.

2. Chill in the refrigerator for 2 hours.

3. Just before serving, add the champagne and whisk to combine. Add the sugar slowly, tasting as you go, making sure you have just enough to emphasize the melon's flavor.

4. Pour into bowls and serve with Crispy Mint Leaves and Champagne Espuma.

CRISPY MINT LEAVES

1. Place oil in a small saucepan and cook until it reaches a temperature of 350°F.

2. Gently place a few of the leaves in the oil and fry until crispy but still green.

3. Use a slotted spoon or tongs to gently lift the leaves from the oil. Place on a paper towel to drain.

4. Repeat with the remaining leaves.

CHAMPAGNE ESPUMA

1. Reserve ¼ cup of the champagne and combine with the gelatin powder.

2. Place the remaining champagne into a small saucepan. Bring to a simmer and then remove from the stove.

3. Combine contents of the saucepan and the gelatin mixture. Strain and pour into Isi whipped cream gun.

4. Place in fridge for 1 hour before use.

INGREDIENTS:

2   CANTALOUPES, HALVED, FLESH CHOPPED INTO BITE-SIZED PIECES, SHELLS RESERVED

2   TEASPOON GINGER, PEELED AND GRATED

2   TABLESPOONS LEMON JUICE

4   CUPS CHAMPAGNE, CHILLED

¼   CUP SUGAR

TO SERVE:
CRISPY MINT LEAVES
CHAMPAGNE ESPUMA

CRISPY MINT LEAVES
1   CUP VEGETABLE OIL
8   MINT LEAVES

CHAMPAGNE ESPUMA
1½ CUPS CHAMPAGNE, CHILLED
1   TABLESPOON GELATIN POWDER

CHILLED MANGO, COCONUT, *and* CURRY SOUP

YIELD: 4 TO 6 SERVINGS / ACTIVE TIME: 15 MINUTES / TOTAL TIME: 45 MINUTES

I created this dish as an intermezzo in Great Britain. It's a modern take on the smoothie. Don't be scared about the curry—the flavor is very mild and refreshing.

1. Combine chopped mango, coconut milk, and curry in a food processor and blend until it has a soupy consistency.

2. Pass through a fine sieve. Serve in chilled bowls or glasses, and top with Coconut Froth.

COCONUT FROTH

Place all ingredients in a bowl and use a hand blender to combine. Blend until frothy, and serve.

INGREDIENTS:

3   CUPS OF RIPE MANGO, PEELED AND CHOPPED

3   14 OZ. CANS OF COCONUT MILK

4   TEASPOONS CURRY POWDER

TO SERVE:
COCONUT FROTH

COCONUT FROTH

½   CUP COCONUT MILK

½   CUP MILK

1   TABLESPOON HEAVY CREAM

1   TABLESPOON SUGAR

CHILLED AVOCADO SOUP
with CRAB *and* MANGO SALSA

YIELD: 6 SERVINGS / ACTIVE TIME: 25 MINUTES / TOTAL TIME: 45 MINUTES

This is a great summer soup. The fat from the avocados gives this soup a very creamy mouth-feel. Paired with the crab and mango salsa, it's a wonderfully balanced dish. If you feel like splurging, change the crab to lobster.

1. Add all the ingredients to a food processor and puree. Strain through a fine sieve and chill in the refrigerator for a minimum of 1 hour.

2. Place the tower of crab and mango salsa on a chilled plate. Remove ring cutter.

3. Pour soup around the already plated food. Place a dollop of crème fraiche on top and garnish with fresh chives.

CRAB AND MANGO SALSA

1. In a bowl, add the mango, red bell pepper, red onion, chives, rice wine vinegar, and olive oil, and stir gently until combined. Season with salt and chill in refrigerator until ready to serve.

2. Just before serving, use a ring cutter to make a tower out of the mango salsa. Top with the crab meat and serve.

INGREDIENTS:

3	RIPE AVOCADOS, PEELED AND CUT INTO CHUNKS
5	CUPS VEGETABLE STOCK
	JUICE OF 2 LIMES
1	TEASPOON CUMIN
2	TEASPOONS SALT
¼	TEASPOON CAYENNE PEPPER
	CHIVES, FOR GARNISH
	CRÈME FRAICHE, FOR GARNISH

TO SERVE:
CRAB AND MANGO SALSA

CRAB AND MANGO SALSA

½	CUP RIPE MANGO, PEELED AND FINELY CHOPPED
½	CUP RED BELL PEPPER, PEELED, SEEDED, AND FINELY CHOPPED
3	TABLESPOONS RED ONION, FINELY CHOPPED
1	TEASPOON CHIVES, FINELY CHOPPED
1	TEASPOON RICE WINE VINEGAR
2	TABLESPOONS EXTRA VIRGIN OLIVE OIL
	SALT
8	OZ. PEEKYTOE CRAB MEAT, CLEANED, COOKED, AND FREE OF SHELL

CHILLED CORN SOUP *with* GARLIC CUSTARD

YIELD: 4 SERVINGS / ACTIVE TIME: 30 MINUTES / TOTAL TIME: 2 HOURS AND 15 MINUTES

This recipe is easily made the day before. Have this lovely appetizer prepared in advance to limit stress on the day of your dinner. Corn cobs have a lot of nutrients and flavor, and this corn stock is the secret of this soup.

1. Remove the corn kernels from the cob.

2. In a large stockpot, add the water, the corn cobs, bay leaf, thyme, peppercorns, and 1 of the chopped onions, and bring to a boil.

3. Reduce the heat so that the stock simmers and cook for 1 hour.

4. Strain through a fine sieve and reserve the stock.

5. In a medium saucepan, melt the butter. Add the remaining onion and the garlic, and cook over medium heat for 5 minutes, or until soft.

6. Add the corn kernels, while reserving 2 tablespoons for garnish, and reduce the heat to low. Cook for 5 minutes.

7. Transfer the corn mixture to a food processor and combine with 4 cups of the corn stock. Puree, adding more if necessary to produce a creamy consistency.

8. Season with lemon juice, salt, and pepper. Chill in refrigerator for at least 1 hour.

9. Place the Garlic Custard, reserved corn kernels, and cilantro leaves in the middle of chilled bowls. Pour the soup around the center and serve.

GARLIC CUSTARD

1. Preheat oven to 325°F.

2. Grease four 4 oz. ramekins. Place them on a baking tray.

3. In a small saucepan, melt the butter. Add the garlic and cook over low heat for 5 minutes, or until soft.

4. Add the cream and the salt. Increase heat to medium and bring to a simmer.

5. Remove from heat, let stand for 10 minutes, and strain through a fine sieve.

Continued . . .

INGREDIENTS:

8	EARS SWEET CORN
10	CUPS WATER
1	BAY LEAF
12	THYME SPRIGS
6	PEPPERCORNS
2	ONIONS, PEELED AND CHOPPED
2	TABLESPOONS BUTTER
4	GARLIC CLOVES, MINCED
2	TABLESPOONS LEMON JUICE
	SALT AND PEPPER, TO TASTE
	CORN KERNELS, FOR GARNISH
	CILANTRO, FOR GARNISH

TO SERVE:
GARLIC CUSTARD

GARLIC CUSTARD

1	TABLESPOON BUTTER
3	GARLIC CLOVES, MINCED
1	CUP HEAVY CREAM
½	TEASPOON SALT
	PEPPER, TO TASTE
2	MEDIUM EGGS
	YOLK FROM 1 MEDIUM EGG
1½	TEASPOONS CHIVES, CHOPPED

6. Add the eggs and the yolk to a medium-sized bowl and whisk until combined. Add chives and whisk until combined.

7. Add the garlic mixture and whisk until combined. Season with additional salt and pepper, if necessary.

8. Divide the mixture between the ramekins and place the tray in the oven. Before closing the door, pour enough hot water on the baking tray to go halfway up the ramekins.

9. Cook for 18 minutes, or until the custard is firm and a knife comes out clean when inserted.

10. Remove the tray from the oven and chill the custard in the refrigerator for 1 hour.

11. When ready to serve, use a knife to remove the custard from the ramekin.

GAZPACHO *with* PARSLEY OIL

YIELD: 4 TO 6 SERVINGS / ACTIVE TIME: 1 HOUR / TOTAL TIME: 14 HOURS

Gazpacho is a cold soup made of raw blended vegetables. A classic of Spanish cuisine, it is enjoyed far and wide during the summer months. If you prefer a more refined version, strain through a fine sieve after pureeing it.

1. Combine all ingredients in a large bowl, cover, and place in refrigerator to marinate overnight.

2. Transfer the soup to a food processor and puree to desired consistency. Chill in refrigerator for 1 hour.

3. Adjust seasoning to taste, and serve in chilled bowls with Parsley Oil, Herb Salad, and Vegetable Kabob.

PARSLEY OIL

1. In a small saucepan, bring 4 cups of water to boil. Add the parsley leaves and spinach, cook for 1 minute, drain, and submerge in ice water.

2. Remove from ice water and squeeze out any excess water.

3. In a food processor, add the parsley, spinach, and vegetable oil, and puree for 3 to 4 minutes. Strain through cheesecloth and reserve until ready to serve.

INGREDIENTS:

4	TOMATOES, CHOPPED
½	RED ONION, PEELED AND CHOPPED
½	CUCUMBER, CHOPPED
1	RED BELL PEPPER, SEEDED AND CHOPPED
1	CELERY STALK, CHOPPED
1	CUP CRUSTY BREAD, CHOPPED
2	TABLESPOONS PARSLEY, LEAVES REMOVED AND CHOPPED
2	TABLESPOONS CHIVES, CHOPPED
1	GARLIC CLOVE, MINCED
¼	CUP RED WINE VINEGAR
2	TABLESPOONS EXTRA VIRGIN OLIVE OIL
1	TEASPOON LEMON JUICE
1	TEASPOON SUGAR
2	TEASPOONS TABASCO™
1	TEASPOON WORCESTERSHIRE SAUCE
2	CUPS TOMATO JUICE
	SALT AND PEPPER, TO TASTE

TO SERVE:
PARSLEY OIL
HERB SALAD
VEGETABLE KABOB

PARSLEY OIL:
1	CUP PARSLEY, CHOPPED
1	CUP BABY SPINACH
1	CUP VEGETABLE OIL

Continued . . .

HERB SALAD

1. Gently rinse the herbs and dry in paper towels.

2. In a small mixing bowl combine the cleaned herbs and add Parsley Oil.

3. Mix together gently and season with salt and pepper.

VEGETABLE KABOB

1. Prepare your vegetables and place on a wooden skewer.

2. Drizzle parsley oil over the skewers and season with salt and pepper.

3. Place in refrigerator until ready to serve.

INGREDIENTS (CONTINUED):

HERB SALAD

1	SMALL BUNCH CHIVES, CUT INTO 1 ½-INCH BATONS
1	SMALL BUNCH CILANTRO, LEAVES REMOVED
1	SMALL BUNCH PARSLEY, LEAVES REMOVED
2	TEASPOONS PARSLEY OIL
	SALT AND PEPPER

VEGETABLE KABOB

8–12	CHERRY TOMATOES, CUT IN HALF
¼	RED BELL PEPPER, SEEDS REMOVED AND CHOP INTO ½ INCH CUBES
¼	CUCUMBER, SEEDS REMOVED AND CHOPPED
¼	RED ONION, CHOPPED INTO ½-INCH CUBES
¼	CELERY, THINLY SLICED
1	TABLESPOON PARSLEY OIL
	SALT AND PEPPER

CURRIED YOGURT SOUP

YIELD: 4 SERVINGS / ACTIVE TIME: 25 MINUTES / TOTAL TIME: 1 HOUR

This traditional Indian soup is made with chickpea flour. You'll learn to love its dazzling color.

1. Combine the yogurt, chickpea flour, chili powder, and turmeric in a bowl. Transfer to a saucepan, add the jalapeños and vegetable stock, and bring to a simmer. Cook for approximately 10 minutes, while stirring occasionally, taking care not to let the soup boil over.

2. Heat the vegetable oil in a sauté pan. Add the remaining spices, garlic, and ginger and cook until the dried curry turns black. Stir in the cilantro and sugar and then add the contents of the sauté pan to the soup. Cover and let stand for 10 minutes.

3. Strain the soup through a fine sieve and adjust seasoning to taste.

4. Serve in bowls with Dried Cilantro Leaves and yogurt.

DRIED CILANTRO LEAVES

This dried cilantro garnish is a great way to make a dried herb and still obtain a nice color, texture, and flavor. This technique can be utilized with most soft herbs.

1. Tightly wrap a plate with plastic wrap and then sprinkle with oil.

2. Use a paper towel to spread the oil into an even layer on the plastic wrap. Lay the leaves on the plate and cover tightly with more plastic wrap.

3. Microwave for 4 to 5 minutes, until crispy. Remove from microwave and serve.

INGREDIENTS:

- 4   CUPS PLAIN YOGURT, PLUS MORE FOR SERVING
- ½   CUP CHICKPEA FLOUR
- 1   TEASPOON CHILI POWDER
- 1   TEASPOON TURMERIC
- ½   TEASPOON JALAPEÑO, CHOPPED
- 1   CUP VEGETABLE STOCK
- ½   CUP VEGETABLE OIL
- 1   DRIED RED CHILI
- 1   TEASPOON CUMIN
- 2   TEASPOONS DRIED CURRY LEAVES, CHOPPED
- 6   GARLIC CLOVES, CRUSHED
-       2-INCH PIECE OF GINGER, PEELED AND CRUSHED
- 4   TABLESPOONS CILANTRO, CHOPPED
- 1   TEASPOON SUGAR
-       SALT AND PEPPER, TO TASTE

TO SERVE:
DRIED CILANTRO LEAVES

DRIED CILANTRO LEAVES
- ¼   TEASPOON OLIVE OIL
- 12   LARGE CILANTRO LEAVES

CHILLED GARLIC *and* PINE NUT SOUP *with* BALSAMIC ROASTED GRAPES

YIELD: 4 SERVINGS / ACTIVE TIME: 35 MINUTES / TOTAL TIME: 50 MINUTES

This is based on an ancient Moorish soup from Southern Spain, a region rich in pine nuts. Toasting the pine nuts concentrates their flavor and blanching the garlic gives it a more palatable taste.

1. Preheat oven to 375°F.

2. Place the pine nuts on a baking tray and then place the tray in the oven. Cook for 4 minutes, remove tray, and stir the pine nuts. Return to oven for 4 minutes, or until the pine nuts are lightly browned. Remove, let cool, and then use a mortar and pestle, or a coffee grinder, to grind into a powder.

3. Bring water to boil in a small saucepan. Add the garlic and boil for 4 minutes. Remove and rinse under cold water.

4. Place the bread in a bowl and add 2 cups of water. Soak for 8 to 10 minutes.

5. Remove the bread from the bowl, squeeze out excess water, and set aside. Reserve soaking water.

6. Add the nuts, garlic, bread, and 1 teaspoon of salt to a food processor and blend until it forms a paste.

7. Add the olive oil and white wine vinegar to the food processor and blend to combine. Slowly add the remaining water until the mixture has a nice velvety texture (you might need to add or subtract water depending on the bread you use).

8. Add the sherry, season to taste with salt and pepper, and chill in refrigerator until ready to serve with Balsamic Roasted Grapes.

BALSAMIC ROASTED GRAPES

1. Preheat oven to 375°F.

2. Add grapes, olive oil, thyme, and marjoram to a bowl and toss lightly.

3. Place grapes on a baking tray and bake for 10 minutes.

4. Remove from oven and drizzle with balsamic vinegar. Return to oven for another 10 minutes, or until the grapes wrinkle and split.

INGREDIENTS:

¾	CUP PINE NUTS
6	GARLIC CLOVES, MINCED
7	OZ. DAY-OLD BREAD, CRUST REMOVED
2 TO 4	CUPS WATER
½	CUP ALMONDS, BLANCHED
1	TEASPOON SALT
	SALT AND PEPPER, TO TASTE
½	CUP EXTRA VIRGIN OLIVE OIL
1	TABLESPOON WHITE WINE VINEGAR
2	TABLESPOONS DRY SHERRY

TO SERVE:
BALSAMIC ROASTED GRAPES

BALSAMIC ROASTED GRAPES

1½	CUPS OF RED GRAPES
2	TABLESPOONS EXTRA VIRGIN OLIVE OIL
2	TEASPOONS THYME, LEAVES REMOVED AND FINELY CHOPPED
1	TEASPOON MARJORAM, LEAVES REMOVED AND FINELY CHOPPED
1½	TEASPOONS BALSAMIC VINEGAR
	SALT AND PEPPER, TO TASTE

CHILLED PEA SOUP

YIELD: 4 TO 6 SERVINGS / ACTIVE TIME: 15 MINUTES / TOTAL TIME: 1 HOUR AND 15 MINUTES

This is a far cry from army-green split pea soup. Cooking the peas briefly retains their vibrant color, and the addition of spinach keeps the finished soup looking, and tasting, bright. Delicious warm or chilled, this one is guaranteed to become a springtime staple.

1. In a medium saucepan, add the olive oil and onions and cook over medium heat for 5 minutes, or until the onions are soft.

2. Add the mint sprig and stir.

3. After 1 minute, add the stock and bring to a boil. Remove from heat and add the frozen peas.

4. Transfer the soup to a food processor, add the spinach, and puree until smooth.

5. Strain through a fine sieve, season with salt and pepper, and serve with Cheese Gougeres.

CHEESE GOUGERES

1. Preheat oven to 400°F.

2. In a medium saucepan, add the milk, water, salt, and butter and bring to a boil. Add the flour and stir constantly until a ball of dough forms.

3. Remove dough from pan and place in a standing mixer. Mix slowly until dough stops steaming.

4. Add the 5 eggs one at a time. Add the cheese and mix until combined.

5. Line a baking tray with a baking mat or parchment paper and spoon the dough onto it.

6. In a small bowl, add the remaining egg and 2 tablespoons of water and whisk until combined. Brush this wash on top of dough and place tray in oven. Bake for 20 minutes, or until golden brown, then remove and let cool on a wire rack.

INGREDIENTS:

1	TABLESPOON EXTRA VIRGIN OLIVE OIL
½	ONION, PEELED AND DICED
1	MINT SPRIG
4	CUPS VEGETABLE STOCK
3	POUNDS PEAS, FROZEN
4	CUPS SPINACH
	SALT AND PEPPER, TO TASTE

TO SERVE:
CHEESE GOUGERES

CHEESE GOUGERES

¾	CUP MILK
¾	CUP WATER
⅛	TEASPOON SALT
7	TABLESPOONS BUTTER
1¼	CUPS ALL-PURPOSE FLOUR
5	EGGS, PLUS 1 EGG FOR EGG WASH
1¼	CUPS GRUYÈRE CHEESE, GRATED

CHILLED STRAWBERRY *and* TOMATO GAZPACHO *with* ROASTED STRAWBERRIES

YIELD: 4 TO 6 SERVINGS / ACTIVE TIME: 1 HOUR / TOTAL TIME: 14 HOURS

Love Gazpacho? Try this exciting twist to an old classic. At the restaurant, we used to serve this with balsamic ice cream, which was an absolute crowd-pleaser.

1. Combine all of the ingredients in a large bowl, cover, and marinate overnight.

2. Transfer the soup to a food processor, puree to desired consistency, and return to refrigerator for 1 hour.

3. Adjust seasoning and ladle into chilled bowls. Serve with Balsamic Roasted Strawberries and garnish with mint leaves.

BALSAMIC ROASTED STRAWBERRIES

1. Preheat oven to 350°F.

2. Place all ingredients in a mixing bowl and toss gently.

3. Place coated strawberries on a lined baking tray and bake for 8 to 10 minutes. Remove from oven and let cool before serving.

INGREDIENTS:

4	POUNDS RIPE TOMATOES, CHOPPED
1	ONION, CHOPPED
2	RED BELL PEPPERS, CHOPPED
6	GARLIC CLOVES, CHOPPED
2	TABLESPOONS BALSAMIC VINEGAR
2	TABLESPOONS EXTRA VIRGIN OLIVE OIL
½	BAGUETTE, CHOPPED
4	CUPS RIPE STRAWBERRIES, STEMS REMOVED, CHOPPED
	ZEST AND JUICE OF 1 LEMON
⅛	TEASPOON CAYENNE PEPPER
	SALT AND PEPPER, TO TASTE
	MINT LEAVES, FOR GARNISH

TO SERVE:

BALSAMIC ROASTED STRAWBERRIES

BALSAMIC ROASTED STRAWBERRIES

2	CUPS STRAWBERRIES, STEMS REMOVED, QUARTERED
1	TABLESPOON HONEY
2	TABLESPOONS BALSAMIC VINEGAR

GOLDEN GAZPACHO
with GRILLED CHEESE

YIELD: 4 TO 6 SERVINGS / ACTIVE TIME: 30 MINUTES / TOTAL TIME: 2 HOURS AND 30 MINUTES

If you love Gazpacho, try this spectacular version that is a twist on the classic. Using only yellow vegetables gives it its special color and transforms the flavor.

1. Combine all the ingredients in a mixing bowl and let chill in refrigerator for at least 30 minutes and up to 1 hour.

2. Transfer the soup to a food processor, blend until smooth, and strain through a fine sieve.

3. Season with salt and pepper, return to refrigerator, and chill for at least 1 hour.

4. Ladle into chilled bowls, garnish with parsley, and serve with Grilled Cheese.

GRILLED CHEESE

1. Preheat the oven to 350°F.

2. Spread the softened butter on each slice of bread.

3. Sprinkle the cheese on the non-buttered sides of the bread. Make sandwiches out of the pieces of bread.

4. Place a large sauté pan over medium heat and add the sandwiches to the pan. Cook until golden brown, flip, and repeat on the other side.

5. Remove sandwiches on the pan and place in the oven for 5 minutes, or until heated through.

6. Remove from oven, cut in half, and serve.

INGREDIENTS:

6   EARS OF CORN, KERNELS REMOVED

9   GOLDEN TOMATOES, CHOPPED

2   YELLOW BELL PEPPERS, SEEDS REMOVED AND CHOPPED

1   ONION, CHOPPED

3   GARLIC CLOVES, MINCED

½   CUP EXTRA VIRGIN OLIVE OIL

4   TABLESPOONS APPLE CIDER VINEGAR

    SALT AND PEPPER, TO TASTE

    PARSLEY, CHOPPED, FOR GARNISH

TO SERVE:
GRILLED CHEESE

GRILLED CHEESE
8–12 SLICES BRIOCHE

½   CUP BUTTER, SOFTENED

2–3   CUPS FONTINA CHEESE, GRATED

RED BELL PEPPER SOUP
with SAMBUCA CREAM

YIELD: 6 SERVINGS / ACTIVE TIME: 25 MINUTES / TOTAL TIME: 55 MINUTES

Take the Sambuca out from behind the bar and bring it into the kitchen. Once mixed in, the Sambuca Cream brings out the flavors of the fennel seed, herbs, and jalapeño.

1. In a medium saucepan, add half the oil and cook over medium heat until warm. Add the onion, fennel seed, thyme, bay leaf, garlic, basil, and jalapeño, reduce heat to low, and cook for 5 minutes, or until onion is soft.

2. Add the flour and cook, while stirring constantly, for 5 minutes.

3. Add the stock, tomato, and tomato paste and bring to a boil.

4. Meanwhile, in a large sauté pan, add the remaining oil and the red bell peppers. Cook over medium until the peppers blister and char slightly.

5. Add the peppers to the soup and cook, while stirring occasionally, for 20 minutes.

6. Transfer the soup to a food processor, puree until smooth and creamy, and pass through a fine sieve.

7. Return the pureed soup to the pan, bring to a simmer, and add the cream and sugar. Season with salt and pepper.

8. Just before serving, add the Sambuca. Ladle into bowls, serve with Sambuca Cream, and garnish with basil.

SAMBUCA CREAM

1. Place cream in a bowl and whisk until soft peaks form.

2. Add the remaining ingredients to the bowl. Whisk until stiff peaks form. Refrigerate until ready to serve.

INGREDIENTS:

- ¾ CUP EXTRA VIRGIN OLIVE OIL
- 1 CUP ONION, CHOPPED
- 1 TABLESPOON FENNEL SEED
- ¼ TEASPOON THYME, LEAVES REMOVED AND CHOPPED
- 1 BAY LEAF
- ½ TEASPOON GARLIC, MINCED
- 1 TABLESPOON BASIL, CHOPPED, PLUS MORE FOR GARNISH
- 1 TABLESPOON JALAPEÑO, STEM AND SEEDS REMOVED, DICED
- ¼ CUP ALL-PURPOSE FLOUR
- 5 CUPS CHICKEN STOCK
- ½ CUP TOMATO, CONCASSE (SEE PAGE 89) AND CHOPPED
- 1 TEASPOON TOMATO PASTE
- 6 LARGE RED BELL PEPPERS, HALVED, SEEDED, AND CHOPPED
- 1 CUP HEAVY CREAM
- PINCH OF SUGAR
- SALT AND PEPPER, TO TASTE
- 4 TABLESPOONS SAMBUCA

TO SERVE:
SAMBUCA CREAM

SAMBUCA CREAM
- ½ CUP HEAVY CREAM
- ¼ TEASPOON LEMON JUICE
- ⅛ TEASPOON LEMON ZEST
- 2 TABLESPOONS SAMBUCA

FONTINA CHEESE SOUP
in a SOURDOUGH BREAD BOWL

YIELDS: 4 SERVINGS / ACTIVE TIME: 30 MINUTES / TOTAL TIME: 1 HOUR

A delicious cheesy soup finished in the fashion of a San Francisco Sourdough Bread Soup. Use smaller rolls for an amuse-bouche or intermezzo or larger ones as a main course. The cheesy soup absorbs nicely into the bread and allows you to eat your "bowl" when you finish. You might argue that the leftover soaked bread is even better than the soup

1. In a medium saucepan on medium heat, melt the butter.

2. Add the onion and thyme and cook for 5 minutes or until soft.

3. Add the flour and cook for 5 minutes.

4. Add the chicken stock and milk and bring to a boil.

5. Remove the pan from heat, add the cheese, and whisk until combined.

6. In a food processor blend until smooth and strain through a fine sieve.

7. Return to a clean pan and season with salt and pepper.

8. With a small serrated knife, remove the tops of the sourdough bread, remove the innards, and toast. Pour the soup in the middle and garnish with chopped chives.

INGREDIENTS:

½ CUP BUTTER

2 ONIONS, CHOPPED

2 THYME SPRIGS, LEAVES REMOVED AND CHOPPED

4 TABLESPOONS ALL-PURPOSE FLOUR

4 CUPS CHICKEN STOCK

4 CUPS MILK

8 CUPS FONTINA CHEESE, GRATED

SALT AND PEPPER

4 SOURDOUGH BREAD ROLLS OR 1 LARGE BOULE

CHIVES, TO GARNISH

VICHYSSOISE

YIELD: 4 SERVINGS / ACTIVE TIME: 40 MINUTES / TOTAL TIME: 2 HOURS

Vichyssoise is traditionally served cold, but it can be eaten hot.

1. In a medium saucepan, add the butter and cook over medium heat until warm. Add the leeks and shallots and cook for 5 minutes, or until soft.

2. Add the potato and cook for 3 minutes.

3. Add the chicken stock and bring to a boil. Reduce to a simmer, partially cover the pan, and cook until potato is soft.

4. Transfer to a food processor, puree until creamy, and strain through a fine sieve.

5. Season with salt, pepper, and nutmeg. Add the heavy cream and place the soup in the refrigerator to chill.

6. Serve in chilled bowls with Chive Oil and Simple Croutons.

CHIVE OIL

1. In a small saucepan, bring 4 cups of water to boil.

2. Add the chives and spinach, cook for 1 minute, remove, and submerge in ice water.

3. Remove from ice water and squeeze out any excess water.

4. In a food processor, add the chives, spinach, and the oil. Puree for 3 to 4 minutes, strain through cheesecloth, and reserve until ready to use.

SIMPLE CROUTONS

1. Preheat the oven to 350°F.

2. Spread the brioche out on a baking tray.

3. Drizzle with olive oil and bake for 5 minutes, or until golden brown.

4. Remove, season with salt and pepper, and place on a paper towel to cool.

INGREDIENTS:

- 4 TABLESPOONS BUTTER
- 6 LEEKS, WHITE PART ONLY, THINLY SLICED
- 3 LARGE SHALLOTS, CHOPPED
- 1 IDAHO POTATO, PEELED AND CUBED
- 6 CUPS CHICKEN STOCK
- 1 CUP HEAVY CREAM
  SALT AND PEPPER, TO TASTE
  PINCH OF NUTMEG

TO SERVE:
CHIVE OIL

SIMPLE CROUTONS

CHIVE OIL
- 1 CUP CHIVES, CHOPPED
- 1 CUP BABY SPINACH
- 1 CUP VEGETABLE OIL

SIMPLE CROUTONS
- SLICED BRIOCHE, CUT INTO ¼-INCH CUBES
- 1 TABLESPOON EXTRA VIRGIN OLIVE OIL
  SALT AND PEPPER, TO TASTE

CHILLED WATERMELON *and* CHERRY SOUP *with* WATERMELON ICE CUBES

YIELD: 4 SERVINGS / ACTIVE TIME: 20 MINUTES / TOTAL TIME: 13 HOURS AND 35 MINUTES

This makes for a great intermezzo or amuse-bouche, and consistently appeared on The White Barn Inn menu in the summer. The ice cubes float to the bottom and keeps the soup chilled without watering it down.

1. Add the watermelon, cherries, and Riesling to a food processor and puree until smooth. Strain through a fine sieve and chill in the refrigerator.

2. Right before serving, add the champagne and Watermelon Ice Cubes. Serve in chilled glasses.

WATERMELON ICE CUBES

Combine the watermelon, kirsch, lime zest, lime juice, vanilla bean seeds, and the vanilla pod in a bowl and chill in the refrigerator for 1 hour. Transfer to a baking tray and freeze overnight. Cut into cubes and serve.

INGREDIENTS:

- 1½ CUPS WATERMELON, PEELED AND CHOPPED
- ¾ CUP CHERRIES, PITTED, FRESH OR FROZEN
- 1 CUP RIESLING
- 1 CUP CHAMPAGNE

TO SERVE:
WATERMELON ICE CUBES

WATERMELON ICE CUBES

- 1 CUP WATERMELON, CUT INTO 1/2-INCH CUBES
- 1 TABLESPOON KIRSCH
  ZEST AND JUICE OF 1 LIME
- ½ VANILLA BEAN, SEEDS SCRAPED AND POD RESERVED

CHILLED CHERRY SOUP
with BRIOCHE FRENCH TOAST

YIELD: 4 TO 6 SERVINGS / **ACTIVE TIME:** 30 MINUTES / **TOTAL TIME:** 1 HOUR AND 40 MINUTES

A great end to any meal, and certain to wow your guests. Fresh cherries are preferred, but frozen are suitable if out of season or unavailable. Drying out the brioche prior to cooking allows the bread to better absorb the egg mixture.

1. In a large saucepan, combine water, Riesling, sugar, vanilla bean, cinnamon stick and lemon juice. Bring to a boil, then reduce heat so that the soup simmers. Cook for 5 minutes, reduce heat, and let stand for 30 minutes.

2. Strain the liquid through a fine sieve.

3. Reserve 12 cherries for garnish and put the rest in a saucepan. Cover with liquid from large saucepan and bring to a boil. Reduce heat so that the soup simmers and cook for 5 minutes.

4. Transfer the soup to a food processor and puree. Pass through a fine sieve, then add the kirch and lemon zest and chill.

5. Once chilled, whisk in the sour cream. Pour into 4 chilled bowls, garnish with sour cream, fresh mint, and reserved cherries, and serve with Brioche French Toast and Dried Vanilla Beans.

BRIOCHE FRENCH TOAST

1. Slice the bread a few hours in advance and leave uncovered.

2. Whisk together the sugar, cinnamon, nutmeg, and flour in a bowl.

3. In a separate bowl, whisk together the eggs, cream, and vanilla extract.

4. Add the wet ingredients to the dry and whisk to combine.

5. Divide the batter between 4 saucers and soak the bread for 2 minutes on each side, until absorbed, but not too soggy.

6. Preheat a nonstick pan or a griddle.

7. Over medium heat, add the bread to the pan or griddle and cook for 2 to 3 minutes on each side, until golden brown.

8. Serve immediately.

Continued . . .

INGREDIENTS:

1   CUP WATER

1   CUP RIESLING

¼   CUP SUGAR

1   VANILLA BEAN, SCRAPED, POD RESERVED

2   CINNAMON STICKS

¼   CUP LEMON JUICE

2 ½ POUNDS RED CHERRIES, PITTED, FRESH OR FROZEN

¼   CUP KIRSCH

2   TEASPOONS LEMON ZEST

½   CUP SOUR CREAM, PLUS MORE FOR GARNISH

     MINT LEAVES, CHIFFONADE, FOR GARNISH

TO SERVE:
BRIOCHE FRENCH TOAST

DRIED VANILLA BEANS

BRIOCHE FRENCH TOAST

4   SLICES BRIOCHE, CUT ¼-INCH THICK

1   TABLESPOON SUGAR

½   TEASPOON CINNAMON

¼   TEASPOON NUTMEG

1   TABLESPOON ALL-PURPOSE FLOUR

2   LARGE EGGS

½   CUP HEAVY CREAM

1   TEASPOON VANILLA EXTRACT

DRIED VANILLA BEANS

1. Preheat oven to 200°F.

2. Cut the vanilla pod lengthwise into very thin slices and place them on a baking tray.

3. Place tray in oven for 10 minutes, or until the bean slices are nice and stiff. Remove and serve.

INGREDIENTS (CONTINUED):

DRIED VANILLA BEANS
  RESERVED VANILLA POD
  FROM SOUP

CHILLED RHUBARB CHAMPAGNE SOUP
with LEMON POPPY SEED MASCARPONE

YIELD: 4 SERVINGS / ACTIVE TIME: 45 MINUTES / TOTAL TIME: 50 MINUTES

The tart flavor of rhubarb is wonderful in the spring. If you want to wow your guests, use some dry ice. Don't be nervous, it's easy. Carefully place the soup bowl on top of dry ice and gently add hot water around the bowl.

1. In a medium saucepan, add the rhubarb, raspberries, orange juice, and water and bring to a boil. Reduce heat so that the soup simmers and cook for 20 minutes.

2. Transfer the soup to a food processor and puree. Slowly add the champagne until the soup has a creamy texture, then strain through a fine sieve.

3. Chill in refrigerator until ready to serve.

4. Serve with a dollop of Lemon Poppy Seed Mascarpone and Raspberry Couli and garnish with mint.

LEMON POPPY SEED MASCARPONE

Combine all ingredients in a bowl and whisk to combine. Chill in refrigerator until ready to serve.

RASPBERRY COULI

1. In a small saucepan, combine all ingredients and bring to a simmer. Cook for 10 minutes, turn off heat, and let stand.

2. When cool, strain through a fine sieve and chill in refrigerator until ready to serve.

INGREDIENTS:

4	CUPS RHUBARB, CHOPPED
1	CUP RASPBERRIES
1	CUP ORANGE JUICE
1	CUP WATER
2	CUPS CHAMPAGNE
	MINT SPRIGS, FOR GARNISH

TO SERVE:
LEMON POPPY SEED MASCARPONE

RASPBERRY COULI

LEMON POPPY SEED MASCARPONE

½	CUP MASCARPONE
1	TABLESPOON LEMON JUICE
1	TABLESPOON POPPY SEEDS
1	TABLESPOON SUGAR

RASPBERRY COULI

¼	CUP SUGAR
½	CUP RASPBERRIES
¼	CUP RED WINE

STRAWBERRY CONSOMMÉ
with CARDAMOM BUTTERMILK PANNA COTTA
and SCOTTISH SHORTBREAD

YIELD: 4 SERVINGS / ACTIVE TIME: 30 MINUTES / TOTAL TIME: 4 HOURS AND 30 MINUTES

This strawberry consommé is named for its clarity, not the technique. Adding sugar to the strawberries pulls out their flavor—try one when they're done, you'll see that all their flavor is in the soup.

1. Combine all ingredients in a metal bowl and cover with plastic wrap.

2. Bring water to boil in a medium saucepan. Place the bowl over the top and lower the flame so that it simmers. Cook for 1 hour.

3. Turn off the heat and let stand for 1 hour.

4. Strain the soup through a fine sieve and chill in refrigerator for at least 1 hour before serving.

CARDAMOM BUTTERMILK PANNA COTTA

Resting the panna cotta in the refrigerator prior to setting allows the mix to become viscous and keeps the seeds suspended. If you don't do this, the flavor will be fine, but all the seeds will float down to the bottom, affecting the look of the panna cotta.

1. Place half of the buttermilk in a bowl and set aside.

2. Combine the remaining buttermilk, heavy cream, vanilla seeds, vanilla pod, cardamom seeds, and sugar in a small saucepan and bring to a simmer. Turn off heat, and let stand for 10 minutes.

3. Add the gelatin powder to the bowl of cold buttermilk and stir quickly until combined.

4. Bring the contents of the saucepan to a boil and add the gelatin mixture.

5. Remove saucepan from heat and stir gently for 2 minutes.

6. Strain through a fine sieve and chill in the refrigerator for 15 minutes, removing to stir every 5 minutes.

7. Pour into serving dishes and refrigerate for 1 hour before serving.

INGREDIENTS:

8	CUPS STRAWBERRIES, STEMS REMOVED, CHOPPED
½	CUP SUGAR
1	VANILLA POD, HALVED, SEEDS REMOVED
1	CINNAMON STICK
1	STAR ANISE
	JUICE AND ZEST OF 2 LEMONS
1	MINT SPRIG
2	TABLESPOONS GRAND MARNIER

TO SERVE:

CARDAMOM PANNA COTTA

SCOTTISH SHORTBREAD

CARDAMOM PANNA COTTA

¾	CUP BUTTERMILK
¾	CUP HEAVY CREAM
½	VANILLA BEAN, SEEDS REMOVED AND POD RESERVED
2	CARDAMOM PODS, SEEDS REMOVED, CHOPPED
⅛	CUP SUGAR
1¼	TEASPOONS GELATIN POWDER

Continued . . .

SCOTTISH SHORTBREAD

Grating the butter and freezing it commits you to very little mixing, which keeps the dough for the shortbread, well, short.

1. Preheat oven to 325°F.

2. Grate the butter and place in the freezer for 30 minutes.

3. Combine ½ cup of the sugar, flour, salt, and frozen butter in the bowl of your mixer and blend slowly until it is fine like sand. Be careful not to overmix.

4. Place mixture in an 8" x 8" baking tray and cook for 1 hour and 15 minutes.

5. Remove from oven and sprinkle on the remaining sugar.

6. Let cool and then serve.

INGREDIENTS (CONTINUED):

SCOTTISH SHORTBREAD

1   CUP BUTTER, PLUS 4 TABLESPOONS

½   CUP SUGAR, PLUS 2 TABLESPOONS

2½   CUPS ALL-PURPOSE FLOUR

1   TEASPOON SALT

COCONUT *and* TAPIOCA SOUP *with* MINT-INFUSED MANGO

YIELD: 4 TO 6 SERVINGS / ACTIVE TIME: 30 MINUTES / TOTAL TIME: 2 HOURS AND 40 MINUTES

This soup is based on a dessert I made when working in England. Tapioca is not seen much these days, but it was very popular back in the '80s.

1. In a large saucepan, add the milk, sugar, vanilla seeds, and vanilla pod and bring to a boil. Reduce heat so that the soup simmers and add the tapioca pearls. Cook for 10 minutes, or until the tapioca pearls are soft.

2. Remove pan from heat, add coconut milk, and let stand until cool.

3. Serve in a chilled glass. Or return to a simmer (adjusting consistency with more milk, if necessary) and ladle into warm bowls.

4. Serve with Coconut Tuile and Mint-Infused Mango and garnish with mint leaves.

COCONUT TUILE

1. In a mixing bowl, combine the coconut, powdered sugar, and flour and combine with a whisk.

2. In a separate bowl, add the melted butter and the egg white and whisk vigorously until combined.

3. Add the coconut mixture to the butter-and-egg mixture and combine. Chill in refrigerator for 2 hours.

4. Preheat oven to 350°F.

5. Spread the chilled tuile on baking mat and then place on a baking tray.

6. Place the tray in the oven and cook for 8 minutes, or until golden brown.

INGREDIENTS:

- 5 CUPS MILK, PLUS MORE IF NECESSARY
- ½ CUP SUGAR
- 1 VANILLA BEAN, HALVED AND SCRAPED
- 1 CUP SMALL TAPIOCA PEARLS
- 1 14 OZ. CAN OF COCONUT MILK

  MINT LEAVES, FOR GARNISH

TO SERVE:

COCONUT TUILE

MINT-INFUSED MANGO

COCONUT TUILE

- ⅓ CUP COCONUT, SHREDDED AND UNSWEETENED
- ¼ CUP POWDERED SUGAR
- 1 TABLESPOON FLOUR
- 1 TABLESPOON BUTTER, MELTED
- 1 EGG WHITE

Continued . . .

MINT-INFUSED MANGO

This infused mango is magical, and the lime and mint come through incredibly well. Just make sure you buy a nice, ripe mango, one with very little green on the peel.

1. In a small saucepan, add the water, white wine, sugar, and lime zest and bring to a boil. Remove from heat, add the mint sprigs, and cover. Let stand until cool.

2. Once cool, place in a bowl with the mango and let chill in refrigerator for at least 2 hours before serving.

INGREDIENTS (CONTINUED):

MINT-INFUSED MANGO

½ CUP WATER

½ CUP WHITE WINE

½ CUP SUGAR

ZEST OF 1 LIME

2 MINT SPRIGS, LEAVES REMOVED AND CHOPPED

1 CUP MANGO, CUBED

HUNGARIAN CHERRY SOUP
with ROASTED VANILLA CHERRIES

YIELD: 4 SERVINGS / ACTIVE TIME: 20 MINUTES / TOTAL TIME: 1 HOUR AND 30 MINUTES

In Central Europe, seasonal fruits are often employed in soup—a great way to celebrate ingredients at their freshest. This soup is delicious with a scoop of sour cream and the roasted cherries. The demerara sugar provides a great smoky flavor. If using fresh cherries with this technique, it's important to pit them after roasting, as this will allow the cherry to hold its shape.

1. In a large saucepan, combine cherries, water, sugar, cinnamon stick, and red wine. Bring to a boil, then reduce heat so the mixture simmers. Cook for 20 minutes.

2. Transfer the soup to a food processor and puree. Transfer the pureed soup to a container and chill in the refrigerator.

3. When the soup is chilled, add the sour cream to a bowl and then slowly add the milk and heavy cream. Stir until it has a smooth consistency.

4. Combine the chilled cherry puree and the sour cream mixture by hand. Return to the refrigerator and chill until ready to serve. Ladle into chilled bowls, garnish with sour cream, and serve with Roasted Vanilla Cherries.

INGREDIENTS:

1¼ POUNDS CHERRIES, HALVED AND PITTED

¾ CUP WATER

¾ CUP SUGAR

1 CINNAMON STICK

2 CUPS RED WINE

¾ CUP SOUR CREAM, PLUS MORE FOR GARNISH

¼ CUP MILK

¼ CUP HEAVY CREAM

TO SERVE:
ROASTED VANILLA CHERRIES

Continued . . .

ROASTED VANILLA CHERRIES

1. Combine all the ingredients in a bowl and place in the refrigerator to marinate overnight.

2. Preheat oven to 400°F.

3. Pass the contents of the bowl through a fine sieve. Place the cherries on a baking tray and reserve the liquid.

4. Place cherries in the oven for 5 minutes. Remove and carefully add half of the liquid. Stir gently and return to oven for 5 minutes.

5. Remove from oven, add the remaining liquid, and stir gently. Return to oven for 5 more minutes, remove from oven, and chill in refrigerator. When chilled, pit the cherries and serve.

INGREDIENTS (CONTINUED):

ROASTED VANILLA CHERRIES

24   CHERRIES

2   TABLESPOONS DEMERARA SUGAR

   PINCH OF SEA SALT

¼   CUP BRANDY

½   VANILLA BEAN, SCRAPED

ALMOND SOUP
with MIXED BERRY COULI

YIELD: 4 TO 6 SERVINGS / ACTIVE TIME: 20 MINUTES / TOTAL TIME: 13 HOURS AND 10 MINUTES

A great chilled dessert for any season. The creaminess of the almond soup balances nicely with the berries' tartness. This recipe works well with all types of nuts, so experiment and have fun.

1. Preheat oven to 350°F.

2. Place almonds on a baking tray and then place in oven. Roast for 15 minutes.

3. Remove from oven and transfer to a bowl. Add water.

4. Add sugar, vanilla bean seeds, and vanilla pod and soak overnight.

5. Transfer contents of bowl to a medium saucepan. Bring contents to a boil, reduce heat so that the soup simmers, and cook for 20 minutes.

6. Transfer soup to a food processor and puree until creamy.

7. Strain soup through a fine sieve. Serve with Mixed Berry Couli and garnish with mint.

MIXED BERRY COULI

1. Combine all the ingredients in a medium saucepan and cook over low heat for 15 minutes, occasionally using a fork to smash the berries.

2. Cool and serve.

INGREDIENTS:

3   CUPS RAW ALMONDS

8   CUPS WATER

4   TABLESPOONS SUGAR

1   VANILLA BEAN, SEEDS SCRAPED

   FRESH MINT SPRIGS, FOR GARNISH

TO SERVE:

MIXED BERRY COULI

MIXED BERRY COULI

½   CUP STRAWBERRIES, STEMS REMOVED

½   CUP BLACKBERRIES

½   CUP BLUEBERRIES

1   TABLESPOON GRAND MARNIER, TRIPLE SEC, OR ORANGE JUICE

½   CUP SUGAR

½   VANILLA BEAN, SEEDS SCRAPED

1   TABLESPOON LEMON JUICE

HOT CHOCOLATE COCONUT SOUP
with BRULÉED BANANAS

YIELD: 4 SERVINGS / ACTIVE TIME: 25 MINUTES / TOTAL TIME: 45 MINUTES

Do your kids not like soup? Well, this recipe will change that. Using two different techniques I learned in pastry, I decided to brulée the bananas and candy some fresh coconut for garnish.

1. In a medium saucepan, add milk, coconut milk, cream, vanilla bean pod, and vanilla seeds and bring to a simmer.

2. Turn off the heat and let stand for 20 minutes.

3. Remove vanilla pod and return to a simmer. Turn off heat, add chocolate and whisk until the chocolate is melted.

4. Pass soup through a fine sieve. Serve in hot bowls with the Bruléed Bananas and Candied Coconut.

INGREDIENTS:

2	CUPS MILK
1	14 OZ. CAN OF COCONUT MILK
1	CUP HEAVY CREAM
1	VANILLA BEAN, SCRAPED
12	OZ. 60% DARK CHOCOLATE

TO SERVE:
BRULÉED BANANAS
CANDIED COCONUT

BRULÉED BANANAS

2	BANANAS
	SUGAR

CANDIED COCONUT

½	FRESH COCONUT
¾	CUP SUGAR
½	CUP WATER

BRULÉED BANANAS

1. Peel and cut your bananas along the bias.

2. Dip the angled piece into the sugar.

3. Using a kitchen torch, caramelize the sugar until golden brown.

CANDIED COCONUT

1. Preheat the oven to 350°F.

2. Remove the outer shell of the coconut and use a spoon to remove the meat. Slice coconut meat very thinly and set aside.

3. In a small saucepan, add the sugar and water and bring to a boil. Remove from heat and let stand until cool.

4. Once the syrup is cool, dip the coconut slices into the syrup and place on a baking tray lined with parchment or a baking mat.

5. Place tray in oven and bake for 8 minutes, or until the coconut is golden brown. Remove and serve.

SOUPS
for KIDS

For me, this chapter was a lot of fun. I didn't want to just make smaller versions, or stereotypical choices—I wanted to be creative with different preparations and photograph them in a way that would be attractive to both adults and kids. While doing my research for this section, I reached out to my neighbors, who have several children. They pretty much all said, "My kids won't touch soup, they like chicken nuggets and junk food." I hope that when they see some of these soups and the fun that can be had with them, maybe they will change their minds.

BROCCOLI SOUP

YIELD: 4 SERVINGS / ACTIVE TIME: 10 MINUTES / TOTAL TIME: 30 MINUTES

This very healthy and quick soup just may get your kids to eat their vegetables.

1. In a medium saucepan, add the butter and cook over medium heat until it is melted.

2. Add the onion, celery, garlic, and carrots and cook for 5 minutes, or until soft.

3. Add the broccoli and chicken stock and bring to a boil.

4. Reduce heat so that the soup simmers. Cook for 10 minutes, or until the broccoli is soft.

5. Transfer the soup to a food processor and puree until smooth.

6. Return to a clean pan. Bring to a simmer and season with salt and pepper.

7. Serve in bowls garnished with grated cheddar cheese.

INGREDIENTS:

¼ CUP BUTTER

1 ONION, PEELED AND DICED

2 CELERY STALKS, CHOPPED

2 GARLIC CLOVES

2 CARROTS, PEELED AND CHOPPED

1½ POUNDS BROCCOLI FLORETS

4 CUPS CHICKEN STOCK

SALT AND PEPPER, TO TASTE

CHEDDAR CHEESE, GRATED, FOR GARNISH

BAKED POTATO SOUP

YIELD: 4 SERVINGS / ACTIVE TIME: 20 MINUTES / TOTAL TIME: 1 HOUR AND 30 MINUTES

Based off the classic baked potato, this is a soup your kids will absolutely love. Garnishing the soup with chopped bacon gives it a very authentic taste and texture.

1. Preheat oven to 400°F.

2. Use a fork to pierce the potatoes. Place them on a baking tray and bake for 1 hour, or until tender.

3. When potatoes are cooked, remove from oven and allow them to cool slightly. Peel and mash with a fork.

4. Meanwhile, in a medium saucepan add the butter and cook over medium heat until it is melted.

5. Add the flour and stir until combined.

6. Add the milk and bring soup to a simmer, while stirring constantly. Cook for 5 minutes, or until the soup thickens.

7. Add the mashed potatoes and half of the cheese. Stir until the cheese melts.

8. Remove the pan from heat and stir in the sour cream.

9. Season with salt and pepper and serve in bowls garnished with scallions and the bacon.

INGREDIENTS:

2	LARGE IDAHO POTATOES
¼	CUP BUTTER
⅓	CUP ALL-PURPOSE FLOUR
4	CUPS MILK
1½	CUPS SHARP CHEDDAR CHEESE
½	CUP SOUR CREAM
	SALT AND PEPPER, TO TASTE
⅔	CUP SCALLIONS, CHOPPED, FOR GARNISH
8	SLICES THICK-CUT BACON, COOKED AND CHOPPED, FOR GARNISH

CHILLED PEANUT BUTTER *and* JELLY SOUP

YIELD: 4 CHILD-SIZED SERVINGS / ACTIVE TIME: 15 MINUTES / TOTAL TIME: 1 HOUR AND 15 MINUTES

Who doesn't love the classic peanut butter and jelly sandwich? How about a chilled version as a soup? Make each soup separately, chill, and then combine in a chilled bowl. It's guaranteed to wow anyone.

PEANUT SOUP

1. In a small saucepan, add the butter and cook over medium heat until it is melted. Add the celery and onions and cook for 3 minutes, or until soft.

2. Add the flour and cook for 2 minutes.

3. Slowly add the chicken stock and milk to the pan. Let soup simmer for 5 minutes, or until it has thickened.

4. Transfer the soup to a food processor and blend until smooth.

5. Return to the pan and add the peanut butter. Whisk until combined and then chill in the refrigerator for 1 hour.

STRAWBERRY SOUP

Combine all ingredients in a food processor and puree until smooth. Place in the refrigerator and chill for 1 hour.

INGREDIENTS:

PEANUT SOUP

2	TABLESPOONS BUTTER
1	CELERY STALK, CHOPPED
½	ONION, CHOPPED
1	TABLESPOON ALL-PURPOSE FLOUR
2	CUPS CHICKEN STOCK
½	CUP MILK
½	CUP PEANUT BUTTER

STRAWBERRY SOUP

2	CUPS STRAWBERRIES, GREENS REMOVED AND CHOPPED
1½	CUPS GREEK YOGURT
	JUICE OF 1 LIME
1	TEASPOON SALT
1	CUP POWDERED SUGAR, SIEVED
¼	CUP HEAVY CREAM

LASAGNA SOUP

YIELD: 4 SERVINGS / ACTIVE TIME: 20 MINUTES / TOTAL TIME: 45 MINUTES

This warm, rich soup is great for a birthday party, or when your childrens' friends come over to play.

1. Cook the lasagna noodles according to manufacturer's instructions. Drain and set aside.

2. In a medium saucepan, add the olive oil and cook over medium heat until warm.

3. Add the onion and cook for 5 minutes, or until soft.

4. Add the sausage, garlic, and oregano and cook for about 3 minutes, or until sausage is browned. Break the sausage up with a wooden spoon so it cooks evenly.

5. Add the tomato paste, beef stock, and tomatoes and bring to a boil.

6. Reduce heat so that the soup simmers and cook for 10 minutes.

7. Stir in the noodles, basil, parmesan, and heavy cream. Simmer for 2 minutes to melt the cheese.

8. Serve in bowls garnished with ricotta and basil.

INGREDIENTS:

- 12 LASAGNA NOODLES, BROKEN INTO PIECES
- 2 TABLESPOONS EXTRA VIRGIN OLIVE OIL
- 1 ONION, PEELED AND CHOPPED
- 1 POUND GROUND ITALIAN SAUSAGE
- 2 GARLIC CLOVES, MINCED
- 2 TEASPOONS DRIED OREGANO
- 2 TABLESPOONS TOMATO PASTE
- 4 CUPS BEEF STOCK
- 2 14 OZ. CANS OF CRUSHED TOMATOES
- ½ CUP BASIL, CHOPPED, RESERVE SOME FOR GARNISH
- ¼ CUP PARMESAN CHEESE, GRATED
- ¼ CUP HEAVY CREAM
- 1 CUP RICOTTA, FOR GARNISH

MACARONI *and* CHEESE SOUP

YIELD: 4 SERVINGS / ACTIVE TIME: 15 MINUTES / TOTAL TIME: 40 MINUTES

Turn this children's classic into a soup and you're sure to be the favorite chef.

1. Cook the pasta according to the manufacturer's instructions. Drain and set aside.

2. In a medium saucepan, add the butter and cook over low heat until it is melted.

3. Add the onion, carrots, and celery. Stirring frequently, cook for 5 minutes, or until the vegetables are soft.

4. Add the flour and cook for 5 minutes.

5. Add the chicken stock and milk and bring to a boil. Reduce heat so that the soup simmers and cook for 10 minutes.

6. Remove pan from heat and add the grated cheddar cheese. Mix together with a whisk.

7. Season with salt and pepper, add cooked pasta, and serve in bowls.

INGREDIENTS:

1½ CUPS ELBOW PASTA

¼ CUP BUTTER

1 ONION, PEELED AND CHOPPED

2 CARROTS, PEELED AND CHOPPED

2 CELERY STALKS, CHOPPED

2 TABLESPOONS ALL-PURPOSE FLOUR

4 CUPS CHICKEN STOCK

2 CUPS MILK

4 CUPS SHARP CHEDDAR CHEESE, GRATED

SALT AND PEPPER, TO TASTE

PURPLE CAULIFLOWER SOUP

YIELD: 4 SERVINGS / ACTIVE TIME: 15 MINUTES / TOTAL TIME: 45 MINUTES

Who says food can't look fun? This beautiful purple soup is certain to look inviting to your children.

1. In a medium saucepan, add the butter and cook over medium heat until melted.

2. Add the onions, chopped cauliflower, and beets and cook for 5 minutes or until soft.

3. Add the stock and bring to a boil.

4. Reduce the heat so that the soup simmers and cook for 5 minutes.

5. Add the cream and simmer for 10 minutes.

6. Transfer the soup to a food processor and puree until creamy. Strain through a fine sieve, return to a clean pan, and bring to a simmer.

7. Serve in warmed bowls and garnish with parmesan.

INGREDIENTS:

¼ CUP BUTTER

1 ONION, PEELED AND DICED

1 PURPLE CAULIFLOWER, FLORETS REMOVED FROM STEM AND CHOPPED

½ CUP BEETS, PEELED AND CHOPPED

4 CUPS VEGETABLE STOCK

2 CUPS HEAVY CREAM

   SALT AND PEPPER, TO TASTE

½ CUP PARMESAN CHEESE, GRATED, FOR GARNISH

VEGETABLE MINESTRONE

YIELD: 4 SERVINGS / ACTIVE TIME: 20 MINUTES / TOTAL TIME: 45 MINUTES

This is a healthy vegetable soup that is perfect for your kids, who will be drawn to the orzo and the parmesan.

1. In a medium saucepan, add the olive oil and cook over medium heat until warm.

2. Add the onion, leek, celery, and carrots and cook for 5 minutes, or until soft.

3. Stir in the tomatoes and garlic and simmer for 10 minutes.

4. Add the vegetable stock, cabbage, oregano, bay leaf, and tomato paste.

5. Bring to a boil, reduce heat so that the soup simmers, and cook for 10 minutes.

6. Add the orzo and cook for 10 minutes, or until pasta is al dente.

7. Season with salt and pepper and ladle into warm bowls, and garnish with the grated parmesan cheese.

INGREDIENTS:

- 2 TABLESPOONS EXTRA VIRGIN OLIVE OIL
- 1 ONION, CHOPPED
- 1 LEEK, CHOPPED
- 2 CELERY STALKS, CHOPPED
- 2 CARROTS, PEELED AND CHOPPED
- 2 14 OZ. CANS OF DICED TOMATOES
- 2 GARLIC CLOVES, MINCED
- 4 CUPS VEGETABLE STOCK
- 2 CUPS GREEN CABBAGE, CHOPPED
- 2 TEASPOONS OREGANO, CHOPPED
- 1 BAY LEAF
- ¼ CUP TOMATO PASTE
- ½ CUP ORZO
  SALT AND PEPPER, TO TASTE
- ½ CUP PARMESAN, GRATED, FOR GARNISH

TACO SOUP

YIELD: 4 SERVINGS / ACTIVE TIME: 20 MINUTES / TOTAL TIME: 45 MINUTES

Tacos are great, but they can be messy. Cut down on your cleanup time by tossing everything into this one-pot soup.

1. In a medium saucepan, add the oil and cook over medium heat until warm.

2. Add the onion and bell peppers and cook for 5 minutes, or until soft.

3. Add the ground beef and taco seasoning and cook for 5 minutes.

4. Add the beef stock, spaghetti sauce, and diced tomatoes and bring to a simmer. Cook for 10 minutes.

5. Add the black beans, kidney beans, and corn kernels. Return to a simmer, add salsa, and simmer for 5 additional minutes.

6. Serve in bowls, and garnish with tortilla chips, Monterey Jack cheese, and sour cream.

INGREDIENTS:

- 2 TABLESPOONS VEGETABLE OIL
- 1 ONION, CHOPPED
- 1 RED BELL PEPPER, SEEDS REMOVED AND CHOPPED
- 1 GREEN BELL PEPPER, SEEDS REMOVED AND CHOPPED
- 1 POUND GROUND BEEF
- 2 TABLESPOONS TACO SEASONING
- 2 CUPS BEEF STOCK
- 2 CUPS SPAGHETTI SAUCE
- 2 14 OZ. CANS OF DICED TOMATOES
- 2 CUPS COOKED BLACK BEANS
- 2 CUPS COOKED KIDNEY BEANS
- 2 CUPS COOKED CORN KERNELS
- ½ CUP SALSA
- 4 CUPS TORTILLA CHIPS, FOR GARNISH
- 2 CUPS MONTEREY JACK CHEESE, GRATED, FOR GARNISH
- 1 CUP SOUR CREAM, FOR GARNISH

TOMATO ALPHABET SOUP

YIELD: 4 SERVINGS / ACTIVE TIME: 15 MINUTES / TOTAL TIME: 30 MINUTES

This is not just a tasty soup, it's fun. You could also serve the letters separately and let the kids practice the alphabet.

1. Cook the pasta according to the manufacturer's instructions. Drain and set aside.

2. In a medium saucepan, add the butter and cook over medium heat until melted.

3. Add the onions, carrots, and celery and cook for 5 minutes, or until soft.

4. Add the vegetable stock, basil, and tomatoes and bring to a boil.

5. Reduce heat so that the soup simmers and cook for 10 minutes.

6. Transfer soup to a food processor and puree until smooth.

7. Return to a clean pan, bring to a simmer, and add the cooked pasta. Season with salt and pepper and serve in warmed bowls.

INGREDIENTS:

1   CUP ALPHABET PASTA

¼   CUP BUTTER

2   ONIONS, CHOPPED

4   CARROTS, CHOPPED

2   CELERY STALKS, CHOPPED

3   CUPS VEGETABLE STOCK

2   TEASPOONS BASIL, CHOPPED

4   14 OZ. CANS OF DICED TOMATOES

     SALT AND PEPPER, TO TASTE

WAGON WHEEL BEEF SOUP

YIELD: 4 SERVINGS / ACTIVE TIME: 15 MINUTES / TOTAL TIME: 30 MINUTES

A great, comforting soup that is easy to prepare. Your children will get a healthy meal, all while having fun with the wagon wheels. Feel free to add other types of ground meat or switch the kidney beans out for other legumes or vegetables that they like.

1. Cook pasta according to manufacturer's instructions. Drain and set aside.

2. In a medium saucepan, add the vegetable oil and cook over medium heat until warm. Add onions and cook for 5 minutes, or until soft.

3. Add the ground beef and cook for an additional 5 minutes.

4. Add the spaghetti sauce, oregano, beef stock, and kidney beans and bring to a gentle simmer. Cook for 10 minutes.

5. Add the cooked pasta, season with salt and pepper, and serve in warmed bowls.

INGREDIENTS:

1   CUP WAGON WHEEL PASTA

2   TABLESPOONS VEGETABLE OIL

1   CUP ONION, CHOPPED

1   POUND GROUND BEEF

4   CUPS SPAGHETTI SAUCE

½   TEASPOON GROUND OREGANO

2   CUPS BEEF STOCK

2   CUPS KIDNEY BEANS, DRAINED AND COOKED

    SALT AND PEPPER, TO TASTE

30 MINUTES
or LESS

The secret to a lot of great soups is time. But in this chapter, we touch on a few soups that you can whip up quickly. Bear in mind, having a well-developed stock on hand is a big help for these quick preparations, as it will be tasked with providing a lot of the soup's flavor. To cut down on cooking time, I've employed a couple tricks such as grating the vegetables and using tender cuts of meat.

BOUILLABAISSE

YIELD: 4 SERVINGS / ACTIVE TIME: 20 MINUTES / TOTAL TIME: 30 MINUTES

Prepare all your ingredients in advance so that once your guests arrive, you can quickly put together this classic.

1. Preheat oven to 200°F. Place four bowls in the oven.

2. In a medium saucepan, add 1 tablespoon of the oil and the lobster tails, flesh side down. Cook over medium heat.

3. Add the clams and cook for 2 minutes.

4. Add the mussels, lobster stock, orange zest, orange juice, and saffron, cover, and cook for 5 minutes, or until the clams and mussels are open.

5. In a medium sauté pan, add 1 tablespoon of the vegetable oil and the shrimp, and cook over medium heat. Cook the shrimp for 2 minutes on each side.

6. Add the shrimp to the broth in the saucepan, cover, and cook for an additional 2 minutes.

7. Remove the shellfish with a slotted spoon and place in four warmed bowls in the oven.

8. Strain the broth through a fine sieve and then return to the pan. Simmer until it is reduced by half.

9. Place the sole in a mixing bowl and gently combine it with the flour, until both sides of each piece are coated.

10. Gently tap the fish to remove any excess flour, season with salt and pepper, and place in a medium sauté pan with the remaining oil. Cook for 2 minutes on each side.

11. When the stock has reduced, add the butter to the broth slowly, whisking constantly.

12. Season the broth with salt and pepper.

13. Remove the warmed bowls from the oven, pour the broth over the seafood, and then add the cooked sole. Garnish with chopped parsley, and serve with crusty bread.

INGREDIENTS:

- 4 TABLESPOONS VEGETABLE OIL
- 2 WHOLE RAW LOBSTER TAILS, CUT IN HALF IN THE SHELL AND RINSED
- 16 CLAMS
- 24 MUSSELS
- 4 CUPS LOBSTER STOCK
- ZEST AND JUICE OF 1 ORANGE
- ⅛ TEASPOON SAFFRON
- 16 SHRIMP, CLEANED
- 1 POUND DOVER SOLE, SKIN REMOVED AND CUT INTO 2-INCH PIECES
- ¼ CUP FLOUR
- SALT AND PEPPER, TO TASTE
- ½ CUP BUTTER, CUT INTO SMALL PIECES AND CHILLED
- 2 TABLESPOONS PARSLEY, CHOPPED, FOR GARNISH

ACORN SQUASH SOUP
with FENNEL SALAD

YIELD: 4 SERVINGS / ACTIVE TIME: 15 MINUTES / TOTAL TIME: 30 MINUTES

Serve this fall-flavored soup with a refreshing fennel salad.

1. In a medium saucepan, add the vegetable oil and cook over medium heat.

2. Add the bacon and cook for 5 minutes, or until crispy.

3. Use a slotted spoon to remove the bacon from the pan. Set to drain on a paper towel. Reserve ¼ cup for garnish.

4. Add the acorn squash and onion to the pan and cook for 5 minutes, or until soft.

5. Add the remaining bacon, apple, five-spice powder, cayenne pepper, and chicken stock and bring to a boil.

6. Reduce heat so that the soup simmers and cook for 10 minutes.

7. Remove the soup from the pot. Transfer to a food processor, puree until smooth, and strain through a fine sieve.

8. Return the soup to a clean pan and bring to a simmer.

9. Add the heavy cream and cook for 5 minutes.

10. Season with salt and pepper and serve in warmed bowls with the reserved bacon and Fennel Salad.

FENNEL SALAD

1. Using a mandolin, slice the fennel as thin as possible. Place the slices in a serving bowl.

2. Add the remaining ingredients and toss gently.

3. Season with salt and pepper and set aside until the soup is done.

INGREDIENTS:

1	TABLESPOON VEGETABLE OIL
8	SLICES OF THICK-CUT BACON, CHOPPED
2	ACORN SQUASH, PEELED, HALVED, SEEDS REMOVED, AND GRATED
1	ONION, PEELED AND CHOPPED
2	APPLES, PEELED AND GRATED
1	TEASPOON FIVE-SPICE POWDER
¼	TEASPOON CAYENNE PEPPER
4	CUPS CHICKEN STOCK
2	CUPS HEAVY CREAM
	SALT AND PEPPER, TO TASTE

TO SERVE:
FENNEL SALAD

FENNEL SALAD

½	FENNEL BULB, OUTER LAYER REMOVED
	ZEST AND JUICE OF 1 ORANGE
1	TABLESPOON PERNOD
2	TABLESPOONS EXTRA VIRGIN OLIVE OIL
2	TABLESPOONS FENNEL FRONDS
1	TABLESPOON FENNEL POLLEN
	SALT AND PEPPER, TO TASTE

CHILLED HONEYDEW MELON SOUP
with CRISPY PROSCIUTTO DI PARMA

YIELD: 4 SERVINGS / ACTIVE TIME: 15 MINUTES / TOTAL TIME: 30 MINUTES

A refreshing, classical preparation of melon and prosciutto, all in no time flat.

1. Puree the melon and lemon juice in a food processor and then strain through a fine sieve.

2. Chill in the refrigerator for 20 minutes.

3. Just before serving, add the chilled white wine, whisk until combined, and then season with just enough sugar to emphasize the melon flavor.

4. Ladle into chilled bowls, serve with Crispy Prosciutto di Parma, and garnish with fresh grapes and lemon zest.

CRISPY PROSCIUTTO DI PARMA

1. Preheat oven to 375°F.

2. Line a baking tray with a baking mat or parchment paper.

3. Place the slices of prosciutto on the tray.

4. When oven is preheated, place tray in oven and bake for 5 to 10 minutes, or until the prosciutto is crispy.

5. Remove tray from oven and place prosciutto on a paper towel to drain.

INGREDIENTS:

1   HONEYDEW MELON, PEELED, HALVED, SEEDS REMOVED

1   TABLESPOON LEMON JUICE

2   CUPS DRY WHITE WINE, CHILLED

⅛   CUP SUGAR

    FRESH GRAPES, FOR GARNISH

    LEMON ZEST, FOR GARNISH

TO SERVE:
CRISPY PROSCIUTTO DI PARMA

CRISPY PROSCIUTTO DI PARMA
8   SLICES PROSCIUTTO

CREAM OF BROCCOLI SOUP

YIELD: 4 SERVINGS / ACTIVE TIME: 15 MINUTES / TOTAL TIME: 30 MINUTES

A childhood favorite of mine. It seems criminal that such a wonderful trip back to the past can be ready in 30 minutes.

1. In a medium saucepan, add the butter and olive oil and cook over medium heat until the butter is melted.

2. Add the onion and cook for 5 minutes, or until soft.

3. Add the broccoli and herbs and cook for an additional 3 minutes.

4. Add the stock and bring to a boil.

5. Reduce the flame so that the soup simmers and cook for 5 minutes.

6. Add the heavy cream and simmer for 10 minutes, or until the broccoli is tender.

7. Remove pan from heat and transfer soup to a food processor. Puree until the soup is creamy.

8. Return the soup to a clean pan, bring to a simmer, and season with salt and pepper.

9. Serve in warmed bowls.

INGREDIENTS:

- 2 TABLESPOONS BUTTER
- 1 TABLESPOON EXTRA VIRGIN OLIVE OIL
- 1 ONION, DICED
- 1 CROWN OF BROCCOLI, FLORETS REMOVED AND CHOPPED
- 1 SPRIG THYME, LEAVES REMOVED AND CHOPPED
- 1 SPRIG ROSEMARY, LEAVES REMOVED AND CHOPPED
- 4 CUPS CHICKEN OR VEGETABLE STOCK
- 2 CUPS HEAVY CREAM
- SALT AND PEPPER, TO TASTE

CREAM OF TOMATO
with SOURDOUGH GARLIC BREAD

YIELD: 4 SERVINGS / ACTIVE TIME: 20 MINUTES / TOTAL TIME: 30 MINUTES

A quick, classic soup served with its favorite partner: garlic bread. Perfect for those nights when you need to simplify.

1. Add the butter to a large saucepan and cook over medium heat until melted.

2. Add the onion and cook for 5 minutes, or until soft.

3. Stir in the tomatoes, carrots, chicken stock, parsley, and thyme and bring to a boil.

4. Reduce to a simmer and cook for 10 minutes, or until the vegetables are tender.

5. Remove soup from heat and transfer to a food processor. Puree the soup and pass through a fine sieve.

6. Return the soup to the pan and add the cream. Reheat gently and season with salt and pepper.

7. Serve with Sourdough Garlic Bread and garnish with parmesan.

SOURDOUGH GARLIC BREAD

1. Preheat oven to 425°F.

2. In a bowl, whisk the butter for 2 minutes by hand in order to lighten it.

3. Add the remaining ingredients, except the bread, to the bowl, season with salt and pepper, and combine.

4. Spread the butter on each slice of bread.

5. Make 2 stacks of buttered bread and wrap each in aluminum foil.

6. Place in oven for 10 to 15 minutes, until the butter is melted and the edges are crispy.

INGREDIENTS:

2	TABLESPOONS BUTTER
1	ONION, CHOPPED
2	14 OZ. CANS OF STEWED TOMATOES
2	CARROTS, PEELED AND GRATED
5	CUPS CHICKEN STOCK
2	TABLESPOONS PARSLEY, CHOPPED
½	TEASPOON THYME, CHOPPED
6	TABLESPOONS HEAVY CREAM
	SALT AND PEPPER, TO TASTE
	PARMESAN CHEESE, GRATED, FOR GARNISH

TO SERVE:
SOURDOUGH GARLIC BREAD

SOURDOUGH GARLIC BREAD

1	CUP BUTTER, SOFTENED
1½	TEASPOONS LEMON JUICE
2	GARLIC CLOVES, MINCED
3	TABLESPOONS PARSLEY, CHOPPED
	SALT AND PEPPER, TO TASTE
8	SLICES SOURDOUGH BREAD

CREAMED PARSNIP SOUP
with ARUGULA PESTO

YIELD: 4 SERVINGS / ACTIVE TIME: 15 MINUTES / TOTAL TIME: 30 MINUTES

Grating the parsnips speeds up the cooking time dramatically. If they're going to be sitting around for a bit, leave them in cold water with a splash of lemon juice so that they don't oxidize.

1. In a medium saucepan, add the butter and cook over medium heat until it is melted.

2. Add the onion, garlic, and thyme to the pan and cook for 5 minutes, or until soft.

3. Add the parsnips and cook for 5 minutes.

4. Add the stock and bring to a boil.

5. Reduce the heat so that the soup simmers and cook for 10 minutes.

6. Remove the pan from the heat and transfer to a food processor. Puree the soup until it is smooth and then strain through a fine sieve.

7. Return to the soup to a clean pan, bring to a simmer, and add heavy cream.

8. Simmer for 5 minutes and season with salt and pepper.

9. Ladle into warm bowls, serve with Arugula Pesto, and garnish with parsley.

ARUGULA PESTO

1. Combine all the ingredients in a food processor and puree until it reaches desired consistency.

2. Season with salt and pepper and serve.

INGREDIENTS:

2	TABLESPOONS BUTTER
1	ONION, CHOPPED
1	GARLIC CLOVE, MINCED
2	THYME SPRIGS, LEAVES REMOVED AND CHOPPED
5	PARSNIPS, PEELED AND GRATED
6	CUPS VEGETABLE STOCK
2	CUPS HEAVY CREAM
	SALT AND PEPPER, TO TASTE
	PARSLEY, CHOPPED, FOR GARNISH

TO SERVE:
ARUGULA PESTO

ARUGULA PESTO

1	CUP ARUGULA
1	CUP SPINACH
1	GARLIC CLOVE, MINCED
⅓	CUP PINE NUTS
2	TABLESPOONS PARMESAN CHEESE, FINELY GRATED
3	TABLESPOONS EXTRA VIRGIN OLIVE OIL
	SALT AND PEPPER, TO TASTE

FAST PHO

YIELD: 4 SERVINGS / ACTIVE TIME: 15 MINUTES / TOTAL TIME: 30 MINUTES

All this in just 30 minutes? That can't be pho real.

1. In a medium saucepan, add the oil and cook over medium heat until warm.

2. Add the onion and ginger, and cook for 5 minutes, or until soft.

3. Meanwhile, in a sauté pan, add the spices and cook over medium heat for 2 to 3 minutes, until they become nice and fragrant. Add to the saucepan.

4. Add the beef stock and bring to a boil. Reduce heat so broth simmers and cook for 10 minutes.

5. Strain the soup into a fresh clean pot. Season with fish sauce, hoisin, and Sriracha and return to a simmer.

6. Place the rice noodles into a bowl and cover with boiling water. Leave to soak for 4 minutes, or according to manufacturer's instructions.

7. Combine rice noodles and soup in warm bowls. Garnish with sliced jalapeño, bean sprouts, lime wedges, and Thai basil and serve.

INGREDIENTS:

- 2 TABLESPOONS VEGETABLE OIL
- 1 SMALL YELLOW ONION, PEELED AND CHOPPED
- 1-INCH PIECE OF GINGER, UNPEELED
- 2 CINNAMON STICKS
- 3 STAR ANISE
- 2 CARDAMOM PODS, SEEDS REMOVED AND CHOPPED
- 1 CUP CILANTRO
- 5 CLOVES
- 1 TABLESPOON CORIANDER SEED
- 1 TABLESPOON FENNEL SEED
- 6 CUPS BEEF STOCK
- 1 TABLESPOON BLACK PEPPERCORNS
- 1 TABLESPOON FISH SAUCE
- 1 TABLESPOON HOISIN
- 1 TEASPOON SRIRACHA
- 3 OZ. RICE NOODLES
- 1 JALAPEÑO, SLICED FOR GARNISH
- BEAN SPROUTS, FOR GARNISH
- LIME WEDGES, FOR GARNISH
- THAI BASIL, FOR GARNISH

CREAMY SPRING SWEET PEA SOUP
with CRÈME FRAICHE

YIELD: 4 SERVINGS / ACTIVE TIME: 10 MINUTES / TOTAL TIME: 20 MINUTES

This soup can be served hot or cool, and makes a delicious snack or light meal. Use frozen peas to lower the broth's temperature and maintain its lovely green color.

1. In a medium saucepan, add butter and cook over medium heat until melted.

2. Add the leek and onion and cook for 5 minutes, or until soft.

3. Add the vegetable stock and bring to a boil.

4. Reduce heat until the soup simmers. Add frozen peas and cook for 5 minutes.

5. Remove the pan from heat and add the soup and parsley to a food processor. Puree the soup until it is smooth.

6. Return soup to a clean pan and bring to a simmer. Add crème fraiche, season with salt and pepper, and serve.

INGREDIENTS:

2 TABLESPOONS BUTTER

1 LEEK, WHITE PART ONLY, CHOPPED

1 ONION, PEELED AND CHOPPED

4 CUPS VEGETABLE STOCK

1½ POUNDS FROZEN PEAS

4 PARSLEY SPRIGS, LEAVES REMOVED AND CHOPPED

1 CUP CRÈME FRAICHE

SALT AND PEPPER, TO TASTE

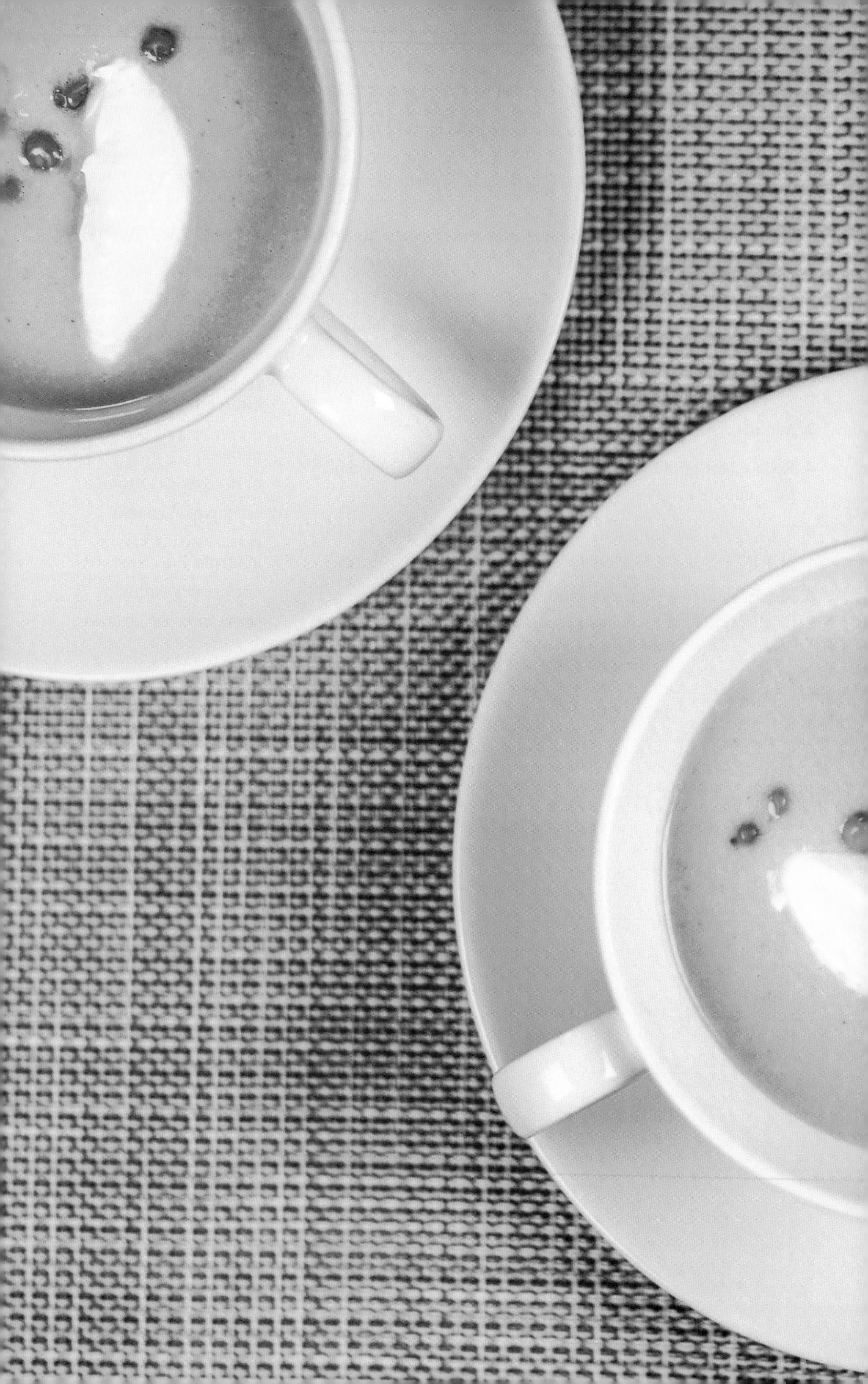

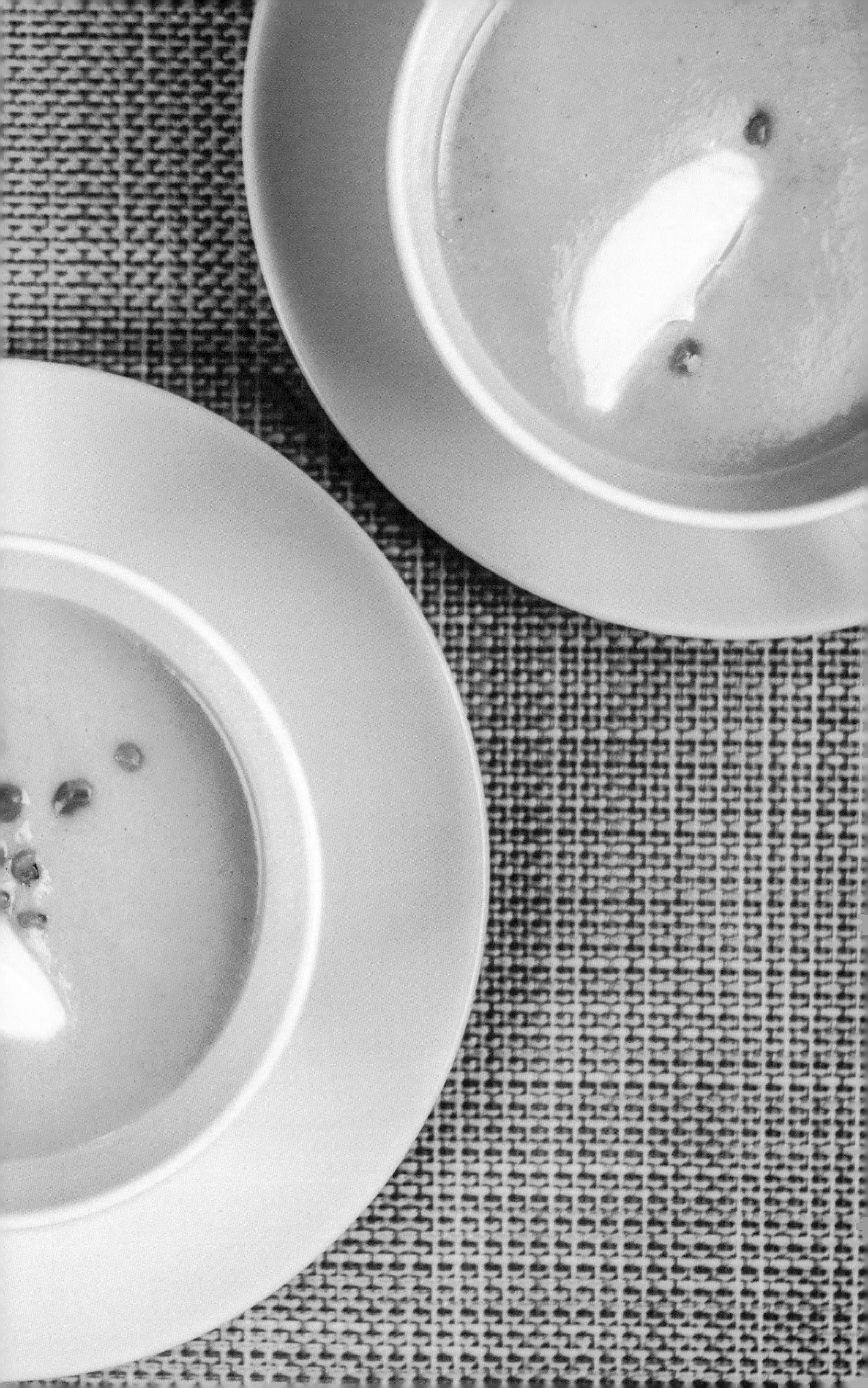

KOREAN BEEF *and* RICE SOU

YIELD: 4 SERVINGS / ACTIVE TIME: 15 MINUTES / TOTAL TIME: 3(

This aromatic, refreshing soup has just a slight bit of heat. It's per
pressed for time.

1. In a medium saucepan, add 1 tablespoon of oil and cook over medium-high heat until warm.

2. Add the beef chuck and cook for 3 to 5 minutes, while turning, until nicely browned.

3. Add the garlic, beef stock, and rice, increase temperature to high, and bring to a boil.

4. Reduce heat so that the soup simmers and cook for 15 minutes.

5. Meanwhile, in an ungreased sauté pan, add the sesame seeds, red chili flakes, star anise, and cinnamon stick and cook for 3 minutes over medium heat while stirring often, until the pan gives off a nice aroma.

6. Remove sauté pan from heat and stir in the sesame oil, fish sauce, soy sauce, rice vinegar, and the remaining vegetable oil. Set aside to cool.

7. Once the rice in the soup is tender, add the scallion whites and celery, and cook for 5 minutes, or until the celery is soft.

8. Season the soup with salt and pepper, serve in warmed bowls and garnish with the infused oil and scallion greens.

INGREDIENTS:

2 TABLESPOONS VEGETABLE OIL

1 POUND BONELESS BEEF CHUCK, CUT INTO ½-INCH PIECES

2 GARLIC CLOVES, MINCED

8 CUPS BEEF STOCK

1 CUP LONG-GRAIN RICE

2 TABLESPOONS SESAME SEEDS

1 TEASPOON RED CHILI FLAKES

1 STAR ANISE

1 CINNAMON STICK

2 TABLESPOONS SESAME OIL

2 TABLESPOONS FISH SAUCE

2 TABLESPOONS SOY SAUCE

1 TABLESPOON RICE WINE VINEGAR

4 SCALLIONS, SLICED, GREENS RESERVED FOR GARNISH

4 CELERY STALKS, CHOPPED

SALT AND PEPPER, TO TASTE

FENNEL-SCENTED OLIVE *and* TOMATO SOUP
with HORIATIKI SALAD

YIELD: 4 SERVINGS / ACTIVE TIME: 15 MINUTES / TOTAL TIME: 30 MINUTES

A quick Mediterranean soup with a Greek side salad. If you have a few minutes, blend the soup to make this a touch more refined.

1. In a medium saucepan, add the olive oil and cook over medium heat until warm.

2. Add the onion, garlic, and fennel and cook for 5 minutes, or until soft.

3. Add the remaining ingredients and bring to a boil.

4. Reduce heat so that soup simmers and cook for 12 minutes, or until the vegetables are tender.

5. Season with salt and pepper and ladle into warm bowls. Garnish with the fennel fronds and serve with the Greek Horiatiki Salad.

HORIATIKI SALAD

1. In a mixing bowl, add the cucumber, cherry tomatoes, feta, onion, olives, and dried oregano and stir gently until combined.

2. Right before serving, drizzle with the olive oil and season with salt and pepper.

3. Gently toss and serve in chilled bowls.

INGREDIENTS:

2   TABLESPOONS EXTRA VIRGIN OLIVE OIL

1   ONION, PEELED AND CHOPPED

2   GARLIC CLOVES, MINCED

2   FENNEL BULBS, CHOPPED, FENNEL FRONDS RESERVED FOR GARNISH

½   CUP KALAMATA OLIVES, PITTED AND CHOPPED

2   ROSEMARY SPRIGS, LEAVES REMOVED AND CHOPPED

2   THYME SPRIGS, LEAVES REMOVED AND CHOPPED

1   TABLESPOON ORANGE ZEST

1½   TABLESPOONS TOMATO PASTE

2   14 OZ. CANS OF STEWED TOMATOES

4   CUPS CHICKEN STOCK

SALT AND PEPPER, TO TASTE

TO SERVE:
HORIATIKI SALAD

GREEK HORIATIKI SALAD

½   CUCUMBER, PEELED, HALVED LENGTHWISE, SEEDS REMOVED, AND CUT INTO HALF-MOONS

½   CUP CHERRY TOMATOES, HALVED

½   CUP FETA CHEESE CRUMBLES

½   ONION, PEELED AND CHOPPED

¼   CUP KALAMATA OLIVES, PITTED AND SLICED

1   TEASPOON DRIED OREGANO

¼   CUP EXTRA VIRGIN OLIVE OIL

SALT AND PEPPER, TO TASTE

LEMON ASPARAGUS SOUP

YIELD: 4 SERVINGS / ACTIVE TIME: 15 MINUTES / TOTAL TIME: 30 MINUTES

When spring rolls around we are presented with beautiful asparagus. It's a very quick vegetable to cook, making it perfect for this chapter.

1. In a medium saucepan, add the butter and cook over medium heat until melted. Add the leek and cook for 5 minutes, or until soft.

2. Add the chopped asparagus. Add the vegetable stock and bring to a boil. Reduce the heat so that the soup simmers and cook for 6 to 8 minutes, or until the vegetables are tender.

3. Remove the pan from heat and transfer the soup to a food processor. Blend until smooth and then pass through a fine sieve.

4. Return soup to a clean pan and add cream and lemon zest. Season with salt and pepper and bring to a simmer.

5. Serve in warmed bowls with Grated Parmesan with Lemon Zest and Parsley.

GRATED PARMESAN WITH LEMON ZEST AND PARSLEY

Add the ingredients to a bowl and gently stir until combined.

INGREDIENTS:

- 2 TABLESPOONS BUTTER
- 1 LEEK, CHOPPED
- 1½ POUNDS GREEN ASPARAGUS, PEELED AND CHOPPED
- 5 CUPS OF VEGETABLE STOCK
- ½ CUP HEAVY CREAM
- ZEST OF 2 LEMONS
- SALT AND PEPPER, TO TASTE

TO SERVE:
GRATED PARMESAN WITH LEMON ZEST AND PARSLEY

GRATED PARMESAN WITH LEMON ZEST AND PARSLEY

- ½ CUP PARMESAN CHEESE, GRATED
- 2 TABLESPOONS LEMON ZEST
- 2 TABLESPOONS PARSLEY, LEAVES REMOVED AND CHOPPED

MOROCCAN CHICKPEA STEW
with CARROT *and* MINT SALAD

YIELD: 4 SERVINGS / ACTIVE TIME: 15 MINUTES / TOTAL TIME: 30 MINUTES

This classic Moroccan soup will make your day—particularly when served alongside a refreshing carrot and mint salad.

1. In a medium saucepan, add the oil and cook over medium heat.

2. When the oil is warm, add the onion and carrots and cook for 5 minutes, or until soft.

3. Add the spices and cook for 2 minutes.

4. Add the veal stock, garlic, tomatoes, and tomato paste and bring to a boil.

5. Add the chickpeas and reduce heat so that the soup simmers.

6. After 5 minutes, season with salt and pepper and serve in warmed bowls with the Carrot and Mint Salad.

CARROT AND MINT SALAD

Combine all ingredients in a bowl and mix gently until combined.

INGREDIENTS:

2	TABLESPOONS EXTRA VIRGIN OLIVE OIL
1	ONION, CHOPPED
2	CARROTS, PEELED AND GRATED
1	TEASPOON GROUND CORIANDER
1	TEASPOON CUMIN
2	CINNAMON STICKS
4	CUPS VEAL STOCK
2	GARLIC CLOVES, MINCED
2	14 OZ. CANS OF STEWED TOMATOES, CHOPPED
1	TABLESPOON TOMATO PASTE
1	14 OZ. CAN OF CHICKPEAS, DRAINED
	SALT AND PEPPER, TO TASTE

TO SERVE:
CARROT AND MINT SALAD

CARROT AND MINT SALAD

2	CARROTS, PEELED AND GRATED
1	TABLESPOON EXTRA VIRGIN OLIVE OIL
2	TEASPOONS APPLE CIDER VINEGAR
½	TEASPOON CUMIN
1	TABLESPOON MINT, LEAVES REMOVED AND CHOPPED
	SALT AND PEPPER, TO TASTE

CAMBODIAN CHICKEN *and* JASMINE RICE SOUP
with SHRIMP

YIELD: 4 SERVINGS / ACTIVE TIME: 15 MINUTES / TOTAL TIME: 30 MINUTES

After a long day at work, it can be brutal thinking up something everyone will love. With this soup, and an assist from a rotisserie chicken from the grocery store, you now have nothing to fear.

1. Cut the chicken breasts into ½-inch pieces, and remove the meat from the thighs and drumsticks.

2. In a medium saucepan, add the vegetable oil and cook over medium heat until warm.

3. Add the ginger and garlic and cook for 3 minutes, or until soft.

4. Add the stock, fish sauce, honey, and cooked rice and bring to a boil.

5. Reduce heat so that the soup simmers, add the chicken pieces, and cook for 5 minutes.

6. Add the shrimp and simmer for 2 minutes.

7. Stir in the lime juice, cilantro, basil, and chili. Season with salt and pepper and serve in warmed bowls with lime wedges.

INGREDIENTS:

- 1   3-POUND ROTISSERIE CHICKEN, LEGS AND BREASTS REMOVED
- 1   TABLESPOON VEGETABLE OIL
- 2   TABLESPOONS GINGER, MINCED
- 2   GARLIC CLOVES, MINCED
- 6   CUPS CHICKEN STOCK
- 3   TABLESPOONS FISH SAUCE
- 1   TEASPOON HONEY
- 1   CUP JASMINE RICE, COOKED
- 12   SHRIMP, SHELLED, DEVEINED, AND HALVED
- 2   TABLESPOONS LIME JUICE
- ¼   CUP CILANTRO, CHOPPED
- 2   TABLESPOONS BASIL, CHOPPED
- 1   THAI CHILI, SEEDS REMOVED AND SLICED
-     SALT AND PEPPER, TO TASTE
-     LIME WEDGES, FOR GARNISH

PASTA FAGIOLI

YIELD: 4 SERVINGS / ACTIVE TIME: 15 MINUTES / TOTAL TIME: 30 MINUTES

Like many other Italian favorites, including pizza and polenta, this started out as a peasant dish, and is composed of inexpensive ingredients.

1. In a medium saucepan, add oil and cook over medium heat.

2. When oil is warm, add onion, carrots, celery, and garlic and cook for 5 minutes, or until soft.

3. Add the stock, tomatoes, and Mediterranean Herbs and bring to a boil.

4. Reduce heat so that soup simmers, add elbow pasta, and cook for 10 minutes.

5. Add the pinto beans and cook for an additional 5 minutes.

6. Season with salt and pepper, garnish with parmesan cheese, and serve in warmed bowls.

MEDITERRANEAN HERBS

Mix all the ingredients together in a small bowl and then store in an airtight container until ready to use.

INGREDIENTS:

- 2 TABLESPOONS EXTRA VIRGIN OLIVE OIL
- 1 ONION, PEELED AND CHOPPED
- 2 CARROTS, PEELED AND GRATED
- 2 CELERY STALKS, CHOPPED
- 1 GARLIC CLOVE, MINCED
- 4 CUPS CHICKEN STOCK
- 1 14 OZ. CAN OF STEWED TOMATOES, CHOPPED
- 2 TABLESPOONS MEDITERRANEAN HERBS
- 1 CUP ELBOW PASTA
- 1 14 OZ. CAN OF PINTO BEANS
  SALT AND PEPPER, TO TASTE
- 1 CUP PARMESAN CHEESE, SHAVED, FOR GARNISH

MEDITERRANEAN HERBS

- 1 TABLESPOON DRIED ROSEMARY
- 2 TEASPOONS CUMIN
- 2 TEASPOONS GROUND CORIANDER
- 1 TEASPOON DRIED OREGANO
- ⅛ TEASPOON SALT

QUICK LAMB STEW

YIELD: 4 SERVINGS / ACTIVE TIME: 15 MINUTES / TOTAL TIME: 30 MINUTES

Want to put together a hearty meal for the whole family, but crunched for time? This quick lamb stew will come to the rescue.

1. In a medium saucepan, add the oil and cook over medium heat.

2. When the oil is warm, add the onion and lamb and cook for 5 minutes, or until lamb is browned all over.

3. Add the garlic, cumin, rosemary, and tomatoes and cook for an additional 5 minutes.

4. Add the stock and potatoes, increase heat to high, and bring to a boil.

5. Reduce heat so that the soup simmers. Cook for 10 minutes, or until the potatoes are tender.

6. Add the green beans and cook for 5 minutes.

7. Season with lemon juice, salt, and pepper and serve in warmed bowls garnished with a sprig of rosemary.

INGREDIENTS:

- 2 TABLESPOONS VEGETABLE OIL
- 1 ONION, PEELED AND CHOPPED
- 1 POUND LAMB LOIN, FAT REMOVED AND CUT INTO ½-INCH PIECES
- 2 GARLIC CLOVES
- 1 TABLESPOON CUMIN
- 1 TABLESPOON ROSEMARY, LEAVES REMOVED AND CHOPPED, PLUS 4 SPRIGS FOR GARNISH
- 2 14 OZ. CANS OF DICED TOMATOES
- 4 CUPS LAMB STOCK
- 2 POTATOES, PEELED AND CUT INTO ½-INCH PIECES
- 2 CUPS GREEN BEANS, CHOPPED
- JUICE OF 1 LEMON
- SALT AND PEPPER, TO TASTE

SEMI-HOMEMADE RAMEN

YIELD: 4 SERVINGS / ACTIVE TIME: 15 MINUTES / TOTAL TIME: 30 MINUTES

Pull out the ramen, throw out the seasoning packet, and make this grownup version of your old college standby.

1. In a medium saucepan, add the sesame oil and cook over medium heat.

2. When the oil is warm, add the chicken and cook, while turning, for 5 minutes.

3. Add the onion, ginger, garlic cloves, and chili flakes and cook for an additional 5 minutes.

4. Add the soy sauce and stock and bring to a boil.

5. Reduce the heat so that the soup simmers and cook for 10 minutes.

6. Add the Ramen noodles and cook for 5 additional minutes.

7. When the noodles are cooking, prepare your poached eggs.

8. Divide the soup between four bowls, add the poached egg, garnish with the scallion greens and bean sprouts, and serve.

POACHED EGGS

1. Crack the eggs, one at a time, into small, individual bowls.

2. In a medium saucepan, add 3 cups water and 2 tablespoons white vinegar and bring to a boil.

3. Reduce the heat so that the water simmers and gently add your eggs one at a time.

4. Cook for 3 minutes, gently basting the eggs with the water.

5. Gently remove the eggs from the pan with a slotted spoon. Place on a paper towel to dry.

6. Season each egg with salt and pepper and serve immediately.

INGREDIENTS:

2   TABLESPOONS SESAME OIL

2   CHICKEN BREASTS, SKIN REMOVED AND CHOPPED INTO ½-INCH PIECES

1   ONION, PEELED AND CHOPPED

1-INCH PIECE OF GINGER

2   GARLIC CLOVES

¼   TEASPOON RED CHILI FLAKES

4   TABLESPOONS SOY SAUCE, OR TO TASTE

8   CUPS CHICKEN STOCK

NOODLES FROM 4 PACKETS OF RAMEN

4   POACHED EGGS

SALT AND PEPPER, TO TASTE

4   SCALLIONS, SLICED, GREENS RESERVED FOR GARNISH

BEAN SPROUTS, FOR GARNISH

KED CHORIZO *and* CABBAGE SOUP

LD: 4 SERVINGS / ACTIVE TIME: 15 MINUTES / TOTAL TIME: 30 MINUTES

t use of European ingredients and techniques!

1. In a medium saucepan, add the oil and cook over medium heat.

2. When the oil is warm, add the onion and cook for 5 minutes, or until soft.

3. Add the thyme, chorizo, cabbage, cumin seeds, and cinnamon stick, cover, and cook for 5 minutes, stirring occasionally.

4. Add the stock, raise the heat to high, and bring to a boil.

5. Reduce heat so that the soup simmers and cook for an additional 10 minutes.

6. Season with salt and pepper and serve in warmed bowls.

INGREDIENTS:

2	TABLESPOONS EXTRA VIRGIN OLIVE OIL
1	ONION, CHOPPED
4	THYME SPRIGS, LEAVES REMOVED AND CHOPPED
1	POUND DRIED SMOKED CHORIZO, SLICED INTO ¼-INCH PIECES
1	GREEN CABBAGE, HALVED, CORE REMOVED, AND CUT INTO ¼-INCH SLICES
1	TABLESPOON CUMIN SEEDS
1	CINNAMON STICK
6	CUPS CHICKEN STOCK
	SALT AND PEPPER, TO TASTE

SAUSAGE, SPINACH, *and* BEAN SOUP

YIELD: 4 SERVINGS / ACTIVE TIME: 15 MINUTES / TOTAL TIME: 30 MINUTES

It seems impossible that a soup this tasty could take anything less than a day to make.

1. In a medium saucepan, add the oil and cook over medium heat.

2. When the oil is warm, add the sausage and cook for 3 to 5 minutes, while turning, until nicely browned.

3. Add the garlic, chili flakes, and baby spinach, cover and cook, stirring frequently until the spinach is wilted, approximately 5 minutes.

4. Add the beans, stock, and bay leaf, increase the heat to high, and bring to a boil.

5. Reduce heat so that the soup simmers and cook for 10 minutes.

6. Remove the bay leaf, season soup with salt and pepper, and serve in warmed bowls with a sprinkle of parmesan cheese.

INGREDIENTS:

2 TABLESPOONS EXTRA VIRGIN OLIVE OIL

1 POUND HOT ITALIAN SAUSAGE, CUT INTO ½-INCH SLICES

2 GARLIC CLOVES, MINCED

½ TEASPOON RED CHILI FLAKES

1 POUND BABY SPINACH

1 14 OZ. CAN OF CANNELLINI BEANS, RINSED, DRAINED, AND COOKED

6 CUPS CHICKEN STOCK

1 BAY LEAF

   SALT AND PEPPER, TO TASTE

1 CUP PARMESAN CHEESE, GRATED, FOR GARNISH

THAI CHICKEN *and* COCONUT S

YIELD: 4 SERVINGS / ACTIVE TIME: 15 MINUTES / TOTAL TIME: 30 M

This refreshing, spicy soup is perfect for the end of a cold day.

1. In a medium saucepan, add the oil and cook over medium heat.

2. When the oil is warm, add the chicken and onion and cook for 5 minutes, or until chicken is browned.

3. Add the stock, ginger, finely chopped Thai chili, lemongrass, and carrots. Increase the heat to high and bring to a boil.

4. Reduce heat so that the soup simmers. Cook for 5 minutes and then add the coconut milk. Simmer for an additional 5 minutes, or until the carrots are soft.

5. Remove the lemongrass and add fish sauce, lime juice, salt, and pepper.

6. Serve in warm bowls and garnish with sliced Thai chili and Thai basil.

INGREDIENTS:

2   TABLESPOONS VEGETABLE OIL

2   CHICKEN BREASTS, SKIN REMOVED, CHOPPED INTO ½-INCH PIECES

1   ONION, PEELED AND CHOPPED

4   CUPS CHICKEN STOCK

    2-INCH PIECE OF GINGER, PEELED AND MINCED

2   THAI CHILIES, SEEDS REMOVED, 1 FINELY CHOPPED, 1 SLICED

2   LEMONGRASS STALKS, HALVED AND BRUISED WITH THE BACK OF A KNIFE

4   CARROTS, PEELED AND CHOPPED

2   14 OZ. CANS OF COCONUT MILK

3   TABLESPOONS FISH SAUCE

    JUICE OF 1 LIME

    SALT AND PEPPER, TO TASTE

    THAI BASIL LEAVES, FOR GARNISH

QUICK KIMCHI RAMEN

YIELD: 4 SERVINGS / ACTIVE TIME: 10 MINUTES / TOTAL TIME: 30 MINUTES

The out-of-this-world flavor in this soup is thanks to the kimchi. Kimchi is made of fermented cabbage, and while I purchased mine, feel free to make your own; it's typically ready in under a week.

1. In a medium saucepan, add the vegetable oil and cook over medium-high heat until warm.

2. Add the shiitakes to the pan and cook for 3 minutes.

3. Add the kimchi, kimchi juice, chicken stock, chili powder, sugar, and sesame oil and bring to a boil.

4. Reduce heat so that the soup simmers, cook for 5 minutes, and then season with salt and pepper.

5. Cook Ramen noodles per manufacturer's instructions. Divide them between four bowls and then pour the broth over them. Garnish with scallions and serve.

INGREDIENTS:

¼ CUP VEGETABLE OIL

2 SHIITAKE MUSHROOMS, THINLY SLICED

2 CUPS KIMCHI, CHOPPED

1 CUP KIMCHI JUICE

6 CUPS CHICKEN STOCK

½ TEASPOON CHILI POWDER, OR TO TASTE

1 TEASPOON SUGAR

1 TABLESPOON SESAME OIL

SALT AND PEPPER, TO TASTE

NOODLES FROM 2 PACKETS OF RAMEN

4 SCALLIONS, SLICED, FOR GARNISH

TOM YUM KOONG SOUP

YIELD: 4 SERVINGS / ACTIVE TIME: 10 MINUTES / TOTAL TIME: 30 MINUTES

This soup has a very aromatic citrus smell and flavor. It is meant to be spicy, so make sure you tailor the amount of chilies and curry paste to your taste.

1. In a large saucepan, combine the chicken stock, lemongrass, galangal root, lime leaves, chilies, fish sauce, lime juice, sugar, and curry paste. Bring to a boil, reduce the heat so that the soup simmers, and cook for 5 minutes.

2. Turn off heat and let stand for 20 minutes.

3. Strain the soup through a fine sieve and return to a clean pan.

4. Bring soup to a simmer. Add shrimp and mushrooms and cook for 5 minutes.

5. Season with salt and pepper. Serve in warmed bowls garnished with cilantro leaves.

INGREDIENTS:

- 6   CUPS CHICKEN STOCK
- 2   LEMONGRASS STALKS, BRUISED WITH THE BACK OF A KNIFE
-     2-INCH PIECE OF GALANGAL ROOT
- 4   KAFFIR LIME LEAVES
- 2   THAI CHILIES, SEEDS REMOVED AND SLICED
- 2   TABLESPOONS FISH SAUCE
-     JUICE OF 3 LIMES
- 1½   TEASPOONS SUGAR
- 1   TABLESPOON THAI RED CURRY PASTE
- 12   OZ. SHRIMP, PEELED AND DEVEINED
- 24   SHIITAKE MUSHROOMS, HALVED
-     SALT AND PEPPER, TO TASTE
-     CILANTRO LEAVES, FOR GARNISH

CHILLED MAINE BLUEBERRY
and YOGURT SOUP

YIELD: 4 SERVINGS / ACTIVE TIME: 5 MINUTES / TOTAL TIME: 30 MINUTES

Enjoy this refreshing Maine staple on a warm summer day.

1. Place all ingredients in a food processor and gently pulse until combined.

2. Season with sugar to taste and place in the refrigerator for 15 minutes.

3. Serve in chilled bowls, or champagne flutes, with fresh blueberries.

INGREDIENTS:

2　CUPS MAINE BLUEBERRIES, PLUS MORE FOR GARNISH

4　CUPS GREEK YOGURT

1　CUP ORANGE JUICE

1　CUP CHAMPAGNE

1　VANILLA BEAN, SCRAPED

1　TEASPOON CINNAMON

　　SUGAR, TO TASTE

CHILLED MANGO SOUP

YIELD: 4 SERVINGS / ACTIVE TIME: 5 MINUTES / TOTAL TIME: 25 MINUTES

Want a healthy snack or light finish to a warm summer day? Try this delicious, fruity soup.

1. In a food processor, combine the mango, orange juice, honey, and yogurt. Puree until smooth and chill in the refrigerator for 20 minutes.

2. Remove from refrigerator, serve in chilled bowls, and garnish with mint leaves, blood orange segments, and fresh kiwi.

INGREDIENTS:

2   LARGE RIPE MANGOES, PEELED AND DICED

2   CUPS ORANGE JUICE

2   TEASPOONS HONEY, OR TO TASTE

1   CUP YOGURT

    MINT LEAVES, FOR GARNISH

    BLOOD ORANGE SEGMENTS, FOR GARNISH

    FRESH KIWI, FOR GARNISH

WHITE CHOCOLATE SOUP

YIELD: 4 SERVINGS / ACTIVE TIME: 10 MINUTES / TOTAL TIME: 25 MINUTES

Whip up this one for a special treat after dinner, or for watching a movie.

1. In a medium saucepan, add milk, cream, vanilla pod, and the vanilla bean seeds and bring to a simmer over medium heat.

2. Turn off heat and let sit for 10 minutes.

3. Remove vanilla pod and return to a simmer. When soup is simmering, turn off heat.

4. Add chocolate and whisk until melted. Strain soup through a fine sieve and then serve in coffee cups garnished with fresh mint.

INGREDIENTS:

3 CUPS MILK

1 CUP HEAVY CREAM

1 VANILLA BEAN, SCRAPED

1 POUND WHITE CHOCOLATE

MINT LEAVES, FOR GARNISH

METRIC EQUIVALENTS

WEIGHTS
1 ounce = 28 grams
2 ounces = 57 grams
4 ounces (¼ pound) = 113 grams
8 ounces (½ pound) = 227 grams
16 ounces (1 pound) = 454 grams

VOLUME MEASURES
⅛ teaspoon = 0.6 ml
¼ teaspoon = 1.23 ml
½ teaspoon = 2.5 ml
1 teaspoon = 5 ml
1 tablespoon (3 teaspoons) = ½ fluid ounce = 15 ml
2 tablespoons = 1 fluid ounce = 29.5 ml
¼ cup (4 tablespoons) = 2 fluid ounces = 59 ml
⅓ cup (5 ⅓ tablespoons) = 2.7 fluid ounces = 80 ml
½ cup (8 tablespoons) = 4 fluid ounces = 120 ml
⅔ cup (10 ⅔ tablespoons) = 5.4 fluid ounces = 160 ml
¾ cup (12 tablespoons) = 6 fluid ounces = 180 ml
1 cup (16 tablespoons) = 8 fluid ounces = 240 ml

LENGTH MEASURES
1⁄16-inch = 1.6 mm
⅛-inch = 3 mm
¼-inch = 6.25 mm
½-inch = 1.25 cm
¾-inch = 2 cm
1-inch = 2.5 cm

TEMPERATURE EQUIVALENTS

°F	°C	Gas Mark
225	110	¼
250	130	½
275	140	1
300	150	2
325	170	3
350	180	4
375	190	5
400	200	6
425	220	7
450	230	8
475	240	9
500	250	10

RESOURCES

I never stop consulting these books—they are outstanding resources.

The Professional Chef, 9th edition (Wiley, 2011)
By Culinary Institute of America

The French Laundry Cookbook, 2nd edition
(Artisan, 1999)
By Thomas Keller & Deborah Jones

*The Inn at Little Washington Cookbook:
A Consuming Passion* (Random House, 1996)
By Patrick O'Connell

*Patrick O'Connell's Refined American Cuisine:
The Inn at Little Washington* (Bulfinch, 2004)
By Patrick O'Connell

The White Barn Inn Cookbook (Running Press
Book Publishers, 2003)
By Jonathan Cartwright, Susan Sully & Phillipe
Schaff

*On Food and Cooking: The Science and Lore of
the Kitchen* (Scribner, 2004)
By Harold McGee

Momufuku (Clarkson Potter, 2009)
By David Change & Peter Meehan

Grand Finales: The Art of the Plated Dessert
(Wiley, 1996)
By Tish Boyle & Timothy Moriarty

*The Professional Pastry Chef: Fundamentals of
Baking and Pastry, 4th edition* (Wiley 2002)
By Bo Friberg

Eleven Madison Park: The Cookbook (Little
Brown and Company, 2011)
By Daniel Humm & Will Guidara

The NoMad Cookbook (Ten Speed Press, 2015)
By Daniel Humm, Will Guidra & Leo
Robitchek

ACKNOWLEDGMENTS

Taking on a project of this size is a feat for an army, but when you take it on alone, you need help along the way. I am very fortunate to have developed relationships throughout my career, relationships that lent a hand, product, space, and knowledge along this journey. I want to take a moment to recognize them and thank them for their assistance.

CIDER MILL PRESS

This project couldn't have happened without my publisher. I was humbled that John Whalen approached me with this opportunity. From day one, he had the confidence in me to take on this project and his encouragement along the way kept the candle lit and made me push through at the toughest of times. His team both past and present have brought this book to life. They have been helpful, inspiring, and willing to tackle any question or task, large or small.

JONATHAN CARTWRIGHT

Jonathan Cartwright, for many young chefs (his alumni stretch throughout the world), has provided so many opportunities not only to me but to culinary professionals all over the world. Chef Cartwright always has a way of pulling the best out of us. His encouragement motivates people to go farther than they think they can go. He has a very keen eye for upcoming chefs and is able to lift them to the next level. Although, I got my kitchen legs 5 years prior to starting at the White Barn Inn (on my first tour of duty), my career truly started the day I entered the White Barn Inn. This book couldn't have happened without Chef Cartwright. I thank him for his kind words in the Foreword, but more importantly for his leadership and friendship over the years.

STEVEN TITMAN

Over the years, working with so many chefs, its natural to live day by day, knowing we all will eventually go our separate ways. I met Chef Titman on my orientation at the White Barn Inn. More than most, he has seen me at my weakest and strongest in the kitchen. He was one of the few chefs over the years who has always put in the effort to stay in contact so when we do get to see one another, we jump right back to were we left off. Chef Titman has always been approachable and understanding and offered me the amazing opportunity to work with him in England. This opportunity both as a chef and a person has completely changed who I am. I thank him for his lovely quote and his sincere friendship and guidance throughout the years.

DANIEL BOULUD

Chef Daniel Boulud, originally from Lyon, France, is one of the America's leading culinary visionaries. With 13 national and international acclaimed restaurants, eating at Daniel, with its coveted 2 Michelin stars, was by far one of the greatest dining experiences of my life. His book *Letters to a Young Chef* is a must read for any future culinarian. I read his book when it first came out and it was very inspiring. I am honored and humbled for his quote in this book, but more so for his ability to keep the culinary world on its toes. Every time I have met him, or was a was a guest in one of his restaurants, he has made me feel at home.

PATRICK O'CONNELL

I would like to both thank and congratulate Chef Patrick O'Connell. This year The Inn at Little Washington is celebrating its 40th Anniversary. Over the years, chef has continued to deliver exceptional dining and lodging and has truly given his guests an authentic and unique experience. It was an honor to be invited into his world and have him mentor me, as he has done for many aspiring chefs. Working in his kitchen was a dream come true, an experience filled with countless valuable lessons that I still reflect on to this day. Chef is the definition of "hospitality," one of the many reasons he is the recipient of two Michelin stars. I am humbled and honored that he took the time to write such nice words about this book, and thank him dearly.

JASON BANGERTER

Chef Bangerter, amongst a slew of awards and years of training in different parts of Europe alongside some of the world's greatest chefs, is now manning the ship at the Langdon Hall Country House Hotel. His approach to obtaining sustainable products is at the forefront of Canadian cuisine. His commitment to the cause resulted in him receiving the 2017 Pinnacle Award for chef of the year. I have had the pleasure of meeting Chef Bangerter at several Relais Chateaux events and have listened to him speak about his experiences, commitments to our industry, and, most importantly, educating future generations of chefs. I thank him for his gracious words in this book, but most importantly for being a leader in North American cuisine, and his artistic approach to truly sustainable cuisine.

WARREN BARR

I met Chef Warren Barr at the Gourmet Fest in Carmel, California when our restaurants were paired together for the first event of the weekend. Neither restaurant was prepared for what was to come. We both thought we would be cooking out of a stocked kitchen, but to our surprise the event was at a vineyard in an outdoor setting with none of the luxuries we were used to, or prepared for. What started out as a challenging day, finished with us enjoying a glass of wine as we looked out over the Carmel Valley. Together, along with our teams, we pulled off a stunning event. It was a incredible reflection of teamwork. I thank Chef Warren Barr, for that incredible day and the many following. Chef Warren Barr is a chef and an artist, utilizing the abundance of great products from the Pacific Northwest. He is an asset to the culinary world and is creating magical experiences for his diners. I am blessed to have many talented chefs speak on my behalf for this book, and very grateful for his kind words.

DANIEL HOSTETTLER

I want to both thank and congratulate Daniel Hostettler for his contributions to hospitality, his commitment to excellence, and his recent appointment as President of Relais Chateaux, North America. Not only is he the Ambassador of the Finest Relais Chateaux Properties of North America, Daniel is the President and Group Managing Director of Ocean House Management Group. The Ocean House under the OHM umbrella is one of few hotels in North America receiving 15 Forbes stars, 5 each for the restaurant, hotel, and spa. I thank him for his kinds words and his mentoring over the years.

CHEFS OVER THE YEARS

It is imperative for me to thank the countless chefs that I've had the honor to work with over the years. Every single one of you has a piece in this book. Every success or failure we have had with a dish has molded who I am as a person and a chef. As I fellow chef once told me: "Every day's a school day." That saying really comes to light in this book. Thank you all for your support and encouragement through my career, and a select few who have supported me through this book. You know who you are....

I am also greatly indebted to the following producers.

VILLEROY AND BOCH

Based in Germany, Villeroy and Boch is one of the largest producers of premium porcelain and ceramic products worldwide. Family-owned since 1748, Villeroy and Boch is an award-winning, innovative company rooted in a time-honored tradition. Their products are suitable for the finest of restaurants, yet comfortable enough for your home collection. Villeroy and Boch plates have been the canvas for me to plate my food on, in most of the restaurants where I have worked. Our continued relationship presented the opportunity for me to be given several bowls to plate up these lovely soups. I thank them for their very kind gesture

STEELITE INTERNATIONAL

Steelite International is a leading manufacturer of dinnerware and tabletop solutions. Their products allow you to marry the perfect food with the perfect plate, for a perfect course. Made in Great Britian, the company has won numerous awards for their sustainability. Steelite was very kind with giving me a few soup bowl pieces from their newest collections. I thank them for this generous offering

GEORGETOWN POTTERY

Georgetown Pottery is a local potter in Maine with three locations in Georgetown, Freeport, and Woolwich. Owner Jeff Peters invited me into his shop and gave me a fantastic tour. He allowed me to borrow some beautiful porcelain pieces. He has an amazing operation and a beautiful and impressive showroom. I'm very grateful for Georgetown Pottery's assistance. It's great working with and supporting local artisans. It fills me with pride that this book created in Maine, with Maine ingredients, and some of these soups were also photographed in Maine pottery.

PREVIN

I have been working with Jay Previn, owner of Previn Incorporated in Philadelphia, for years. I buy all my personal and business products through this world-class restaurant supplier. Any tools in this book can be ordered through the company. I highly recommend purchasing kitchen equipment through them and am very appreciative that they sent me some plates and bowls for the production of this book.

INDEX

ABOUT THE AUTHOR

Derek Bissonnette has been a chef for the past 22 years, and is the former Executive Chef at the White Barn Inn in Kennebunk, Maine. He stepped out of the kitchen to focus on his passion for photography and opened up Derek Bissonnette Photography. Visit him online at dbmainephotography.com.

ABOUT CIDER MILL PRESS BOOK PUBLISHERS

Good ideas ripen with time. From seed to harvest, Cider Mill Press brings fine reading, information, and entertainment together between the covers of its creatively crafted books. Our Cider Mill bears fruit twice a year, publishing a new crop of titles each spring and fall.

KENNEBUNKPORT, MAINE

"Where Good Books Are Ready for Press"

Visit us online at

www.cidermillpress.com

or write to us at

PO Box 454
12 Spring St.
Kennebunkport, Maine 04046